AFGHANISTAN WAR

AFGHANISTAN WAR

A Documentary and Reference Guide

Ryan Wadle

Documentary and Reference Guides

 GREENWOOD™

An Imprint of ABC-CLIO, LLC
Santa Barbara, California • Denver, Colorado

Library of Congress Cataloging-in-Publication Data

Names: Wadle, Ryan, 1980– author.
Title: Afghanistan war : a documentary and reference guide / Ryan Wadle.
Description: Santa Barbara, California : Greenwood, an imprint of ABC-CLIO,
    LLC, [2018] | Series: Documentary and reference guides | Includes
    bibliographical references and index.
Identifiers: LCCN 2018016630 (print) | LCCN 2018017345 (ebook) | ISBN
    9781440857478 (Ebook) | ISBN 9781440857461 (hard copy : alk. paper)
Subjects: LCSH: Afghan War, 2001– | Afghanistan—History—Soviet occupation,
    1979–1989. | Counterinsurgency—Afghanistan—Sources. | Postwar
    reconstruction—Afghanistan—Sources. | Afghan War, 2001—Sources. |
    Afghanistan—History—Soviet occupation, 1979–1989—Sources. |
    Afghanistan—History, Military—21st century—Sources.
Classification: LCC DS371.412 (ebook) | LCC DS371.412 .W33 2018 (print) | DDC
    958.104/7—dc23
LC record available at https://lccn.loc.gov/2018016630

ISBN: 978–1–4408–5746–1 (print)
        978–1–4408–5747–8 (ebook)

22 21 20 19 18   1 2 3 4 5

This book is also available as an eBook.

Greenwood
An Imprint of ABC-CLIO, LLC

ABC-CLIO, LLC
130 Cremona Drive, P.O. Box 1911
Santa Barbara, California 93116-1911
www.abc-clio.com

This book is printed on acid-free paper ∞

Manufactured in the United States of America

CONTENTS

READER'S GUIDE TO RELATED DOCUMENTS

INTRODUCTION

The nation of Afghanistan has been embroiled in conflict for, at the time of this writing, nearly 40 years. This incessant conflict has embroiled two superpowers and dozens of other nations and has taken an incredible toll on the economy, the infrastructure, the institutions, and most important, the people of Afghanistan. The roots of this conflict have been long in the making, but the first spark came in April 1978 when a coup against President Mohammed Daoud Khan brought to power an unpopular and internally divided Communist regime that led to an insurgency in the Afghan countryside. This, in turn, triggered a Soviet invasion in December 1979 to install a new Communist leader, Babrak Kamal, and the deployment of forces to quell the Afghan uprising. A decade of Soviet occupation caused the deaths of thousands of Soviet troops and millions of Afghans but left the *mujahedeen* intact, leading to the Soviet withdrawal in 1989. A civil war between the remaining factions appeared to end in 1993, but a new group, the Taliban, emerged late the following year, seeking to implement their own conservative religious doctrines upon the entire country. The Taliban succeeded in taking over most of Afghanistan by 2001, partially because many Afghans preferred the Taliban's imperfect order to the anarchy that had preceded them. The Taliban, however, had chosen to give shelter to the Saudi Arabian terrorist Osama bin Laden, and a group of 19 of his al-Qaeda operatives attacked the World Trade Center and the Pentagon on September 11, 2001. The Taliban quickly became the focus of an international military campaign to drive them from power, but even after 16 years of combat, the Taliban still persist as a major threat to the Afghan government.

These events have involved people and institutions at the highest levels of power down to the soldiers and local Afghanis who lived this conflict. Capturing the entirety of this story is the duty of the historian, and since this conflict has occurred in the ages of both mass media and the dawn of social media, it has provided an endless variety of sources from which one can analyze the war in Afghanistan. The documents included in this volume have their own varied origins; some are messages drawn from firsthand observations of events, while others are transcripts of speeches and press conferences delivered by world leaders before audiences of millions to announce significant changes in policies. Others still come from the websites created by the insurgents themselves that allow them to maintain a portal for their followers in the region and their sympathizers around the globe. While the World Wide Web may appear to be ephemeral, it is a treasure trove of sources on the war in Afghanistan.

First, a brief note on the sources. Many of the following documents have been excerpted from their originals to display the most pertinent sections for readers to understand the conflict. Links are provided so that readers may find the original documents if they so choose. In addition, readers should take a critical eye toward each of these documents. History is, at its core, a search for truth, but the perspectives of those making history and those interpreting it always matter. Unless readers interrogate these sources to understand their meaning and context, one's understanding of the past will remain at the surface level.

The documents in this volume chronicle the evolution of the war in Afghanistan with particular emphasis upon the U.S.-led campaigns since 2001. Yet, to understand how that war has evolved, one must take a step back to learn how Afghanistan transformed from a poor, peaceful nation into a hotbed of international conflict. Chapter 1, "Documents from the Soviet Invasion and Civil War, 1979–2001," covers the period of the Soviet occupation and the years of the civil war that followed. Afghans had struggled internally for some time with how to modernize and incorporate Western culture and influences without alienating the more conservative tribes in the countryside, but the 1978 coup and the imposition of Communism transformed this cultural struggle into open conflict. The Soviets intervened out of extreme confidence in their martial abilities but found themselves bogged down in a fight far more difficult than they had imagined. Their withdrawal only left anarchy in its wake, and the Taliban, with their al-Qaeda allies, ably filled this power vacuum by the late 1990s.

For most Americans, the conflict in Afghanistan had receded from the political and national security zeitgeist by 2001, but it quickly became the dominant national security issue on September 11, 2001. Chapter 2, "Documents from Operation Enduring Freedom and the Beginning of Reconstruction, 2001–2003," begins in the immediate aftermath of the al-Qaeda attacks on New York and Washington. In a matter of weeks, the United States harnessed an international coalition to invade Afghanistan that ruthlessly drove the Taliban from power and their leaders, along with their al-Qaeda allies, into hiding. The work of building a new government almost entirely from scratch then commenced, but in spite of the incredible progress made by 2003, the Taliban never completely disappeared.

The U.S.-led invasion of Iraq in March 2003 and the subsequent occupation seemingly left the war in Afghanistan as a secondary effort. In Chapter 3, "Documents from the Return of the Taliban and Counterinsurgency, 2003–2009," the Coalition and the new Afghan government sought to rebuild Afghanistan while neutralizing the remaining pockets of Taliban and al-Qaeda fighters in southern and eastern Afghanistan. The Coalition had the resources to conduct these limited tasks, but the Taliban—from their sanctuaries in Pakistan—gradually rebuilt their cadres and frustrated the Afghan government's efforts to extend its legitimacy into the countryside. As the Taliban returned by the middle of the decade, it became increasingly clear that the optimism that had marked the sudden collapse of the Taliban in 2001 had faded and that vanquishing the group may require a large-scale counterinsurgency campaign. Unfortunately, the resources did not exist to fully execute that kind of campaign.

The fourth and final chapter, "Documents from the Surge, Withdrawal, and an Uncertain Future, 2009–2017," reflects the significant shifts in Afghanistan's fortunes since 2009. The period brought about renewed hope as President Barack Obama devoted more resources and forces to the conflict, bringing about a "surge" of U.S. forces similar to that which had been given credit for the recent success in Iraq. In addition, the United States finally located and killed Osama bin Laden in his Pakistani hideout in May 2011, bringing about the most notable success of the linked war against terrorism. The "surge," however, came to an end, and the massive commitment by the Obama administration gradually faded so that few U.S. forces remained by the end of his presidency. By the end of 2017 and in spite of hopes to the contrary, the United States continues to deploy troops to Afghanistan to fight the persistent Taliban with little sign that this 16-year commitment will end anytime soon. In effect, the war has already engulfed multiple generations of Afghans and is on the cusp of doing the same in the United States.

This book is dedicated to the fallen Afghan, U.S., and Coalition personnel who struggled to bring about a peaceful, stable Afghanistan.

1

DOCUMENTS FROM THE SOVIET INVASION AND CIVIL WAR, 1979–2001

- **Document 1: President Jimmy Carter, Speech on Afghanistan**
- **When:** January 4, 1980
- **Where:** Washington, D.C.
- **Significance:** This was the first major statement made by the United States following the Soviet invasion of Afghanistan in late December 1979.

DOCUMENT

I come to you this evening to discuss the extremely important and rapidly changing circumstances in Southwest Asia.

I continue to share with all of you the sense of outrage and impatience because of the kidnaping of innocent American hostages and the holding of them by militant terrorists with the support and the approval of Iranian officials. Our purposes continue to be the protection of the long range interests of our Nation and the safety of the American hostages.

We are attempting to secure the release of the Americans through the International Court of Justice, through the United Nations, and through public and private diplomatic efforts. We are determined to achieve this goal. We hope to do so without bloodshed and without any further danger to the lives of our 50 fellow Americans. In these efforts, we continue to have the strong support of the world community. The unity and the common sense of the American people under such trying circumstances are essential to the success of our efforts.

Recently, there has been another very serious development which threatens the maintenance of the peace in Southwest Asia. Massive Soviet military forces have invaded the small, nonaligned, sovereign nation of Afghanistan, which had hitherto not been an occupied satellite of the Soviet Union. Fifty thousand heavily armed Soviet troops have crossed the border and are now dispersed throughout Afghanistan, attempting to conquer the fiercely independent Muslim people of that country.

The Soviets claim, falsely, that they were invited into Afghanistan to help protect that country from some unnamed outside threat. But the President, who had been the leader of Afghanistan before the Soviet invasion, was assassinated along with several members of his family after the Soviets gained control of the capital city of Kabul. Only several days

DID YOU KNOW?

Afghanistan through the 19th Century

The territory comprising the modern nation of Afghanistan has been occupied by many of the most powerful empires in human history. It has sometimes acquired strategic importance because the land lay along the so-called Silk Road of trade between China and the various empires in the Middle East and Europe. These invaders included the Persians and the Greeks under Alexander the Great, the latter of whom left behind a partially Greek culture that survived in Afghanistan for more than three centuries. Later came the Huns and then the Arabs, who introduced Islam to Afghanistan in 642 CE. The Mongols caused much suffering during their invasions in the early 13th century CE, but Afghanistan became a critical part of the Mongol ruler Tamerlane's vast empire in the centuries that followed. By the 19th century, the Pashtuns had risen to control Afghanistan just as the Russian and British Empires sought to control the region. Two British invasions in the mid-19th century led to disastrous defeats for the British, which ultimately allowed Afghanistan to remain an independent nation.

later was the new puppet leader even brought into Afghanistan by the Soviets. This invasion is an extremely serious threat to peace because of the threat of further Soviet expansion into neighboring countries in Southwest Asia and also because such an aggressive military policy is unsettling to other peoples throughout the world.

This is a callous violation of international law and the United Nations Charter. It is a deliberate effort of a powerful atheistic government to subjugate an independent Islamic people.

We must recognize the strategic importance of Afghanistan to stability and peace. A Soviet-occupied Afghanistan threatens both Iran and Pakistan and is a steppingstone to possible control over much of the world's oil supplies.

The United States wants all nations in the region to be free and to be independent. If the Soviets are encouraged in this invasion by eventual success, and if they maintain their dominance over Afghanistan and then extend their control to adjacent countries, the stable, strategic, and peaceful balance of the entire world will be changed. This would threaten the security of all nations including, of course, the United States, our allies, and our friends.

DID YOU KNOW?

Soviet Invasion of Afghanistan

In April 1978, a group of Marxist officers in the Afghan army killed Prime Minister Mohammad Daoud Khan and his family following his crackdown against the People's Democratic Party of Afghanistan (PDPA). Once in power, the PDPA, led by Nur Mohammad Taraki, initiated a series of reforms far more radical than any enacted by Daoud or the shah. This caused the tribes to revolt, and, as 1979 wore on, Afghanistan slipped into chaos. Even the replacement and execution of Taraki by his deputy, Hafizullah Amin, only exacerbated the problems. Rather than risk Afghanistan becoming an American client state, Soviet premier Leonid Brezhnev elected to invade Afghanistan in December 1979. Fifty thousand Soviets poured into Afghanistan on Christmas Eve ostensibly to support Amin, but, thanks to clever sabotage of the Afghan army by Soviet advisers, the Soviets swiftly took over communications facilities and government buildings on the December 27. The Soviets killed Amin, replacing him with Babrak Karmal. The invasion had been an efficient and successful operation, but it made the revolt among the tribes a Soviet problem.

Therefore, the world simply cannot stand by and permit the Soviet Union to commit this act with impunity. Fifty nations have petitioned the United Nations Security Council to condemn the Soviet Union and to demand the immediate withdrawal of all Soviet troops from Afghanistan. We realize that under the United Nations Charter the Soviet Union and other permanent members may veto action of the Security Council. If the will of the Security Council should be thwarted in this manner, then immediate action would be appropriate in the General Assembly of the United Nations, where no Soviet veto exists.

In the meantime, neither the United States nor any other nation which is committed to world peace and stability can continue to do business as usual with the Soviet Union.

I have already recalled the United States Ambassador from Moscow back to Washington. He's working with me and with my other senior advisers in an immediate and comprehensive evaluation of the whole range of our relations with the Soviet Union. The successful negotiation of the SALT II treaty has been a major goal and a major achievement of this administration, and we Americans, the people of the Soviet Union, and indeed the entire world will benefit from the successful control of strategic nuclear weapons through the implementation of this carefully negotiated treaty.

However, because of the Soviet aggression, I have asked the United States Senate to defer further consideration of the SALT II treaty so that the Congress and I can assess Soviet actions and intentions and devote our primary attention to the legislative and other measures required to respond to this crisis. As circumstances change in the future, we will, of course, keep the ratification of SALT II under active review in consultation with the leaders of the Senate.

The Soviets must understand our deep concern. We will delay opening of any new American or Soviet consular facilities, and most of the cultural and economic exchanges currently under consideration will be deferred. Trade with the Soviet Union will be severely restricted.

I have decided to halt or to reduce exports to the Soviet Union in three areas that are particularly important to them. These new policies are being and will be coordinated with those of our allies. I've directed that no high technology or other strategic items will be licensed for sale to the Soviet Union until further notice, while we revise our licensing policy.

Fishing privileges for the Soviet Union in United States waters will be severely curtailed.

The 17 million tons of grain ordered by the Soviet Union in excess of that amount which we are committed to sell will not be delivered. This grain was not intended for human consumption but was to be used for building up Soviet livestock herds.

I am determined to minimize any adverse impact on the American farmer from this action. The undelivered grain will be removed from the market through storage and price support programs and through purchases at market prices. We will also increase amounts of grain devoted to the alleviation of hunger in poor countries, and we'll have a massive increase of the use of grain for gasohol production here at home.

After consultation with other principal grain-exporting nations, I am confident that they will not replace these quantities of grain by additional shipments on their part to the Soviet Union.

These actions will require some sacrifice on the part of all Americans, but there is absolutely no doubt that these actions are in the interest of world peace and in the interest of the security of our own Nation, and they are also compatible with actions being taken by our own major trading partners and others who share our deep concern about this new Soviet threat to world stability.

Although the United States would prefer not to withdraw from the Olympic games scheduled in Moscow this summer, the Soviet Union must realize that its continued aggressive actions will endanger both the participation of athletes and the travel to Moscow by spectators who would normally wish to attend the Olympic games.

Along with other countries, we will provide military equipment, food, and other assistance to help Pakistan defend its independence and its national security against the seriously increased threat it now faces from the north. The United States also stands ready to help other nations in the region in similar ways. Neither our allies nor our potential adversaries should have the slightest doubt about our willingness, our determination, and our capacity to take the measures I have outlined tonight. I have consulted with leaders of the Congress, and I am confident they will support legislation that may be required to carry out these measures.

History teaches, perhaps, very few clear lessons. But surely one such lesson learned by the world at great cost is that aggression, unopposed, becomes a contagious disease.

The response of the international community to the Soviet attempt to crush Afghanistan must match the gravity of the Soviet action.

With the support of the American people and working with other nations, we will deter aggression, we will protect our Nation's security, and we will preserve the peace. The United States will meet its responsibilities.

Thank you very much.

Source: Carter, Jimmy. *Public Papers of the Presidents of the United States: Jimmy Carter, 1980–81, Book 1.* Washington, D.C.: Government Printing Office, 1981, 21–24.

ANALYSIS

President Carter, much of whose foreign policy had emphasized human rights, framed the Soviet invasion of Afghanistan as an affront to the self-determination of peoples. He also noted the geostrategic consequences of the move when he mentioned that the Soviet presence in Afghanistan places their forces closer to Middle Eastern oil fields.

The measures Carter proposed in response to the invasion—deferring action on the SALT II treaty, new trade restrictions, and threatening to withdraw the U.S. team from the Summer Olympics in Moscow—were harsh and sought to isolate the Soviet regime for its decisions. Carter eventually enacted all of these policies, but they ultimately failed in bringing a quick end to the Soviet occupation.

- **Document 2: Central Intelligence Agency, Directorate of Intelligence, Office of Political Analysis, "The Soviets and the Tribes of Southwest Asia"**
- **When:** September 23, 1980
- **Where:** Langley, Virginia
- **Significance:** A Central Intelligence Agency (CIA) analysis of how the tribes in Afghanistan and neighboring countries viewed the Soviet occupation.

DOCUMENT

The Tribes

There are hundreds of tribes belonging to more than a dozen ethnic groups in Afghanistan and neighboring areas of Iran and Pakistan. Most are loosely organized with little or no central authority, but in some the power of the tribal chief is nearly absolute. Some have only a few thousand members; others, several hundred thousand. Some tribesmen are nomadic, most are settled farmers, and a few have abandoned the tribal way of life almost entirely.

These variations occur even within tribes. Pashtun Mohmands (living on both sides of the Pakistan-Afghan border near the Khyber Pass) include both nomads and farmers, and some members of the tribe have broken with traditional ways altogether to become urban laborers or even physicians and lawyers.

Tribes in Afghanistan

Tribal loyalties have more importance among the Pashtun of eastern and southern Afghanistan than among most of the ethnic groups. Among the Uzbeks of northern Afghanistan, for example, tribal ties area weak, and they probably are not much stronger for many of the Turkmen of northwest Afghanistan. Even for the Pashtuns, tribal membership usually means little more than a feeling of identity with others in the tribe. Organized action by an entire tribe is rare. An attack on one part of a tribe may bring some response from other tribesmen not directly affected, but each extended family or village usually determines its own course without reference to the rest of the tribe or to the ostensible tribal leaders.

Those who cling most closely to the traditional tribal ways are the least likely to be influenced by Communism. To the extent that the tribesmen have an ideology it is a belief that a combination of Islam and even older tribal traditions is the proper guide for action. Among most tribes, the traditional views include such things as the obligation to seek revenge, masculine superiority, an emphasis on personal bravery and honor, and suspicion of outsiders. Tradition also tends to sanctify everything from rules governing property ownership to ways of treating illness. Any change in the traditional way of life is considered wrong, and modern ideas—whether Communist or Western—are seen as a threat.

The Afghan insurgency has been strongest among the most traditionally minded such as the Pushtuns of Paktia Province and the Nuristanis and Tajiks farther north along the Pakistani border. They resist the Afghan Marxists and the Soviets more to preserve the old ways than to fight Communism. Some of the reforms that have incensed the tribes—education of women for example—are neither Communist nor anti-Islamic, but they conflict with the tribesmen's perception of what is right.

[Redacted]

Attitudes developed generations ago when they were nomads are still strong among settled tribesmen, but these are weakening gradually as they experience life as farmers and villagers and have more contact with the outside world. In particular, their traditional tendency to resort to and glorify fighting has waned. Insurgency has been less of a problem among long-settled Pashtun tribes such as the Popalzai in the Qandahar area, than among the nomads and seminomads of the mountains.

In the tribal villages it is in the interests of the most influential men—local landowners, religious leaders, or both—to reject reforms, especially Communist ones, that threaten both their property and their political power. Nevertheless, Communist programs may have some appeal to the settled tribes. Landless laborers would benefit from land reform, and those already exposed to modern influence would see benefits from increased education—even for women—and better medical care.

[Redacted]

A major problem for the Soviets is to convince the tribes that it is to their advantage to support the government. The Soviets can bolster their arguments with offers of weapons and money. They can also threaten retaliation against tribesmen who will not cooperate, or threaten to support their traditional enemies.

Ethnic ties between groups in the USSR and in northern Afghanistan such as the Turkmen, Tajiks, and Uzbeks could also be exploited, although there is little evidence that the Soviets have sought to do so. Such an effort could be especially difficult among the Uzbeks; many Uzbeks fled from the USSR before World War II to escape Communist rule.

[Redacted]

Even were the tribesmen motivated by more than an opportunity to steal, they would probably regard any arrangement with the Soviets as a temporary expedient and would turn against them as soon as it seemed advantageous to do so. The Soviets are aware of the unreliability of tribal allies. In the past, tribesmen fighting for outsiders have changed alliance in response to offers of better pay, or even when they decided their pay inadequate. A recent book review published in Tashkent made much of Britain's problems in the 19th century in trying to keep Afghan tribes loyal.

[Redacted]

Tribes in Pakistan

The tribes in the remote and rugged area along the northern part of the Afghan-Pakistani border are probably too small and isolated to be a useful target for the USSR.

To the south are the Pakistani Pashtuns, some of whom are actively supporting the Afghan insurgents, and almost all of whom sympathize with their cause. In the past, the Pashtuns have tended to support politicians with ties to Moscow and Kabul, and perhaps the leading Pakistani Communist is a tribesmen—although from the most "civilized" of all the Pashtun tribes.

The Pakistani Pashtuns have long resented domination by the Punjabis to the east and have sought greater autonomy or outright independence. The Soviets could attempt to exploit this desire, but with Soviets fighting Pashtuns in Afghanistan, the prospects for a positive response from the Pakistani Pashtuns have never been so poor.

. . .

Source: Central Intelligence Agency Library. Available online at https://www.cia.gov/library/readingroom/document/cia-rdp81b00401r000400110005-4.

ANALYSIS

This analysis argued that culture and social structure were the most important reasons why the Afghan countryside resisted the Soviet occupation. The heavy-handed attempts to radically remake Afghan society in the Marxist image had completely alienated the tribesmen. Also of note is the belief that the Pashtuns of southern and eastern Afghanistan constituted the core of the Afghan resistance. Many of the problems identified in this report would recur during the American-led reconstruction of Afghanistan after 2001.

- **Document 3: UN Resolution 35/37**
- **When:** November 20, 1980
- **Where:** New York, New York

- **Significance:** The UN General Assembly called for a withdrawal of troops and a peaceful settlement to the war in Afghanistan.

DOCUMENT

The General Assembly,

Having considered the item entitled "The situation in Afghanistan and its implications for international peace and security",

Recalling its resolution ES-6/2 of 14 January 1980 adopted at its sixth emergency special session,

Reaffirming the purposes and principles of the Charter of the United Nations and the obligation of all States to refrain in their international relations from the threat or use of force against the sovereignty, territorial integrity and political independence of any State,

Reaffirming further the inalienable right of all peoples to determine their own form of government and to choose their own economic, political, and social system free from outside intervention, subversion, coercion, or constraint of any kind whatsoever;

Gravely concerned at the continuing foreign armed intervention in Afghanistan, in contravention of the above principles, and its serious implications for international peace and security,

Deeply concerned at the increasing outflow of refugees from Afghanistan,

Deeply conscious of the urgent need for a political solution of the grave situation in respect of Afghanistan,

Recognizing the importance of the continuing efforts and initiatives of the Organization of the Islamic Conference for a political solution of the situation in respect of Afghanistan,

1. *Reiterates* that the preservation of the sovereignty, territorial integrity, political independence and non-aligned character of Afghanistan is essential for a peaceful solution of the problem;

2. *Reaffirms* the right of the Afghan people to determine their own form of government and to choose their economic, political and social system free from outside intervention, subversion, coercion or constraint of any kind whatsoever;

3. *Calls* for the immediate withdrawal of the foreign troops from Afghanistan;

4. *Also calls upon* all parties concerned to work for the urgent achievement of a political solution and the creation of the necessary conditions which would enable the Afghan refugees to return voluntarily to their homes in safety and honour;

5. *Appeals* to all States and national and international organizations to extend humanitarian relief assistance, with a view to alleviating the hardship of the Afghan refugees, in co-ordination with the United Nations High Commissioner for Refugees;

6. *Expresses in its appreciation* of the efforts of the Secretary-General in the search for a solution to the problem and hopes that he will continue to extend assistance, including the appointment of a special representative, with a view to promoting a political solution in accordance with the provisions of the present resolution, and the exploration of securing appropriate guarantees for non-use of force, or threat of

use of force, against the political independence, sovereignty, territorial integrity and security of all neighbouring States, on the basis of mutual guarantees and strict non-interference in each other's internal affairs and with full regard for the principles of the Charter of the United Nations;

7. *Requests* the Secretary-General to keep Member States and the Security Council concurrently informed of progress towards the implementation of the present resolution and to submit to Member States a report on the situation at the earliest appropriate opportunity;

8. *Decides* to include in the provisional agenda of its thirty-sixth session the item entitled "The situation in Afghanistan and its implications for international peace and security".

70th plenary meeting
20 November 1980

Source: UN General Assembly Resolution 35/37, November 20, 1980. Available online at http://www.un.org/documents/ga/res/35/a35r37e.pdf.

ANALYSIS

By the end of 1980, the wave of refugees that eventually numbered more than 3 million had begun to flee the violence in Afghanistan. The majority of these refugees went to Pakistan and Iran, but a large Afghan diaspora community also arose in many other nations. Finding a peaceful settlement thus constituted a major regional humanitarian and security issue.

Unfortunately, this resolution from the General Assembly carried little weight behind it. Power in the United Nations rests with the Security Council, but Afghanistan, as with many other Cold War security issues, remained untouchable due to the Soviet ability to veto any resolution that another member of the Security Council proposed.

- **Document 4: President Ronald Reagan, Remarks on Signing the Afghanistan Day Proclamation**
- **When:** March 10, 1982
- **Where:** Washington, D.C.
- **Significance:** President Reagan proclaimed Afghanistan Day as a show of support for Afghan resistance against the Soviet Union.

DOCUMENT

I can't help but say—thank you all very much—but I can't help but recall that I was in Iran on the day that the first coup took place by the Soviet Union in their overthrow there of the government.

DID YOU KNOW?

Mohammad Zahir Shah

Mohammad Zahir Shah was the last king of Afghanistan, ruling from 1933 to 1973. Born in 1914, Shah was the son of Mohammad Nadir Khan, a member of the royal family and army general. Nadir Khan assumed the throne in 1929 after executing Habibullah Kalakani following the latter's coup against the monarchy. Nadir Khan was himself assassinated in 1933, allowing his son to take power. During Zahir Shah's reign, he kept Afghanistan largely neutral, avoiding taking sides in World War II and courting both the United States and the Soviets in the Cold War. He also sought to gradually modernize Afghanistan, which had been a relatively poor and isolated country when he took power. He created a modern parliament, held free elections, and also advocated for women's rights. He abdicated in 1973 when his cousin, Mohammad Daoud Khan, staged a coup and established a new government. He attempted to broker peace during the Soviet occupation and the civil war in the 1990s to no avail. In 2002, he chaired the Loya Jirga that chose Hamid Karzai as the new Afghan president. He then lived in Kabul with no official title but much public respect until his death in 2007.

I take particular satisfaction in signing today the proclamation authorized by Joint Resolution No. 142, which calls for the commemoration of March 21st as Afghanistan Day throughout the United States. This resolution testifies to America's deep and continuing admiration for the Afghan people in the face of brutal and unprovoked aggression by the Soviet Union.

A distinguished former Secretary of State, William P. Rogers, is coordinating the observance of Afghan Day in the United States. He not only has my strong support but that of former Presidents Carter, Ford, and Nixon and former Secretaries of State Muskie, Vance, Kissinger, and Rusk.

The Afghans, like the Poles, wish nothing more, as you've just been so eloquently told, than to live their lives in peace, to practice their religion in freedom, and to exercise their right to self-determination. As a consequence, they now find themselves struggling for their very survival as a nation. Nowhere are basic human rights more brutally violated than in Afghanistan today.

I have spoken on occasion of the presence of unsung heroes in American life. Today, we recognize a nation of unsung heroes whose courageous struggle is one of the epics of our time. The Afghan people have matched their heroism against the most terrifying weapons of modern warfare in the Soviet arsenal. Despite blanket bombing and chemical and biological weapons, the brave Afghan freedom-fighters have prevented the nearly 100,000-strong Soviet occupation force from extending its control over a large portion of the countryside.

Their heroic struggle has carried a terrible cost. Many thousands of Afghans, often innocent civilians, women and children, have been killed and maimed. Entire villages and regions have been destroyed and depopulated. Some 3 million people have been driven into exile—that's one out of every five Afghans. The same proportion of Americans would produce a staggering 50 million refugees.

We cannot and will not turn our backs on this struggle. Few acts of international aggression have been so universally condemned. The United Nations has repeatedly called for the withdrawal of Soviet forces. The Islamic Conference, deeply troubled over this assault on Moslem religion, has four times condemned the Soviet occupation. The nonaligned movement has added its voice to the demands for withdrawal of foreign troops.

Most recently, as you've been told, the European Parliament took the leadership in advancing the idea of a worldwide commemoration of Afghanistan Day. On behalf of all Americans, I want to thank the members of the European Parliament for this action and welcome today the participation of Egon Klepsch, Vice President of the European Parliament, and his distinguished colleagues.

I also want to express the hope that people the world over will respond with eagerness and determination. And in that connection, I want to express my particular appreciation that we're joined here today by members of the parliaments of Japan, Kenya, Panama, Thailand, and Austria.

We must go beyond public condemnation of the Soviet puppet regime in Kabul to bring relief and an early end to the Afghan tragedy. We have a human responsibility to the Afghan refugees. The United States has given generous support to the U.N.'s refugee effort. And I'm pleased to announce today an additional commitment of $21.3 million worth of food. This contribution will bring the total U.S. support for the refugees to over $200 million in the past 2 years. But I ask that all Americans supplement these funds with personal donations to organizations which work with Afghan refugees and the cause of a free Afghanistan.

Beyond this, the United States is determined to do everything politically possible to bring the Soviet Union to the negotiating table. We and our allies have made clear that Afghanistan will remain a central issue in U.S. [Soviet][1] Government and East-West relations as long as Soviet forces continue to occupy that nation. We have used, and will continue to use, every available opportunity, including the last meeting between Secretary Haig and Soviet Foreign Minister Gromyko, to urge the Soviets to enter into genuine negotiations for a peaceful settlement of the Afghan crisis.

In that spirit I want to address the claim made by the Soviet Union—that its troops entered Afghanistan and must remain there as a result of foreign intervention against the Kabul government. The world is well aware that this is nothing more than propaganda designed to divert international attention from the sordid reality. The foreign interference in Afghanistan comes from the nearly 100,000 Soviet armed invaders. The United States has consistently followed a policy of noninterference in Afghanistan's internal affairs. We similarly supported the nonaligned character of the previous Afghanistan Governments. The fire of resistance in Afghanistan is being kindled and sustained not by outside forces, but by the determination of the Afghan people to defend their national independence.

We and most other members of the international community have repeatedly stressed to the Soviets both publicly and privately that we have no objectives in Afghanistan beyond those set forth in the U.N. General Assembly resolutions. These are the withdrawal of the Soviet forces, the free exercise of self-determination for the Afghan people, the restoration of Afghanistan's nonaligned status, and the safe and honorable return of Afghan refugees to their homes. Unfortunately, the Soviet Union has to date rejected all attempts to move toward an internationally acceptable solution.

In 1980 it refused to receive emissaries of the Islamic Conference, who wished to travel to Moscow to discuss a political solution. In 1981 it was the British foreign minister who was rudely rebuffed when he presented a very sensible proposal of the European Community for a two-tiered international conference, which is still on the table. Finally, the Soviets have evaded the issue, insisting that the U.N. Secretary-General seek a solution in Kabul, Islamabad, and Tehran rather than at the source of the aggression in Moscow.

---

[1]White House correction.

The Soviet Union bears a grave responsibility for the continuing suffering of the Afghan people, the massive violations of human rights, and the international tension which has resulted from its unprovoked attack. The Soviet Union must understand that the world will not forget, as it has not forgotten the peoples of the other captive nations from Eastern Europe to Southwest Asia—who have suffered from Soviet aggression. This is the meaning of Afghanistan Day, that the Afghan people will ultimately prevail.

Coincidentally, the day after Afghanistan Day, this country plans to launch the third *Columbia* space shuttle. Just as the *Columbia*, we think, represents man's finest aspirations in the field of science and technology, so too does the struggle of the Afghan people represent man's highest aspirations for freedom. The fact that freedom is the strongest force in the world is daily demonstrated by the people of Afghan. Accordingly, I am dedicating on behalf of the American people the March 22d launch of the *Columbia* to the people of Afghanistan.

And in that same spirit I call on all Americans to observe Afghanistan Day in their thoughts, their prayers, their activities, and in their own renewed dedication to freedom. With the help of those assembled here today, the unanimous backing of the Congress, and the support of the American people, I'm confident that this day will mark a true celebration, and not just for freedom in Afghanistan, but, for freedom wherever it is threatened or suppressed the world over. Now, I shall sign the proclamation.

Source: Reagan, Ronald. *Public Papers of the Presidents of the United States. Ronald Reagan, 1982, Book 1.* Washington, D.C.: Government Printing Office, 1983, 272–274.

ANALYSIS

President Reagan's rhetoric framed the Afghan resistance, known as the *mujahedeen*, as "brave … freedom fighters" and sought to link their struggle against the Soviets with the contemporary political resistance posed by the Solidarity movement in Poland. This label of the mujahedeen would carry over into popular depictions of the war in Afghanistan.

President Reagan's claim that the mujahedeen was a self-sustaining movement and not reliant upon outside support masked the money and arms that the United States had provided as early as 1980 under President Carter. This support, funneled through the CIA and Pakistan, would only grow in the years ahead.

- **Document 5: Defense Intelligence Agency, Directorate for Research, "The Economic Impact of Soviet Involvement in Afghanistan"**
- **When:** May 1983
- **Where:** Washington, D.C.
- **Significance:** A summary of economic trends in Afghanistan since the Soviet invasion in 1979.

DOCUMENT

SUMMARY

The effect of the Soviet occupation of Afghanistan has been catastrophic for the development of the Afghan economy. The evidence suggests a serious decline in the gross national product (GNP) and the abandonment of many Soviet-aided industrial products which had been completed or were under construction in 1979. With its agricultural base adversely affected by war and collectivization, the country has also become a net importer of food after being a net exporter in previous years. In addition, Soviet involvement in Afghanistan has lessened the prospects for beneficial Western economic involvement through both trade and aid transactions. Although living conditions were never high by world standards, the current situation at best can be considered grim.

Source: National Security Archive. Available online at http://nsarchive2.gwu.edu//NSAEBB/NSAEBB57/us4.pdf.

DID YOU KNOW?

Abdul Rashid Dostum

Abdul Rashid Dostum is an Afghan general and politician who has served on multiple sides during the long-running conflict in Afghanistan. Born in 1954, he welcomed the growth of communism in Afghanistan and joined the Afghan army in 1978. Unlike many prominent figures in Afghanistan, however, he remained on the Soviet side during their occupation, rising to command Afghan militias fighting the mujahedeen. After the Soviets withdrew in 1989, he remained loyal to the Najibullah government, but, just as forces of Ahmad Shah Massoud closed on Kabul, Dostum joined them and participated in the downfall of the government. During the civil war in the 1990s, he switched sides numerous times, at times supporting the new government and at times opposing it. He viewed the Taliban as a major threat and helped to form the Northern Alliance in 1998, but he spent several years in exile in Turkey. He returned in 2001 but had a checkered relationship with the Karzai government because of his brutality, causing him to return to exile. Surprisingly, he returned to Afghanistan and became first vice president in 2014 under President Ashraf Ghani. Still, his reputation for brutality continues to dog him.

ANALYSIS

Just over three years after the invasion, Afghanistan's economy had crumbled under the weight of the fighting that had in turn created massive disruptions caused by death and the movements of large numbers of refugees both inside and outside Afghanistan. The humanitarian crisis that had started with the invasion had only worsened, and the need for aid would only continue.

- **Document 6: Central Intelligence Agency, Directorate of Intelligence, "The Soviet Invasion of Afghanistan: Five Years After"**
- **When:** May 1985
- **Where:** Langley, Virginia
- **Significance:** A CIA analysis of the war in Afghanistan that concluded that the Soviets had failed to pacify the country.

DOCUMENT

Key Judgments

More than five years after the Soviets invaded Afghanistan, they are bogged down in a guerilla war of increasing intensity. The Soviets have had little success in reducing the insurgency or winning acceptance by the Afghan people, and the Afghan resistance continues to grow stronger and to command widespread popular support. Fighting has gradually spread to all parts of Afghanistan. The Soviets control less territory than they did in 1980, and their airfields, garrisons, and lines of communication are increasingly subject to insurgent attack.

The serious shortcomings of the Afghan Army have forced the Soviets to shoulder more of the combat burden than they had anticipated. But the Soviets have shown little imagination in developing counterinsurgency tactics, and they have relied upon stereotyped search and destroy operations that often give the insurgents advance warning of an assault. Poor intelligence has also been a continuing problem.

Although Soviet military tactics are clearly designed to minimize losses of personnel and equipment, we estimate they have suffered roughly 23,000 casualties, including about 8,000 killed, and lost over 600 helicopters and fixed-wing aircraft and thousands of armored vehicles and trucks. We estimate casualties in the Afghan Army at about 67,000 and insurgent casualties at some 40,000, excluding civilian sympathizers.

Meanwhile, the Soviet program to transform Afghanistan into a reliable Communist client state is having little impact:

- Efforts at media indoctrination of Afghans fail because of Afghan illiteracy, distrust of the regime, religious beliefs, and adherence to traditional values.
- The regime has bought only temporary loyalties by bribery and occasional truces with insurgent groups.
- The Afghan school system is in a shambles, and trainees sent to the USSR often become antagonistic toward the Soviet system. Many cannot find appropriate or attractive positions upon their return to Afghanistan.
- The Afghan ruling party is riven by factionalism.

The insurgents have serious problems of their own. They have few local leaders of quality, rivalries among insurgent leaders and factions inhibit cooperation and often result in bloody fighting, and inadequate training and supply shortages are common.

We believe the fighting in Afghanistan will increase in the next two years. The insurgents are likely to show greater aggressiveness as they receive better weapons and more training. The Soviets are showing renewed resolve to break the military stalemate and have begun to adopt a more aggressive posture. They are stepping up efforts to halt insurgent infiltration, and we expect to see a greater use of airpower along the Pakistani and Iranian borders.

Over the next two years, as improvements in the insurgency become evident, we believe it most likely that the Soviets will increase their forces incrementally, perhaps by another 5,000 to 10,000 men. Such an augmentation would probably include contingents of specialized forces, such as security battalions and specialized combat and support units. Less likely—either because of continuing frustration or if their situation deteriorates more drastically than we believe probable—the Soviets could expand their forces by several divisions, possibly as many as 50,000 men, and increase efforts to garrison and hold large areas. Even then, however, they would not have enough troops to maintain control in much of the countryside as long as insurgents have access to strong external support and open borders.

We cannot rule out a more serious deterioration of the Soviet position in Afghanistan, which could arise if the insurgents improve their coordination, adjust their tactics, and assimilate increased outside assistance more rapidly than we anticipate. This train of events would probably force the Soviets to review their basic options in Afghanistan and could result in a greatly expanded military commitment and an even wider war.

We also cannot rule out greater progress by the Soviets in building a political and military infrastructure in Afghanistan. This development would be more likely if Soviet pressure or internal instability in Pakistan resulted in Islamabad's limiting its support for the resistance. Even so, the Soviets could not completely pacify the country and withdraw a sizable number of forces.

The Soviets, in our view, are unlikely to make real progress toward quelling the insurgency in the next two years. The more aggressive Soviet tactics over the past year, however, suggest that Moscow continues to hope its policies will, over the long term, grind down the will of the insurgents to resist and allow the Kabul government to consolidate Communist rule in Afghanistan. Soviet officials claim and probably expect that their efforts to rebuild the Afghan armed forces and gain converts by indoctrination, bribery, and internal reforms will bear fruit in the long term.

War weariness does not appear to present a problem for either side, and the Soviets have shown no interest in compromising their maximum demands. Prospects for a political settlement remain dim because of Soviet opposition.

Soviet losses, together with the trains of a counterinsurgency campaign, have worsened morale and discipline problem in the Army and produced more grumbling at home. We believe that Moscow's effort to limit the human and financial costs of the war have held domestic political and social dissatisfaction to a level acceptable to the leadership. Moscow probably believes it has weathered the worst of the international censure for its actions in Afghanistan.

Although the new CPSU General Secretary Gorbachev presumably will want to solve the Afghanistan problem in some way and may eventually put his stamp on Soviet Afghan policy, we believe that he will be occupied over the next year or so with consolidating his power to the Soviet leadership. In our view, he has a strong interest in avoiding positions that might make him look weak or adventuristic. He is unlikely, therefore, to seek sharp revisions in Soviet goals or strategy.

. . .

Source: National Security Archive. Available online at http://nsarchive2 .gwu.edu//NSAEBB/NSAEBB57/us5.pdf.

ANALYSIS

The Soviet war effort in Afghanistan bogged down for many reasons, perhaps most importantly because they could not send enough forces to counter the mujahedeen without fundamentally compromising their interests in Europe or elsewhere. Meanwhile, the mujahedeen, who enjoyed popular support, had external allies, and had a much-deeper understanding of the politics and geography of their own country and could devote all of their energies on eliminating the Soviet threat.

Furthermore, the hatred of the illegitimate regime in Kabul and their Soviet masters masked many of the cleavages between mujahedeen factions that, absent that outside agitator, would easily have turned on one another. This also helps explain why the resistance failed to coalesce into a coherent national government after the Soviet withdrawal.

- **Document 7: Central Intelligence Agency, Special National Intelligence Estimate 11/37/88, "USSR: Withdrawal from Afghanistan"**
- **When:** March 1988
- **Where:** Langley, Virginia
- **Significance:** A declassified intelligence estimate that concluded that the nearly decade-long Soviet occupation of Afghanistan would soon end.

DOCUMENT

Key Judgments

We believe Moscow has made a firm decision to withdraw from Afghanistan. The decision stems from the war's effect on the Soviet regime's ability to carry out its agenda at home and abroad and its pessimism about the military and political prospects for creating a viable client regime:

- Although Afghanistan has been a controversial issue, we believe General Secretary Gorbachev has built a leadership consensus for withdrawal. The regime is aware that its client's chances of surviving without Soviet troops are poor. We do not believe that Moscow will attempt a partition of Afghanistan or start withdrawal and then renege.
- The Soviets want to withdraw under the cover of the Geneva accords. We believe they would prefer to withdraw without an agreement, however, rather than sign one that formally restricts their right to provide aid and further undermines the legitimacy of the Kabul regime.
- In our view, the Soviets will begin withdrawal this year even if the Geneva talks are deadlocked. Under such conditions, however, the Soviet leadership would

not feel constrained by the provisions of the draft accords, and withdrawal would more likely be accompanied by heavy fighting. Although the Soviets in this case would have been the option of delaying or prolonging the withdrawal process, we believe that—once begun in earnest—geographic, political, and military factors would lead them to opt for a relatively rapid exit.

– There is an alternative scenario. A more chaotic situation accompanying withdrawal than the Soviets expect or a political crisis in Moscow could fracture the Politburo consensus for withdrawal and lead them to delay or even reverse course. We believe the odds of this scenario are small—perhaps less than one in five.

We judge that the Najibullah regime will not long survive the completion of Soviet withdrawal even with continued Soviet assistance. The regime may fall before withdrawal is complete.

> ## DID YOU KNOW?
>
> ### Stinger Missiles
>
> First developed in 1981, the FIM-92 Stinger is a Man Portable Air Defense System (MANPADS). At the behest of U.S. Representative Charlie Wilson and others, the CIA began funneling these missiles through Pakistan to the mujahedeen in 1986. To that point, the Soviets relied heavily upon fixed-wing aircraft and helicopters to support their operations because the mujahedeen had few means to effectively shoot them down. The Stingers, however, when combined with effective tactics, finally allowed the mujahedeen to knock out Soviet aircraft, including the large, heavily armored Mi-24 Hind helicopter gunship. Estimates of Soviet aircraft losses from Stingers vary widely, but their presence had a notable effect on Soviet tactics. The United States ceased supplying Stingers to the mujahedeen in 1988 and sought to buy back the remaining weapons, but not all were recovered.

Despite infighting, we believe the resistance will retain sufficient supplies and military strength to ensure the demise of the Communist government. We cannot confidently predict the composition of the new regime, but we believe it initially will be an unstable coalition of traditionalist and fundamentalist groups whose writ will not extend far beyond Kabul and the leaders' home areas. It will be Islamic—possibly strongly fundamentalist, but not as extreme as Iran. While anti-Soviet, it will eventually establish "correct"—not friendly—ties to the USSR We cannot be confident of the new government's orientation toward the West; at best it will be ambivalent and at worst it may be actively hostile, especially toward the United States.

There are two alternative scenarios. There is some chance—less than 1 in 3 in our view—that fighting among resistance groups will produce so much chaos that no stable government will take hold for an extended period after the Afghan Communist regime collapses. We also cannot rule out a scenario in which the Kabul regime manages to survive for a protracted period after withdrawal, due to an increasingly divided resistance. The odds of this outcome, in our view, are very small. Both scenarios would complicate relief efforts, reduce the prospects that refugees would return, and increase opportunities for Soviet maneuvering.

The impact of the Soviet withdrawal will depend on how it proceeds and what kind of situation the Soviets leave behind. At home, we believe that ending the war will be a net plus for Gorbachev, boosting his popularity and his reform agenda. Nonetheless, withdrawal will not be universally popular and is sure to cause recriminations. There is some chance—if it proves to have a more damaging impact on Soviet interests over the long term than either we or Gorbachev anticipate—that the decision could eventually form part of a "bill of attainder" used by his opponents in an effort to oust him.

Moscow's defeat in Afghanistan will have significant international costs. It is an implicit admission that Soviet-supported revolutions can be reversed. It will demonstrate that there are limits on Moscow's willingness and ability to use its power abroad, tarnish its prestige among some elements of the Communist movement, and lead other beleaguered Soviet clients to question Soviet resolve.

Nevertheless, we—as well as the Soviets—believe the withdrawal will yield important benefits for Moscow. The move will be popular even among some Soviet allies. Moscow will net substantial public relations gains in the rest of the world— particularly in Western Europe—that could ultimately translate into more concrete diplomatic benefits. Gorbachev expects the withdrawal to have a positive impact on US-Soviet relations.

By enhancing the Soviet Union's image as a responsible superpower, withdrawal will present new challenges to Western diplomacy. In South Asia, US relations with Pakistan will be complicated. But Soviet withdrawal under the conditions we anticipate will also produce substantial benefits for the West:

- It will be seen as a triumph for Western policy.
- If it produces the benefits Gorbachev expects, withdrawal will probably add impetus to the ongoing rethinking in Moscow about the utility of military power in Third World conflicts and accelerate efforts to reach negotiated solutions on other issues.

Source: National Security Archive. Available online at http://nsarchive2 .gwu.edu/NSAEBB/NSAEBB57/us9.pdf.

ANALYSIS

This intelligence estimate proved extremely accurate as the Soviets would soon agree to withdraw their forces as part of the Geneva Accords (Document 8). By 1988, the war had begun to eat into Soviet defense spending and had prompted elements of the public to question the regime with unprecedented frequency. This estimate mostly calculates the foreign policy costs to the war on the Soviets, but the long war carried with it serious domestic consequences, too.

- **Document 8: The Geneva Accords of 1988 (Afghanistan)**
- **When:** April 14, 1988
- **Where:** Geneva, Switzerland
- **Significance:** The Geneva Accords formalized relations between Afghanistan and Pakistan while setting a timetable for the withdrawal of Soviet forces.

DOCUMENT

Annex I
AGREEMENTS ON THE SETTLEMENT OF THE SITUATION RELATING TO AFGHANISTAN

Bilateral Agreement
Between the Republic of Afghanistan and the Islamic Republic of Pakistan on the Principles of Mutual Relations, in particular on Non-Interference and Non-Intervention

The Republic of Afghanistan and the Islamic Republic of Pakistan, hereinafter referred to as the High Contracting Parties,

Desiring to normalize relations and promote good-neighborliness and co-operation as well as to strengthen international peace and security in the region,

Considering that full observance of the principle of non-interference and non-intervention in the internal and external affairs of States is of the greatest importance for the maintenance of international peace and security and for the fulfillment of the proposes and principles of the Charter of the United Nations,

Reaffirming the inalienable right of States freely to determine their own political, economic, cultural and social systems in accordance with the will of their peoples, without outside intervention, interference, subversion, coercion or threat in any form whatsoever.

Mindful of the provisions of the Charter of the United Nations as well as the resolutions adopted by the United Nations on the principle of non-interference and non-intervention, in particular the Declaration on Principles of International Law concerning Friendly Relations and Co-operation among States in accordance with the Charter of the United Nations, of 24 October 1970, as well as the Declaration on the Inadmissibility of Intervention and Interference in the Internal Affairs of States, of 9 December 1981,

Have agreed as follows:

Article I

Relations between the High Contracting Parties shall be conducted in strict compliance with the principle of non-interference and non-intervention by States in the affairs of other States.

Article II

For the purpose of implementing the principle of non-interference and non-intervention, each High Contracting Party undertakes to comply with the following obligations:

(1) to respect the sovereignty, political independence, territorial integrity, national unity, security and non-alignment of the other High Contracting Party, as well as the national identity and cultural heritage of its people;

(2) to respect the sovereign and inalienable right of the other High Contracting Party freely to determine its own political, economic, cultural and

social systems, to develop its international relations and to exercise permanent sovereignty over its natural resources. In accordance with the will of its people, and without outside intervention, interference, subversion, coercion or threat in any form whatsoever;

(3) to refrain from the threat or use of force in any form whatsoever so as not to violate the boundaries of each other, to disrupt the political, social or economic order of the other High Contracting Party, to overthrow or change the political system of the other High Contracting Party or its Government, or to cause tension between the High Contracting Parties;

(4) to ensure that its territory is not used in any manner which would violate the sovereignty, political independence, territorial integrity and national unity or disrupt the political, economic and social stability of the other High Contracting Party;

(5) to refrain from armed intervention, subversion, military occupation or any other form of intervention and interference, overt or covert, directed at the other High Contracting Party, or any act of military political or economic interference in the internal affairs of the other High Contracting Party, including acts of reprisal involving the use of force;

(6) to refrain from any action or attempt in whatsoever form or under whatever pretext to destabilize or to undermine the stability of the other High Contracting Party or any of its institutions;

(7) to refrain from the promotion, encouragement or support, direct or indirect, of rebellious or secessionist activities against the other High Contracting Party, under any pretext whatsoever, or from any other action which seeks to disrupt the unity or to undermine or subvert the political order of the other High Contracting Party;

(8) to prevent within its territory the training, equipping, financing and recruitment of mercenaries from whatever origin for the purpose of hostile activities against the other High Contracting Party, or the sending of such mercenaries into the territory of the other High Contracting Party and accordingly to deny facilities, including financing for the training, equipping and transit of such mercenaries;

(9) to refrain from making any agreements or arrangements with other States designed to intervene or interference in the internal and external affairs of the other High Contracting Party;

(10) to abstain from any defamatory campaign, vilification or hostile propaganda for the purpose of intervening or interfering in the internal affairs of the other High Contracting Party;

(11) to prevent any assistance to or use of or tolerance of terrorist groups, saboteurs or subversive agents against the other High Contracting Party;

(12) to prevent within its territory the presence, harbouring, in camps and bases of otherwise, organizing, training, financing, equipping and arming of individuals and political, ethnic and any other groups for the purpose of creating subversion, disorder or unrest in the territory of the other High Contracting Party and accordingly also to prevent the use of mass media and the transportation of arms, ammunition and equipment by such individuals and groups.

(13) not to resort to or to allow any other action that could be considered as interference or intervention.

Article III

The present Agreement shall enter into force on 15 May 1988.

Article IV

Any steps that may be required in order to enable the High Contracting Parties to comply with the provisions of Article II of this Agreement shall be completed by the date on which this

Agreement enters into force.

Article V

This Agreement is drawn up in the English, Pashtu and Urdu languages, all texts being equally authentic. In case of any divergence of interpretation, the English text shall prevail.

Done in five original copies at Geneva this fourteenth day of April 1988.

(Signed by Afghanistan and Pakistan)

Declaration on International Guarantees

The Government of the Union of Soviet Socialist Republics and of the United States of America,

Expressing support that the Republic of Afghanistan and the Islamic Republic of Pakistan have concluded a negotiated political settlement designed to normalize relations and promote good-neighbourliness between the two countries as well as to strengthen international peace and security in the region;

Wishing in turn to contribute to the achievement of the objectives that the Republic of Afghanistan and the Islamic Republic of Pakistan have set themselves, and wish a view to ensuring respect for their sovereignty, independence, territorial integrity and non-alignment;

Undertake to invariably refrain from any form of interference and intervention in the internal affairs of the Republic of Afghanistan and the Islamic Republic of Pakistan and to respect the commitments contained in the bilateral Agreement between the Republic of Afghanistan and the Islamic Republic of Pakistan on the Principles of Mutual Relations, in particular on Non- Interference and Non-Intervention;

Urge all States to act likewise.

The present Declaration shall enter into force on 15 May 1988.

Done at Geneva, this fourteenth day of April 1988 in five original copies, each in the English and Russian languages, both texts being equally authentic.

(Signed by the USSR and the USA)

Bilateral Agreement between the Republic of Afghanistan and the Islamic Republic of Pakistan on the Voluntary Return of Refugees

The Republic of Afghanistan and the Islamic Republic of Pakistan, hereinafter referred to as the High Contracting Parties,

Desiring to normalize relations and promote good-neighbourliness and co-operation as well as to strengthen international peace and security in the region,

Convinced that voluntary and unimpeded repatriation constitutes the most appropriate solution for the problem of Afghan refugees present in the Islamic Republic of Pakistan and having ascertained that the arrangements for the return of the Afghan refugees are satisfactory to them,

Have agreed as follows:

Article I

All Afghan refugees temporarily present in the territory of the Islamic Republic of Pakistan shall be given the opportunity to return voluntarily to their homeland in accordance with the arrangements and conditions set out in the present Agreement.

Article II

The Government of the Republic of Afghanistan shall take all necessary measures to ensure the following conditions for the voluntary return of Afghan refugees to their homeland:

(a) All refugees shall be allowed to return in freedom to their homeland;

(b) All returnees shall enjoy the free choice of domicile and freedom of movement within the Republic of Afghanistan;

(c) All returnees shall enjoy the right to work, to adequate living conditions and to share in the welfare of the State;

(d) All returnees shall enjoy the right to participate on an equal basis in the civic affairs of the Republic of Afghanistan. They shall be ensured equal benefits from the solution of the land question on the basis of the Land and Water Reform;

(e) All returnees shall enjoy the same rights and privileges, including freedom of religion, and have the same obligations and responsibilities as any other citizens of the Republic of Afghanistan without discrimination.

The Government of the Republic of Afghanistan undertakes to implement these measures and to provide, within its possibilities, all necessary assistance in the process of repatriation.

Article III

The Government of the Islamic Republic of Pakistan shall facilitate the voluntary, orderly and peaceful repatriation of all Afghan refugees staying within its territory and undertakes to provide, within its possibilities, all necessary assistance in the process of repatriation.

. . .

Agreement on the Interrelationships for the Settlement of the Situation Relating to Afghanistan

1. The diplomatic process initiated by the Secretary-General of the United Nations with the support of all Governments concerned and aimed at achieving, through negotiations, a political settlement of the situation relating to Afghanistan has been successfully brought to an end.

2. Having agreed to work towards a comprehensive settlement designed to resolve the various issues involved and to establish a framework for good-neighbourliness and co-operation, the Government of the Republic of Afghanistan and the Government of the Islamic Republic of Pakistan entered into negotiations through

the intermediary or the Personal Representative of the Secretary-General at Geneva from 16 to 24 June 1982. Following consultations held by the Personal Representative in Islamabad, Kabul and Teheran from 21 January to 7 February 1983, the negotiations continued at Geneva from 11 to 22 April and from 12 to 24 June 1983. The Personal Representative again visited the area for high level discussions from 3 to 15 April 1984. It was then agreed to change the format of the negotiations and, in pursuance thereof, proximity talks through the intermediary of the Personal Representative were held at Geneva from 24 to 30 August 1984. Another visit to the area by the Personal Representative from 25 to 31 May 1985 preceded further rounds of proximity talks held at Geneva from 20 to 25 June, from 27 to 30 August and from 16 to 19 December 1985. The Personal Representative paid an additional visit to the area from 8 to 18 March 1986 for consultations. The final round of negotiations began as proximity talks at Geneva on 5 May 1986, was suspended on 23 May 1986, and was resumed from 31 July to 8 August 1986. The Personal Representative visited the area from 20 November to 3 December 1986 for further consultations and the talks at Geneva were resumed again from 25 February to 9 March 1987, and from 7 to 11 September 1987. The Personal Representative again visited the area from 18 January to 9 February 1988 and the talks resumed at Geneva from 2 March to 8 April 1988. The format of the negotiations was changed on 14 April 1988, when the instruments comprising the settlement were finalized, and, accordingly, direct talks were held at that stage. The Government of the Islamic Republic of Iran was kept informed of the progress of the negotiations throughout the diplomatic process.

3. The Government of the Republic of Afghanistan and the Government of the Islamic Republic of Pakistan took part in the negotiations with the expressed conviction that they were acting in accordance with their rights and obligations under the Charter of the United Nations and agreed that the political settlement should be based on the following principles of international law:

– The principle that States shall refrain in their international relations from the threat of use of force against the territorial integrity or political independence of any State, or in any other manner inconsistent with the purposes of the United Nations;

– The principle that States shall settle their international disputes by peaceful means in such a manner that international peace and security and justice are not endangered;

– The duty not to intervene in matters within the domestic jurisdiction of any State, in accordance with the Charter of the United Nations;

– The duty of States to co-operate with one another in accordance with the Charter of the United Nations;

– The principle of equal rights and self-determination of peoples;

– The principle of sovereign equality of States;

– The principle that States shall fulfil in good faith the obligations assumed by them in accordance with the Charter of the United Nations.

The two Governments further affirmed the right of the Afghan refugees to return to their homeland in a voluntary and unimpeded manner.

4. The following instruments were concluded on this date as component parts of the political settlement:

A Bilateral Agreement between the Republic of Afghanistan and the Islamic Republic of Pakistan on the Principles of Mutual Relations, in particular on Non-interference and Non-intervention;

A Declaration on International Guarantees by the Union of Soviet Socialist Republics and the United States of America;

A Bilateral Agreement between the Republic of Afghanistan and the Islamic Republic of Pakistan on the Voluntary Return of Refugees;

The present Agreement on the Interrelationships for the Settlement of the Situation Relating to Afghanistan.

5. The Bilateral Agreement on the Principles of Mutual Relations, in particular on Non-interference and Non-intervention; the Declaration on International Guarantees; the Bilateral Agreement on the Voluntary Return of Refugees; and the present Agreement on the Interrelationships for the Settlement of the Situation Relating to Afghanistan will enter into force on 15 May 1988. In accordance with the time-frame agreed upon between the Union of Soviet Socialist Republics and the Republic of Afghanistan there will be a phased withdrawal of the foreign troops which will start on the date of entry into force mentioned above. One half of the troops will be withdrawn by 15 August 1988 and the withdrawal of all troops will be completed within nine months.

6. The interrelationships in paragraph 5 above have been agreed upon in order to achieve effectively the purpose of the political settlement, namely, that as from 15 May 1988, there will be no interference and intervention in any form in the affairs of the Parties; the international guarantees will be in operation; the voluntary return of the refugees to their homeland will start and be completed within the time-frame specified in the agreement on the voluntary return of the refugees; and the phased withdrawal of the foreign troops will start and be completed within the time-frame envisaged in paragraph 5. It is therefore essential that all the obligations deriving from the instruments concluded as component parts of the settlement be strictly fulfilled and that all the steps required to ensure full compliance with all the provisions of the instruments be completed in good faith.

. . .

The representatives of the Parties, being duly authorized thereto by their respective Governments, have affixed their signatures hereunder. The Secretary-General of the United Nations was present.

Done, at Geneva, this fourteen day of April 1988, in five original copies each in the English, Pashtu, Russian and Urdu languages, all being equally authentic. In case of any dispute regarding the interpretation the English text shall prevail.

(Signed by Afghanistan and Pakistan)

In witness thereof, the representatives of the States-Guarantors affixed their signatures hereunder:

(Signed by the USSR and USA).

. . .

Source: Agreements on the Settlement of the Situation Relating to Afghanistan. United Nations. Available online at https://peacemaker.un.org/node/641.

ANALYSIS

The Geneva Accords took effect on May 15, 1988, and formally ended the Soviet intervention in Afghanistan. As part of the Agreement on the Interrelationships for the Settlement of the Situation Relating to Afghanistan, the Soviets agreed to withdraw their forces within nine months. The last Soviet troops withdrew, on schedule, on February 15, 1989.

The agreement, however, was not without flaws. The negotiating parties consisted of the Soviet-backed Afghan government, Pakistan, the Soviet Union, and the United States. Crucially, no part of the mujahedeen was invited to participate in the talks. Thus, while it brought the Soviet occupation to an end, it did little to bring about a political reconciliation in Afghanistan that could end all of the fighting.

- **Document 9: U.S. Army, "Lessons from the War in Afghanistan"**
- **When:** May 1989
- **Where:** Arlington, Virginia
- **Significance:** An internal Army study that sought to distill the military lessons of the war in Afghanistan.

DOCUMENT

Lessons from the War in Afghanistan
Part I. Introduction

. . .

The Soviets installed in power a new Afghan communist leader, Babrak Karmal, and hoped to shore up the Democratic Republic of Afghanistan (later renamed the Republic of Afghanistan) military to the point where it could control the insurgency. What was clearly perceived by the insurgents as a foreign invasion, however, further inflamed the situation. What had earlier been a disjointed "Jihad" (Holy War) against the communist government in Kabul, now took on greater urgency and served as the strongest unifying factor for the insurgents. As one Soviet news commentator remarked in the newspaper IZVESTIYA in late 1988, "The Afghan people now had invading infidels against whom to unite." Due to this, and the continuing ineffectiveness of the Afghan Army, the Soviets were compelled to go over to the offensive. But no Soviet textbook had prepared them for the tactical problems of counterinsurgency (COIN) warfare.

While the insurgency reflected the classic threat—no fixed battle lines; low technology insurgent warfare; small, short duration insurgent targets—several factors gave the Soviet campaign in Afghanistan a unique set of characteristics. For one, the Kremlin obviously imposed limitations on the size of the Soviet force deployment. There would be no significant build-up in force strength. The Soviet name for their forces in Afghanistan, "Limited Contingent," was as real as it was propagandistic. This had a significant effect on the conduct of operations: insufficient forces were available to expand appreciably 40th Army's area of physical control, or to identify and attack many insurgent targets at the same time. When major operations were conducted in one part of the country, forces had to be drawn from other areas, leaving those areas vulnerable to insurgent activities. Moreover, early in the war, especially after Brezhnev's death, Soviet leaders apparently assigned a high priority to minimizing personnel and equipment losses. This in turn caused Soviet operations to exhibit an unusual degree of caution and lack of boldness when employing troops at the tactical level.

Other factors influencing the nature of the Afghan War were:

- Geographic proximity to the USSR, with direct access to well developed and secure Soviet internal LOCs
- Rugged, desolate terrain where movement was limited to a few established routes and often difficult to conceal
- Deep-rooted religious and tribal/regional divisions among both the client and insurgent forces in an environment where there was no well-developed traditional sense of nationalism
- Primitive nature of the Afghan economic infrastructure and extremely limited LOCs

These objectives and characteristics created a combat environment very different from the European war scenario against NATO which the conscript-based Soviet Armed Forces were trained and equipped to fight. Afghanistan was not a high-intensity war fought by large armored and air forces, with massed formations penetrating deep into enemy rear areas to strike a crippling blow at the enemy's ability to resist. Instead, the 40th Army settled into bases along the primary LOCs and near key cities and towns. It found itself in a protracted war, albeit often intense and at a high tempo, fought at the tactical level, where two-thirds of its forces were committed to resupply or defensive security missions. The elusive insurgents were dispersed throughout the country. With no railways, logistic support for 40th Army and the Afghan economy depended primarily on the sparse, exposed road network, creating a constant, but unavoidable Soviet vulnerability.

<u>Applicability of the Lessons</u>

        . . .

<u>Counterinsurgency</u>

Many lessons from the Soviet COIN experience will appear very familiar to students of the U.S. involvement in Vietnam. They represent many of the tactical dilemmas found in any COIN operation. Soviet failure to learn from the U.S. and other applicable COIN experiences caused them to make many of the same errors.

. . .

Tactical Lessons from the Mujahideen Experience

LESSON: Do not provide COIN forces with large, lucrative targets.

. . .

LESSON: Know the enemy's tactics and routines.

. . .

LESSON: Be aware of personal and group rivalries and conflicts.

. . .

Convoy Ambushes

. . .

LESSON: Locate and destroy vehicle marshalling areas.

. . .

Intelligence and Security

LESSON: Take full advantage of the cultural and linguistic identities between insurgent and government personnel.

. . .

Air Defense

. . .

LESSON: Position base camps so as to reduce the effectiveness of air attacks.

. . .

LESSON: Know the effects of terrain on air recce.

. . .

LESSON: The use of light-weight, easily operated surface-to-air missiles (SAM) help to overcome the massive fire superiority usually characteristic of COIN forces.

. . .

Part III. Counterinsurgency
Soviet Objectives

Rather than being an "invasion," the introduction of Soviet combat forces in December 1979 was an "intervention" in a COIN effort which had begun shortly after the Afghan Communist Party coup in April 1978. The USSR sent its forces into Afghanistan primarily for the purpose of taking over security responsibilities, so that government forces could concentrate on putting down the ever-growing insurgency. Thus the initial Soviet objectives were to:

- Control the cities and towns
- Secure the major lines of communications (LOC)
- Train and equip government forces

As the insurgency expanded and the Afghan Army proved inadequate to the task, the Soviet "Limited Contingent" in Afghanistan soon found itself enmeshed in full-fledged COIN operations. Thus, by mid-1980 the Soviets acquired the following additional missions:

- Eliminate insurgent centers
- Separate insurgents from the population
- Deny by interdiction outside aid and sanctuary

Nonetheless, this "low-intensity conflict" was to be conducted with a minimum of losses in personnel and equipment. As pointed out above, there would be no significant troop buildup, nor great expansion of the logistics and transportation infrastructures. The Soviets partially succeeded in only the first three of the above missions.

. . .

Command and Control

LESSON: Decentralize planning and execution of low-level operations.

. . .

LESSON: Train battalion commanders and staffs to operate with combined arms task forces.

. . .

Maneuver

. . .

LESSON: Use dismounted infantry or air assault teams to identify and destroy antitank ambushes.

. . .

LESSON: Constantly review and reassess the effectiveness of tactics being applied against insurgent forces.

. . .

LESSON: Use smoke as a defensive measure when caught in an ambush.

. . .

Fire Support

. . .

LESSON: Helicopter operations at night require extensive training and familiarity with the terrain.

. . .

LESSON: Use air transport whenever possible.

. . .

Source: National Security Archive. Available online at http://nsarchive2.gwu.edu//NSAEBB/NSAEBB57/us11.pdf.

ANALYSIS

This analysis suggested that the Soviets significantly handicapped their own war effort and that this was perhaps the biggest factor in explaining their defeat. The

Chapter 1 • The Soviet Invasion and Civil War   29

Soviet army was already poorly trained and equipped to fight an insurgency, but the lack of troops and a political desire to limit the casualties of the committed forces made it nearly impossible for the Soviets to overcome all of the political and social issues that this analysis did not even touch upon.

- **Document 10: Islamabad Accord**
- **When:** March 7, 1993
- **Where:** Islamabad, Pakistan
- **Significance:** These accords unsuccessfully attempted to end the fighting among the various factions vying for control of the post-Soviet Islamic State of Afghanistan.

DOCUMENT

LETTER DATED 17 MARCH 1993 FROM THE CHARGE D'AFFAIRES A.I. OF THE PERMANENT MISSION OF AFGHANISTAN TO THE UNITED NATIONS ADDRESSED TO THE SECRETARY-GENERAL

As you are aware, after intensive negotiations between the President of the Islamic State of Afghanistan and other Afghan leaders, a peace accord was signed on 7 March 1993.

The negotiations and consultations took place in Islamabad where the President and other Afghan leaders met at the invitation of the Prime Minister of Pakistan, H.E. Muhammad Nawaz Sharif. Prince Turki al-Faisal of Saudi Arabia and Dr. Alaedin Broujerdi, the Deputy Foreign Minister of the Islamic Republic of Iran were also present during the negotiations.

I have the honour to enclose the text of the Afghan Peace Accord and request that this letter, along with its enclosures, the Peace Accord and its annex, "Division of Powers", be circulated as a document of the Security Council.

(Signed) ABDUL RAHIM GHAFOORZAI
Ambassador

Deputy Permanent Representative
Charge d'affaires a.i.

Annex I
Afghan Peace Accord

Given our submission to the will of Allah Almighty and commitment to seeking guidance from the Holy Quran and Sunnah,

DID YOU KNOW?

Durand Line

The Durand Line, named after British diplomat Sir Henry Mortimer Durand, was fixed in 1896 to delineate the border between India and Afghanistan. Britain had attempted two invasions of Afghanistan in the 19th century, seeking to add the territory to its holdings in India. The Afghans, however, repelled these attacks. The Russian Empire resented these attempted British seizures and sought to keep Afghanistan as a buffer state between the two nations' respective territories. Thus, in 1893, Durand negotiated with the Afghan emir, Abdur Rahman Khan, to set a border that, following extensive surveys, was fixed in 1896. The boundary, however, cut through the middle of ethnic Pashtun lands and left members of the group living in Afghanistan and India. Pashtun nationalism remained dormant, however, until after the partition of India and Pakistan in 1947, and has since grown into a major issue for the Afghan and Pakistani governments.

Recalling the glorious success of the epic Jehad waged by the valiant Afghan people against foreign occupation,

Desirous of ensuring that the fruits of this glorious Jehad bring peace, progress and prosperity for the Afghan people,

Having agreed to bringing armed hostilities to an end,

Recognizing the need for a broad-based Islamic Government in which all parties and groups representing all segments of Muslim Afghan society are represented so that the process of political transition can be advanced in an atmosphere of peace, harmony and stability,

Committed to the preservation of unity, sovereignty and territorial integrity of Afghanistan,

Recognizing the urgency of rehabilitation and reconstruction of Afghanistan and of facilitating the return of all Afghan refugees,

Committed to promoting peace and security in the region,

Responding to the call of Khadim Al-Harmain Al-Sharifain His Majesty King Fahd Bin Abdul Aziz to resolve the differences among Afghan brothers through a peaceful dialogue,

Appreciating the constructive role of good offices of Mr. Muhammad Nawaz Sharif, Prime Minister of the Islamic Republic of Pakistan and his sincere efforts to promote peace and conciliation in Afghanistan,

Recognizing the positive support for these efforts extended by the Governments of the Kingdom of Saudi Arabia and the Islamic Republic of Iran, who have sent their Special Envoys for the conciliation talks in Islamabad,

Having undertaken intensive intra-Afghan consultations separately and jointly to consolidate the gains of the glorious Jehad,

All the parties and groups concerned have agreed as follows:

1. To the formation of a Government for a period of 18 months in which President Burhanuddin Rabbani would remain President and Eng. Gulbadin Hikmatyar or his nominee would assume the office of Prime Minister. The powers of the President and Prime Minister and his cabinet which have been formulated through mutual consultations will form part of this Accord and is annexed;

2. The Cabinet shall be formed by the Prime Minister in consultations with the President, and leaders of Mujahideen Parties within two weeks of the signing of this Accord;

3. The following electoral process is agreed for implementation in a period of not more than 18 months with effect from 29 December 1992:

(a) The immediate formation of an independent Election Commission by all parties with full powers;

(b) The Election Commission shall be mandated to hold elections for a Grand Constituent Assembly within eight months from the date of signature of this Accord;

(c) The duly elected Grant Constituent Assembly shall formulate a Constitution under which general elections for the President and the Parliament shall be held within the prescribed period of 18 months mentioned above;

4. A Defence Council comprising two members from each party will be set up to, inter alia,

(a) Enable the formation of a national Army;

(b) Take possession of heavy weapons from all parties and sources which may be removed from Kabul and other cities and kept out of range to ensure the security of the Capital;

(c) Ensure that all roads in Afghanistan are kept open for normal use;

(d) Ensure that State funds shall not be used to finance private armies or armed retainers;

(e) Ensure that operational control of the armed forces shall be with the Defence Council;

5. There shall be immediate and unconditional release of all Afghan detainees held by the Government and different parties during the armed hostilities;

6. All public and private buildings, residential areas and properties occupied by different armed groups during the hostilities shall be returned to their original owners. Effective steps shall be taken to facilitate the return of displaced persons to their respective homes and locations;

7. An All Party Committee shall be constituted to supervise control over the monetary system and currency regulations to keep it in conformity with existing Afghan banking laws and regulations;

8. A cease-fire shall come into force with immediate effect. After the formation of the Cabinet, there shall be permanent cessation of hostilities;

9. A Joint Commission comprising representatives of the Organization of the Islamic Conference and of all Afghan parties shall be formed to monitor the cease-fire and cessation of hostilities.

In confirmation of the above Accord, the following have affixed their signatures hereunder, on Sunday, 7 March 1993 in Islamabad, Pakistan.

(Signed)
Prof. Burhan-ud-Din Rabbani
Jamiat-e-Islami
President of the Islamic State
of Afghanistan

(Signed)
Moulvi Muhammad Nabi Muhammadi
Harkat-e-Inqilab-e-Islami

(Signed)
Engr Gulbadin Hikmatyar
Hizb-e-Islami

(Signed)
With my reservation to the
President time.
Prof. Sibghatullah Mujjadidi
Jabha-e-Nijat-e-Milli

(Signed)
Pir Syed Ahmed Gaillani
Mahaz-e-Milli
Sheikh Asif Mohseni
Harkat-e-Islami

(Signed)
With my reservation to the
President time.
Engineer Ahmed Shah
Ahmadzai Ittehad-e-Islami

(Signed)
Ayatullah Fazil
Hizb-e-Wahdat-e-Islami

. . .

Source: Afghan Peace Accord. United Nations. Available online at https://peacemaker.un.org/node/643.

ANALYSIS

Following the Soviet withdrawal in 1989, its client government continued to fight on until its collapse in 1992. Without the common threat posed by the Communist government, however, the former mujahedeen leaders began to fight among themselves. The bulk of the mujahedeen leaders formed the new Islamic State of Afghanistan, but Gulbuddin Hekmatyar fought the new state. These accords sought to create a power-sharing agreement by allowing Hekmatyar to become prime minister within the government. He soon reneged on the agreement and resumed fighting the government. As a result, a state of anarchy persisted throughout much of Afghanistan.

- **Document 11: U.S. Consulate (Peshawar), Cable, "New Fighting and New Forces in Kandahar"**
- **When:** November 3, 1994

- **Where:** Peshawar, Pakistan
- **Significance:** This U.S. State Department cable was among the first official notices of the emergence of the Taliban in late 1994 and provided some early estimates of the group's origins and ultimate goals.

DOCUMENT

FM AMCONSUL PESHAWAR
TO SECSTATE WASHDC
. . .
SUBJECT: NEW FIGHTING AND NEW FORCES IN KANDAHAR
. . .

2. Summary. Fighting broke out earlier this week in Kandahar Province between an alliance of established HiG and NIFA commanders and a new movement, the Taliban ("Seekers"). Jamiat commander Naqib has remained aloof so far from the fighting, which has strained Pakistan's much-publicized truck caravan to central Asia. While speculation is rife about who the Taliban actually support and are being supported by, it appears that the well-armed movement—largely drawn from religious students that did not fight in the jihad—may represent a new phenomenon independent from party politics. End Summary.

NEW FIGHTING IN KANDAHAR PROVINCE

3. According to multiple sources, troops belonging to Hekmetyar commander Sar Kateb ("Head Clerk"), Governor Gul Agha (nominally NIFA), commander Lalai (also nominally NIFA, but reportedly with Sayaaf contacts), and commander Mansur (a former Khalqi militia leader for the Achikzai tribe, now free lance commander) attacked on Tuesday, November 1, the village of Takht-E Pul astride the Chaman-Kandahar Highway and held by a new factor in the Afghan equation, the new Taliban. According to sources just returned from Kandahar, the Tuesday attack was repulsed as was a follow-up attack on Wednesday. No numbers of forces committed are available. A small force (estimated at 90 or less) of well-armed and experienced troops under Mullah Yar Mohammed (a Khalis commander whose troops previously fought under the name of the Taliban) have reportedly left their stronghold in Arghistan District south of the Kandahar Airport to support the besieged Taliban by attacking the commanders' alliance from the rear.

4. New Taliban forces have told our sources that on the afternoon of November 1 they attacked and

DID YOU KNOW?

Gulbuddin Hekmatyar

Gulbuddin Hekmatyar is an Afghan political and military leader. Born in 1947, Hekmatyar adopted a conservative Islamic worldview after being exiled from the communist People's Democratic Party of Afghanistan in the early 1970s. He founded Hezb-i-Islami (HiG) in 1975 and advocated for an Islamic takeover of the Afghan government. He led his group as part of the mujahedeen against the Soviets, but, after the Soviet withdrawal, he battled with other mujahedeen factions for control and briefly served as prime minister in 1992. His forces caused the deaths of many civilians in Kabul, which caused his popularity to drop rapidly. His Pakistani benefactors switched their support for the Taliban after 1994, compelling Hekmatyar to ally with the government in Kabul. He briefly served as prime minister again in 1996, but his unpopularity forced him into exile in Iran until 2003. From exile, he condemned both Pakistan and the U.S. occupation, leading the State Department to label him a terrorist. He eventually returned to Afghanistan to direct his forces against the Karzai government. Ever the dealmaker, however, Hekmatyar negotiated a peace deal with President Ashraf Ghani in 2016 and received a pardon.

took two hilltop positions belonging to HiG Commander Sar Kateb near Bara Pul west of Kandahar city. So far, it is reported, the Taliban forces have not advanced toward Sar Kateb's headquarters, but our sources speculate that if they are going to be successful—Jamiat commander Naqibullah may break the truce in effect between his forces and Sar Kateb's and move in on the side of the Taliban. Taliban forces are said, by some journalist sources, to have now "cleaned up" the Kandahar-Herat Road as far as the eastern edge of Farah Prov nce.

THE LONG AND WINDING ROAD GETS ROCKIER

5. Caught up in this new conflict is the much publicized first Pakistani convoy of aid supplies to Afghanistan and the NIS. This 30-plus vehicle convoy, a manifestation of Pakistani Interior Minister Babar's vision of opening up trade between Pakistan and the central Asian states via Chaman, Kandahar, and Herat, was reportedly originally scheduled to enter Afghanistan on October 15, but the departure was [redacted] held up because of objections of the new Taliban holding the Afghan border town of Spin Boldak.

6. [Redacted] New Taliban spokesman Mullah Mohammad Ghaus had set the following conditions to allow the convoy to enter Afghanistan:

–For sovereignty's sake, the convoy arrangements should be vetted by Governor Gul Agha rather than unilaterally established by the government of Pakistan;

–The convoy must include Afghan transports, rather than just Pakistani vehicles;

–Pakistan must agree to release Afghan transit goods being held, some for more than two years, in Karachi; and,

–Pakistan and Afghanistan must come to a comprehensive agreement regarding the transit trade.

7. [Redacted] modestly noting his own role as a facilitator, told us that the Taliban and Pakistani Ministry of Interior teams had been negotiating over the past two weeks, and had apparently reached some unspecified compromise. According to embassy sources, Taliban members along with Pakistan's consul in Kandahar, Col (ret'd) Iman, joined the convoy which reportedly cleared the border and passed through Spin Boldak without incident on October 31. According to press reports, generally confirmed by [redacted] embassy sources, the presence of the upstart Taliban convoy was too much of a provocation (and the riches of the convoy perhaps too much of a temptation) to the troops of Gul Agha, Lalai, and Mansur who stopped the convoy south of Kandahar with demands that Kandahar's share of the supplied be off-loaded. [Redacted] the drivers were "roughed up," but there were no casualties and the trucks remain—at least as of Wednesday evening—in Kandahar.

8. The conflicts has [sic] caused cancellation of special envoy Mestiri's scheduled visit to Kandahar this week. Reportedly, Kandahari members of the UN's Advisory Council are traveling to Kandahar in their tribal/religious leader capacities to attempt to stop the fighting and resolve the caravan dispute.

TALIBAN—A NEW VARIABLE

9. During the jihad, a group of fighters calling themselves the Taliban ("Seekers," a term applied to religious students) were active in the Kandahar region under Khalis commander Mullah Yar Mohammad. In early summer, however, another group using the Taliban name surfaced in Kandahar province under the leadership of Mullah Mohammad Omar and his deputy, a Mullah Ehsanullah. These new Taliban are

mainly made up of teenage and early 20's religious students that did not fight in the jihad. The movement's initial goal, according to their spokesman, was to "clean up" the Chaman-Kandahar Highway and one of their first acts was a summary Shariat trial of Mullah Fatah Mohammad, a free lance commander who had maintained a "toll booth" in Arghistan District, extracting arbitrary payments (and selected merchandise) from trucks en route to and from Kandahar. Fatah Mohammad had reportedly refused the Taliban's orders to open the road, so after a short firefight and Fatah Mohammad's capture, he was tried and hanged for brigandage. Independent toll stations along the Chaman-Kandahar Highway reportedly drastically reduced in number following this example.

10. These initial actions led to some speculation that the Taliban—who [redacted] in what is almost certainly an exaggeration, says now number in the low thousands—were being supported by Pakistani and Afghan businessmen. It also led to some tension in the province between this new force and most of the established commanders, particularly Lalai and Sar Kateb, who derived significant revenues from toll collections and may have felt threatened by the evolution of a new force motivated by something other than party considerations. Main Jamiat commander in Kandahar Mullah Naqib, however, publicly supported the Taliban actions.

11. On October 13, the Taliban occupied the formerly HiG dominated border town of Spin Boldak following a night attack begun on October 12 supported by, according to one generally reliable source, rocket artillery from the south. Casualties are said to have included five HiG and three Taliban dead. The campaign had started on October 9, with Taliban cleaning up a number of "free lance" checkposts between Kandahar and the border in an effort that reportedly enjoyed the initial tacit approval of Governor Gul Agha. In an October 14/15 interview with BBC, Taliban deputy Ehsanullah said that his group had taken the action to:

–Eliminate the Wahabi and Salifi (another term for certain fundamentalists, usually associated with certain Hekmetyar supporters) influence from the area; and,

–Open the highway to free traffic.

Ehsanullah also took the opportunity of the interview to state that the Taliban support the Mestiri process, and believe in a Loya Jirga as an essential step in selecting a government. Ehsanullah also reportedly belittled the defenders of the Spin Boldak, including the commander Mohammad Nabi who was associated with the earlier kidnapping of European drug enforcement personnel in the area.

12. Few observers thought that the timing of the Spin Boldak was independent of Pakistani Interior Minister Babar's announced plans to open the highway to central Asia. The recruiting of young Taliban members from the madrasas (religious schools) of Quetta and Peshawar with, according to some reports, the assistance of Pakistan's Fazl Rehman's JUI Party coupled, with the reported arming of the Taliban with brand new weapons (*still in their grease* according to some sources) led to a suspicion in many quarters that the new Taliban had formed with the active support of the GOP.

13. In their own defense, Taliban members reportedly say that they are independent of Pakistan, and point to their delay of the convoy as evidence. According to embassy sources in the Pakistani government, the Taliban are acting as Rabbani or Sayaaf surrogates—although why Rabbani would need surrogates beyond powerful commander Naqib is open to question.

14. According to [redacted] who says he had been "supporting" the Taliban in their early stages, the armed opposition to the Taliban was actually being stage-managed by Sayaaf who [redacted] says despatched Ittehad military chief Capt Musa to the area on Sunday. [Redacted] went on to note that he suspects Sayaaf was still stinging over the Taliban's anti-Wahabi stance and was trying to take advantage of the resentment the pious and apparently austere Taliban had already engendered among the established leaders.

COMMENT

15. The Taliban have been characterized as being simultaneously Pakistani tools and anti-Pakistan, and pro- and anti-Sayaaf. All observers agree that they appear to be anti-Hekmetyar. There are elements to support all of these various characterizations, leading one to believe that Taliban is a sui generis phenomenon fueled in part by frustration at the party leaders' failure to achieve peace, disgust at the venal actions of many of the various party commanders, and possibly a sincere desire to establish an Islamic peace. Since their elders had their jihad, the new Taliban may wish to seek glory by playing their part in reforming Afghanistan.

16. It is very possible that the Taliban have received support from a number of sources, including Pakistan, the business community, commander Naqib, and even nominal NIFA elements. If the Taliban was created by secular or outside forces, however, it is very possible that their backers may find that they have created a tiger that is more than willing to take independent action and not be anyone's tool.

Smyth

. . .

Source: National Security Archive. Available online at http://nsarchive2.gwu.edu/NSAEBB/NSAEBB97/tal1.pdf.

ANALYSIS

Some of the details included in this first analysis of the Taliban would be called into question by further information, but the consular officials accurately assessed the Taliban's threat to the existing factions in Afghanistan and the possibility that the group might become a force to be reckoned with in Afghan politics. Given the continued infighting among the Afghan government (see Document 17), the Taliban's offers of stability and security appeared attractive to a war-ravaged populace.

- **Document 12: U.S. Embassy (Islamabad), Cable, "The Taliban—Who Knows What the Movement Means?"**
- **When:** November 28, 1994
- **Where:** Islamabad, Pakistan
- **Significance:** A U.S. State Department cable that further analyzed the origins and goals of the Taliban soon after the group's emergence.

DOCUMENT

FM AMEMBASSY ISLAMABAD
TO SECSTATE WASHDC

. . .

SUBJECT: THE TALIBAN—WHO KNOWS WHAT THE MOVEMENT
MEANS?

. . .

2. This message was principally drafted by consulate in Peshawar and coordinated with embassy Islamabad.

SUMMARY

3. The origins, goals, and sponsors of the "Taliban" (religious students) movement remain unclear, even to well-informed Afghans. The organization appears to have its origins in the Jehadi group of the same name, which consisted of Pashtun madrasa students from Afghanistan's southwest who fought with distinction against the Soviets. After the war, the students returned to their religious schools and now to have been re-mobilized through a combination of frustration with extortionist party commanders and foreign financing—probably by conservative religious groups in Pakistan. Taliban leaders are political Islamists who have declared Sharia law in Kandahar, and are reported to follow a conservative, traditionalist religious line.

4. The Taliban now control most of Kandahar province, have moved into Zabul and Ghazni, and appear to enjoy the open admiration of most Afghans for taking action against extortionist party commanders and unresponsive party leadership. The uncontroversial, conservative values espoused by the traditionalist, mullah-led group (freeing the roads from bandits, restoring law and order and respect for traditional religious norms, etc.) have made it difficult for both factional and neutral Afghan activists to publicly express their reservations about the popular movement's patrons and possible ulterior motives.

5. Privately, however, party leaders are worried by both the rapid growth of the Taliban movement and its obvious popularity. Both Rabbani and Hekmetyar are looking for ways to cooperate with or coopt the organization, with Hekmetyar particularly worried by the support the group has received from pro-Rabbani Mullah Naqib in Kandahar. A number of Afghan political opportunists and has-beens are flocking to the Taliban in hopes of resuscitating moribund political careers. How successful outside elements—be they Afghans or Pakistanis—will be in controlling or influencing the Taliban remains very much in doubt.

6. Some Afghan observers argue that, despite probable assistance from Pakistan's JUI, the Taliban lack the logistics, training, administrative experience and financial backing to expand much farther. The consternation of the Afghan factions would tend to suggest otherwise. Although much else about the Taliban is murky, one fact is clear: the strong support the Taliban receive from the Afghan people reflects popular frustration with the party leaders and a strong desire for peace and stability. End Summary.

MEET THE NEW BOSS

. . .

8. Following sharp fighting with HiG and Ittehad-affiliated commanders, and the apparent cooption of the major Jamiat commander in the region (Mullah Naqib), the Taliban control all but two or three northern districts in Kandahar province, are seeking to bring independent commanders in Oruzgan to heel, and have a significant presence in Helmand Province. Helmand Governor Ghaffour Akhunzada of Harakat, himself a cleric, has reportedly declared "I am a Talib," although whether this should be read as welcoming the presence of the Taliban or indicating that they are unnecessary in Helmand is unclear.

9. According to embassy sources, the Taliban are said to have made agreements with the governor of Zabul and Ghazni Governor Qari Baba to allow them to police the Kandahar-Kabul Road. Recent Taliban successes in Ghazni and Zabul, however, in contrast to earlier ones, are said to depend upon bribing commanders than fighting them. Yet despite this significant activity, the specifics of the group's sponsorship, membership, and objectives remain murky.

. . .

SAME AS THE OLD BOSS?

11. According to embassy sources, the current Taliban movement draws its inspiration (and some of its leaders) from the old Taliban organization. A group of religious students and mullas who fought with distinction in the Kandahar region during the jehad. Following the end of the war, many of these Taliban returned home to study and teach in religious schools (madrasas). This older group, joined by younger students from the area, now comprise the core of the contemporary movement, knowledgeable Kandaharis report. These observers believe that the Taliban enjoy the support of the bazaaris, whose commercial activities have been hampered by the highway "toll booths." Giving a black eye to "arrogant" local commanders and causing a discomfort to the stubborn party leaders are in and of themselves activities with enormous mass appeal, leading some southern party commanders such as Abdul Razak (Hizb-i-Islami-Khalis) [redacted] to pitch in their lot with the Taliban.

. . .

THE TALIBAN—THREAT OR MENACE TO THE PARTIES?

17. Despite this reported early approval from the Rabbani government, official spokesmen from the major parties (including both Hekmetyar son-in-law Humayun Jarir and Jamiat's Masood Khalili) have been careful to avoid either direct criticism or praise of the movement in both their public statements and in meeting with embassy and consulate officers. When pressed for an official position, Dr. Taleeb of Hezb-i-Wahdat and the Peshawar resident representative for the Supreme Co-ordination Council would only say—officially—that the SCC had no formal position, and had dispatched a delegation led by Dr. Hasmatullah Mojadeddi to Quetta to assess the situation.

18. Influential players outside the party structure are also reluctant to publicly criticize the movement. [Redacted] noting that "it is too early to tell whether they are good or bad" and [redacted] close associate, [redacted] telling embassy officers that the Taliban actions have "so far been free of anything to criticize."

[Redacted] has stated bluntly that Hekmatyar, Rabbani, and Masood are bewildered even though one of them (which one he refrained from identifying) supports them.

19. Privately, however, activists from outside the Taliban will express their fears. [Redacted] has told Peshawar PO and Islamabad POLOFF that the Taliban are "quite dangerous—even more dangerous than the party leaders (sic)." The party leaders, he claims, can at least talk to each other either directly or through their "educated supporters." The Taliban, however, "are half-educated and naïve." Abdul Haq, while unwilling to characterize the movement, admits to the dangers it poses saying, "If this gets out of hand, all of the UN work could be for nothing. It looks like Afghanistan was first destroyed by the Communists, then by the fundamentalists, and now we might be destroyed by the mullahs."

20. Even some of the movement's apparent supporters have expressed unease. [Redacted] who is apparently cooperating with the Taliban in Helmand Province, has been quoted by Jamiat sources as saying, "I'm a Talib, but we must see where the movement is going." Kandahar's [redacted] who post believes looks upon the Taliban as his vehicle for getting back on the national stage, admits "that there have been a few too many unnecessary hangings."

INTENSE ATTRACTION

21. The Taliban movement holds out hope for war-weary Afghans disgusted with the failure of national-level leaders to compromise and the failure of local commanders to establish local security. Most Afghans perceive local commanders as the greatest threats to residents and travelers alike.

PRESSURE ON THE PARTIES—COPY-CAT CRUSADERS?

22. The Taliban's apparent freedom of action has factional leaders concerned that their own monopoly on power and the political process is at stake. However, several sources—including those from HiG, SCC, Jamiat, the UN's Advisory Council, and the Council for Understanding and National Unity—doubt the staying power of the Kandahari Taliban. "They're trained to be mullas," said one source, "and they don't understand logistics or administration. How far can they go?"

. . .

27. [Redacted] dismissed earlier reports that Hekmetyar had dispatched members of his young wing to work with him. "I pray the day will never come when I need help from Hekmetyar," the [redacted] said, noting that Hekmetyar had been a very poor theology student during the HiG leader's Peshawar days.

. . .

QUO BONO?

29. Just as there are conflicting reports on the sponsors of the Taliban, there is wildly conflicting speculation on exactly who will benefit from their actions. [Redacted] explicitly noted that the Taliban will "perhaps" be useful in bringing the party leaders, particularly Hekmetyar, Khalis, Rabbani, and Sayaaf, together to face a common threat. [Redacted] a third force advocate and supporter of the UN process, says the challenge will be to "get them on our side." Other observers feel that the local success at breaking the major parties' monopolies

will give renewed heart to the non-partisan traditionalists/royalists of Kandahar, or the perennially mentioned compromise candidate for president and traditionalist Harakat leader Nabi Mohammadi, or even the largely marginalized Hamid Karzai.

COMMENT

26. The Taliban's origins and future remain an enigma, with even the most well-informed speculation confronted with paradoxes. It does appear, however, that the Taliban are certainly not acting to the exclusive benefit of any of the established vested interests, and even those that have longed for a "third force" seem surprised at what has developed. The strong support the Taliban have received thus far from the Afghan people reflects the degree of popular frustration with the party leaders and a strong desire for peace and stability. End Comment.

MONJO

Source: National Security Archive. Available online at http://nsarchive2 .gwu.edu/NSAEBB/NSAEBB97/tal3.pdf.

ANALYSIS

Just weeks after the first cable discussing their emergence, the Taliban had taken control of most of Kandahar Province in southern Afghanistan. Although a somewhat closed group, even at this early stage, the Taliban showed their deftness by sometimes coopting local leaders willing to join their movement rather than risk a violent takeover.

Perhaps surprisingly, given the centrality of the Taliban's conservative religious views to their identity, the group was initially seen as friendly to commercial interests. Local business owners favored the stability the Taliban offered, and the cable argued that Pakistan used the Taliban as a means of opening up land trade routes to central Asia.

Also of interest is the brief mention of future Afghan president Hamid Karzai, whom the ambassador described as "largely marginalized" as of late 1994. Identifying a leader who could unite the disparate factions in Afghanistan has long been a challenge.

- **Document 13: U.S. Embassy (Islamabad), Cable, "[Redacted] Believe Pakistan Is Backing Taliban"**
- **When:** December 6, 1994
- **Where:** Islamabad, Pakistan
- **Significance:** A U.S. State Department cable that clearly identified Pakistan as supporting the nascent Taliban in Afghanistan.

DOCUMENT

FM AMEMBASSY ISLAMABAD
TO SECSTATE WASHDC
...
SUBJECT: [REDACTED] BELIEVE PAKISTAN IS BACKING TALIBAN
...

2. Summary: A well-informed [redacted] source claims that the burgeoning Taliban (students) movement in Afghanistan is being directly supported by Pakistan. [Redacted] believes Pakistan's Interior Minister is the principal patron of the Taliban, and that ISI advised against supporting them. End Summary.

3. [Redacted] confided to POLOFF November 29 that he had accompanied [redacted] to Kabul at a meeting with ISI DIRGEN LTGEN. General Ashraf the previous week. In the meeting, [redacted] Ashraf had vehemently denied that his agency had any role in supporting the Afghan Taliban movement in Kandahar.

4. The ISI DIRGEN reportedly told [redacted] that he had strongly recommended to PM Bhutto that the GOP not support the Taliban in any way. [Redacted] The general predicted that the Taliban could become a dangerous and uncontrollable force which could harm both Afghanistan and—potentially—Pakistan.

5. [Redacted] commented that Ashraf's remarks tracked with other information [redacted] had received about the Taliban. According to [redacted], the Taliban's September seizure of the Spin Boldak armory was preceded by artillery shelling of the base —from Pakistani Frontier Corps positions. The ensuing confusion had helped the Taliban to capture the well-defended outpost. [Redacted] claimed to have evidence that three separate Taliban units were involved in assaulting the base, with coordination provided by Pakistani officers on the scene. The Taliban's military competence (quickly routing two major battle-tested commanders in Kandahar—NIFA commander Lalaie and HiG commander Sar Khatib), and their use of tanks and helicopters, strongly suggested Pakistani tutelage or direct control [redacted].

5. Comment: [Redacted] is an extremely well-informed and reliable source and we do not doubt that the he has accurately characterized Ashraf's comments [redacted]. There appears to be little doubt that some elements in Pakistan (private and/or governmental) have supported the Taliban. Whether that support continues, is as much as [redacted] believe, and, if so, whether it gave the GOP much leverage over the Taliban, remains very much in doubt. End comment.
MONJO

Source: National Security Archive. Available online at http://nsarchive2 .gwu.edu/NSAEBB/NSAEBB97/tal5.pdf.

ANALYSIS

While earlier cables had noted the strong possibility of Pakistan supporting the Taliban, the reported presence of Pakistani officers and fire support offered greater credence for this case. Furthermore, this cable offered greater clarity on who in the

Pakistani government did—or did not—seek to support the Taliban. Pakistan, as with Afghanistan, had many competing factions with different agendas and interests, and the Taliban was yet another sign of this.

- **Document 14: U.S. Embassy (Islamabad), Cable, "The Taliban: What We've Heard"**
- **When:** January 26, 1995
- **Where:** Islamabad, Pakistan
- **Significance:** A U.S. State Department cable that discussed the goals of the Taliban and their governing style.

DOCUMENT

FM AMEMBASSY ISLAMABAD
TO SECSTATE WASHDC
. . .
SUBJECT: THE TALIBAN: WHAT WE'VE HEARD
. . .
2. Recent visitors to Kandahar city say the Taliban are well-armed, militarily proficient, and eager to expand their influence. Practicing a heavy-handed style of conservative Islam, the Taliban nonetheless profess support for the U.N. peace efforts and say they have no interest in sectarianism. Although denied by the group's leaders, both U.N. and Western journalist sources believe the Taliban continue to receive foreign support. [Redacted] End Summary.

3. What follows is a compilation of reports from several sources who have traveled recently (within the past ten days) to Kandahar, and a round-up of what we have heard here in Islamabad. [Redacted]

WHAT THEY BELIEVE IN

4. Taliban leaders told [redacted] that they intend to liberate Kabul, and as much of the rest of Afghanistan as possible, from the menace of the Communists. Similar comments were made to [redacted] who met with the Taliban January 22. A recurrent theme in these conversations, we have been told, is the Taliban's desire to replace the ad hoc banditry and local rule of small militias with strict Sharia law. As examples of their interpretation of Islamic orthodoxy, [redacted] says the Taliban in Kandahar have banned the playing of chess and marbles, although a three-week ban on soccer had to be lifted after widespread protest. [Redacted] all were told that women have been ordered to stay in the home, and male doctors have been refused permission to treat female patients, leaving doubts as to where the women and girls of Kandahar will be able to turn for medical treatment. Women who taught elementary school for boys have also been sent home, leaving much of the young male population without teachers. However, reports that the Taliban would force all adult males to grow beards are not correct, [redacted] found. [Redacted] who says he saw

a dozen or so ex-Communists who now do the "smart work" for the Taliban (writing reports, signing checks for employees, etc.), suggested that the decision not to force the growing of beard may reflect a Taliban desire to accommodate the generally moustachioed (but not bearded) ex-Communists in the administration.

. . .

POPULAR REACTION TO THE TALIBAN

6. Both [redacted] report that the educated elite of Kandahar are "terrified" of the Taliban. One female physician told [redacted] that the Taliban are "a bunch of ignorant thugs," who are willful and capricious. [Redacted] speculated that many of the elite either worked for or had close ties to the previous Gul Agha administration, and probably worry that they will be singled out for punishment by the new order. The powerful bazaaris of Kandahar city, however, told [redacted] they are pleased with the restoration of stability and seem less threatened by the orthodoxy preached by the Taliban.

TALIBAN FINANCES

7. All visitors to Kandahar have told us they believe that the Taliban must have access to considerable funding. On several occasions, Taliban representatives told [redacted] that they had over 4,000 fighters on the payroll. [Redacted] sources in Islamabad say ex-Communist military officers, who apply intermittently for visas to visit relatives in the CIS, reported the Taliban were able to offer salaries "three times" that which commanders could pay. One group of officers told [redacted] that "at least" 40-50 ex-officers had joined with the Taliban, and that many more were considering signing up. Bourke said experienced ex-Communist regime bureaucrats were also being hired by the Taliban—he saw a dozen or so, but expected there were more. [Redacted] sources have heard reports that the Taliban are hiring former regime police officers to set up a police academy in Kandahar city. [Redacted] added that the food, fuel, and other inputs for Taliban military operations must be costly. When he asked Taliban representatives about their finances, [redacted] said he was told that funds come from a combination of customs duties and a tax levied on local merchants. Yet local bazaaris deny that the Taliban are taxing them at all, although several told [redacted] they would happily pay if asked. There are reports that the Taliban have received financial assistance from other Afghan factions, particularly Rabbani, although probably not in amounts large enough to pay the kinds of bills observers believe the religious students must be racking up. The apparent gap between obvious sources of funding and expenditures suggests to our interlocutors that the Taliban have other benefactors.

THE TALIBAN MILITARY

. . .

9. In terms of actual military capability, the Taliban claim to possess 200 tanks, of which they say 100 are fully operational. They also say they have an air force comprising 11 MiGs piloted by ex-militiamen and 9 transport helicopters. Driving in from Chaman, [redacted] said he was impressed by the orderly Taliban checkpoints, plus the "very large amount" of heavy ammunition and RPGs stacked at each control point. He did not see any tanks or artillery, but believed the Taliban had placed them behind numerous visible revetments. The [redacted] seconded earlier observations that the Taliban had "new AK-47s, RPGs, and light machineguns."

. . .

SUPPORT FROM PAKISTAN

11. [Redacted] to Kandahar January 22 report that the Taliban leaders they spoke with seemed "coached" in what questions to ask and what kinds of assistance to ask for. Fuel in Kandahar city, which for the past several years has been supplied from Iran, had been replaced with diesel from Pakistan, the manager of the major "official" gas station in Kandahar city told one [redacted]. The manager said he dispensed fuel for all the Taliban vehicles in Kandahar. The [redacted] said that, given recently-imposed tight border controls at Chaman, it is unlikely the large amounts of fuel the manager said he dispensed could be smuggled in easily, [redacted].

[Redacted]

13. Comment: The impressions reported raise more questions than they answer. Embassy will continue to report on the Taliban, [redacted]

HOLZMAN

Source: National Security Archive. Available online at http://nsarchive2 .gwu.edu/NSAEBB/NSAEBB97/tal6.pdf.

ANALYSIS

The Taliban quickly took over Kandahar Province and positioned themselves as a significant problem for the disorganized government in Kabul. The question of how much support the Taliban received from Pakistan continued to be raised without reaching a fully satisfactory conclusion. The draconian cultural restrictions imposed by the Taliban, however, did not escape the notice of the consular officials. These overbearing rules and harsh punishments became defining features of Taliban rule, even as many Afghans resented them but quietly accepted the stability they appeared to offer.

- **Document 15: U.S. Embassy (Islamabad), Cable, "Meeting with the Taliban in Kandahar: More Questions Than Answers"**
- **When:** February 15, 1995
- **Where:** Islamabad, Pakistan
- **Significance:** A U.S. State Department cable following the first formal American meeting with the Taliban in Kandahar, Afghanistan.

DOCUMENT

FM AMEMBASSY ISLAMABAD
TO SECSTATE WASHDC

. . .

SUBJECT: MEETING WITH THE TALIBAN IN KANDAHAR: MORE QUESTIONS THAN ANSWERS

. . .

2. Summary: The Taliban say they will take Kabul, disarm all the commanders, and install one government across Afghanistan which will institute Shariah law. They refused to be drawn out on their leaders and sources of religious advice, but denied receiving any outside support. Taliban representatives claimed to support the Mestiri mission yet appeared unwilling to participate in the U.N.'s interim governing coalition. They appeared well-disposed towards the United States and said they would welcome future visits. On drugs policy, the Taliban waffled, saying poppy growing was unIslamic, but that economic conditions left the people little alternative. The Taliban representatives seemed unlikely candidates to lead a movement which has swept across southwestern Afghanistan up to the gates of Kabul. Their secretiveness leaves lingering questions about the Taliban's leadership and intentions. End Summary.

3. Peshawar PO and Islamabad POLOFF met with representatives of the Taliban in Kandahar city, February 13, at the provincial governor's office. Speaking for the Taliban was Maulavi Abul-Abbas, the mayor of Kandahar and a member of the Taliban Shura. Also present were Mullah Attiqullah, in charge of U.N. affairs and foreign visitors, Maulavi Abdul Hadim, in charge of industry for the Shura, Maulavi Abdur-Razzaq, in charge of administrative affairs, Maulavi Abdul-Shukkur, in charge of electricity, and Maualavis Abdul Zahir and Abdul Halim, Shura members. Average age of the Taliban representatives appeared to be about 40. Translation was provided by a U.N. employee Khan Mohammed, the brother of deposed Jamiat commander Mullah Naqibullah.

. . .

5. Asked about the goals of the movement, the mayor said the Taliban seek to establish one government in Afghanistan and to restore peace to their country. The first objective will be disarmament of all the commanders, after which Shariah law will be established throughout Afghanistan. Our movement, he noted, is the wish of the Afghan people. Abul-Abbas commented that students in other countries go on strike and seek to effect social change—as Islamic students the Taliban were simply doing the same. The mayor said the efforts of the Taliban are aimed at bringing peace "to the whole world." This is something for which all Taliban will sacrifice, he observed. Asked about relations with the Shi'a, Tajiks, Uzbeks, and other ethnic and religious minorities, Abul-Abbas commented ominously that "anyone who gets in our way will be crushed."

6. POLOFF asked the mayor about the Taliban's relationship with Special Envoy Mahmoud Mestiri, noting that the U.S. supports the peace process. Abul-Abbas said the Taliban had had discussions with Mestiri and "we agree with him." When queried about the announced February 20 convening of an interim governing mechanism in Kabul, the mayor said the Taliban had not received any formal notification or official contact on the matter and therefore could not respond.

7. Abul-Abbas was asked the number of members in the Taliban Shura, but refused to respond. "This cannot be told," he said. Inquiries into the membership of the Taliban movement were also turned aside. Encouragement for the formation of the movement came from madrasa teachers and the people of Afghanistan, who had tired of the behavior of the commanders, the mayor noted. The Taliban did not receive any support from outsiders, he volunteered.

8. Financial support for the movement derives form taxes levied in accordance with Shariah law, Abul-Abbas said. (Note: U.N. and NGO sources say no taxes

other than road tolls are being collected. End note) These funds are collected according to the advice of Taliban religious leaders, he observed, but refused to name which leaders in particular the Taliban followed. "All can help advise us," he noted. Although the Taliban named no specific source of guidance, several flags of the Pakistani Islamist JUI (F) Party were observed flying in downtown Kandahar, and pro-JUI (F) graffiti was in evidence on the walls outside the governor's office. Asked if Maulavi Tarakhel was an influential figure in the movement, Abul-Abbas responded very negatively, saying Tarakhel was a politician not a religious leader and was disliked by the Taliban. While noting the importance of religious advice, PO Smyth noted that sometimes practical and technical knowledge was needed. Abul-Abbas accepted this point, responding that the religious leaders gave broad policy direction to the Taliban while engineers and technocrats dealt with practical matters.

9. The Taliban were asked about their commitment to counter-narcotics efforts and offered participation in a training program in the U.S. Abul-Abbas, in a commentary which generated considerable discussion and obvious dissent amongst the assembled Shura members, said the Taliban did not have any special counter-narcotics office or coordinator and did not need to focus special attention on this area. "Narcotics is prohibited in Islam, this is very clear," Abul-Abbas intoned. "Islam is a complete religion—all issues and matters are answered in it," he continued. Abul-Abbas declined the offer of training in the U.S. saying the Taliban Shura will not let the people grow drugs, which is the best way to stop it. The health department and police will follow-up as a second step to ensure no illicit drugs are grown, he added.

10. The mayor's categorical comments generated considerable heated interjection from other Shura members. His subsequent response to a specific question about drug production in Helmand was far less categorical. "Drugs in Helmand are an economic issue," he noted. The people are poor and have small plots of land—until economic alternatives exist it is not possible to stop the growing of poppy, the mayor commented. As an example of the deterioration in the economy, Abul-Abbas said agricultural lands are no longer properly irrigated and that cotton production has shrunk to one percent of previous output. POLOFF asked if the Shura would be willing to continue discussions on anti-narcotics cooperation with the U.S., and was told that such a delegation—and any other U.S. visitors—would be welcomed.

11. Comment: The meeting with the Taliban representatives was more significant for what was omitted than for what was said. Some of the Taliban responses appeared coached and the overall impression was one of disingenuity and a degree of deception. The assembled Shura members seemed unlikely candidates to lead an organization which has swept across southwest Afghanistan up to the very gates of Kabul. Their unwillingness to comment on their leaders, who their advisors are, and the need to mask their intentions behind platitudinous Islamist generalizations left the interlocutors with more questions than answers. End comment.

12. This cable has been coordinated with consulate Peshawar.
MONJO

Source: National Security Archive. Available online at http://nsarchive2 .gwu.edu/NSAEBB/NSAEBB97/tal7.pdf.

ANALYSIS

This first meeting with a member of the Taliban, as mentioned in the cable's subject line, did little to clarify the intentions of the movement. This opacity, combined with the "coached" answers, did little to dispel the rumor that the Taliban was merely the puppet of powerful Pakistani interests. The only signs of optimism came from the lack of hostility toward counternarcotics—an increasing U.S. concern—or in the possibility of working with the UN mission in Kabul.

- **Document 16: U.S. Embassy (Islamabad), Cable, "Finally, a Talkative Talib: Origins and Membership of the Religious Students' Movement"**
- **When:** February 20, 1995
- **Where:** Islamabad, Pakistan
- **Significance:** A U.S. State Department cable that, for the first time, gave U.S. officials insight into the nature and the structure of the Taliban.

DOCUMENT

FM AMEMBASSY ISLAMABAD
TO SECSTATE WASHDC
SUBJECT: "FINALLY, A TALKATIVE TALIB: ORIGINS AND MEMBER-SHIP OF THE RELIGIOUS STUDENTS' MOVEMENT"

. . .

2. Summary: A Taliban insider says the movement is not supported by foreign governments, but does have connections to Pashtuns in Pakistan and, via madrasas, conservative Pakistani religious parties. The Taliban, he says, do not wish to interfere with the Shi'a and will protect the rights of ethnic minorities. The religious students do not appear averse to elections, but only in the context of an Islamic government ruling through Shariah law. Once there is greater stability in Afghanistan and refugees have been repatriated, a national Shura and provincial Shuras could be elected, with the Taliban Shura determining who could run for office. The Taliban desire good relations with the U.S. and the U.N., which they perceive as unbiased, but doubt the motivations of Saudi Arabia and the Pakistani government. End Summary.

3. POLOFF was contacted February 16 by [redacted] who claimed to have a good friend among the senior leadership of the Taliban. [Redacted] who said he lived "just across the border" from the Taliban official, [redacted] noted that [redacted] was visiting Islamabad, and suggested a meeting. [Redacted] added that [redacted] was tipped to become a "senior foreign affairs official" for the Taliban, and was in Islamabad for introductory and low-key contacts with the U.N. and other "friendly elements" and very much desired to meet representatives of the U.S.

4. POLOFF met with [redacted] and [redacted] February 17, although [redacted] spoke some English, for most of the conversation he relied on [redacted] to translate his Pashto. [Redacted] began the conversation by asking that the meeting be kept confidential. He noted that press reports were suggesting erroneously that the Taliban were subject to foreign influence and that these allegations could have a negative impact on the Taliban's efforts to bring peace to Afghanistan. The Taliban leadership had issued strict instructions that meetings with foreign representatives—which easily could be misconstrued and played by the Taliban's enemies—should be avoided [redacted] said. However, since the United States was an important and unbiased friend, [redacted] said he had decided to make initial contact.

ORIGINS OF THE TALIBAN

5. [Redacted] outlined for POLOFF the origins of the Taliban movement. [Redacted] and a resident of the Maroof district of Kandahar, [redacted] said he had been in an excellent position to observe the rise of the Taliban. [Redacted] and while [redacted] admitted that he was not an original member of the Taliban, he claimed to be very familiar with all the major players.

6. [Redacted] said the Taliban began in the Meiwand District of Kandahar, at the Madrasa of a prominent trader, Haji Bashar. Haji Bashar had been a Hizb-i-Islami (Khalis) commander during the jehad, and one of his soldiers was a poor man named Mohammed Omar from the Hotak sub-clan (descended from the Mirwais Hotak who briefly ruled Afghanistan before Ahmed Shah Durrani). Omar's clan was small and undistinguished, occupying only one house in Meiwand. Omar himself had received an Islamic education "on a small scale," only barely achieving the level Maulavi. Mullah Omar had earned a reputation for bravery and soldiering during the jehad, losing an eye in the process, and after the war had returned to the madrasa funded by Haji Bashar. There Omar's reputation for honesty and sincerity grew—despite his being neither particularly charismatic nor articulate.

7. During the summer of 1994, the situation in Kandahar city had become very bad, [redacted] related, reaching a new low when several madrasa students were gang-raped by a local commander. At about this time, Mullah Omar went to Haji Bashar and related a vision in which the Prophet Mohammed had appeared to him and told him of the need to bring peace to Afghanistan. Haji Bashar believed Mullah Omar, and drawing upon family resources and local business and political connections (including the bazaaris and Jamiat commander Mullah Naqibullah), raised 8 million Pakistani rupees (USD 250,000) for the cause and contributed six pick-up trucks. Arms and ammunition came initially from stocks left over from the jehad.

8. The movement soon had about 200 adherents and took over the administration of the Meiwand District, [redacted] claimed. The seizure of the important town of Boldak soon followed, motivated by stories of "very bad and un-Islamic" behavior by the Hekmetyar commander there—and with the capture of the town came access to the large amount of military supplies at the Spin Boldak armory. [Redacted] denied the report that the Taliban were supported in seizing the armory by Pakistani Interior Minister Babar's Frontier Corps. He noted that Babar had not even consulted with the fledgling Taliban movement when planning the GOP's central Asian convoy, preferred to deal with more established Kandahari commanders.

9. [Redacted] observed that Pakistan had begun to pay attention to the Taliban when the group stopped the central Asian convoy at Boldak. The Taliban had objected to Pakistan's "high-handedness" in not notifying Afghan authorities in Kabul about the convoy, [redacted] noted. However, after holding the convoy for several days, the Taliban had been convinced by the senior Pakistani escort, [redacted] that the convoy was good "for Muslims." [Redacted] said the Taliban had been persuaded by [redacted] argument that Pakistan was a Muslim country and that there was also a broader Islamic duty to assist the Muslim brothers in central Asia. The Taliban then agreed to escort the convoy across Kandahar, [redacted] noted. As the 30 Pakistani trucks moved down the road with their Taliban escort, [redacted] said the religious students began cutting the chains laid across the road by toll-hungry commanders. "There were chains almost every kilometer," [redacted] commented, "but there was no initial resistance to our actions." He said that as word spread of what the Taliban were doing, the people of Kandahar began actively to support them, bringing the religious students food and weapons.

10. [Redacted] said no one was more surprised than the Taliban by how quickly the movement caught on. When faced by armed opposition by some of the powerful commanders in Kandahar, [redacted] commented that the "madrasa network" in Pakistan's NWFP and Baluchistan was able to provide willing recruits in a short period of time. Most of the "thousands" of Afghans (and few Pakistani Pashtuns) who joined the Taliban came from madrasas run by the Pakistanis [redacted] commented. To assist in training the Taliban and operating sophisticated weapons (including aircraft, tanks and helicopters) the movement had recruited former regime pilots and generals, who were being paid twice the usual salary of 20,000 afghanis a month. The Taliban themselves, however, were volunteers, [redacted] noted, who depended upon support from the Afghan people to feed themselves.

STRUCTURE OF THE MOVEMENT

11. Asked about the structure of the movement, [redacted] said there is a "High Council" of eight and lower Shura of 22. The members of the High Council are: Mohammed Omar, Haji Bashar, Mohammed Hassan (governor of Kandahar), Baz Mohammad, Ahmadullah, Abdur-Rahman, Qari Ihsanullah and Abdul-Salam. The first three names are the most important, [redacted] observed, with Mohammed Omar occasionally changing the other five. All are maulavis except for Haji Bashar, and all fought during the jehad, he noted. Also important is the Taliban military operations in Kabul. The 22-member Shura, of which [redacted] said he was a member, deals with more administrative issues than policy matters and all its members are "from the bottom to the middle of the ulema."

12. The Taliban's immediate aim, [redacted] said, is to disarm all of Afghanistan and establish one Muslim government for the country. Asked about elections, [redacted] said the Taliban believe in elections, but would want to wait until all the refugees return to the country and there was a more peaceful atmosphere. [Redacted] said he imagined a government set-up in which there would be one national shura and also individual provincial shuras. He suggested that the current Taliban shura would decide who could run in the elections. Commenting on the success of the disarmament campaign in Kandahar, [redacted] joked that when his son had been born a few days previously, there were no guns in the district to

announce the event to the village (traditionally, guns are fired into the air to signal the birth of a son).

NOT AGAINST THE SHI'A OR MINORITIES

13. Asked about concerns that the Pashtun, Sunni Taliban would not be accepted by the Shi'a and ethnic minorities, [redacted] said Pashtuns are 70 percent of Afghanistan's population, but that the Taliban thought it more important to make the minorities happy. He claimed there was a large Shi'a population in the Taliban-controlled province of Oruzgan, and said there had been no problems. "The Shi'a are Muslims, we have lived with them for 200 years," [redacted] declared. "They have Imam Baras and we have mosques, but we will not interfere with them," he added. The Shi'a Hizb-i-Wahdat Party in Kabul had begun negotiations with the Taliban, [redacted] said, and both sides were pleased with the discussions.

14. On the ethnic issue, [redacted] said the Taliban would do "too much" to keep the minorities happy. "We will make an Uzbek governor in Paktia and a Tajik governor in Kandahar," he commented, "all this to keep them happy." Citing the example of Dostam and fears that the country could be divided, the [redacted] said Dostam will be free to participate in the political process in Afghanistan, but must surrender his weapons and abide by the Shariah law. "Everyone will be subject to the law," [redacted] noted.

15. [Redacted] said Dostam had recently sent emissaries to the Taliban, promising to surrender once "certain conditions" are met. Rabbani had sent similar messages, [redacted] noted, but Masoud "wants to fight." In Kabul, Harakat's commander Siddiqullah is ready to defect to the Taliban, and [redacted] said he had accompanied representatives of Khalis, Sayyad and Mohemmadi to Kandahar where they had pledged to support the movement. Asked about Ismael Khan's relations with the Taliban, [redacted] said "Ismael Khan is a good man, not the best, but good." Khan is ready to surrender to the Taliban, [redacted] judged, and could be counted on to obey the movement. Ismael Khan's commanders around Shindand Air Base and in half of Herat province already had pledged support to the Taliban, he noted.

COMMITMENT TO DRUG ERADICATION

16. Responding to a question concerning the Taliban's commitment to drug eradication, [redacted] said he could best describe developments in his home district of Maroof. There, he said, the Taliban leader Abdul-Samad had been approached by poppy farmers and asked whether they could continue to grow their crop. Abdul-Samad had called together 30 members of the Ulema, who issued a public statement opposing the growing and trading of narcotics, after which the farmers had been told that they would be punished under the Shariah if they continued poppy production. In conclusion, [redacted] observed that "the Taliban believe narcotics are bad."

ATTITUDES TOWARDS OTHER COUNTRIES

17. Since he expected to have a leadership role in foreign affairs once the Taliban succeeded in removing all the commanders from Afghanistan, [redacted] was eager to talk about the Taliban's attitudes towards other countries. He said the movement sought good relations with the Islamic countries, but did not like Saudi Arabia's efforts to interfere in Afghan religious matters. Similarly, the Pakistani government's desire to interfere in internal affairs, and the efforts of ISI to treat

Afghanistan "like another province" are not appreciated, he observed. Saying that he knew personally [redacted] commented that "Afghans are proud people who do not like the Pakistanis always trying to run things and place the Afghans at a lower level." The Taliban want very good relations with the U.S., he noted, particularly since the U.S. had been so helpful in the jehad. [Redacted] said that the Taliban realize the U.S. and the U.N. do not want to do anything but help the Afghans.

18. Asked to comment on the Taliban's relations with the U.N., [redacted] said the best thing would be to arrange a meeting with Haji Bashar and Mohammed Omar to discuss the matter. Haji Bashar would return from performing Umra February 26, after which a meeting "in secret" could be arranged. The secrecy was necessary, he said, because of efforts by the enemies of the Taliban to portray them as stooges of outside powers. "People are saying Babar, the U.S. or the U.K. are behind us," the maulavi noted, "and we cannot do anything which might give support to this view." [Redacted] promised to be in touch through [redacted] about the meeting.

19. At the close of the conversation, [redacted] raised the topic of Pashtunistan. [Redacted] said the Durand Accord, like the lease of Hong Kong, "was about to expire." Pakistan had tried to pressure Rabbani into extending the agreement, but had failed, [redacted] claimed. [Redacted] said the issue of Pashtunistan could be addressed later, but noted that the Taliban are now caught up in fighting, trying to bring peace to Afghanistan.

20. Comment: [Redacted] appeared to be about [redacted] years old, spoke a little English, and clearly was well-disposed towards the United States. His in-depth knowledge of Taliban events and personalities lends credence to his claim to be one of the movement's insiders. End comment.

MONJO

Source: National Security Archive. Available online at http://nsarchive2.gwu.edu/NSAEBB/NSAEBB97/tal8.pdf.

ANALYSIS

For the first time since the Taliban's emergence in November 1994, the United States finally gained a much-clearer picture of the movement. Unlike Afghanistan's other prominent figures who had a more traditional political background or were charismatic warlords, the base of the Taliban's support was in religious leaders. As the United States learned in this conversation, religion dictated much about the group's structure.

Of great interest are the Taliban references to Pashtunistan, or the idea of a unified Pashtun state. This reflects that ethnicity clearly defined the Taliban just as much as their religious conservatism, and the group would encounter resistance to its agenda as they came into contact with other ethnic groups in Afghanistan. It also helps make clear why the Taliban were able to find support in Pakistan since the Pashtuns in that country often provided support for the group.

- **Document 17: U.S. Embassy (Islamabad), Cable, "A/S Raphel Discusses Afghanistan"**
- **When:** April 22, 1996
- **Where:** Islamabad, Pakistan
- **Significance:** A U.S. State Department cable reporting on the visit of Assistant Secretary of State Robin Raphel with the major factions in Afghanistan.

DOCUMENT

FM AMEMBASSY ISLAMABAD
TO RUEHC/SECSTATE WASHDC

. . .

SUBJECT: A/S RAPHEL DISCUSSES AFGHANISTAN

. . .

2. Summary: Discussions with GOP, Kabul government and Taliban officials suggest the door is not yet closed for an Afghan peace process—but it will take hard work to keep it open, let alone go through it. The GOP has recognized that its support for the Taliban has back-fired and is looking for alternatives, and neither the Taliban nor the Kabul government can be sufficiently sure that they will win the expected next round of fighting to rule out completely negotiations. Nonetheless, it will take skillful management—and a bit of luck—to break through the rigid positions espoused by Kabul and the Taliban. An arms embargo (perhaps to be discussed via an international conference) and support for an all-party Afghan conference could be useful tools to break the current dead-lock. End Summary.

. . .

PAKISTAN: LOOKING FOR A WAY OUT

4. A consensus has emerged among the top leadership of the GOP that Pakistan needs to broaden its Afghan policy. PM Bhutto told A/S Raphel that the GOP is pursuing an enhanced dialogue with the Kabul government; FM Assef Ali said Islamabad would welcome a visit by a Rabbani/Masood delegation, which would be reciprocated, and also offered to meet with Kabul regime Minstate for Foreign Affairs Lafraie on the margins of the upcoming Ashgabat Eco Conference. The move to repair relations in Kabul, in large part derives from GOP dissatisfaction with the direction in which the Taliban are moving; Coas Karamat went so far as to refer to the Taliban as "a millstone around our necks." Fonsec Shaikh outlined Pakistan's repeated efforts to get the Taliban to agree to negotiations and expressed disappointment that the recent Kandahar Ulema Majlis opted for hard-line rejectionism; FM Assef Ali said the only good result of that gathering was the possibility that Maulavi Mohammed Omar's elevation to "Leader of the Faithful" would give him more power to make decisions. PM Bhutto emphasized that Pakistan was not providing military support to the Taliban and insisted that only minimal, non-lethal aid was being delivered.

. . .

6. At heart, Paksitan's need to pursue a pro-Pashtun policy for the sake of its own domestic political and security agenda represents a hurdle which the GOP acknowledges, but feels the Tajik-dominated Kabul government is doing little to help out on. Efforts to resuscitate relations with Kabul are hampered, Shakir and Assef Ali remarked, by Rabbani and Masood's bickering over modalities and their unwillingness to engage in good faith negotiations aimed at creating a broad-based government. Pakistan appears to focus more on ways to get the Afghan factions themselves to put their house in order, and is less fixated on the issue of curbing outside interference, the latter being seen more as a contributing—rather than a causal—factor. While accepting the need to work both internal and external tracks, the GOP would prefer an Afghan all-party conference in Jalalabad to an international gathering, senior officials noted, since Islamabad believes the key to (and responsibility for) a solution must lie with the Afghan factions themselves. They believe either gathering would require careful preparation and a pre-agreed agenda.

KABUL GOVERNMENT: SELF-RIGHTEOUSNESS MASKS DEEP INSECURITY

7. The Kabul government's dialogue with A/S Raphel emphasized Rabbani and Masood's perception of themselves as the legitimate government of Afghanistan. They blamed Pakistan and the Taliban for almost all of their problems, with Lafraie and Masood going so far as to allege that "Pakistan is as much to blame for the destruction in Afghanistan as the Soviets;" a perception with which A/S Raphel strongly took issue. A pre-occupation with fixing the blame (on the Taliban and Pakistan), rather than fixing the problem of Afghanistan, was a recurring theme in discussions with Lafraie, Masood, and Rabbani. Lafraie, in particular, took a hard-line suggesting that it was for those opposed to the government to make peace overtures; Masood observed that "we are ready to talk to anybody and have said we are prepared to transfer power, that is all we need to do."

. . .

10. Missing from the Kabul government's approach was a sense of how to get from the current stalemate to the rosy, democratic future both Rabbani and Masood envisioned. Masood said he thought a Jalalabad conference probably would be useful only in giving the "minor factions" of Gallani, Mojadeddi, Nabi Mohammedi and Khalis the opportunity to sign-on with the government. Kabul-SCC discussions were separate from the Jalalabad moot, Masood noted, and the difficulty facing progress with the Taliban and Dostam was their "arrogance and pursuit of their own interests at the expense of Afghanistan." It was the latter factor, Masood added, which made the Kabul government reluctant to accept the idea of federalism, which would only divide—or obliterate—the nation of Afghanistan.

. . .

THE TALIBAN: IMAGE CONSCIOUS BUT RELUCTANT TO CHANGE

12. Taliban leaders asked A/S Raphel to help improve their image in the international community. They denied being human rights violators and claimed to have opened many more schools in the area under their control than had existed previously. Differences of culture lay at the heart of much of the misunderstanding, they alleged, "in France you cannot wear the veil, by law, and here women have to,

by law" Maulavi Motaqi commented. The Taliban claimed Iran and Russia accused them of being terrorists. On the contrary, they noted, the Taliban had within two years brought peace and security to half of Afghanistan; soon the whole country would be safe and at peace, god willing.

   . . .

14. The Taliban had few ideas to put forward on what the future government of Afghanistan should be, or how it could be achieved. Motaqi said the shape of the government would be "determined by the people" once the nation was disarmed and peace restored. Motaqi did embrace the idea of an arms embargo, however, saying that the Taliban supported this proposal and invited the U.S. to judge for itself the evidence on who received more outside help: the Taliban or Kabul. When pressed to engage in meaningful negotiations, Motaqi replied simply that "we are students; we will take your advice to our Shura and try to implement it." However, while the basic Taliban message was naïve, simplistic and rigid, their concern about their image and request that A/S Raphel "tell President Clinton and the West that we are not bad people" demonstrated a growing awareness, previously absent, of their own limitations—which may be the modality through which they can be coaxed, over time, to the negotiating table.

COMMENT: FLEXIBILITY OR FIGHTING?

15. A/S Raphel's discussion took place against the backdrop of general expectations that heavy fighting between the Kabul regime and the Taliban will be an inevitability this summer. Yet all sides genuinely appear to desire a way out—at least in part because none can be confident that the fighting will go their way. That insecurity has created renewed opportunities for a reinvigorated U.N. mission to move forward—particularly now that Pakistan appears willing to engage more positively. An arms embargo (perhaps to be discussed via an international conference), plus support for an all-party Afghan conference, could be useful tools to break past the knee-jerk, rigid positions of the Afghan factions and to start coalescing support for a resolution to the crisis there. The bottom-line is that there still appears to be reason for a limited optimism that, properly managed, there may now be opportunities to move the peace process forward. End comment.

SIMONS

Source: National Security Archive. Available online at http://nsarchive2 .gwu.edu/NSAEBB/NSAEBB97/tal15.pdf.

ANALYSIS

The series of meetings showed the confused policies of the major players—the Taliban, the Afghan government, and Pakistan—involved in the Afghan Civil War and insight into why the country remained embroiled in a civil war. The Pakistani government recognized that supporting the Taliban had created many unforeseen consequences, yet that support did not entirely cease nor could it because of, as the memo noted, domestic political concerns with its own Pashtun population. Meanwhile, the Afghan government remained riven with factionalism and, even in the face of a concerted Taliban challenge, unable to fully unite and overcome its problems. The Taliban, curiously, showed concern over their international image, which is rare given that many of their stated policies ran counter to any prevailing international mood.

- **Document 18: U.S. Embassy (Islamabad), Cable, "Afghanistan: Jalaluddin Haqqani's Emergence as a Key Taliban Commander"**
- **When:** January 7, 1997
- **Where:** Islamabad, Pakistan
- **Significance:** A U.S. State Department cable that noted the rise of Jalaluddin Haqqani within the Taliban.

DOCUMENT

FM AMEMBASSY ISLAMABAD
TO RUEHC/SECSTATE WASHDC

. . .

SUBJECT: AFGHANISTAN: JALALUDDIN HAQQANI'S EMERGENCE AS A KEY TALIBAN COMMANDER

. . .

SUMMARY

2. Recent reports indicate that former Afghan resistance commander Jalaluddin Haqqani may now be in charge of the Taliban's forces north of Kabul. Views of Haqqani's role with the Taliban are mixed. Some observers see him as an effective military leader with socially moderate views. Others express concern about Haqqani's links to Islamic extremists. Observers tend to agree that Haqqani at this time probably has more influence with the Taliban on military strategy than on political or social issues. End Summary.

NEW ROLE AS KEY COMMANDER NORTH OF KABUL

3. Recent press and radio reports indicate that former Afghan resistance commander Jalaluddin Haqqani may now be in charge of the Taliban's forces north of Kabul. There has been no confirmation from the Taliban that Haqqani has been placed in such a position and his formal Taliban title remains "Acting Minister of Tribes and Borders." If Haqqani has assumed the lead role north of Kabul, the war's most important sector—he will have taken over a position previously held by Mullah Borjan, formerly the Taliban's chief military commander, who was killed near Kabul in late September 1996.

4. Haqqani, 50, has been a commander for the Taliban since the group's beginning in 1994. Before 1994, he was a major commander for Hezb-i-Islami (Khalis) in Paktia Province during the Soviet-Afghan War. Reportedly, he commands the respect of his fellow Zadran tribesmen from the Paktia-Paktika area and has brought a large number of them with him to the Kabul front. A mullah, Haqqani studied for sixteen years in Afghan and Pakistani madrasas.

A TOUGH MILITARY LEADER

5. Abdul Wahab, First Secretary at the Afghan Embassy in Islamabad and a Taliban supporter, told POLOFF January 1, that he could not confirm that Haqqani has assumed the role of chief commander on the Kabul front. He thought, however, that Haqqani had become one of the "Taliban's key military commanders because he is known for his toughness and military effectiveness." Wahab, a former Hezb-i-Islami (Khalis) commander like Haqqani, claimed that Haqqani played a key role in the Taliban's defeat of Hezb-i-Islami (Hekmetyar) forces in eastern Afghanistan in August-September 1996. He explained that Ghilzais (a major branch of the Pashtun ethnic group) in eastern Afghanistan had "defected from Hekmetyar to the Taliban largely because of Haqqani's successful efforts to turn them against the Kabul regime." (Note: Gulbuddin Hekmetyar served as the former Kabul regime's prime minister for several months before the Taliban seized Kabul in September 1996.)

PORTRAYED AS A "SOCIAL MODERATE"

6. Asked about Haqqani's views on the Taliban's social policies, Wahab replied that he thought that of Haqqani as a "social moderate, who is not strongly supportive of the Taliban's positions on the treatment of women." He explained that Haqqani's tribe, the Zadrans, are considered more liberal in their treatment of women than the tribes in the Kandahar area. (Note: Most influential Taliban leaders are from Kandahar Province.) Wahab commented, however, that Haqqani functions more in the military area, and is not a force in setting Taliban political or social issues.

HAQQANI SEEN AS INFLUENCED BY ISLAMIC EXTREMISTS

7. In a January 6 conversation with POLOFF, [redacted] a Taliban supporter [redacted] said he knows Haqqani and agrees that he is an effective military strategist. He argued that Haqqani "should be seen in his proper context and he has clear links with Islamic extremists." Warming to this theme [redacted] asserted that Haqqani had developed a close relationship with various radical Arab groups during the jihad. These relationships, [redacted] asserted, have continued, and, in exchange for weapons and money, Haqqani is "offering shelter for various Arabs in areas of Paktia Province." Brushing aside POLOFF's request for further information on this subject, [redacted] stated that he did not have the details, but that Haqqani's role with the "Arabs" is "well-known." (Note: Reporting in other channels indicate that Haqqani maintains these links.)

NOT SEEN AS INFLUENTIAL WITH TALIBAN

8. Turning to the issue of Haqqani's relationship with the Taliban, [redacted] concurred with Wahab's assessment that Haqqani probably did not have significant influence with the Taliban on political or social issues. "Although he is a mullah," he related, "Haqqani is not considered to be a Taliban and he has little credibility with them on issues outside of the military realm." He observed that Haqqani's ties to Islamic extremists are also opposed by a number of Taliban officials, including "Acting Foreign Minister" Ghaus. (Note: In a meeting with DCM in early December, Mullah Ghaus, when asked about Haqqani's relationship with the Taliban, was dismissive and intimated that Haqqani was not important in the Taliban leadership hierarchy.) Nonetheless, [redacted] advised, "Haqqani could prove to have a negative influence on the Taliban by making them more prone to accept the advice of Islamic radicals."

ONE OF THE "HARD MEN"

9. General Payenda, Dostam's representative in Islamabad, told POLOFF January 3 that members of the Supreme Defense Council are aware of Haqqani's emergence as an important Taliban commander and they see his rise as a manifestation of a Taliban policy to place "hard men" in key military positions. (Note: Payenda characterized the Taliban's recent selection of Abdul Razaq as Governor of Herat as part of this Taliban policy.) Haqqani's Zadran tribesmen are "quite wild," he continued, "and the Taliban want them on the front-lines to harass our forces." Payenda evinced little concern about Haqqani, however, asserting that he and his forces generally lack discipline and will inevitably develop tensions with the Taliban.

COMMENT

10. The presence of Haqqani's forces north of Kabul—whether Haqqani is overall commander of the sector or not—is significant and has undoubtedly added to the military clout of the Taliban. At the same time, there is little evidence to suggest that he is influential in Taliban circles. Because of Haqqani's links to extremists, however, his relationship with the Taliban bears scrutiny.

SIMONS

Source: National Security Archive. Available online at http://nsarchive2 .gwu.edu//NSAEBB/NSAEBB295/doc05.pdf.

ANALYSIS

Jalaluddin Haqqani, like many in the Afghan Civil War, first rose to prominence as a mujahedeen commander during the Soviet occupation. As this memo noted, by 1997, he parlayed this experience—which trumped his disagreements with the Taliban's social policies—to become one of the group's most effective military commanders against the former Afghan government, which now called itself the Northern Alliance. He also again showed the willingness of the Taliban to accommodate some degree of dissension within their ranks in order to accomplish their larger goal of ruling Afghanistan.

Haqqani became the senior Taliban military leader by 2001 and resisted peace overtures from the new Afghan government. He later formed the quasi-independent Haqqani Network in Pakistan and continued to fight the American occupation. He is rumored to have died in 2014.

- **Document 19: U.S. Consulate (Peshawar), Cable, "Afghanistan: Taliban Agree to Visits of Militant Training Camps, Admit Bin Ladin Is Their Guest"**
- **When:** January 9, 1997
- **Where:** Peshawar, Pakistan
- **Significance:** The United States attempted to persuade the Taliban to expel Osama bin Laden from their territory for his support of international terrorism.

DOCUMENT

FM AMCONSUL PESHAWAR
TO SECSTATE WASHDC

. . .

SUBJECT: AFGHANISTAN: TALIBAN AGREE TO VISITS OF MILITANT
TRAINING CAMPS, ADMIT BIN LADIN IS THEIR GUEST

. . .

SUMMARY
2. In a meeting with DCM/Islamabad on Jan 6 in Kandahar, senior Taliban leader
Mullah Mohammad Rabbani agreed the USG, through the Taliban ambassador in
Islamabad, should propose names of delegation and dates to follow up Acting FM
Mullah Ghaus' offer to visit militant training camps, which the Taliban claim have
been closed. Rabbani and Mullah Mohammad Hassan (acting head of the interim
Shura in Kabul) acknowledged that Usama Bin Ladin is their "guest," adding that
he has been asked not to carry out terrorist activities against other countries. Post
suggests USG urge Saudi and Egyptian authorities to take more active approach
with the Taliban on bin Ladin. End Summary.

VISITING THE MILITANT TRAINING CAMPS

3. In separate meetings with senior Taliban leaders on Jan 5 and 6, DCM accepted acting FM Mullah Ghaus' offer that US officers visit militant training camps which the Taliban claim they have closed (reftels). He raised the mechanics of doing so. Kandahar governor Mullah Mohammad Hassan, after asking who are the terrorists and being told one of the groups training in the camps is the Harakat Ul-Ansar (HUA), said there is a Taliban council in Kabul with whom the matter should be discussed. He added that the Taliban do not permit anyone with the name terrorist to train in their territory to carry out terrorist acts in the outside world. Deputy FM Abdul Jalil replied similarly, stating that the Taliban did not establish these training camps, they had been established during the jihad, adding Kashmiris had been trained there. He continued that when the Taliban came to power in those areas, they had told the persons there they would live as refugees but they could not engage in "hostilities." Jalil reiterated that USG officers could visit the camps but the subject should be raised in Kabul, as Taliban authorities there are close to the camps. DCM left with Jalil a non-paper describing the tree areas of camps (along the Kabul/Jalalabad/Torkham Road, in northern Paktia Province, and in southeastern Paktika Province (note: better

DID YOU KNOW?

Osama bin Laden

Osama bin Laden was born in 1957 to the family of a Saudi billionaire. He left the kingdom in 1979 to join the mujahedeen fighting the Soviets in Afghanistan. He used his wealth to funnel money and arms to the mujahedeen and helped build up the ranks of foreign fighters. In 1988, he formed a new group called al-Qaeda with other Saudis and Egyptians. He sought to use his new group to defend Saudi Arabia after Iraqi leader Saddam Hussein invaded Kuwait in 1990, but the king rejected his overtures. Bin Laden, already opposed to U.S. involvement in the Middle East, became incensed when King Fahd invited U.S. forces into the kingdom and then allowed them to remain after Hussein withdrew from Kuwait. He sought exile in Sudan but moved to Afghanistan in 1997, where he established terrorist training camps and supported the Taliban. He masterminded a series of deadly attacks against the United States, including the 1998 U.S. Embassy bombings, the 2000 attack on the USS Cole, and finally the September 11 attacks in 2001. He escaped the advancing Coalition in late 2001 and fled to Pakistan, eventually settling in Abbottabad in 2005. There he remained until a SEAL team killed him in a raid on his compound on May 2, 2011.

described in Khost Province) and giving coordinates where known.)

4. The next morning DCM raised the matter with Mullah Mohammad Rabbani (described variously as Chairman of the interim caretaker government and Chairman of the interim Shura in Kabul, but then sitting in Kandahar). Rabbani, with whom Mullahs Hassan and Jalil had probably spoken before the meeting, asked many questions about the locations of the camps USG officers wish to visit. He noted the third complex of camps are in Khost Province, not Paktia Province. Like Jalil, Rabbani noted that the camps were established during the jihad, when the mujahedin received assistance from Islamic and non-Islamic states, for which they were most grateful. Now, however, the Taliban's opponents—naming Hekmetyar, Masood, Dostam, and Rabbani—because they had suffered defeats at the hands of the Taliban, were spreading propaganda to defame the Taliban. Rabbani said "government policy" was not to permit others to use its territory to use terrorism against other countries.

> ### DID YOU KNOW?
>
> **Pashtunwali**
>
> Pashtunwali is a set of unwritten rules and codes of conduct that defines the way of life in rural Pashtun culture. Pashtunwali has evolved for as long as the Pashtuns have existed as a distinct culture and tribe in modern-day Afghanistan and Pakistan, which dates back more than two millennia. Among the norms passed down as part of Pashtunwali include "melmastia" or hospitality toward guests. This hospitality extends to all guests in a Pashtun's home, regardless of race, culture, or religion. This protection of guests has been used by the Taliban to justify the harboring of Osama bin Laden in the late 1990s as well as the protection provided to SEAL Marcus Luttrell by a Pashtun tribesman after he was wounded and his comrades captured as part of Operation Red Wings in 2005. Other principles included in Pashtunwali include "badal" or revenge and justice against wrongdoers, "tureh" or personal bravery, and "nang" or the honor of one and one's family.

. . .

USAMA BIN LADIN, TALIBAN GUEST, WARNED AGAINST TERRORISM

6. With Rabbani in Kandahar Jan 6, DCM pressed hard on the presence of Usama bin Ladin in Taliban territory. He noted that the US continues to receive reports that bin Ladin, who has been linked to a number of terrorist attacks, is planning terrorist attacks against countries like Saudi Arabia, which are friends of the Taliban. It would be useful if the Taliban could tell us where he is located and ensure that he is not able to carry out these attacks.

7. Rabbani responded that bin Ladin came to Afghanistan when Haji Qadir controlled Nangarhar Province. The Taliban would not allow anyone to use their territory for terrorist activities. Rabbani acknowledged that bin Ladin was in the Jalalabad area, adding he was living there as "a guest, as a refugee." While the Taliban can arrest anyone in areas they control, bin Ladin is living like an ordinary man, "like an Afghan refugee in the United States." Rabbani volunteered that the Taliban had talked to bin Ladin, telling him not to carry out terrorist activities. He told the Taliban he would not, Rabbani stated.

8. DCM again stated that the US had information that he is planning terrorist acts. Rabbani retorted that bin Ladin had promised the Taliban he would not, adding that "others" might be telling us otherwise. Mullah Abdul Jalil, who also attended the meeting with Rabbani, interjected that bin Ladin had lived in caves south of Tora Bora and the Taliban had become suspicious. They told him to move out, to live in an ordinary house.

9. DCM tried another track; if, for example, Saudi Arabia or Egypt came to the Taliban with information that bin Ladin had committed terrorist acts against their countries, would the Taliban take action against bin Ladin? Rabbani responded that if something happened in the past during the pre-Taliban period, that was not the Taliban's concern. However, if bin Ladin did something now in the Taliban period, the Taliban could do something. Rabbani again stressed that in the past the Taliban did not have control over the areas in which bin Ladin lived. DCM explained that bin Ladin was involved in crimes before he came to Afghanistan, that he was now using Afghanistan by seeking refuge, making Afghanistan appear associated with his past terrorist crimes. Rabbani reiterated that while bin Ladin might have committed crimes earlier, he had promised the Taliban he would not commit them now. "Bin Ladin is with us as a guest, a refugee."

10. DCM continued that bin Ladin is identified with terrorism with good reason. All counties, even as big and powerful as the US need friends. Afghanistan, especially, needs friends—the international agencies, the US, others. For Afghanistan and the Taliban to be associated with bin Ladin hurts. The Taliban do not owe bin Ladin anything. He is using Afghanistan for his own purposes, not for the Taliban's purposes. Bin Ladin is the Taliban's problem now, a problem which will hurt the Taliban. If, for example, bin Ladin carried out terrorist acts against Saudi Arabia and it became known he planned the operation in Afghanistan, it would be a terrible blow to Afghanistan and the Taliban. While he respected the Taliban's need to treat a guest with respect and hospitality, this man is poison. Rabbani returned to his theme of Pashtun hospitality and provision of refuge. "In this part of the world there is a law that when someone seeks refuge, he should be granted asylum, but if there are people who carry out terrorist activities, then you can point these out; we have our senses will not permit anyone to carry out these filthy activities."

11. In Kabul Jan 7, DCM also raised the presence of bin Ladin with Mullah Mohammad Hassan, acting head of the interim Shura there. Hassan replied that "this person was already told he should not carry out activities against other countries. The Taliban cannot expel them (note: apparently referring to bin Ladin and his entourage), because they are strangers and as Muslims, they can live in this country."

COMMENT

12. Embassy Islamabad will propose to the Taliban ambassador in Islamabad soon details of the visit to test the Taliban's offer for USG officers to visit militant training camps. As for bin Ladin, the Taliban appear to have concluded that it is in their interest to give him refuge. How hard they may have pressed him not to commit terrorist acts is unknown. Reporting in other channels suggests bin Ladin is paying off some individual Taliban. Post suggests further approaches to the Saudis and Egyptians to intensify their approaches with the Taliban on bin Ladin. Co-religionists may have a better chance convincing the Taliban bin Ladin is poison to them.

HANSON

Source: National Security Archive. Available online at http://nsarchive2 .gwu.edu//NSAEBB/NSAEBB295/doc06.pdf.

ANALYSIS

By 1997, the United States had become increasingly frustrated by the Taliban's support for militant and terrorist organizations and sought to convince the Taliban that this issue would eventually force the international community to become hostile toward their regime. Whereas the Taliban had expressed concern about their image in their 1995 meeting with Assistant Secretary of State Robin Raphel, regarding bin Laden they showed no such concern. It is believed that some in the Taliban did not agree with the decision to harbor bin Laden, but the United States remained unable to fully exploit those internal differences.

- **Document 20: UN Secretary General, "The Situation in Afghanistan and Its Implications for International Peace and Security"**
- **When:** November 14, 1997
- **Where:** New York, New York
- **Significance:** An acknowledgment of the Taliban's continued military success against the Afghan government and the failure of the warring factions to reach an accommodation.

DOCUMENT

. . .

II. RECENT DEVELOPMENTS IN AFGHANISTAN

A. Military situation

4. The military balance between the Afghan warring factions see-sawed wildly in 1997. The factions fought hard for control of northern Afghanistan and the northern approaches to Kabul. However, despite the expenditure of large quantities of externally supplied ammunition and equipment, and the loss of many lives and the displacement of civilian populations, neither side succeeded in recording sizeable gains of territory or significant political advantage. By early November 1997, the predominantly Pushtun Taliban continued to hold approximately two thirds of the country but had not been able to capture the territories in the north, which are largely populated by the Tajik, Uzbek and Hazara ethnic groups.

5. The Afghan antagonists were the Taliban and the five-party Northern Alliance which is formally known as the Islamic and National Front for the Salvation of Afghanistan. The Taliban continued to control most provinces in the south, south-west and south-east, including Kabul and the cities of Kandahar, Herat and Jalalabad. The Northern Alliance, which operated from the provincial capitals of Mazar-i-Sharif, Bamyan, Taloqan and Maimana, was in control of the provinces in northern and central Afghanistan. The Alliance at present comprises the Jamiat-i-Islami, led by Burhanuddin Rabbani and his chief military commander, Ahmad

Shah Massoud; the Hezb-i-Wahdat led by Karim Khalili; the National Islamic Front of Afghanistan (NIMA), led by General Rashid Dostum and General Abdul Malik; the Harakat-i-Islami, led by Sheik Asef Mohseini; and the breakaway faction of the Hezb-i-Wahdat, led by Mohammed Akbari.

. . .

B. Political situation

12. As the fighting continued, the political situation in Afghanistan remained deadlocked. The deepening division of the country along ethnic lines, reinforced by external military and political support, continued to inhibit efforts to engender political dialogue among the factions. Throughout 1997, neither the Taliban nor its rivals appear to have given serious consideration to a political, as opposed to a military, solution to the conflict.

13. An unsettled leadership problem within the Northern Alliance also affected the political environment. Infighting was most pronounced in the predominantly Uzbek Jumbish movement, whose leader, General Dostum, was forced into exile in Turkey for four months by his rival, General Malik, after the latter's short-lived defection to the Taliban in May. While General Malik subsequently turned against the Taliban and helped to drive its forces out of Mazar, the return of General Dostum to Afghanistan on 12 September led to further political uncertainty in the north. Adding to the complex leadership problem was the death of newly designated Prime Minister Abdul Rahim Ghafoorzai in an aircraft accident at Bamyan airport in August.

. . .

15. Of similar concern is the Taliban's refusal to start negotiations with the Northern Alliance as a whole without preconditions, as well as its social and administrative practices. The mistreatment of girls and women, such as the denial of their rights to employment, health care and education, is especially worrying. Furthermore, Afghanistan has become the world's largest producer of heroin, with the vast majority of the poppies used for that purpose cultivated in areas controlled by the Taliban. The United Nations International Drug Control Programme recently announced that the Taliban had agreed to work out ways and means to eliminate poppy cultivation. I sincerely hope that the Taliban will ensure that the agreement is implemented faithfully and effectively.

16. The Taliban have made new efforts during 1997 to gain international recognition and support. Taliban representatives undertook a series of missions abroad, in particular to East Asia, the Gulf region and the United States of America. While the Governments of Pakistan, Saudi Arabia and the United Arab Emirates recognized the Taliban as the legitimate government of Afghanistan in May, other Governments have withheld their decision to extend de jure recognition.

. . .

18. Foreign military support to the two sides continued unabated throughout 1997. Reliable eyewitnesses reported many sorties of military deliveries in unmarked aircraft to bases of the Northern Alliance, as well as numerous deliveries by truck caravans of arms, ammunition and fuel to Taliban-controlled territory. United Nations employees also reported an encounter with an unidentified foreign military

training unit of several hundred persons near Kabul. Such blatant violations of General Assembly and Security Council resolutions which call for a halt to foreign military intervention seriously undermine United Nations peacemaking efforts and serve to prolong the Afghan conflict. They also raised suspicions and worsened relations among the countries in the region.

. . .

V. OBSERVATIONS AND CONCLUSIONS

36. Afghanistan, which was once a flashpoint of super-Power rivalry, has since become a typical post-cold war regional and ethnic conflict, where the major Powers no longer see a strategic incentive to get involved. It has also become a place where even responsible local political authorities, let alone a central government, have virtually ceased to exist. Herein lies much of the explanation why repeated international attempts to bring peace to the country have not borne fruit.

37. Since the early 1990s, the Afghan factions and warlords have failed to show the will to rise above their narrow factional interests and to start working together for national reconciliation. The United Nations successfully mediated the withdrawal of foreign forces from Afghanistan in the late 1980s. But, although the Najibullah regime was ready to hand over power to a broad-based transition mechanism, the Mujahideen parties were unable to agree among themselves on how to form such a mechanism. Their disagreements escalated to the point where Kabul was plunged into chaos and bloodshed once the Najibullah regime collapsed in April 1992. Since that time, the situation has only become worse.

38. Even today, the Afghan parties seem determined to go on fighting, while outside Powers continue to provide material, financial and other support to their respective clients inside Afghanistan. Meanwhile, although those major Powers that have potential influence in Afghanistan have recently started to show interest, they have yet to demonstrate the necessary degree of determination to move the situation forward.

39. In these circumstances, it is illusory to think that peace can be achieved. How can peace be imposed on faction leaders who are determined to fight it out to the finish and who receive seemingly unlimited supplies of arms from outside sponsors? It is this continued support from some outside Powers—combined with the apathy of the others who are not directly involved—which has strengthened the belief among the warlords and parties in Afghanistan that they can achieve their political, religious and social goals by force.

. . .

Conclusions

53. As described in the preceding sections of the present report, a peaceful settlement in Afghanistan remains elusive notwithstanding the untiring efforts of the United Nations to broker peace among the country's warring factions. In the meantime, Afghanistan's civil war has continued to exact a staggering toll in terms of human lives and suffering as well as material destruction. What we are witnessing is a seemingly endless tragedy of epic proportions in which the Afghan people's yearning for peace is being systematically and continually betrayed by leaders and warlords driven by selfish ambitions and thirst for power.

54. In earlier reports I have observed that the Afghan parties and their external supporters, while continuing to pursue military solutions, often also profess support for resolutions of the General Assembly and the Security Council calling for a peaceful settlement. Regrettably, their actions seldom seem to be motivated, however, by a desire to contribute to the implementation of those resolutions. Similarly, it is discouraging that with few exceptions, the international community as a whole has shown only limited interest in adopting tangible measures to discourage the Afghan parties and their outside supporters from pursuing their bellicose aims and objectives.

55. There is no doubt that a number of Governments both inside and outside the region would be in a favourable position, should they so decide, to encourage the Afghan parties to overcome their differences and seek a peaceful settlement. It is also clear, however, that as long as those Governments choose not to exercise their influence with the parties in a positive and constructive manner, the efforts made by my representatives, however dedicated and skilled, will not suffice to bring peace to Afghanistan. Sadly, it could be argued that in these circumstances the role of the United Nations in Afghanistan is little more than that of an alibi to provide cover for the inaction—or worse—of the international community at large.

56. Over the past several years, it has become increasingly difficult to justify the continuation of United Nations peace efforts and the attendant costs in the absence of any positive signs suggesting a fundamental change of attitude on the part of those Governments that are capable of contributing decisively to a peaceful solution of the conflict. Recently, I have been somewhat encouraged, however, by the increased level of attention to the situation in Afghanistan now being manifested by a number of countries that have begun to discuss among themselves the adoption of practical measures to persuade the Afghan parties to embark on serious negotiations. But much more needs to be done by Governments with a greater sense of unity in order for the peace efforts spearheaded by the United Nations to stand a realistic chance of success.

. . .

Source: United Nations. General Assembly/Security Council. A/52/682; S/1997/894. Available online at http://www.un.org/en/ga/search/view_doc.asp?symbol=A/52/682.

ANALYSIS

By the time this summary appeared in late 1997, the war had turned badly for the Northern Alliance. Its leaders had unified to some degree, but strong disagreements remained and helped to explain their poor military position. Fortunately for them, as they retreated into northern Afghanistan, the ethnic groups of that part of the country—Uzbeks, Tajiks, Hazaras, and others—favored the Northern Alliance over the Pashtun-dominated Taliban.

Also of note was the increasing frustration on the part of the United Nations for the warring parties to reach a political settlement. The United Nations had sought peace in Afghanistan since 1980, but its representatives could not force the faction-alized Northern Alliance and the unwilling Taliban to come together in a mediated environment. With the Taliban controlling a majority of the country, there appeared to be even less incentive to negotiate.

- **Document 21: U.S. Embassy (Islamabad), Cable, "Afghanistan: Taliban Decision-Making and Leadership Structure"**
- **When:** December 30, 1997
- **Where:** Islamabad, Pakistan
- **Significance:** A U.S. State Department cable that identified Taliban leader Mullah Omar as the most influential member of the group.

DOCUMENT

FM AMEMBASSY ISLAMABAD
TO SECSTATE WASHDC

. . .

1. Summary: Mullah Omar plays the key role in Taliban decision-making, while his advisers—Wakil Ahmed, Mullah Jalil, and others—are believed to play key roles in policy implementation. Although they do not seriously rival Omar for influence, several Taliban leaders, including Talban Deputy Leader Mullah Rabbani, reportedly maintain an independent power base. Because of Omar's highly-personalized leadership style, Taliban institutions, such as the "inner" Shura, have weakened from disuse, although the "Ulema" Shura is believed to maintain some authority. While the movement is under the sway of Omar, it does not appear reliant on his survival—Afghanistan's mullahs are mobilized and the Taliban will probably remain the leading force in the Pashtun community into the foreseeable future. End Summary.

MULLAH OMAR: LEADERSHIP FROM THE TOP

2. Mullah Mohammad Omar plays the key role in Taliban decision-making. The Taliban's twin policies of continuing the war until victory and imposing "Sharia'h Law" on Afghanistan bear his imprint. Within the Taliban movement, Mullah Omar's legitimacy springs from his reputation as a pious Muslim with a vision of an "Islamic" government in Afghanistan, and an effective (if relatively unknown) commander during the Afghan-Soviet War, and from his role in opposing "corrupt mujahedin" commanders in the Kandahar area. Omar's preeminent role in the Taliban movement was recognized in April 1996 when he was named "Amir Al-Mu-Minin" (Commander of the Faithful) by a group of (Taliban-picked) religious scholars in Kandahar. In September 1996 after the Taliban captured Kabul, the Taliban announced that Omar would serve as the leader of the "Islamic State of Afghanistan" which was recently renamed "The Islamic Emirate of Afghanistan" in his honor.

3. Observers agree that Mullah Omar maintains an idiosyncratic, almost obscurantist, style of leadership. A man of few words, Omar is said to listen to visitors carefully and then say a few polite words. At this point in the meeting, if the issue can be dealt with immediately, Omar may issue an order for the visitor to be issued money or weapons by initializing a piece of paper. Otherwise, Omar retires to his spartan offices near the Kandahar governor's guesthouse to make decisions. Since the Taliban capture of Kabul, Mullah Omar is said to have devolved many decisions concerning policy implementation to his advisors or to the "caretaker council" in Kabul. According to [redacted] a former resistance commander with links to the Taliban, Mullah Omar now focuses more on the big picture—"Omar sees himself as a religious figure of historical importance and he prefers to pronounce only on what he considers the important issues."

4. Omar reportedly maintains tight reins over the Taliban movement and the population in Taliban-controlled areas through the activities of the religious police, a.k.a. "The Department to Propagate Virtue and Prevent Vice." (Note: Among other responsibilities, the religious police are responsible for ensuring that Afghans in Taliban-controlled areas maintain proper beard-length and that women are clothed according to Islamic law.) [Redacted] at the Taliban-controlled Afghan Embassy in Islamabad, told POLOFF that Mullah Qalamuddin, the head of the religious police, reports to Mullah Turabi, the Taliban "Acting Minister of Justice," who, in turn, reports directly to Mullah Omar. Some sources have told POLOFF that Maulawi Khairullah Khairkhwah, the "Acting Minister of Interior" who maintains responsibilities for the Taliban's civilian intelligence organization, also reports directly to Omar.

. . .

THE COMMANDERS

7. While observers claim that the Taliban's chief military strategist is Mullah Omar himself, they mention a number of commanders who are believed to hold key positions in the Taliban military structure, including

. . .

THE INSTITUTIONAL FRAMEWORK

8. The Taliban have created four major institutional structures that technically maintain the ability to weigh in on policy issues and policy implementation. They are:

–The "Inner" Shura: The Inner Shura used to be considered the Taliban's collective leadership. However, since Mullah Omar assumed the title of Amir and developed his highly-personalized leadership style, the Inner Shura has lost much of its importance. The Inner Shura reportedly has 23-members, including most of the Taliban leaders mentioned above. Other well-known Taliban, including former "Acting Foreign Minister" Ghaus, are also members. [Redacted] a member, told POLOFF that the Inner Shura meets "occasionally and during crises."

–The "Outer" Shura: This Shura is believed to have over 100 members, including many religious figures and provincial notables. It is considered relatively unimportant and we not know when it meets. [Redacted] asserted that the Outer Shura is meant to advise the Inner Shura.

–"The Caretaker Council": The Caretaker Council is headed by Mullah Rabbani, although Abdul Kabir, the Deputy Head, has chaired most of its meetings of late. The Council, which was formed after the Taliban capture of Kabul, does not have any policy-making role. Its role is primarily policy implementation: it has responsibility for issues directives to Taliban "government" ministries based in Kabul.

–The "Ulema" Shura: Not much is known about this Shura, which meets in Kandahar. It is believed to have some influence on social policies and to play a key role in advising Mullah Omar on Islamic law. [Redacted] told POLOFF in a brief meeting in Kandahar in May that it has 24 members and its purpose is to "implement Sharia'h (Law) in Afghanistan."

WHAT IF SOMETHING HAPPENED TO OMAR?

9. Although Mullah Omar is firmly in charge of the Taliban at this time, given the volatile political/military situation in Afghanistan it is always possible that unexpected event or chain of events could remove Mullah Omar from the scene. For example, if Mullah Omar was killed in an internal coup, which no one sees as likely at this time, leadership of the Taliban—if it doesn't splinter—would probably be won on the battlefield. However, if Omar dies in an accident or is killed by a lone gunman acting without political support, the Taliban collective leadership, i.e., the Inner Shura and the Ulema Shura, would probably meet to choose a new leader. (Note: It is not known whether Omar has a designated successor or whether his choice would be respected by Shura members, if he has named one.) At this time, most observers say that Mullah Rabbani or Regional Governor Mullah Hassan Rahmani would probably be chosen to assume leadership. While he agreed that Rabbani or Hassan are the favorites, [redacted] observed that it is possible that a number of dark horse candidates could emerge in a leadership contest. Queried for information on this point, [redacted] replied that Omar has forced numerous Taliban from positions of influence because of personal dislike or displeasure with their performance and it is possible that some could be rehabilitated, such as Mullah Ghaus, who was blamed for the Taliban's defeat in Mazar-i-Sharif in May. [Redacted] added that the Ulema Shura is a "shadowy organization" that could produce a candidate for leadership who does have wide name recognition.

COMMENT

10. The Taliban leadership structure is opaque—it is extremely difficult to understand what goes on within the walls in Kandahar or how the Taliban relate to one another. What is clear is that the Taliban movement as a whole has accepted the increasingly personalized rule of Mullah Omar. In the process, Omar's role appears to have preempted the growth of Taliban institutions, with the possible exception of the Ulema Shura, which appears to maintain some influence on religious issues. Although the Taliban movement is under the sway of Omar, it does not appear reliant on his survival, however—Afghanistan's mullahs have been mobilized and unless another force can displace them, which appears unlikely for the near term, the Taliban as a movement will probably remain the leading force in the Pashtun community into the foreseeable future.

SIMONS

Source: National Security Archive. Available online at http://nsarchive2 .gwu.edu//NSAEBB/NSAEBB295/doc08.pdf.

ANALYSIS

Mullah Omar had led the Taliban since its birth in 1994, but the evolution of the group's structure by late 1997 had given him much more effective control of the group with few real checks against his power. As mentioned in the analysis for Document 19, Mullah Omar's views on many issues, especially the harboring of Osama bin Laden, had been adopted as policy in spite of the disagreements lodged by other members of the Taliban.

The analysis also presciently noted that the Taliban was a strong enough movement to survive the death of its leader. Mullah Omar remained in control of the Taliban as it went into exile in Pakistan in 2001 and then through its rebirth in the mid-2000s. He eventually died in 2011, though this fact was hidden from the public for several years afterward.

- **Document 22: Department of State (Washington), Cable, "Afghanistan: Taliban Convene Ulema, Iran and Bin Ladin on the Agenda"**
- **When:** September 25, 1998
- **Where:** Washington, D.C.
- **Significance:** A U.S. State Department cable that analyzed whether the Ulema convened by the Taliban would have any appreciable effect on Afghan policy.

DOCUMENT

FM SECSTATE WASHDC
INFO USDEL SECRETARY IMMEDIATE

. . .

SUBJECT: AFGHANISTAN: TALIBAN CONVENE ULEMA, IRAN AND BIN LADIN ON THE AGENDA

. . .

SUMMARY

3. In Kabul, the Taliban have convened some 1,500 Ulema (Islamic Religious Scholars) from all over Afghanistan. Official Taliban sources say the Ulema are discussing Afghanistan's response to the threat of attack from Iran. Usama bin Ladin's presence in Afghanistan—an issue over which the Taliban leadership appears to be split—will also probably figure in the discussion. The convention appears to be an attempt to orchestrate a show of nationwide allegiance to the Taliban in general and to their paramount leader, Mullah Omar, in particular.

. . .

BIN LADIN PROBABLY WILL BE DISCUSSED

8. The other reason for gathering so many Ulema together was to give advice, perhaps a fatwa, to Mullah Omar on several subjects, with (as the Radio Shariat announcement makes clear) Iran at the top of the list. Some have speculated that they would also discuss what to do with Usama bin Ladin, [redacted] often a well-informed contact, suggests that Mullah Omar "authorized" the Ulema to "make a final decision" on bin Ladin's presence in Afghanstan. [Redacted] doubts the Ulema would do anything other than reiterate what Mullah Omar has already said on the subject, i.e., that bin Ladin is their guest, has not been proved to be involved in any bombings, and will be permitted to stay in Afghanistan, but with his political activities curtailed.

. . .

TALIBAN DIVIDED OVER BIN LADIN?

11. [Redacted] according to his sources, said four issues would be discussed: Iran, bin Ladin, relationships with UN and international organizations, and human rights questions on which the Taliban have been so heavily criticized abroad (women's health, girls' education, and allegations of mass killings in the north, perhaps). On Iran, he speculated the group may take a tough line. On bin Ladin, he thought the Taliban were divided into two groups. Mullah Mohammad Rabbani, the convener of this meeting, is known to oppose bin Ladin's presence inside Afghanistan and to argue that, if bin Ladin remains in Afghanistan, his political activities must be strictly controlled. Mullah Omar heads the other camp wishing to keep bin Ladin in Afghanistan. [Redacted] speculated that the Ulema meeting will decide that bin Ladin may stay in Afghanistan but his political activities, especially directed against third countries, must be strictly controlled.

. . .

COMMENT

13. This Ulema meeting could prove quite significant. The last time the Taliban convened such a large gathering of Ulema, in Kandahar in 1996, they anointed Mullah Omar "Amir Ul-Mominin" ("Emir of the Faithful"). It appears to be an attempt at legitimizing Taliban rule in the north of Afghanistan as well as a means of gaining approval for a course of action vis-à-vis Iran, and possibly, bin Ladin. With potential troublemakers almost certainly screened out by the Taliban and (if Radio Shariat is to be believed) an official agenda of laughably loaded questions, we do not expect to see a free-wheeling debate here, much less any decisions that run counter to Mullah Omar's pronounced views.

14. Comment, continued: From time to time, rumors surface that Mullah Mohammad Rabbani holds different, more pragmatic views on various subjects compared to Mullah Omar's. If his role is anything more than just titular convener of the meeting, there may be more going on in the meeting than immediately visible.

Milam UnquoteTalbott

Source: National Security Archive. Available online at http://nsarchive2.gwu.edu//NSAEBB/NSAEBB97/tal26.pdf.

ANALYSIS

As discussed in the analysis for Document 21, the Taliban had plenty of internal disagreements, but Mullah Omar had effectively imposed his views as those of the group's. In this case, the Taliban had convened an Ulema, a meeting of its top scholars, but many correctly anticipated that the meeting would essentially approve the policies already set forth by Mullah Omar. In fact, the Taliban continued to harbor Osama bin Laden, and the group did little to soften its human rights abuses to seek international approval.

- **Document 23: U.S. Consulate (Peshawar), Cable, "Afghanistan: Military Situation Reviewed"**
- **When:** January 12, 2001
- **Where:** Peshawar, Pakistan
- **Significance:** A U.S. State Department cable that cast doubt on the survival of the Northern Alliance.

DOCUMENT

FM AMCONSUL PESHAWAR
TO SECSTATE WASHDC

. . .

SUBJECT: AFGHANISTAN: MILITARY SITUATION REVIEWED

1. Summary: The Taliban made significant advances north of the Hindu Kush mountains during the past year, and are in position to maintain and increase pressure on the opposition when fighting resumes in earnest, as it likely will in the spring of 2001. Despite the Taliban's improved military position, they remain unable to deliver a knock-out blow. On the other side, the opposition's future is inextricably linked to the continued military leadership of Ahmad Shah Masoud and his ability to procure the materiel that he needs to contend with the superior manpower and firepower of the Taliban. End Summary.

. . .

HOW SERIOUS IS MASOUD'S SITUATION?

14. Ref E suggested that Masoud's supply lines are increasingly threatened by the growing accommodation between Uzbekistan and the Taliban. It does indeed appear that Masoud must improve his supply situation, and be ready to defend his supply lines vigorously when fighting resumes in the spring of 2001, if he has any hope of continuing to confront the Taliban. The Taliban's efforts to blockade UIFSA-controlled areas, in Dara-Ye Suf, Kunar, and on the southern side of Panjshir, also appear to be exacting a toll. In Taghab District of Kapisa Province, Taliban pressure on the trade of food and other supplies with Panjshir, in the form

of harsh jail sentences for smugglers, has led to a ten-fold increase in food prices in Panjshir and resultant shortages, according to a relative of one of our FSN's who recently visited the area. Masoud is going to have to dig deeply into his extensive military and technical experience, not to mention his luck, if he is to continue his resistance to the Taliban. We have received a reliable report that Masoud, on a recent visit to Faizabad, Badakhshan Province, angrily blamed the Russians for failing to provide sufficient supplies to the UIFSA. In the same speech, Masoud also decried that lack of support that the UIFSA is receiving from the population of Badakhshan.

15. [Redacted] observed that, in his view, Masoud must turn the tide in the north before winter snows close the roads, or he must be prepared to do so immediately upon the snow melt in spring 2001. [Redacted] noted that of the two sides, Masoud's is the better prepared for cold-weather combat, though fighters on both sides are woefully unprepared for true winter conditions. For exam-

DID YOU KNOW?

Bamiyan Buddhas

The Bamiyan Buddhas were two massive statues of Buddha carved into the side of a cliff in central Afghanistan in the Bamiyan Valley. Buddhism had flourished during Afghanistan's time as part of the Silk Road, and Buddhist monks in the region carved the two statues as well as other monuments sometime between the 3rd and 6th centuries CE. Soon afterward, Islam entered Afghanistan and became the dominant religion, but, despite some occasional threats, the statues remained mostly intact save for the destruction of one face in the late 19th century. The Taliban, however, sought to erase any vestiges of non-Islamic religions during their rule, and Mullah Omar ordered them destroyed in early 2001. This prompted an international outcry from the United Nations Educational, Scientific and Cultural Organization (UNESCO) and other groups seeking to preserve their cultural and historical value to no avail. Afghan authorities have long planned to rebuild the statues, but this has not yet occurred as of 2018.

ple, both sides lack proper winter boots. [Redacted] noted that he thinks it possible that Masoud may still try to push the Taliban out of Taloqan in early 2001. As of late December, rain and wet snows had rendered the region a sea of mud, but [redacted] thought that a few days of sub-zero temperatures prior to any heavy snowfalls, would give Masoud an opportunity to go on the offensive against the Taliban occupiers of Taloqan, who are at present surrounded on three sides by the UIFSA forces. [Redacted] also noted that Masoud had a high incentive to retake Taloqan, and the relatively comfortable residences in the town, before winter progressed any more, since many of Masoud's men are living outside or in tents.

16. Without elaborating on his evidence, [redacted] also said he believes that the GOP is working furiously to ensure that the Taliban have adequate military supplies in advance of the imposition of UNSC Resolution 1333 in mid-January. [Redacted] did not have any comments on the degree to which India, Iranian, and/or Russian supplies to the Northern Alliance may have increased in the recent past.

17. Comment: Using their superior manpower, supplies, and their ideological fervor, the Taliban have used the past year to approach the brink of a complete military occupation of Afghanistan. Indeed, they have been in variations of this position since 1996. Why can't they simply finish the job? Early last summer, just before the Taliban launched their Shomali offensive, we had heard from [redacted] who is among the best-informed and best-connected Afghan watchers in Peshawar, that the year 2000 was going to be different. The Taliban, he said, had decided to try a new approach. Mindful of their economic problems,

including the drought, and mindful of their abysmal international reputation, they were going to adopt a more subtle strategy to winning the entire country. [Redacted] said that high-level Taliban officials had told him that they would focus on development, improving administration, and converting opposition commanders through bribery and diplomacy. [Redacted] had barely told of this "new approach" when the Taliban took the offensive in the Shomali in early July. So much for the new approach.

18. Comment, continued: Among the Taliban's weaknesses is that their only real success has come on the battlefield. They have established security, at least relative to the anarchy that preceded them, and they have managed to extend their military domination across perhaps 95 percent of the country. They've done precious little else, apparently because they lack the capacity to do so. The Taliban are like the proverbial carpenter whose only tool is a hammer, and who thus treats every problem as a nail. Fighting is all they really know how to do. Their martial abilities have gotten them this far, and may eventually enable them to occupy even more of the country, but we still see no evidence that they can begin to do anything else that real governments do.
KATZ

Source: National Security Archive. Available online at http://nsarchive2 .gwu.edu//NSAEBB/NSAEBB295/doc15.pdf.

ANALYSIS

By early 2001, the Northern Alliance's military position had degraded even further, and Ahmad Shah Masoud had become the military leader and clear public face for the group. It barely hung on to the northern territories from which it had drawn much of its political support.

The situation, however, was not entirely positive for the Taliban either. It had acquired a reputation for maintaining order in its early days, but the group was unable or unwilling to be effective stewards of a nation-state. The Northern Alliance, to be fair, had proven little better, but taking control of Kabul had done little to change the culture of the Taliban. The military stalemate and the Taliban's unwillingness to govern continued into the fall of 2001.

- **Document 24: State Department Report, "U.S. Engagement with the Taliban on Usama Bin Laden"**
- **When:** c. July 16, 2001
- **Where:** Washington, D.C.
- **Significance:** A U.S. State Department report that chronicled its attempts to negotiate with the Taliban over Osama bin Laden.

DOCUMENT

U.S. Engagement with the Taliban on Usama Bin Laden

Since the Taliban captured Kabul in 1996, the United States has consistently discussed with them peace, humanitarian assistance, drugs, and human rights. However, we have made clear that Usama bin Laden (UBL) and terrorism is the preeminent issue between the U.S. and the Taliban.

- These concerns over bin Ladin preceded the 1998 bombings.
- For instance, Secretary Christopher wrote to the Taliban Foreign Minister in 1996 that "we wish to work with you to expel all terrorists and those who support terrorism."

In our talks, we have stressed that UBL has murdered Americans and continues to plan attacks against Americans and others and that we cannot ignore this threat.

- Have also emphasized that the international community shares this concern. In 1999 and in 2000, the UN Security Council passed resolutions demanding that UBL be expelled to a country where he can be brought to justice.
- Have told the Taliban that the terrorist problem is not confined to bin Laden and that the Taliban must take steps to shut down all terrorist activities.
- Have told them that the resolution of the bin Laden issue and steps to close the terrorist apparatus would enable us to discuss other issues in an improved atmosphere.
- Conversely, have stressed that if this terrorism issue is not addressed, there can be no improvement in relations.

These talks have been fruitless. The Taliban usually said that they want a solution but cannot comply with UNSCRs. Often the Taliban asked the U.S. to suggest a solution.

- In October 1999, the Taliban suggested several "solutions" including a UBL trial by a panel of Islamic scholars or monitoring of UBL Afghanistan by OIC or UN.
- Taliban consistently maintained that UBL's activities are restricted, despite all evidence to the contrary.

Often our discussions have been followed by Taliban declarations that no evidence exists against UBL and that he will not be expelled as demanded by the UN resolutions. Highlights of our talks with the Taliban follow.

. . .

Source: National Security Archive. Available online at http://nsarchive2.gwu.edu/NSAEBB/NSAEBB97/tal40.pdf.

ANALYSIS

Despite earlier Taliban assurances to the contrary, they ignored repeated American and other international overtures to surrender Osama bin Laden on charges of terrorism. Since the meeting discussed in Document 19, the Taliban refused to modify their stance save for the suggestion of a religious trial that appeared unlikely to alter his legal status.

Since the first meeting in Document 19, the United States had also attempted to solve the problem using force. Following the 1998 U.S. Embassy bombings, the United States had attacked camps in Afghanistan using Tomahawk cruise missiles, but they missed bin Laden himself. The United States also tracked bin Laden using unmanned aerial vehicles by 2000, but these incidents occurred before modifications had been made to allow the aircraft to fire weapons.

Despite these concerted efforts, bin Laden remained beyond America's reach into the fall of 2001.

2

DOCUMENTS FROM OPERATION
ENDURING FREEDOM
AND THE BEGINNING OF
RECONSTRUCTION, 2001–2003

- **Document 25: George W. Bush, Statement by the President in His Address to the Nation**
- **When:** September 11, 2001
- **Where:** Washington, D.C.
- **Significance:** Delivered on the evening of September 11, 2001, President George W. Bush's brief address hinted at a military response for the series of terror attacks earlier that day that killed more than 3,000 people.

DOCUMENT

Good evening. Today, our fellow citizens, our way of life, our very freedom came under attack in a series of deliberate and deadly terrorist acts. The victims were in airplanes, or in their offices; secretaries, businessmen and women, military and federal workers; moms and dads, friends and neighbors. Thousands of lives were suddenly ended by evil, despicable acts of terror.

The pictures of airplanes flying into buildings, fires burning, huge structures collapsing, have filled us with disbelief, terrible sadness, and a quiet, unyielding anger. These acts of mass murder were intended to frighten our nation into chaos and retreat. But they have failed; our country is strong.

A great people has been moved to defend a great nation. Terrorist attacks can shake the foundations of our biggest buildings, but they cannot touch the foundation of America. These acts shattered steel, but they cannot dent the steel of American resolve.

America was targeted for attack because we're the brightest beacon for freedom and opportunity in the world. And no one will keep that light from shining.

Today, our nation saw evil, the very worst of human nature. And we responded with the best of America—with the daring of our rescue workers, with the caring for strangers and neighbors who came to give blood and help in any way they could.

Immediately following the first attack, I implemented our government's emergency response plans. Our military is powerful, and it's prepared. Our emergency teams are working in New York City and Washington, D.C. to help with local rescue efforts.

Our first priority is to get help to those who have been injured, and to take every precaution to protect our citizens at home and around the world from further attacks.

The functions of our government continue without interruption. Federal agencies in Washington which had to be evacuated today are reopening for essential personnel tonight, and will be open for business tomorrow. Our financial institutions remain strong, and the American economy will be open for business, as well.

The search is underway for those who are behind these evil acts. I've directed the full resources of our intelligence and law enforcement communities to find those responsible and to bring them to justice. We will make no distinction between the terrorists who committed these acts and those who harbor them.

I appreciate so very much the members of Congress who have joined me in strongly condemning these attacks. And on behalf of the American people, I thank the many world leaders who have called to offer their condolences and assistance.

America and our friends and allies join with all those who want peace and security in the world, and we stand together to win the war against terrorism. Tonight, I ask for your prayers for all those who grieve, for the children whose worlds have been shattered, for all whose sense of safety and security has been threatened. And I pray they will be comforted by a power greater than any of us, spoken through the ages in Psalm 23: "Even though I walk through the valley of the shadow of death, I fear no evil, for You are with me."

This is a day when all Americans from every walk of life unite in our resolve for justice and peace. America has stood down enemies before, and we will do so this time. None of us will ever forget this day. Yet, we go forward to defend freedom and all that is good and just in our world.

Thank you. Good night, and God bless America.

Source: Public Papers of the President of the United States. George W. Bush, 2001, Book 2. Washington, D.C.: Government Printing Office, 2002, 1099–1100.

ANALYSIS

The address is striking for not specifically naming Osama bin Laden and al-Qaeda for perpetrating the attack or the Taliban for granting the terrorists safe harbor, even though many had made the connection as the events earlier in the day wore on. It is also noteworthy because terrorism had traditionally been a law enforcement matter and was described as such in this speech. No clear indication was given of the pending campaign in Afghanistan.

- **Document 26: U.S. Department of State, Cable, "Deputy Secretary Armitage's Meeting with General Mahmud: Actions and Support Expected of Pakistan in Fight against Terrorism"**
- **When:** September 14, 2001
- **Where:** Washington, D.C.
- **Significance:** The U.S. government formally requested extensive Pakistani support for the campaign against al-Qaeda and the Taliban.

DOCUMENT

FM SECSTATE WASHDC
TO AMEMBASSY ISLAMABAD
…
SUBJECT: DEPUTY SECRETARY ARMITAGE'S MEETING WITH GEN-
ERAL MAHMUD: ACTIONS AND SUPPORT EXPECTED OF PAKISTAN IN
FIGHT AGAINST TERRORISM
…

3. Summary: During a businesslike meeting September 13 with Pakistan Intelligence Chief Mahmud, Deputy Secretary Armitage laid out specific requests we
are making of the Pakistani government for logistical, technical, and other support in the fight against terrorism. Mr. Armitage passed the points over in a nonpaper, asking that Mahmud convey them to his president promptly. Mahmud
assured the Deputy Secretary that Pakistan was with the U.S. in this fight. While
expressing appreciation for these welcome sentiments, Mr. Armitage indicated
we would be looking for an official response from President Musharraf, who the
Secretary hopes to call in the next several hours. [Redacted] Action request:
Ambassador should seek earliest opportunity to double track this message with
President Musharraf, working off the nonpaper in para. 4. End Summary and
Action Request.

4. Deputy Secretary Armitage met on September 13 with Pakistani Inter-Services
Intelligence Directorate (ISI-D) Director General Mahmud Ahmed. Ambassador Lodhi
and DCM Akram attended, as did SA A/S Rocca, S/CT Director Taylor, and SA/PAB Director Young.

5. Mr. Armitage began by reprising his message from the previous day to Mahmud (ref A) about the need for extraordinary action in this perilous time and the importance of Pakistan's stepping up to U.S. requests in the fight against terrorism. He noted with satisfaction President Musharraf's comments to Ambassador Chamberlin in their recent meeting (ref B), as well as the positive public remarks by Musharraf in support of the U.S. He reviewed our encouraging multilateral and bilateral efforts thus far to build an international coalition, underscoring the importance of Pakistan's joining as a full partner in this process. This was a difficult choice for Paki-stan, he repeated, and with that forewarning, read the following points, which were passed over to Gen-eral Mahmud immediately afterwards.

6. Begin text of nonpaper: Specific actions and support to address terrorist attacks

– Stop Al Qaida operatives at your border, inter-cept arms shipments through Pakistan and end all logistical support for bin Ladin;

DID YOU KNOW?

Pervez Musharraf

Pervez Musharraf is a former Pakistani army general and the former president of Pakistan. Born in Delhi in 1943, the Pakistani army commissioned Musharraf as an officer in 1965. He rose through the ranks over the next three decades, eventually reaching the rank of four-star general under Prime Minister Nawaz Sharif. Relations between the two men became strained, however, when Musharraf oversaw a controversial 1999 operation in Kashmir that led to a fierce Indian reprisal. Rather than wait for Sharif to remove him, Musharraf instead conspired with fellow officers to overthrow Sharif's elected government. This action caused much international consternation because Pakistan had openly tested its first nuclear weapon only one year earlier. Musharraf assumed the presidency in 2001, and he quickly moved to cooperate with the U.S. war in Afghanistan. A series of unpopular decisions even-tually turned public opinion against him, causing Mushar-raf to resign from office in August 2008.

– Provide the U.S. with blanket overflight and landing rights to conduct all necessary military and intelligence operations;

– Provide as needed territorial access to U.S. and allied military intelligence, and other personnel to conduct all necessary operations against the perpetrators of terrorism or those that harbor them, including use of Pakistan's naval ports, airbases and strategic locations on borders;

– Provide the U.S. immediately with intelligence, [redacted]

– Continue to publicly condemn the terrorist acts of September 11 and any other terrorist acts against the U.S. or its friends and allies [redacted]

– Cut off all shipments of fuel to the Taliban and any other items and recruits, including volunteers en route to Afghanistan, that can be used in a military offensive capacity or to abet the terrorist threat;

– Should the evidence strongly implicate Usama bin-Ladin and the al Qaida network in Afghanistan and should Afghanistan and the Taliban continue to harbor him and this network, Pakistan will break diplomatic relations with the Taliban government, end support for the Taliban and assist us in the aforementioned ways to Usama bin-Ladin and his al Qaida network. End nonpaper

7. Repeating his earlier statement that the noose was tightening around bin Ladin's and al Qaida's neck, Mr. Armitage said this involved not only Afghanistan, but would encompass terrorist groups elsewhere. He noted President Bush's description that Americans were responding to Tuesday's attacks with unyielding anger, and also noted with regret that this has sometimes manifested itself in ugly attacks and others in the U.S.

[Redacted]

Source: National Security Archive. Available online at http://nsarchive2 .gwu.edu/NSAEBB/NSAEBB325/doc05.pdf.

ANALYSIS

Pakistan had been under U.S. sanctions since its May 1998 test of a nuclear weapon in violation of the Nuclear Test Ban Treaty. Furthermore, elements of the Pakistani government had supported the Taliban since the group's emergence in 1994. Yet, the Bush administration needed the support of Pakistan—as well as other corrupt and unsavory regimes in Uzbekistan and Kyrgyzstan—to establish U.S. bases and supply lines to allow the prosecution of a military campaign in Afghanistan. As a result, the Bush administration completely reversed several major foreign policy decisions enacted by their predecessors.

- **Document 27: U.S. Embassy (Islamabad), Cable, "Musharraf Accepts the Seven Points"**
- **When:** September 14, 2001
- **Where:** Islamabad, Pakistan

- **Significance:** President Pervez Musharraf agreed to cooperate with the United States on all issues raised during the previous day's meeting between Deputy Secretary of State Richard Armitage and General Mahmud.

DOCUMENT

FM AMEMBASSY ISLAMABAD
TO SECSTATE WASHDC IMMEDIATE
. . .
SUBJECT: MUSHARRAF ACCEPTS THE SEVEN POINTS
. . .

1. Summary: General Musharraf accepts the seven actions we are asking of the GOP to support our efforts against international terrorism. His top military commanders concur. Musharraf discussed implementation details remaining to be worked out regarding the points and invited us to send an interagency team to address them. [redacted] End Summary.

2. In a 90-minute meeting with the Ambassador and Polcounselor late September 14, Musharraf said he had studied the points and discussed them in an all-day meeting with his corps commanders and other ranking military officers. He said he accepted the points without conditions and that his military leadership concurred.

3. Reviewing each point in detail, Musharraf enumerated a variety of security and technical issues that need to be addressed. [Redacted] These were among issues that needed to be discussed and he hoped an interagency team would visit Pakistan as soon as possible to address them. These were not conditions, he told the ambassador, but points that required clarification.

4. Musharraf also raised several general issues that he and corps commanders had discussed. He then offered several recommendations for making the operation a success.

[Redacted]

E. We need to think about the political future of Afghanistan. Do we intend to strike UBL and his supporters, or the Taliban as well? It was important, he said, not to alienate the Afghan people. Following any military action, there should be a prompt economic recovery effort. "You are there to kill terrorists, not make enemies," he said. Islamabad, he said, wants a friendly government in Kabul. [Redacted]

F. Pakistan will need full US support as it proceeds with us. [Redacted]

5. Comment: Musharraf is personally on board and so is his military leadership. [Redacted]

CHAMBERLIN

Source: National Security Archive. Available online at http://nsarchive2 .gwu.edu/NSAEBB/NSAEBB325/doc06.pdf.

ANALYSIS

President Musharraf's acceptance of U.S. requests represented a significant change in policy given the previous support elements of the Pakistani government had provided to the Taliban. The possibilities for American monetary aid and the end of sanctions outweighed the potential difficulties that abandoning the Taliban might cause. However, Musharraf's insistence that his government desired "a friendly government in Kabul" hinted at the Pakistani double-dealing of future years.

- **Document 28: Authorization for the Use of Military Force, PL 107-40**
- **When:** September 18, 2001
- **Where:** Washington, D.C.
- **Significance:** The joint resolution of the U.S. Congress authorized hostilities against the perpetrators of the September 11 attacks.

DOCUMENT

Joint Resolution
To authorize the use of United States Armed Forces against those responsible for the recent attacks launched against the United States.

Whereas, on September 11, 2001, acts of treacherous violence were committed against the United States and its citizens; and

Whereas, such acts render it both necessary and appropriate that the United States exercise its rights to self-defense and to protect United States citizens both at home and abroad; and

Whereas, in light of the threat to the national security and foreign policy of the United States posed by these grave acts of violence; and

Whereas, such acts continue to pose an unusual and extraordinary threat to the national security and foreign policy of the United States; and

Whereas, the President has authority under the Constitution to take action to deter and prevent acts of international terrorism against the United States: Now, therefore, be it

Resolved by the Senate and House of Representatives of the United States of America in Congress assembled,

SECTION 1. SHORT TITLE.

This joint resolution may be cited as the "Authorization for Use of Military Force".

SEC. 2. AUTHORIZATION FOR USE OF UNITED STATES ARMED FORCES.

(a) IN GENERAL.—That the President is authorized to use all necessary and appropriate force against those nations, organizations, or persons he determines planned, authorized, committed, or aided the terrorist attacks that occurred on September 11, 2001, or harbored such organizations or persons, in order to prevent any future acts of international terrorism against the United States by such nations, organizations or persons.

(b) WAR POWERS RESOLUTION REQUIREMENTS.—

(1) SPECIFIC STATUTORY AUTHORIZATION.—Consistent with section 8 (a)(1) of the War Powers Resolution, the Congress declares that this section is intended to constitute specific statutory authorization within the meaning of section 5(b) of the War Powers Resolution.

(2) APPLICABILITY OF OTHER REQUIREMENTS.—Nothing in this resolution supercedes any requirement of the War Powers Resolution.

Approved September 18, 2001.

Source: Public Law 107-40, September 18, 2001. 115 Stat. 224. Available online at https://www.gpo.gov/fdsys/pkg/PLAW-107publ40/pdf/PLAW-107publ40.pdf.

ANALYSIS

The Authorization of the Use of Military Force (AUMF) provided broad legislative support for military action against the "nations, organizations, or persons" involved in the September 11 attacks. It did not specifically mention Afghanistan, but the presence of al-Qaeda and the support provided to the group by the Taliban provided the legal justification to make for a just, lawful military campaign.

In the years that followed, the AUMF would be referenced to justify more than 30 military actions around the globe. As of the end of 2017, the 2001 AUMF remains in effect and was most recently cited to justify U.S. intervention in the western African nation of Niger. Attempts to revise or replace the AUMF have, to date, been unsuccessful.

- **Document 29: President George W. Bush, Address to Congress**
- **When:** September 20, 2001
- **Where:** Washington, D.C.
- **Significance:** In a rare presidential appearance before both houses of Congress, President George W. Bush addressed the American public and formally demanded that the Taliban surrender Osama bin Laden and renounce terrorism.

DOCUMENT

Mr. Speaker, Mr. President Pro Tempore, members of Congress, and fellow Americans, in the normal course of events, presidents come to this chamber to report on the state of the union. Tonight, no such report is needed; it has already been delivered by the American people.

We have seen it in the courage of passengers who rushed terrorists to save others on the ground. Passengers like an exceptional man named Todd Beamer. And would you please help me welcome his wife Lisa Beamer here tonight?

We have seen the state of our union in the endurance of rescuers working past exhaustion.

We've seen the unfurling of flags, the lighting of candles, the giving of blood, the saying of prayers in English, Hebrew and Arabic.

We have seen the decency of a loving and giving people who have made the grief of strangers their own.

My fellow citizens, for the last nine days, the entire world has seen for itself the state of union, and it is strong.

Tonight, we are a country awakened to danger and called to defend freedom. Our grief has turned to anger and anger to resolution. Whether we bring our enemies to justice or bring justice to our enemies, justice will be done.

I thank the Congress for its leadership at such an important time.

All of America was touched on the evening of the tragedy to see Republicans and Democrats joined together on the steps of this Capitol singing "God Bless America."

And you did more than sing. You acted, by delivering $40 billion to rebuild our communities and meet the needs of our military. Speaker Hastert, Minority Leader Gephardt, Majority Leader Daschle and Senator Lott, I thank you for your friendship, for your leadership and for your service to our country.

And on behalf of the American people, I thank the world for its outpouring of support.

America will never forget the sounds of our national anthem playing at Buckingham Palace, on the streets of Paris and at Berlin's Brandenburg Gate.

We will not forget South Korean children gathering to pray outside our embassy in Seoul, or the prayers of sympathy offered at a mosque in Cairo.

We will not forget moments of silence and days of mourning in Australia and Africa and Latin America.

Nor will we forget the citizens of 80 other nations who died with our own. Dozens of Pakistanis, more than 130 Israelis, more than 250 citizens of India, men and women from El Salvador, Iran, Mexico and Japan, and hundreds of British citizens.

America has no truer friend than Great Britain.

Once again, we are joined together in a great cause.

I'm so honored the British prime minister has crossed an ocean to show his unity with America.

Thank you for coming, friend.

On September the 11th, enemies of freedom committed an act of war against our country. Americans have known wars, but for the past 136 years they [sic] have been wars on foreign soil, except for one Sunday in 1941. Americans have known the casualties of war, but not at the center of a great city on a peaceful morning.

Americans have known surprise attacks, but never before on thousands of civilians. All of this was brought upon us in a single day, and night fell on a different world, a world where freedom itself is under attack.

Americans have many questions tonight. Americans are asking, "Who attacked our country?"

The evidence we have gathered all points to a collection of loosely affiliated terrorist organizations known as al Qaeda.

They are some of the murderers indicted for bombing American embassies in Tanzania and Kenya and responsible for bombing the USS Cole.

Al Qaeda is to terror what the Mafia is to crime. But its goal is not making money, its goal is remaking the world and imposing its radical beliefs on people everywhere.

The terrorists practice a fringe form of Islamic extremism that has been rejected by Muslim scholars and the vast majority of Muslim clerics; a fringe movement that perverts the peaceful teachings of Islam.

The terrorists' directive commands them to kill Christians and Jews, to kill all Americans and make no distinctions among military and civilians, including women and children. This group and its leader, a person named Osama bin Laden, are linked to many other organizations in different countries, including the Egyptian Islamic Jihad, the Islamic Movement of Uzbekistan.

There are thousands of these terrorists in more than 60 countries.

They are recruited from their own nations and neighborhoods and brought to camps in places like Afghanistan where they are trained in the tactics of terror. They are sent back to their homes or sent to hide in countries around the world to plot evil and destruction. The leadership of al Qaeda has great influence in Afghanistan and supports the Taliban regime in controlling most of that country. In Afghanistan we see al Qaeda's vision for the world. Afghanistan's people have been brutalized, many are starving and many have fled.

Women are not allowed to attend school. You can be jailed for owning a television. Religion can be practiced only as their leaders dictate. A man can be jailed in Afghanistan if his beard is not long enough. The United States respects the people of Afghanistan—after all, we are currently its largest source of humanitarian aid—but we condemn the Taliban regime.

It is not only repressing its own people, it is threatening people everywhere by sponsoring and sheltering and supplying terrorists.

By aiding and abetting murder, the Taliban regime is committing murder. And tonight the United States of America makes the following demands on the Taliban:

— Deliver to United States authorities all of the leaders of Al Qaeda who hide in your land.

— Release all foreign nationals, including American citizens you have unjustly imprisoned.

— Protect foreign journalists, diplomats and aid workers in your country.

— Close immediately and permanently every terrorist training camp in Afghanistan. And hand over every terrorist and every person and their support structure to appropriate authorities.

— Give the United States full access to terrorist training camps, so we can make sure they are no longer operating.

These demands are not open to negotiation or discussion.

The Taliban must act and act immediately.

They will hand over the terrorists or they will share in their fate. I also want to speak tonight directly to Muslims throughout the world. We respect your faith. It's practiced freely by many millions of Americans and by millions more in countries that America counts as friends. Its teachings are good and peaceful, and those who commit evil in the name of Allah blaspheme the name of Allah.

The terrorists are traitors to their own faith, trying, in effect, to hijack Islam itself.

The enemy of America is not our many Muslim friends. It is not our many Arab friends. Our enemy is a radical network of terrorists and every government that supports them.

Our war on terror begins with al Qaeda, but it does not end there.

It will not end until every terrorist group of global reach has been found, stopped and defeated.

Americans are asking "Why do they hate us?"

They hate what they see right here in this chamber: a democratically elected government. Their leaders are self-appointed. They hate our freedoms: our freedom of religion, our freedom of speech, our freedom to vote and assemble and disagree with each other.

They want to overthrow existing governments in many Muslim countries such as Egypt, Saudi Arabia and Jordan. They want to drive Israel out of the Middle East. They want to drive Christians and Jews out of vast regions of Asia and Africa.

These terrorists kill not merely to end lives, but to disrupt and end a way of life. With every atrocity, they hope that America grows fearful, retreating from the world and forsaking our friends. They stand against us because we stand in their way.

We're not deceived by their pretenses to piety.

We have seen their kind before. They're the heirs of all the murderous ideologies of the 20th century. By sacrificing human life to serve their radical visions, by abandoning every value except the will to power, they follow in the path of fascism, Nazism and totalitarianism. And they will follow that path all the way to where it ends in history's unmarked grave of discarded lies. Americans are asking, "How will we fight and win this war?"

We will direct every resource at our command—every means of diplomacy, every tool of intelligence, every instrument of law enforcement, every financial influence, and every necessary weapon of war—to the destruction and to the defeat of the global terror network.

Now, this war will not be like the war against Iraq a decade ago, with a decisive liberation of territory and a swift conclusion. It will not look like the air war above Kosovo two years ago, where no ground troops were used and not a single American was lost in combat.

Our response involves far more than instant retaliation and isolated strikes. Americans should not expect one battle, but a lengthy campaign unlike any other we have ever seen. It may include dramatic strikes visible on TV and covert operations secret even in success.

We will starve terrorists of funding, turn them one against another, drive them from place to place until there is no refuge or no rest.

And we will pursue nations that provide aid or safe haven to terrorism. Every nation in every region now has a decision to make: Either you are with us or you are with the terrorists.

From this day forward, any nation that continues to harbor or support terrorism will be regarded by the United States as a hostile regime. Our nation has been put on notice, we're not immune from attack. We will take defensive measures against terrorism to protect Americans. Today, dozens of federal departments and agencies, as well as state and local governments, have responsibilities affecting homeland security.

These efforts must be coordinated at the highest level. So tonight, I announce the creation of a Cabinet-level position reporting directly to me, the Office of Homeland Security. And tonight, I also announce a distinguished American to lead this effort, to strengthen American security: a military veteran, an effective governor, a true patriot, a trusted friend, Pennsylvania's Tom Ridge.

He will lead, oversee and coordinate a comprehensive national strategy to safeguard our country against terrorism and respond to any attacks that may come. These measures are essential. The only way to defeat terrorism as a threat to our way of life is to stop it, eliminate it and destroy it where it grows.

Many will be involved in this effort, from FBI agents, to intelligence operatives, to the reservists we have called to active duty. All deserve our thanks, and all have our prayers. And tonight a few miles from the damaged Pentagon, I have a message for our military: Be ready. I have called the armed forces to alert, and there is a reason.

The hour is coming when America will act, and you will make us proud.

This is not, however, just America's fight. And what is at stake is not just America's freedom. This is the world's fight.

This is civilization's fight. This is the fight of all who believe in progress and pluralism, tolerance and freedom.

We ask every nation to join us.

We will ask and we will need the help of police forces, intelligence service and banking systems around the world. The United States is grateful that many nations and many international organizations have already responded with sympathy and with support—nations from Latin America to Asia to Africa to Europe to the Islamic world.

Perhaps the NATO charter reflects best the attitude of the world: An attack on one is an attack on all. The civilized world is rallying to America's side.

They understand that if this terror goes unpunished, their own cities, their own citizens may be next. Terror unanswered can not only bring down buildings, it can threaten the stability of legitimate governments.

. . .

Great harm has been done to us. We have suffered great loss. And in our grief and anger we have found our mission and our moment.

Freedom and fear are at war. The advance of human freedom, the great achievement of our time and the great hope of every time, now depends on us.

Our nation, this generation, will lift the dark threat of violence from our people and our future. We will rally the world to this cause by our efforts, by our courage. We will not tire, we will not falter and we will not fail.

It is my hope that in the months and years ahead life will return almost to normal. We'll go back to our lives and routines and that is good.

Even grief recedes with time and grace.

But our resolve must not pass. Each of us will remember what happened that day and to whom it happened. We will remember the moment the news came, where we were and what we were doing.

Some will remember an image of a fire or story or rescue. Some will carry memories of a face and a voice gone forever.

And I will carry this. It is the police shield of a man named George Howard who died at the World Trade Center trying to save others.

It was given to me by his mom, Arlene, as a proud memorial to her son. It is my reminder of lives that ended and a task that does not end.

I will not forget the wound to our country and those who inflicted it. I will not yield, I will not rest, I will not relent in waging this struggle for freedom and security for the American people. The course of this conflict is not known, yet its outcome is certain. Freedom and fear, justice and cruelty, have always been at war, and we know that God is not neutral between them.

Fellow citizens, we'll meet violence with patient justice, assured of the rightness of our cause and confident of the victories to come.

In all that lies before us, may God grant us wisdom and may he watch over the United States of America. Thank you.

Source: Public Papers of the President of the United States. George W. Bush, 2001, Book 2. Washington, D.C.: Government Printing Office, 2002, 1140–1144.

ANALYSIS

President Bush explicitly demanded yet again that the Taliban turn over Osama bin Laden to the United States, cease their support for international terrorist organizations, and end their human rights abuses. Such pleas had fallen on deaf ears since at least 1997, but the speech gave the Taliban one more opportunity to deliver. The speech, along the lines of the mandate delivered in the earlier AUMF, also hinted that Afghanistan may only be the first campaign in a long war against terrorism.

- **Document 30: Statement by NATO Secretary General, Lord Robertson**
- **When:** October 4, 2001
- **Where:** NATO Headquarters, Brussels, Belgium
- **Significance:** The leader of the North Atlantic Treaty Organization (NATO), Lord George Robertson, confirmed the invocation of the North Atlantic Charter's Article 5 for the Alliance to attack international terrorist organizations.

DOCUMENT

Following its decision to invoke Article 5 of the Washington Treaty in the wake of the 11 September attacks against the United States, the NATO Allies agreed to-day—at the request of the United States—to take eight measures, individually and collectively, to expand the options available in the campaign against terrorism. Specifically, they agreed to:

- enhance intelligence sharing and co-operation, both bilaterally and in the appropriate NATO bodies, relating to the threats posed by terrorism and the actions to be taken against it; provide, individually or collectively, as appropriate and according to their capabilities, assistance to Allies and other states which are or may be subject to increased terrorist threats as a result of their support for the campaign against terrorism; take necessary measures to provide increased security for facilities of the United States and other Allies on their territory; backfill selected Allied assets in NATO's area of responsibility that are required to directly support operations against terrorism; provide blanket overflight clearances for the United States and other Allies' aircraft, in accordance with the necessary air traffic arrangements and national procedures, for military flights related to operations against terrorism; provide access for the United States and other Allies to ports and airfields on the territory of NATO nations for operations against terrorism, including for refueling, in accordance with national procedures.

The North Atlantic Council also agreed:

- that the Alliance is ready to deploy elements of its Standing Naval Forces to the Eastern Mediterranean in order to provide a NATO presence and demonstrate resolve; and that the Alliance is similarly ready to deploy elements of its NATO Airborne Early Warning force to support operations against terrorism.

Today's collective actions operationalise Article 5 of the Washington Treaty. These measures were requested by the United States following the determination that the 11 September attack was directed from abroad.

These decisions clearly demonstrate the Allies' resolve and commitment to support and contribute to the U.S.-led fight against terrorism.

Source: NATO Library. Available online at https://www.nato.int/docu/speech/2001/s011004b .htm.

DID YOU KNOW?

North Atlantic Treaty Organization

Formed on April 4, 1949, the North Atlantic Treaty Organization (NATO) is a collective security organization that originally comprised many of the countries of Western Europe and North America, including the United States. The organization came into being after the Soviet blockade of Berlin in 1948 in order to ensure a unified defense in case of further Soviet aggression. Article 5 of the North Atlantic Treaty states that an attack against one member nation will be considered as an attack against every member. Originally, NATO had 12 members but grew over time. The acceptance of West Germany in 1954 led the Soviets to form the corresponding Warsaw Pact in 1955. The organization survived the partial withdrawal of France in 1960 and expanded gradually during the Cold War. After the Soviet Union collapsed in 1991, many former Warsaw Pact nations joined NATO as part of their political and cultural reintegration with the rest of Europe. In addition, NATO oversaw military interventions in the former Yugoslav republics in the 1990s. NATO had 19 members in 2001 and has since grown to 29. This expansion has not gone without controversy as recent Russian aggressiveness toward the rest of Europe has been partially blamed on the expansion of NATO to its borders.

ANALYSIS

For the first time in the Alliance's history, NATO collectively invoked Article 5 of their charter, which considered a foreign attack against one member as an attack on every member nation. This clause had been meant to ensure the collective defense of Europe against Soviet aggression since 1949 but was unexpectedly used to justify a unified Western military response to the attacks on the United States. While this confirmed the outpouring of sympathy and support for the United States after the September 11 attacks, it also conferred a strong degree of international legitimacy for any military campaign that followed.

- **Document 31: President George W. Bush, Address to the Nation**
- **When:** October 7, 2001
- **Where:** Washington, D.C.
- **Significance:** President Bush announced that the United States had initiated a military campaign against the Taliban and al-Qaeda in Afghanistan.

DOCUMENT

THE PRESIDENT: Good afternoon. On my orders, the United States military has begun strikes against al Qaeda terrorist training camps and military installations of the Taliban regime in Afghanistan. These carefully targeted actions are designed to disrupt the use of Afghanistan as a terrorist base of operations, and to attack the military capability of the Taliban regime.

We are joined in this operation by our staunch friend, Great Britain. Other close friends, including Canada, Australia, Germany and France, have pledged forces as the operation unfolds. More than 40 countries in the Middle East, Africa, Europe and across Asia have granted air transit or landing rights. Many more have shared intelligence. We are supported by the collective will of the world.

More than two weeks ago, I gave Taliban leaders a series of clear and specific demands: Close terrorist training camps; hand over leaders of the al Qaeda network; and return all foreign nationals, including American citizens, unjustly detained in your country. None of these demands were met. And now the Taliban will pay a price. By destroying camps and disrupting communications, we will make it more difficult for the terror network to train new recruits and coordinate their evil plans.

Initially, the terrorists may burrow deeper into caves and other entrenched hiding places. Our military action is also designed to clear the way for sustained, comprehensive and relentless operations to drive them out and bring them to justice.

At the same time, the oppressed people of Afghanistan will know the generosity of America and our allies. As we strike military targets, we'll also drop food, medicine and supplies to the starving and suffering men and women and children of Afghanistan.

DID YOU KNOW?

Task Force Dagger

Task Force Dagger was the codename given to the personnel of the U.S. 5th Special Forces Group that infiltrated into Afghanistan in September and October 2001. Two Operational Detachment Alpha (ODA) teams, 555 and 595, of about a dozen men each entered Afghanistan on October 19 to coordinate Coalition air strikes with the movements of Northern Alliance forces on the ground. Once on the ground, ODA 595 was given horses by the Northern Alliance, who themselves relied upon the animals to navigate the tough terrain in Afghanistan. For the next two months, they helped General Abdul Rashid Dostum's forces liberate northern and western Afghanistan while ODA 555 helped forces in eastern Afghanistan liberate Kabul. These teams and others performed incredibly valuable service but would be remembered by the public for riding into battle on horseback. A movie based upon their experiences, *12 Strong*, was released in January 2018.

The United States of America is a friend to the Afghan people, and we are the friends of almost a billion worldwide who practice the Islamic faith. The United States of America is an enemy of those who aid terrorists and of the barbaric criminals who profane a great religion by committing murder in its name.

This military action is a part of our campaign against terrorism, another front in a war that has already been joined through diplomacy, intelligence, the freezing of financial assets and the arrests of known terrorists by law enforcement agents in 38 countries. Given the nature and reach of our enemies, we will win this conflict by the patient accumulation of successes, by meeting a series of challenges with determination and will and purpose.

Today we focus on Afghanistan, but the battle is broader. Every nation has a choice to make. In this conflict, there is no neutral ground. If any government sponsors the outlaws and killers of innocents, they have become outlaws and murderers, themselves. And they will take that lonely path at their own peril.

I'm speaking to you today from the Treaty Room of the White House, a place where American Presidents have worked for peace. We're a peaceful nation. Yet, as we have learned, so suddenly and so tragically, there can be no peace in a world of sudden terror. In the face of today's new threat, the only way to pursue peace is to pursue those who threaten it.

We did not ask for this mission, but we will fulfill it. The name of today's military operation is Enduring Freedom. We defend not only our precious freedoms, but also the freedom of people everywhere to live and raise their children free from fear.

I know many Americans feel fear today. And our government is taking strong precautions. All law enforcement and intelligence agencies are working aggressively around America, around the world and around the clock. At my request, many governors have activated the National Guard to strengthen airport security. We have called up Reserves to reinforce our military capability and strengthen the protection of our homeland.

In the months ahead, our patience will be one of our strengths—patience with the long waits that will result from tighter security; patience and understanding that it will take time to achieve our goals; patience in all the sacrifices that may come.

Today, those sacrifices are being made by members of our Armed Forces who now defend us so far from home, and by their proud and worried families. A Commander-in-Chief sends America's sons and daughters into a battle in a foreign land only after the greatest care and a lot of prayer. We ask a lot of those who wear our uniform. We ask them to leave their loved ones, to travel great distances, to risk injury, even to be prepared to make the ultimate sacrifice of their lives. They are dedicated, they are honorable; they represent the best of our country. And we are grateful.

To all the men and women in our military—every sailor, every soldier, every airman, every coastguardsman, every Marine—I say this: Your mission is defined; your objectives are clear; your goal is just. You have my full confidence, and you will have every tool you need to carry out your duty.

I recently received a touching letter that says a lot about the state of America in these difficult times—a letter from a 4th-grade girl, with a father in the military: "As much as I don't want my Dad to fight," she wrote, "I'm willing to give him to you."

This is a precious gift, the greatest she could give. This young girl knows what America is all about. Since September 11, an entire generation of young Americans has gained new understanding of the value of freedom, and its cost in duty and in sacrifice.

The battle is now joined on many fronts. We will not waver; we will not tire; we will not falter; and we will not fail. Peace and freedom will prevail.

Thank you. May God continue to bless America.

Source: Public Papers of the Presidents of the United States: George W. Bush, 2001, Book 2. Washington, D.C.: Government Printing Office, 2002, 1201–1202.

DID YOU KNOW?

Joint Direct Attack Munition

Joint Direct Attack Munitions, or JDAMs, are precision-guided weapons used by the U.S. military in large numbers for the first time in Afghanistan. Dating back to World War II, the U.S. and other militaries had developed increasingly sophisticated guidance systems to allow air-dropped bombs to hit precise targets. Radio signals eventually gave way to television and wire-guided systems, but during the Vietnam War, the United States began to use bombs guided by a laser beam to a target. More advanced versions of these weapons proved successful in Operation Desert Storm in 1991, but the system could be disrupted by weather and was not cheap. In the late 1990s, JDAMs emerged and were guided on to targets using the Global Positioning System (GPS). First used in Kosovo in 1999, they became the predominant weapon in Afghanistan because they are much cheaper than the older laser-guided systems. In the first months of combat, more than 60 percent of bombs dropped were JDAMs, hitting their intended targets 90 percent of the time. More advanced versions of these weapons remain in use with the United States and allied nations today.

ANALYSIS

The Taliban refused to end their support for international terrorism or to turn over Osama bin Laden to the United States as President Bush had demanded more than two weeks earlier. As a result, the president initiated a military campaign in Afghanistan designed to drive the Taliban from power. He acknowledged that air strikes of Taliban positions had begun earlier that day, but special forces were also preparing to enter Afghanistan and would do so less than two weeks later.

In addition, this brief speech, as did President Bush's earlier address to Congress, implored the American public to support a campaign that might continue beyond the end of hostilities in Afghanistan. Since the United States had the twin goals of destroying a terrorist group and the current government of a sovereign nation, his rhetoric called for vigilance at home and for patience abroad in the weeks and months ahead.

- **Document 32: U.S. Department of State, Memorandum, From Secretary of State Colin Powell to U.S. President George W. Bush, "Your Meeting with Pakistani President Musharraf"**
- **When:** November 5, 2001
- **Where:** Washington, D.C.

- **Significance:** This U.S. State Department memorandum for President George W. Bush outlined the Pakistani steps toward cooperation taken since the September 11 attacks.

DOCUMENT

MEMORANDUM FOR THE PRESIDENT
FROM: Colin L. Powell
SUBJECT: Your Meeting with Pakistan President Musharraf

President Musharraf's decision to fully cooperate with the United States in the wake of September 11, at considerable political risk, abruptly turned our stalled relationship around. At the time of your meeting, [redacted] Musharraf has abandoned the Taliban, frozen terrorist assets, quelled anti-Western protests without unwarranted force, [redacted]. These moves open up bold new possibilities in our relationship, but additional steps are necessary. Your meeting and dinner can serve to assure Musharraf we will assist Pakistan through this difficult time, and underscore our intent to work with Pakistan closely after the current conflict.

During my October 15–16 visit to Islamabad, I affirmed our renewed relationship and discussed our common goal of defeating terrorists and rebuilding Afghanistan. Musharraf is pressing for a future government supportive of its interests and is concerned that the Northern Alliance will occupy Kabul. I assured him that the U.S. supports the formation of a broad-based government in Afghanistan, friendly to its neighbors.

Tensions in Kashmir threaten our efforts in Afghanistan and are a flashpoint for possible Indo-Pakistani conflict. On October 1, a terrorist attack on the state assembly in Kashmir resulted in 38 civilian deaths. India subsequently shelled positions in Pakistan. [redacted]

. . .

Source: National Security Archive. Available online at http://nsarchive2 .gwu.edu/NSAEBB/NSAEBB325/doc09.pdf.

ANALYSIS

The memo confirmed that President Musharraf had followed through on his September promises to end support for the Taliban. Pakistan, however, remained deadlocked in a rivalry with its larger, Hindu neighbor, India, and previous support for groups such as the Taliban and Kashmiri separatists had sought to give Pakistan influence and leverage in the region where India's growing population threatened to outstrip Pakistan's. President Musharraf feared that a Northern Alliance–controlled government would severely limit its influence in Afghanistan—hence, Secretary Powell's assurance that the new Afghan government would be "broad-based." This guarantee seemed to promise Pakistan it would have some input in the makeup of the new Afghan government.

- **Document 33: UN Security Council Resolution 1378**
- **When:** November 14, 2001
- **Where:** New York, New York
- **Significance:** The UN Security Council condemned the Taliban and expressed its support for negotiations to form a new Afghan government.

DOCUMENT

Resolution 1378 (2001)
Adopted by the Security Council at its 4415th meeting, on 14 November 2001

The Security Council,

Reaffirming its previous resolutions on Afghanistan, in particular resolutions 1267 (1999) of 15 October 1999, 1333 (2000) of 19 December 2000 and 1363 (2001) of 30 July 2001,

Supporting international efforts to root out terrorism, in keeping with the Charter of the United Nations, and reaffirming also its resolutions 1368 (2001) of 12 September 2001 and 1373 (2001) of 28 September 2001,

Recognizing the urgency of the security and political situation in Afghanistan in light of the most recent developments, particularly in Kabul,

Condemning the Taliban for allowing Afghanistan to be used as a base for the export of terrorism by the Al-Qaida network and other terrorist groups and for providing safe haven to Usama Bin Laden, Al-Qaida and others associated with them, and in this context supporting the efforts of the Afghan people to replace the Taliban regime,

Welcoming the intention of the Special Representative to convene an urgent meeting of the various Afghan processes at an appropriate venue and calling on the United Front and all Afghans represented in those processes to accept his invitation to that meeting without delay, in good faith and without preconditions,

Welcoming the Declaration on the Situation in Afghanistan by the Foreign Ministers and other Senior Representatives of the Six plus Two of 12 November 2001, as well as the support being offered by other international groups,

Taking note of the views expressed at the meeting of the Security Council on the situation in Afghanistan on 13 November 2001,

Endorsing the approach outlined by the Special Representative of the Secretary-General at the meeting of the Security Council on 13 November 2001,

Reaffirming its strong commitment to the sovereignty, independence, territorial integrity and national unity of Afghanistan,

Deeply concerned by the grave humanitarian situation and the continuing serious violations by the Taliban of human rights and international humanitarian law,

1. *Expresses* its strong support for the efforts of the Afghan people to establish a new and transitional administration leading to the formation of a government, both of which:

– should be broad-based, multi-ethnic and fully representative of all the Afghan people and committed to peace with Afghanistan's neighbours,

– should respect the human rights of all Afghan people, regardless of gender, ethnicity or religion,

– should respect Afghanistan's international obligations, including by cooperating fully in international efforts to combat terrorism and illicit drug trafficking within and from Afghanistan, and

– should facilitate the urgent delivery of humanitarian assistance and the orderly return of refugees and internally displaced persons, when the situation permits;

2. *Calls* on all Afghan forces to refrain from acts of reprisal, to adhere strictly to their obligations under human rights and international humanitarian law, and to ensure the safety and security and freedom of movement of United Nations and associated personnel, as well as personnel of humanitarian organizations;

3. *Affirms* that the United Nations should play a central role in supporting the efforts of the Afghan people to establish urgently such a new and transitional administration leading to the formation of a new government and expresses its full support for the Secretary-General's Special Representative in the accomplishment of his mandate, and calls on Afghans, both within Afghanistan and among the Afghan diaspora, and Member States to cooperate with him;

4. *Calls* on Member States to provide:

– support for such an administration and government, including through the implementation of quick-impact projects,

– urgent humanitarian assistance to alleviate the suffering of Afghan people both inside Afghanistan and Afghan refugees, including in demining, and

– long-term assistance for the social and economic reconstruction and rehabilitation of Afghanistan and welcomes initiatives towards this end;

5. *Encourages* Member States to support efforts to ensure the safety and security of areas of Afghanistan no longer under Taliban control, and in particular to ensure respect for Kabul as the capital for all the Afghan people, and especially to protect civilians, transitional authorities, United Nations and associated personnel, as well as personnel of humanitarian organizations;

6. *Decides* to remain actively seized of the matter.

Source: United Nations. Available online at http://unscr.com/en/resolutions/doc/ 1378.

ANALYSIS

The resolution passed on the same day that the Northern Alliance—with NATO air support—retook Kabul from the Taliban. The UN Security Council resolution sought to keep the organization involved in Afghanistan even though its attempts to mediate the Afghan Civil War in the 1990s had met with failure and, as noted in Document 20, increasing frustration. Still, the United Nations hoped to garner support for the humanitarian assistance that Afghanistan's people desperately needed after having endured so much conflict in recent years.

- **Document 34: Defense Intelligence Agency, Cable, "IIR [Redacted]/The Assassination of Massoud Related to 11 September 2001 Attack"**
- **When:** November 21, 2001
- **Where:** Washington, D.C.
- **Significance:** The cable explained the circumstances leading to the assassination of Northern Alliance commander Ahmed Shah Massoud two days prior to the September 11 attacks on the United States.

DOCUMENT

Subject: IIR [Redacted]—The Assassination of Massoud Related to 11 September 2001 Attack

Summary: The relationship between the assassination of the late Northern Alliance commander Massoud and the terrorist incident of 11 September 2001, including al-Qaida involvement.

Text: Background. In the early 1990s, the Taliban began as a group of religious students who rejected the mujahadin takeover of Afghanistan. Due to the Pakistani government support to Taliban forces, the Taliban became militarily powerful and their forces controlled approximately 90 percent of Afghanistan. Many Afghan opposition forces were outnumbered and outgunned by Taliban forces, and could not fight Taliban forces directly. The former mujahadin commander, Ahmed Shah (Massoud) managed to form the Northern Alliance Forces (NAF) and continued his fight against Taliban forces in northern Afghanistan. [Redacted] On 9 September 2001, Commander Massoud was assassinated in northern Afghanistan.

2. Warning. Through Northern Alliance intelligence efforts, the late Commander Massoud gained limited knowledge regarding the intentions of the Saudi millionaire, Usama bin Ladin (UBL), and his terrorist organization, al-Qaida, to perform a terrorist act against the U.S., on a scale larger than the 1998 bombing of the U.S. embassies in Kenya and Tanzania [redacted]. In April 2001, Massoud addressed the French and European parliaments in Paris. In his televised speech he warned the U.S. government about UBL [redacted]

DID YOU KNOW?

John Walker Lindh

John Walker Lindh is an American citizen born in 1981 who later converted to Islam in 1997. Following his conversion, he studied at a Pakistani madrassa and, like many of his peers, was elected to fight in Afghanistan with the Taliban against the Northern Alliance. In November 2001, he and several other fighters surrendered at Kunduz. While under interrogation at the temporary prison camp at Qala-i-Jangi, other prisoners rebelled against their captors, but Lindh hid with a group of other foreign fighters until his recapture. Only then did his interrogators identify him as an American. He was later charged with 10 crimes, including conspiracy to commit murder and for supporting terrorist organizations. In late 2002, he pled guilty to the charges and was sentenced to 20 years in federal prison. If he remains on good behavior, he could be eligible for early release in 2019.

DID YOU KNOW?

Mazar-i-Sharif Uprising

In November 2001, General Abdul Rashid Dostum allowed U.S. forces to use his former headquarters at the Qala-i-Jangi fortress outside the city of Mazar-i-Sharif to interrogate a large number of Taliban and al-Qaeda prisoners, including the American, John Walker Lindh. On the November 25, a group of prisoners used grenades to kill a CIA agent conducting interviews, Mike Spann, and several guards. They then overran the ammunition depot inside the fortress and armed themselves with a variety of weaponry. For the next two days, aircraft bombed the southern end of the fortress and killed at least 200 of the Taliban fighters, but many more had escaped into the underground parts of the structure. Only after the structure was flooded with irrigation water did the remaining 86 prisoners finally surrender on December 1.

3. Relationships. On 9 September 2001, two Arabs, loyal to UBL and members of the al-Qaida organization deceptively posed as Arab journalists, asked for an interview with Commander Massoud, and killed him with a suicide bomb that was hidden in their camera [redacted] Although Commander Massoud was fighting Taliban forces over the control of Afghanistan, he was not a threat to UBL and the al-Qaida organization. To Massoud, UBL was a Saudi citizen, exiled to Afghanistan due to his challenge to the legitimacy of the Saudi monarchy. After the terrorist strikes on the U.S. embassies in Africa, and receiving intelligence for his forces regarding UBL's future attacks, Massoud began to warn the West of UBL and al-Qaida [redacted]

Source: National Security Archive. Available online at http://nsarchive2.gwu.edu/NSAEBB/NSAEBB97/tal31.pdf.

ANALYSIS

Massoud had been a popular mujahedeen leader during the Afghan-Soviet War and served in the Afghan government during the civil war in the 1990s. He remained the most important Northern Alliance leader during the group's retreat against Taliban advances and at times attempted to warn Europe and the United States about the dangers posed by the Taliban and al-Qaeda. His assassination was part of a coordinated Taliban effort to seize control of the entire country. His death removed one of the most popular non-Taliban leaders from the scene and a possible key player in any attempt in forming a new Afghan government. Massoud's Tajik background would likely have limited his appeal in the new Afghanistan, but he possessed cachet and skills matched by few of his contemporaries.

- **Document 35: Agreement on Provisional Arrangements in Afghanistan Pending the Re-Establishment of Permanent Government Institutions**
- **When:** December 5, 2001
- **Where:** Bonn, Germany
- **Significance:** The Interim Agreement established a temporary governing body in Afghanistan until the Loya Jirga—a traditional gathering of ethnic leaders—could meet the following spring.

DOCUMENT

AGREEMENT ON PROVISIONAL ARRANGEMENTS IN AFGHANISTAN PENDING THE RE-ESTABLISHMENT OF PERMANENT GOVERNMENT INSTITUTIONS

The participants in the UN Talks on Afghanistan,

In the presence of the Special Representative of the Secretary-General for Afghanistan,

Determined to end the tragic conflict in Afghanistan and promote national reconciliation, lasting peace, stability and respect for human rights in the country,

Reaffirming the independence, national sovereignty and territorial integrity of Afghanistan,

Acknowledging the right of the people of Afghanistan to freely determine their own political future in accordance with the principles of Islam, democracy, pluralism and social justice,

Expressing their appreciation to the Afghan mujahidin who, over the years, have defended the independence, territorial integrity and national unity of the country and have played a major role in the struggle against terrorism and oppression, and whose sacrifice has now made them both heroes of jihad and champions of peace, stability and reconstruction of their beloved homeland, Afghanistan,

Aware that the unstable situation in Afghanistan requires the implementation of emergency interim arrangements and expressing their deep appreciation to His Excellency Professor Burhanuddin Rabbani for his readiness to transfer power to an interim authority which is to be established pursuant to this agreement,

Recognizing the need to ensure broad representation in these interim arrangements of all segments of the Afghan population, including groups that have not been adequately represented at the UN Talks on Afghanistan,

Noting that these interim arrangements are intended as a first step toward the establishment of a broad-based, gender-sensitive, multi-ethnic and fully representative government, and are not intended to remain in place beyond the specified period of time,

Recognizing that some time may be required for a new Afghan security force to be fully constituted and functional and that therefore other security provisions detailed in Annex I to this agreement must meanwhile be put in place,

DID YOU KNOW?

Hamid Karzai

Hamid Karzai was born into a politically active family in Kandahar in 1957. During the Soviet occupation, he worked in Pakistan to raise money for the mujahedeen as part of the Afghan National Liberation Front. He worked with the first postcommunist government for a time, but, when he attempted to mediate a dispute between the government and Gulbuddin Hekmatyar, Karzai was arrested and forced to flee Kabul. He initially welcomed the stability of the Taliban, but he abandoned his support for the movement by 1999 because he felt them too beholden to their Pakistani and Arab allies. From exile in Quetta, he lobbied on behalf of the Northern Alliance in Europe. In October 2001, Karzai crossed the border into Afghanistan and worked with the U.S.-led Coalition, but an attempted Taliban assassination forced the United States to remove him from the country. He participated in the Bonn process and emerged as the preferred U.S. candidate to lead the new Afghan government. Because of his Western ties, he proved an able advocate for Afghanistan abroad and won elections in 2004 and 2009 even though his domestic record was tarnished by scandal and corruption. Since leaving office in 2014, Karzai has at times been harshly critical of the United States and its policies in Afghanistan.

Considering that the United Nations, as the internationally recognized impartial institution, has a particularly important role to play, detailed in Annex II to this agreement, in the period prior to the establishment of permanent institutions in Afghanistan,

Have agreed as follows:

THE INTERIM AUTHORITY
I. General provisions

1) An Interim Authority shall be established upon the official transfer of power on 22 December 2001.

2) The Interim Authority shall consist of an Interim Administration presided over by a Chairman, a Special Independent Commission for the Convening of the Emergency Loya Jirga, and a Supreme Court of Afghanistan, as well as such other courts as may be established by the Interim Administration. The composition, functions and governing procedures for the Interim Administration and the Special Independent Commission are set forth in this agreement.

3) Upon the official transfer of power, the Interim Authority shall be the repository of Afghan sovereignty, with immediate effect. As such, it shall, throughout the interim period, represent Afghanistan in its external relations and shall occupy the seat of Afghanistan at the United Nations and in its specialized agencies, as well as in other international institutions and conferences.

4) An Emergency Loya Jirga shall be convened within six months of the establishment of the Interim Authority. The Emergency Loya Jirga will be opened by His Majesty Mohammed Zaher, the former King of Afghanistan. The Emergency Loya Jirga shall decide on a Transitional Authority, including a broad-based transitional administration, to lead Afghanistan until such time as a fully representative government can be elected through free and fair elections to be held no later than two years from the date of the convening of the Emergency Loya Jirga.

5) The Interim Authority shall cease to exist once the Transitional Authority has been established by the Emergency Loya Jirga.

6) A Constitutional Loya Jirga shall be convened within eighteen months of the establishment of the Transitional Authority, in order to adopt a new constitution for Afghanistan. In order to assist the Constitutional Loya Jirga prepare the proposed Constitution, the Transitional Administration shall, within two months of its commencement and with the assistance of the United Nations, establish a Constitutional Commission.

II. Legal framework and judicial system

1) The following legal framework shall be applicable on an interim basis until the adoption of the new Constitution referred to above:

i) The Constitution of 1964, a/ to the extent that its provisions are not inconsistent with those contained in this agreement, and b/ with the exception of those provisions relating to the monarchy and to the executive and legislative bodies provided in the Constitution; and

ii) existing laws and regulations, to the extent that they are not inconsistent with this agreement or with international legal obligations to which Afghanistan is a party, or with those applicable provisions contained in the Constitution of 1964, provided that the Interim Authority shall have the power to repeal or amend those laws and regulations.

2) The judicial power of Afghanistan shall be independent and shall be vested in a Supreme Court of Afghanistan, and such other courts as may be established by the Interim Administration. The Interim Administration shall establish, with the assistance of the United Nations, a Judicial Commission to rebuild the domestic justice system in accordance with Islamic principles, international standards, the rule of law and Afghan legal traditions.

III. Interim Administration

A. *Composition*

1) The Interim Administration shall be composed of a Chairman, five Vice Chairmen and 24 other members. Each member, except the Chairman, may head a department of the Interim Administration.

2) The participants in the UN Talks on Afghanistan have invited His Majesty Mohammed Zaher, the former King of Afghanistan, to chair the Interim Administration. His Majesty has indicated that he would prefer that a suitable candidate acceptable to the participants be selected as the Chair of the Interim Administration.

3) The Chairman, the Vice Chairmen and other members of the Interim Administration have been selected by the participants in the UN Talks on Afghanistan, as listed in Annex IV to this agreement. The selection has been made on the basis of professional competence and personal integrity from lists submitted by the participants in the UN Talks, with due regard to the ethnic, geographic and religious composition of Afghanistan and to the importance of the participation of women.

4) No person serving as a member of the Interim Administration may simultaneously hold membership of the Special Independent Commission for the Convening of the Emergency Loya Jirga.

B. *Procedures*

1) The Chairman of the Interim Administration, or in his/her absence one of the Vice Chairmen, shall call and chair meetings and propose the agenda for these meetings.

2) The Interim Administration shall endeavour to reach its decisions by consensus. In order for any decision to be taken, at least 22 members must be in attendance. If a vote becomes necessary, decisions shall be taken by a majority of the members present and voting, unless otherwise stipulated in this agreement. The Chairman shall cast the deciding vote in the event that the members are divided equally.

C. *Functions*

1) The Interim Administration shall be entrusted with the day-to-day conduct of the affairs of state, and shall have the right to issue decrees for the peace, order and good government of Afghanistan.

2) The Chairman of the Interim Administration or, in his/her absence, one of the Vice Chairmen, shall represent the Interim Administration as appropriate.

3) Those members responsible for the administration of individual departments shall also be responsible for implementing the policies of the Interim Administration within their areas of responsibility.

4) Upon the official transfer of power, the Interim Administration shall have full jurisdiction over the printing and delivery of the national currency and special drawing rights from international financial institutions. The Interim Administration shall establish, with the assistance of the United Nations, a Central Bank of Afghanistan that will regulate the money supply of the country through transparent and accountable procedures.

5) The Interim Administration shall establish, with the assistance of the United Nations, an independent Civil Service Commission to provide the Interim Authority and the future Transitional Authority with shortlists of candidates for key posts in the administrative departments, as well as those of governors and uluswals, in order to ensure their competence and integrity.

6) The Interim Administration shall, with the assistance of the United Nations, establish an independent Human Rights Commission, whose responsibilities will include human rights monitoring, investigation of violations of human rights, and development of domestic human rights institutions. The Interim Administration may, with the assistance of the United Nations, also establish any other commissions to review matters not covered in this agreement.

7) The members of the Interim Administration shall abide by a Code of Conduct elaborated in accordance with international standards.

8) Failure by a member of the Interim Administration to abide by the provisions of the Code of Conduct shall lead to his/her suspension from that body. The decision to suspend a member shall be taken by a two-thirds majority of the membership of the Interim Administration on the proposal of its Chairman or any of its Vice Chairmen.

9) The functions and powers of members of the Interim Administration will be further elaborated, as appropriate, with the assistance of the United Nations.

IV. The Special Independent Commission for the Convening of the Emergency Loya Jirga

1) The Special Independent Commission for the Convening of the Emergency Loya Jirga shall be established within one month of the establishment of the Interim Authority. The Special Independent Commission will consist of twenty-one members, a number of whom should have expertise in constitutional or customary law. The members will be selected from lists of candidates submitted by participants in the UN Talks on Afghanistan as well as Afghan professional and civil society groups. The United Nations will assist with the establishment and functioning of the commission and of a substantial secretariat.

. . .

V. Final provisions

1) Upon the official transfer of power, all mujahidin, Afghan armed forces and armed groups in the country shall come under the command and control of the Interim Authority, and be reorganized according to the requirements of the new Afghan security and armed forces.

2) The Interim Authority and the Emergency Loya Jirga shall act in accordance with basic principles and provisions contained in international instruments on human rights and international humanitarian law to which Afghanistan is a party.

3) The Interim Authority shall cooperate with the international community in the fight against terrorism, drugs and organized crime. It shall commit itself to respect international law and maintain peaceful and friendly relations with neighbouring countries and the rest of the international community.

4) The Interim Authority and the Special Independent Commission for the Convening of the Emergency Loya Jirga will ensure the participation of women as well as the equitable representation of all ethnic and religious communities in the Interim Administration and the Emergency Loya Jirga.

5) All actions taken by the Interim Authority shall be consistent with Security Council resolution 1378 (14 November 2001) and other relevant Security Council resolutions relating to Afghanistan.

6) Rules of procedure for the organs established under the Interim Authority will be elaborated as appropriate with the assistance of the United Nations.

This agreement, of which the annexes constitute an integral part, done in Bonn on this 5th day of December 2001 in the English language, shall be the authentic text, in a single copy which shall remain deposited in the archives of the United Nations. Official texts shall be provided in Dari and Pashto, and such other languages as the Special Representative of the Secretary-General may designate. The Special Representative of the Secretary-General shall send certified copies in English, Dari and Pashto to each of the participants.

. . .

ANNEX I
INTERNATIONAL SECURITY FORCE

1. The participants in the UN Talks on Afghanistan recognize that the responsibility for providing security and law and order throughout the country resides with the Afghans themselves. To this end, they pledge their commitment to do all within their means and influence to ensure such security, including for all United Nations and other personnel of international governmental and non-governmental organizations deployed in Afghanistan.

2. With this objective in mind, the participants request the assistance of the international community in helping the new Afghan authorities in the establishment and training of new Afghan security and armed forces.

3. Conscious that some time may be required for the new Afghan security and armed forces to be fully constituted and functioning, the participants in the UN Talks on Afghanistan request the United Nations Security Council to consider authorizing the early deployment to Afghanistan of a United Nations mandated force. This force will assist in the maintenance of security for Kabul and its surrounding areas. Such a force could, as appropriate, be progressively expanded to other urban centres and other areas.

4. The participants in the UN Talks on Afghanistan pledge to withdraw all military units from Kabul and other urban centers or other areas in which the UN mandated force is deployed. It would also be desirable if such a force were to assist in the rehabilitation of Afghanistan's infrastructure.

* * *

ANNEX II
ROLE OF THE UNITED NATIONS DURING THE INTERIM PERIOD

1. The Special Representative of the Secretary-General will be responsible for all aspects of the United Nations' work in Afghanistan.

2. The Special Representative shall monitor and assist in the implementation of all aspects of this agreement.

3. The United Nations shall advise the Interim Authority in establishing a politically neutral environment conducive to the holding of the Emergency Loya Jirga in free and fair conditions. The United Nations shall pay special attention to the conduct of those bodies and administrative departments which could directly influence the convening and outcome of the Emergency Loya Jirga.

4. The Special Representative of the Secretary-General or his/her delegate may be invited to attend the meetings of the Interim Administration and the Special Independent Commission on the Convening of the Emergency Loya Jirga.

5. If for whatever reason the Interim Administration or the Special Independent Commission were actively prevented from meeting or unable to reach a decision on a matter related to the convening of the Emergency Loya Jirga, the Special Representative of the Secretary-General shall, taking into account the views expressed in the Interim Administration or in the Special Independent Commission, use his/her good offices with a view to facilitating a resolution to the impasse or a decision.

6. The United Nations shall have the right to investigate human rights violations and, where necessary, recommend corrective action. It will also be responsible for the development and implementation of a programme of human rights education to promote respect for and understanding of human rights.

* * *

ANNEX III
REQUEST TO THE UNITED NATIONS BY THE PARTICIPANTS AT THE UN TALKS ON AFGHANISTAN

The participants in the UN Talks on Afghanistan hereby

1. Request that the United Nations and the international community take the necessary measures to guarantee the national sovereignty, territorial integrity and unity of Afghanistan as well as the non-interference by foreign countries in Afghanistan's internal affairs;

2. Urge the United Nations, the international community, particularly donor countries and multilateral institutions, to reaffirm, strengthen and implement their commitment to assist with the rehabilitation, recovery and reconstruction of Afghanistan, in coordination with the Interim Authority;

3. Request the United Nations to conduct as soon as possible (i) a registration of voters in advance of the general elections that will be held upon the adoption of the new constitution by the constitutional Loya Jirga and (ii) a census of the population of Afghanistan.

4. Urge the United Nations and the international community, in recognition of the heroic role played by the mujahidin in protecting the independence of

Afghanistan and the dignity of its people, to take the necessary measures, in co-ordination with the Interim Authority, to assist in the reintegration of the mujahi-din into the new Afghan security and armed forces;

5. Invite the United Nations and the international community to create a fund to assist the families and other dependents of martyrs and victims of the war, as well as the war disabled;

6. Strongly urge that the United Nations, the international community and regional organizations cooperate with the Interim Authority to combat international terrorism, cultivation and trafficking of illicit drugs and provide Afghan farmers with financial, material and technical resources for alternative crop production.

. . .

Source: United Nations. Available online at http://www.un.org/News/dh/latest/afghan/afghan-agree.htm.

ANALYSIS

The Interim Agreement emerged after several weeks of contentious talks between members of the Northern Alliance and other groups over the makeup of the new administration. Given that the Northern Alliance included many individuals who served in the fractious government of the 1990s, other exile groups demanded broader representation. Afghan's aged former monarch, Mohammad Zaher Shah, was involved in the talks but served as a figurehead. Most importantly, the gathering chose Hamid Karzai, an ethnic Pashtun, to serve as the interim leader, believing him able to gather the respect of the Pashtun majority and the various minority groups. This was a marked change in his fortunes from having been "marginalized" as mentioned in Document 12.

- **Document 36: UN Security Council Resolution 1383**
- **When:** December 6, 2001
- **Where:** New York, New York
- **Significance:** The UN Security Council endorsed the Interim Agreement adopted the previous day.

DOCUMENT

Resolution 1383 (2001)
Adopted by the Security Council at its 4434th meeting on 6 December 2001
The Security Council,
Reaffirming its previous resolutions on Afghanistan, in particular its resolution 1378 (2001) of 14 November 2001,
Reaffirming its strong commitment to the sovereignty, independence, territorial integrity and national unity of Afghanistan,

Stressing the inalienable right of the Afghan people themselves freely to determine their own political future,

Determined to help the people of Afghanistan to bring to an end the tragic conflicts in Afghanistan and promote national reconciliation, lasting peace, stability and respect for human rights, as well as to cooperate with the international community to put an end to the use of Afghanistan as a base for terrorism,

Welcoming the letter of 5 December 2001 from the Secretary-General informing the Council of the signature in Bonn on 5 December 2001 of the Agreement on provisional arrangements in Afghanistan pending the re-establishment of permanent government institutions (S/2001/1154),

Noting that the provisional arrangements are intended as a first step towards the establishment of a broad-based, gender sensitive, multi-ethnic and fully representative government,

1. *Endorses* the Agreement on provisional arrangements in Afghanistan pending the re-establishment of permanent government institutions as reported in the Secretary-General's letter of 5 December 2001;

2. *Calls* on all Afghan groups to implement this Agreement in full, in particular through full cooperation with the Interim Authority which is due to take office on 22 December 2001;

3. *Reaffirms* its full support to the Special Representative of the Secretary-General and endorses the missions entrusted to him in annex 2 of the above-mentioned Agreement;

4. *Declares* its willingness to take further action, on the basis of a report by the Secretary-General, to support the Interim institutions established by the above-mentioned Agreement and, in due course, to support the implementation of the Agreement and its annexes;

5. *Calls* on all Afghan groups to support full and unimpeded access by humanitarian organizations to people in need and to ensure the safety and security of humanitarian workers;

6. *Calls* on all bilateral and multilateral donors, in coordination with the Special Representative of the Secretary-General, United Nations Agencies and all Afghan groups, to reaffirm, strengthen and implement their commitment to assist with the rehabilitation, recovery and reconstruction of Afghanistan, in coordination with the Interim Authority and as long as the Afghan groups fulfil their commitments;

7. *Decides* to remain actively seized of the matter.

Source: United Nations. Available online at http://unscr.com/files/2001/01383.pdf.

ANALYSIS

The resolution, passed unanimously by the Security Council, called upon all the parties in Afghanistan to implement the Interim Agreement completed in Bonn. In addition, the resolution called upon international humanitarian aid donors to support Afghan reconstruction and for the parties in Afghanistan to not impede their access. These provisions further reaffirmed the commitment to the international community to support Afghanistan.

- **Document 37: UN Security Council Resolution 1386**
- **When:** December 20, 2001
- **Where:** New York, New York
- **Significance:** This UN Security Council resolution authorized the creation of the International Security Assistance Force (ISAF) called for in the Bonn Agreement that would provide security for Afghanistan's interim government.

DOCUMENT

Resolution 1386 (2001)

Adopted by the Security Council at its 4443rd meeting, on 20 December 2001

The Security Council,

Welcoming developments in Afghanistan that will allow for all Afghans to enjoy inalienable rights and freedom unfettered by oppression and terror,

Recognizing that the responsibility for providing security and law and order throughout the country resides with the Afghan themselves,

Reiterating its endorsement of the Agreement on provisional arrangements in Afghanistan pending the re-establishment of permanent government institutions, signed in Bonn on 5 December 2001 (S/2001/1154) (the Bonn Agreement),

Taking note of the request to the Security Council in Annex 1, paragraph 3, to the Bonn Agreement to consider authorizing the early deployment to Afghanistan of an international security force, as well as the briefing on 14 December 2001 by the Special Representative of the Secretary-General on his contacts with the Afghan authorities in which they welcome the deployment to Afghanistan of a United Nations authorized international security force,

Taking note of the letter dated 19 December 2001 from Dr. Abdullah Abdullah to the President of the Security Council (S/2001/1223),

Welcoming the letter from the Secretary of State for Foreign and Commonwealth Affairs of the United Kingdom of Great Britain and Northern Ireland to the Secretary-General of 19 December 2001 (S/2001/1217), and taking note of the United Kingdom offer contained therein to take the lead in organizing and commanding an International Security Assistance Force,

Stressing that all Afghan forces must adhere strictly to their obligations under human rights law, including respect for the rights of women, and under international humanitarian law,

Reaffirming its strong commitment to the sovereignty, independence, territorial integrity and national unity of Afghanistan,

Determining that the situation in Afghanistan still constitutes a threat to international peace and security,

Determined to ensure the full implementation of the mandate of the International Security Assistance Force, in consultation with the Afghan Interim Authority established by the Bonn Agreement,

Acting for these reasons under Chapter VII of the Charter of the United Nations,

1. *Authorizes*, as envisaged in Annex 1 to the Bonn Agreement, the establishment for 6 months of an International Security Assistance Force to assist the Afghan Interim Authority in the maintenance of security in Kabul and its surrounding areas, so that the Afghan Interim Authority as well as the personnel of the United Nations can operate in a secure environment;

2. *Calls* upon Member States to contribute personnel, equipment and other resources to the International Security Assistance Force, and invites those Member States to inform the leadership of the Force and the Secretary-General;

3. *Authorizes* the Member States participating in the International Security Assistance Force to take all necessary measures to fulfil its mandate;

4. *Calls* upon the International Security Assistance Force to work in close consultation with the Afghan Interim Authority in the implementation of the force mandate, as well as with the Special Representative of the Secretary-General;

5. *Calls* upon all Afghans to cooperate with the International Security Assistance Force and relevant international governmental and non-governmental organizations, and welcomes the commitment of the parties to the Bonn Agreement to do all within their means and influence to ensure security, including to ensure the safety, security and freedom of movement of all United Nations personnel and all other personnel of international governmental and non-governmental organizations deployed in Afghanistan;

6. *Takes note* of the pledge made by the Afghan parties to the Bonn Agreement in Annex 1 to that Agreement to withdraw all military units from Kabul, and calls upon them to implement this pledge in cooperation with the International Security Assistance Force;

7. *Encourages* neighbouring States and other Member States to provide to the International Security Assistance Force such necessary assistance as may be requested, including the provision of overflight clearances and transit;

8. *Stresses* that the expenses of the International Security Assistance Force will be borne by the participating Member States concerned, requests the Secretary-General to establish a trust fund through which contributions could be channelled to the Member States or operations concerned, and encourages Member States to contribute to such a fund;

9. *Requests* the leadership of the International Security Assistance Force to provide periodic reports on progress towards the implementation of its mandate through the Secretary-General;

10. *Calls* on Member States participating in the International Security Assistance Force to provide assistance to help the Afghan Interim Authority in the establishment and training of new Afghan security and armed forces;

11. *Decides* to remain actively seized of the matter.

Source: United Nations. Available online at http://unscr.com/files/2001/01386.pdf.

ANALYSIS

The creation of ISAF represented a significant international commitment to Afghanistan and carried much more weight than Security Council Resolution 1383 (Document 36) passed two weeks earlier. The resolution only authorized ISAF for an initial six-month commitment, but ISAF would remain in existence until 2014. ISAF's primary supporters were the NATO countries, and each of the Alliance's members committed forces to participate in ISAF missions. Leaders of ISAF all came from NATO countries, but from 2007 to 2014, all ISAF commanders were either from the U.S. Army or the U.S. Marine Corps. Many other nations, including Australia, also contributed to the ISAF mission, and a total of 50 countries ultimately participated in ISAF peacekeeping missions.

- **Document 38: Tora Bora Revisited: How We Failed to Get Bin Laden and Why It Matters Today**
- **When:** November 30, 2009
- **Where:** Washington, D.C.
- **Significance:** The report chronicled the strategic choices made in late 2001 as the Taliban and al-Qaeda retreated from the Afghan interior toward the rugged border with Pakistan.

DOCUMENT

TORA BORA REVISITED: HOW WE FAILED TO GET BIN LADEN AND WHY IT MATTERS TODAY

———

A Report to Members
OF THE
COMMITTEE ON FOREIGN RELATIONS
UNITED STATES SENATE
John F. Kerry, Chairman
One Hundred Eleventh Congress
First Session
November 30, 2009

. . .

LETTER OF TRANSMITTAL

———

UNITED STATES SENATE,

COMMITTEE ON FOREIGN RELATIONS,

Washington, DC, November 30, 2009.

DEAR COLLEAGUE: This report by the committee majority staff is part of our continuing examination of the conflict in Afghanistan. When we went to war less than a month after the attacks of September 11, the objective was to destroy Al Qaeda and kill or capture its leader, Osama bin Laden, and other senior figures in the terrorist group and the Taliban, which had hosted them. Today, more than eight years later, we find ourselves fighting an increasingly lethal insurgency in Afghanistan and neighboring Pakistan that is led by many of those same extremists. Our inability to finish the job in late 2001 has contributed to a conflict today that endangers not just our troops and those of our allies, but the stability of a volatile and vital region. This report relies on new and existing information to explore the consequences of the failure to eliminate bin Laden and other extremist leaders in the hope that we can learn from the mistakes of the past.

Sincerely,

JOHN F. KERRY,
Chairman.

TORA BORA REVISITED: HOW WE FAILED TO GET BIN LADEN AND WHY IT MATTERS TODAY

EXECUTIVE SUMMARY

On October 7, 2001, U.S. aircraft began bombing the training bases and strongholds of Al Qaeda and the ruling Taliban across Afghanistan. The leaders who sent murderers to attack the World Trade Center and the Pentagon less than a month earlier and the rogue government that provided them sanctuary were running for their lives. President George W. Bush's expression of America's desire to get Osama bin Laden "dead or alive" seemed about to come true.

Two months later, American civilian and military leaders celebrated what they viewed as a lasting victory with the selection of Hamid Karzai as the country's new hand-picked leader. The war had been conceived as a swift campaign with a single objective: defeat the Taliban and destroy Al Qaeda by capturing or killing bin Laden and other key leaders. A unique combination of airpower, Central Intelligence Agency and special operations forces teams and indigenous allies had swept the Taliban from power and ousted Al Qaeda from its safe haven while keeping American deaths to a minimum. But even in the initial glow, there were concerns: The mission had failed to capture or kill bin Laden.

Removing the Al Qaeda leader from the battlefield eight years ago would not have eliminated the worldwide extremist threat. But the decisions that opened the door for his escape to Pakistan allowed bin Laden to emerge as a potent symbolic figure who continues to attract a steady flow of money and inspire fanatics worldwide. The failure to finish the job represents a lost opportunity that forever altered the course of the conflict in Afghanistan and the future of international terrorism, leaving the American people more vulnerable to terrorism, laying the foundation for today's protracted Afghan insurgency and inflaming the internal strife now endangering Pakistan. Al Qaeda shifted its locus across the border into Pakistan, where it has trained extremists linked to numerous plots, including the July 2005 transit bombings in London and two recent aborted attacks involving people living in the United States. The terrorist group's resurgence in Pakistan has coincided with the rising violence orchestrated in Afghanistan by the Taliban, whose leaders also escaped only to re-emerge to direct today's increasingly lethal Afghan insurgency.

This failure and its enormous consequences were not inevitable. By early December 2001, Bin Laden's world had shrunk to a complex of caves and tunnels carved into a mountainous section of eastern Afghanistan known as Tora Bora. Cornered in some of the most forbidding terrain on earth, he and several hundred of his men, the largest concentration of Al Qaeda fighters of the war, endured relentless pounding by American aircraft, as many as 100 air strikes a day. One 15,000-pound bomb, so huge it had to be rolled out the back of a C-130 cargo plane, shook the mountains for miles. It seemed only a matter of time before U.S. troops and their Afghan allies overran the remnants of Al Qaeda hunkered down in the thin, cold air at 14,000 feet.

Bin Laden expected to die. His last will and testament, written on December 14, reflected his fatalism. "Allah commended to us that when death approaches any of us that we make a bequest to parents and next of kin and to Muslims as a whole," he wrote, according to a copy of the will that surfaced later and is regarded as authentic. "Allah bears witness that the love of jihad and death in the cause of Allah has dominated my life and the verses of the sword permeated every cell in my heart, 'and fight the pagans all together as they fight you all together.' How many times did I wake up to find myself reciting this holy verse!" He instructed his wives not to remarry and apologized to his children for devoting himself to jihad.

But the Al Qaeda leader would live to fight another day. Fewer than 100 American commandos were on the scene with their Afghan allies, and calls for reinforcements to launch an assault were rejected. Requests were also turned down for U.S. troops to block the mountain paths leading to sanctuary a few miles away in Pakistan. The vast array of American military power, from sniper teams to the most mobile divisions of the Marine Corps and the Army, was kept on the sidelines. Instead, the U.S. command chose to rely on airstrikes and untrained Afghan militias to attack bin Laden and on Pakistan's loosely organized Frontier Corps to seal his escape routes. On or around December 16, two days after writing his will, bin Laden and an entourage of bodyguards walked unmolested out of Tora Bora and disappeared into Pakistan's unregulated tribal area. Most analysts say he is still there today.

The decision not to deploy American forces to go after bin Laden or block his escape was made by Secretary of Defense Donald Rumsfeld and his top commander, Gen. Tommy Franks, the architects of the unconventional Afghan battle plan known as Operation Enduring Freedom. Rumsfeld said at the time that he was concerned that too many U.S. troops in Afghanistan would create an anti-American backlash and fuel a widespread insurgency. Reversing the recent American military orthodoxy known as the Powell doctrine, the Afghan model emphasized minimizing the U.S. presence by relying on small, highly mobile teams of special operations troops and CIA paramilitary operatives working with the Afghan opposition. Even when his own commanders and senior intelligence officials in Afghanistan and Washington argued for dispatching more U.S. troops, Franks refused to deviate from the plan.

There were enough U.S. troops in or near Afghanistan to execute the classic sweep-and-block maneuver required to attack bin Laden and try to prevent his escape. It would have been a dangerous fight across treacherous terrain, and the injection of more U.S. troops and the resulting casualties would have contradicted the risk-averse, "light footprint" model formulated by Rumsfeld and Franks. But commanders on the scene and elsewhere in Afghanistan argued that the risks were worth the reward.

After bin Laden's escape, some military and intelligence analysts and the press criticized the Pentagon's failure to mount a full-scale attack despite the tough rhetoric by President Bush. Franks, Vice President Dick Cheney and others defended the decision, arguing that the intelligence was inconclusive about the Al Qaeda leader's location. But the review of existing literature, unclassified government records and interviews with central participants underlying this report removes any lingering doubts and makes it clear that Osama bin Laden was within our grasp at Tora Bora.

For example, the CIA and Delta Force commanders who spent three weeks at Tora Bora as well as other intelligence and military sources are certain he was there. Franks' second-in-command during the war, retired Lt. Gen. Michael DeLong, wrote in his autobiography that bin Laden was "'definitely there when we hit the caves"—a statement he retracted when the failure became a political issue. Most authoritatively, the official history of the U.S. Special Operations Command determined that bin Laden was at Tora Bora. "'All source reporting corroborated his presence on several days from 9-14 December," said a declassified version of the history, which was based on accounts of commanders and intelligence officials and published without fanfare two years ago.

The reasons behind the failure to capture or kill Osama bin Laden and its lasting consequences are examined over three sections in this report. The first section traces bin Laden's path from southern Afghanistan to the mountains of Tora Bora and lays out new and previous evidence that he was there. The second explores new information behind the decision not to launch an assault. The final section examines the military options that might have led to his capture or death at Tora Bora and the ongoing impact of the failure to bring him back "dead or alive."

. . .

Source: U.S. Senate Foreign Relations Committee. Available online at https:// www.foreign.senate.gov/imo/media/doc/Tora_Bora_Report.pdf.

ANALYSIS

The report itself emerged after President Barack Obama had campaigned on refocusing American effort on the "forgotten war" in Afghanistan. Operation Enduring

Freedom had been fought with only limited amounts of American and allied ground troops, who instead provided heavy air support and contingents of special operations forces to coordinate with the Northern Alliance. This model had proven successful in driving the Taliban from power in the preceding weeks, but its limitations became apparent in the face of the siege of Tora Bora. Osama bin Laden and other Taliban and al-Qaeda leaders escaped through the mountains and across the Pakistani border.

- **Document 39: Military Technical Agreement between the International Security Assistance Force (ISAF) and the Interim Administration of Afghanistan ("Interim Administration")**
- **When:** January 4, 2002
- **Where:** Kabul, Afghanistan
- **Significance:** This agreement defined the specific parameters under which ISAF would operate in cooperation with the interim Afghan government.

DOCUMENT

Military Technical Agreement Between the International Security Assistance Force (ISAF) and the Interim Administration of Afghanistan ('Interim Administration')

Preamble

Referring to the "Agreement on Provisional Arrangements in Afghanistan pending the Re-establishment of Permanent Government Institutions", signed in Bonn on 5 December 2001, ("Bonn Agreement"), The Interim Administration welcomes the provisions of United Nations Security Council Resolution (UNSCR) 1386.

The ISAF welcomes the Interim Administration's commitment in the Bonn Agreement to cooperate with the international community in the fight against terrorism, drugs and organised crime and to respect international law and maintain peaceful and friendly relations with neighbouring countries and the rest of the international community.

Article I: General Obligations

1. The Interim Administration understands and agrees that the Bonn Agreement requires a major contribution on its part and will make strenuous efforts to cooperate with the ISAF and with the international organisations and agencies which are assisting it.

2. Interim Administration understands and agrees the Mission of the ISAF is to assist it in the maintenance of the security in the area of responsibility as defined below at Article I paragraph 4(g).

3. The Interim Administration agrees to provide the ISAF with any information relevant to the security and safety of the ISAF mission, its personnel, equipment and locations.

. . .

5. It is understood and agreed that once the ISAF is established, its membership may change.

Article II: Status Of The International Security Assistance Force
The arrangements regarding the Status of the ISAF are at Annex A.

Article III: Provision of Security and Law and Order
1. The Interim Administration recognises that the provision of security and law and order is their responsibility. This will include maintenance and support of a recognised Police Force operating in accordance with internationally recognised standards and Afghanistan law and with respect for internationally recognised human rights and fundamental freedoms, and by taking other measures as appropriate.

2. The Interim Administration will ensure that all Afghan Military Units come under its command and control in accordance with the Bonn Agreement. The Interim Administration agrees it will return all Military Units based in Kabul into designated barracks detailed at Annex C as soon as possible. Such units will not leave those Barracks without the prior approval of the Interim Administration and notification to the ISAF Commander by the Chairman of the Interim Administration.

3. The Interim Administration will refrain from all Offensive Actions within the AOR.

4. A Joint Co-ordinating Body (JCB) will meet on a regular basis. The JCB will comprise of designated Interim Administration officials and senior ISAF representatives. The purpose of the JCB will be to discuss current and forthcoming issues and to resolve any disputes that may arise.

Article IV: Deployment of the ISAF
1. UNSCR 1386 authorises the establishment for six months of an international force to assist the Interim Administration in the maintenance of security in the AOR. The Interim Administration understands and agrees that the ISAF is the international force authorised by UNSCR 1386 and may be composed of ground, air and maritime units from the international community.

2. The Interim Administration understands and agrees that the ISAF Commander will have the authority, without interference or permission, to do all that the Commander judges necessary and proper, including the use of military force, to protect the ISAF and its Mission.

3. The Interim Administration understands and agrees the ISAF will have complete and unimpeded freedom of movement throughout the territory and airspace of Afghanistan. The ISAF will agree with the Interim Administration its use of any areas or facilities needed to carry out its responsibilities as required for its support, training and operations, with such advance notice as may be practicable.

4. In consultation with the Interim Administration, the ISAF Commander is authorised to promulgate appropriate rules for the control and regulation of surface military traffic throughout the AOR.

5. The ISAF will have the right to utilise such means and services as required to ensure its full ability to communicate and will have the right to the unrestricted use of all of the electromagnetic spectrum, free of charge, for this purpose. In implementing this right, the ISAF will make every reasonable effort to co-ordinate with and take into account the needs and requirements of the Interim Administration.

Article V: Illustrative Tasks of the ISAF

1. The ISAF will undertake a range of tasks in Kabul and surrounding areas in support of its Mission. ISAF will make every reasonable effort to co-ordinate with and take into account the needs and requirements of the Interim Administration. Possible tasks, which may be undertaken jointly with Interim Administration Forces, will include protective patrolling.

2. By mutual agreement between the ISAF Commander and the Interim Administration the ISAF may:

a. Assist the Interim Administration in developing future security structures.

b. Assist the Interim Administration in reconstruction.

c. Identify and arrange training and assistance tasks for future Afghan security forces.

3. The ISAF will liaise with such political, social and religious leaders as necessary to ensure that religious, ethnic and cultural sensitivities in Afghanistan are appropriately respected by the ISAF.

Article VI: Identification

1. ISAF personnel will wear uniforms and may carry arms if authorised by their orders. Police Force personnel, when on duty, will be visibly identified by uniform or other distinctive markings and may carry arms if authorised by the Interim Administration.

Article VII: Final Authority to Interpret

1. The ISAF Commander is the final authority regarding interpretation of this Military Technical Agreement.

Article VIII: Summary

1. The purposes of the obligations and responsibilities set out in this Arrangement are as follows:

a. To provide the necessary support and technical arrangements for the ISAF to conduct its Mission.

b. To outline the responsibilities of the Interim Administration in relation to the ISAF.

Article IX: Final Provisions

1. Certified copies of this Military Technical Agreement will be supplied in Dari and Pashto language versions. For the purposes of interpretation the English language version of this Military Technical Agreement is authoritative.

Article X: Entry Into Force

1. This agreement will enter into force upon signature by the Participants.

Signed by the Minister of Interior, QANOUNI

On behalf of the Interim Administration of Afghanistan
Dated 4.01.02

Witnessed by BG DE Kratzer for Lt Gen PT Mikolashek Coalition Forces Land Component Commander

Dated

Signed by General McColl, COMISAF

On behalf of the International Security Assistance Force
Dated 4.01.02

4/01/02

. . .

Source: "Military Technical Agreement between the International Security Assistance Force (ISAF) and the Interim Administration of Afghanistan ('Interim Administration')." U.K. Ministry of Defense. Available online at http://reliefweb.int/sites/reliefweb.int/files/resources/9B11C79DE13BB700C1256 B5300381E4F-unsc-afg-25jan.pdf. U.K. Government Web Archive. It contains public sector information licensed under the Open Government Licence v3.0.

ANALYSIS

The Military Technical Agreement outlined the specific roles and missions to be accomplished by ISAF in Afghanistan. Even though the Taliban had been driven from power by the time this agreement came into existence, it continued to fight the United States and its allies in southern and eastern Afghanistan. ISAF, however, was not part of these active military campaigns, and this first agreement limited ISAF's area of responsibility to the region around Kabul. ISAF only had a few hundred troops in early 2002, but the force would number nearly 5,000 by the end of 2002.

- **Document 40: President George W. Bush, State of the Union Address**
- **When:** January 29, 2002
- **Where:** Washington, D.C.
- **Significance:** In his first State of the Union address since the September 11 attacks, President George W. Bush outlined progress made in the campaign against al-Qaeda and the Taliban while also identifying Iraq, Iran, and North Korea as the "axis of evil" nations supporting international terrorism.

DOCUMENT

THE PRESIDENT: Thank you very much. Mr. Speaker, Vice President Cheney, members of Congress, distinguished guests, fellow citizens: As we gather tonight, our nation is at war, our economy is in recession, and the civilized world faces unprecedented dangers. Yet the state of our Union has never been stronger.

We last met in an hour of shock and suffering. In four short months, our nation has comforted the victims, begun to rebuild New York and the Pentagon, rallied a great coalition, captured, arrested, and rid the world of thousands of terrorists, destroyed Afghanistan's terrorist training camps, saved a people from starvation, and freed a country from brutal oppression.

The American flag flies again over our embassy in Kabul. Terrorists who once occupied Afghanistan now occupy cells at Guantanamo Bay. And terrorist leaders who urged followers to sacrifice their lives are running for their own.

America and Afghanistan are now allies against terror. We'll be partners in rebuilding that country. And this evening we welcome the distinguished interim leader of a liberated Afghanistan: Chairman Hamid Karzai.

The last time we met in this chamber, the mothers and daughters of Afghanistan were captives in their own homes, forbidden from working or going to school. Today women are free, and are part of Afghanistan's new government. And we welcome the new Minister of Women's Affairs, Doctor Sima Samar.

Our progress is a tribute to the spirit of the Afghan people, to the resolve of our coalition, and to the might of the United States military. When I called our troops into action, I did so with complete confidence in their courage and skill. And tonight, thanks to them, we are winning the war on terror. The man and women of our Armed Forces have delivered a message now clear to every enemy of the United States: Even 7,000 miles away, across oceans and continents, on mountaintops and in caves—you will not escape the justice of this nation.

For many Americans, these four months have brought sorrow, and pain that will never completely go away. Every day a retired firefighter returns to Ground Zero, to feel closer to his two sons who died there. At a memorial in New York, a little boy left his football with a note for his lost father: Dear Daddy, please take this to heaven. I don't want to play football until I can play with you again someday.

Last month, at the grave of her husband, Michael, a CIA officer and Marine who died in Mazur-e-Sharif, Shannon Spann said these words of farewell: "Semper Fi, my love." Shannon is with us tonight.

Shannon, I assure you and all who have lost a loved one that our cause is just, and our country will never forget the debt we owe Michael and all who gave their lives for freedom.

Our cause is just, and it continues. Our discoveries in Afghanistan confirmed our worst fears, and showed us the true scope of the task ahead. We have seen the depth of our enemies' hatred in videos, where they laugh about the loss of innocent life. And the depth of their hatred is equaled by the madness of the destruction they design. We have found diagrams of American nuclear power plants and public water facilities, detailed instructions for making chemical weapons, surveillance maps of

American cities, and thorough descriptions of landmarks in America and throughout the world.

What we have found in Afghanistan confirms that, far from ending there, our war against terror is only beginning. Most of the 19 men who hijacked planes on September the 11th were trained in Afghanistan's camps, and so were tens of thousands of others. Thousands of dangerous killers, schooled in the methods of murder, often supported by outlaw regimes, are now spread throughout the world like ticking time bombs, set to go off without warning.

Thanks to the work of our law enforcement officials and coalition partners, hundreds of terrorists have been arrested. Yet, tens of thousands of trained terrorists are still at large. These enemies view the entire world as a battlefield, and we must pursue them wherever they are. So long as training camps operate, so long as nations harbor terrorists, freedom is at risk. And America and our allies must not, and will not, allow it.

Our nation will continue to be steadfast and patient and persistent in the pursuit of two great objectives. First, we will shut down terrorist camps, disrupt terrorist plans, and bring terrorists to justice. And, second, we must prevent the terrorists and regimes who seek chemical, biological or nuclear weapons from threatening the United States and the world.

Our military has put the terror training camps of Afghanistan out of business, yet camps still exist in at least a dozen countries. A terrorist underworld—including groups like Hamas, Hezbollah, Islamic Jihad, Jaish-i-Mohammed—operates in remote jungles and deserts, and hides in the centers of large cities.

While the most visible military action is in Afghanistan, America is acting elsewhere. We now have troops in the Philippines, helping to train that country's armed forces to go after terrorist cells that have executed an American, and still hold hostages. Our soldiers, working with the Bosnian government, seized terrorists who were plotting to bomb our embassy. Our Navy is patrolling the coast of Africa to block the shipment of weapons and the establishment of terrorist camps in Somalia.

My hope is that all nations will heed our call, and eliminate the terrorist parasites who threaten their countries and our own. Many nations are acting forcefully. Pakistan is now cracking down on terror, and I admire the strong leadership of President Musharraf.

But some governments will be timid in the face of terror. And make no mistake about it: If they do not act, America will.

Our second goal is to prevent regimes that sponsor terror from threatening America or our friends and allies with weapons of mass destruction. Some of these regimes have been pretty quiet since September the 11th. But we know their true nature. North Korea is a regime arming with missiles and weapons of mass destruction, while starving its citizens.

Iran aggressively pursues these weapons and exports terror, while an unelected few repress the Iranian people's hope for freedom.

Iraq continues to flaunt its hostility toward America and to support terror. The Iraqi regime has plotted to develop anthrax, and nerve gas, and nuclear weapons for over a decade. This is a regime that has already used poison gas to murder thousands of its own citizens—leaving the bodies of mothers huddled over their dead children. This is a regime that agreed to international inspections—then kicked out the inspectors. This is a regime that has something to hide from the civilized world.

States like these, and their terrorist allies, constitute an axis of evil, arming to threaten the peace of the world. By seeking weapons of mass destruction, these regimes pose a grave and growing danger. They could provide these arms to terrorists, giving them the means to match their hatred. They could attack our allies or attempt to blackmail the United States. In any of these cases, the price of indifference would be catastrophic.

We will work closely with our coalition to deny terrorists and their state sponsors the materials, technology, and expertise to make and deliver weapons of mass destruction. We will develop and deploy effective missile defenses to protect America and our allies from sudden attack. And all nations should know: America will do what is necessary to ensure our nation's security.

We'll be deliberate, yet time is not on our side. I will not wait on events, while dangers gather. I will not stand by, as peril draws closer and closer. The United States of America will not permit the world's most dangerous regimes to threaten us with the world's most destructive weapons.

Our war on terror is well begun, but it is only begun. This campaign may not be finished on our watch—yet it must be and it will be waged on our watch.

We can't stop short. If we stop now—leaving terror camps intact and terror states unchecked—our sense of security would be false and temporary. History has called America and our allies to action, and it is both our responsibility and our privilege to fight freedom's fight.

Our first priority must always be the security of our nation, and that will be reflected in the budget I send to Congress. My budget supports three great goals for America: We will win this war; we'll protect our homeland; and we will revive our economy.

September the 11th brought out the best in America, and the best in this Congress. And I join the American people in applauding your unity and resolve. Now Americans deserve to have this same spirit directed toward addressing problems here at home. I'm a proud member of my party—yet as we act to win the war, protect our people, and create jobs in America, we must act, first and foremost, not as Republicans, not as Democrats, but as Americans.

It costs a lot to fight this war. We have spent more than a billion dollars a month—over $30 million a day—and we must be prepared for future operations. Afghanistan proved that expensive precision weapons defeat the enemy and spare innocent lives, and we need more of them. We need to replace aging aircraft and make our military more agile, to put our troops anywhere in the world quickly and safely. Our men and women in uniform deserve the best weapons, the best equipment, the best training—and they also deserve another pay raise.

My budget includes the largest increase in defense spending in two decades—because while the price of freedom and security is high, it is never too high. Whatever it costs to defend our country, we will pay.

. . .

During these last few months, I've been humbled and privileged to see the true character of this country in a time of testing. Our enemies believed America was weak and materialistic, that we would splinter in fear and selfishness. They were as wrong as they are evil.

The American people have responded magnificently, with courage and compassion, strength and resolve. As I have met the heroes, hugged the families, and looked into the tired faces of rescuers, I have stood in awe of the American people.

And I hope you will join me—I hope you will join me in expressing thanks to one American for the strength and calm and comfort she brings to our nation in crisis, our First Lady, Laura Bush.

None of us would ever wish the evil that was done on September the 11th. Yet after America was attacked, it was as if our entire country looked into a mirror and saw our better selves. We were reminded that we are citizens, with obligations to each other, to our country, and to history. We began to think less of the goods we can accumulate, and more about the good we can do.

For too long our culture has said, "If it feels good, do it." Now America is embracing a new ethic and a new creed: "Let's roll." In the sacrifice of soldiers, the fierce brotherhood of firefighters, and the bravery and generosity of ordinary citizens, we have glimpsed what a new culture of responsibility could look like. We want to be a nation that serves goals larger than self. We've been offered a unique opportunity, and we must not let this moment pass.

My call tonight is for every American to commit at least two years—4,000 hours over the rest of your lifetime—to the service of your neighbors and your nation. Many are already serving, and I thank you. If you aren't sure how to help, I've got a good place to start. To sustain and extend the best that has emerged in America, I invite you to join the new USA Freedom Corps. The Freedom Corps will focus on three areas of need: responding in case of crisis at home; rebuilding our communities; and extending American compassion throughout the world.

One purpose of the USA Freedom Corps will be homeland security. America needs retired doctors and nurses who can be mobilized in major emergencies; volunteers to help police and fire departments; transportation and utility workers well-trained in spotting danger.

Our country also needs citizens working to rebuild our communities. We need mentors to love children, especially children whose parents are in prison. And we need more talented teachers in troubled schools. USA Freedom Corps will expand and improve the good efforts of AmeriCorps and Senior Corps to recruit more than 200,000 new volunteers.

And America needs citizens to extend the compassion of our country to every part of the world. So we will renew the promise of the Peace Corps, double its volunteers over the next five years—and ask it to join a new effort to encourage development and education and opportunity in the Islamic world.

This time of adversity offers a unique moment of opportunity—a moment we must seize to change our culture. Through the gathering momentum of millions of acts of service and decency and kindness, I know we can overcome evil with greater good. And we have a great opportunity during this time of war to lead the world toward the values that will bring lasting peace.

All fathers and mothers, in all societies, want their children to be educated, and live free from poverty and violence. No people on Earth yearn to be oppressed, or aspire to servitude, or eagerly await the midnight knock of the secret police.

If anyone doubts this, let them look to Afghanistan, where the Islamic "street" greeted the fall of tyranny with song and celebration. Let the skeptics look to Islam's own rich history, with its centuries of learning, and tolerance and progress. America will lead by defending liberty and justice because they are right and true and unchanging for all people everywhere.

No nation owns these aspirations, and no nation is exempt from them. We have no intention of imposing our culture. But America will always stand firm for the non-negotiable demands of human dignity: the rule of law; limits on the power of the state; respect for women; private property; free speech; equal justice; and religious tolerance.

America will take the side of brave men and women who advocate these values around the world, including the Islamic world, because we have a greater objective than eliminating threats and containing resentment. We seek a just and peaceful world beyond the war on terror.

In this moment of opportunity, a common danger is erasing old rivalries. America is working with Russia and China and India, in ways we have never before, to achieve peace and prosperity. In every region, free markets and free trade and free societies are proving their power to lift lives. Together with friends and allies from Europe to Asia, and Africa to Latin America, we will demonstrate that the forces of terror cannot stop the momentum of freedom.

The last time I spoke here, I expressed the hope that life would return to normal. In some ways, it has. In others, it never will. Those of us who have lived through these challenging times have been changed by them. We've come to know truths that we will never question: evil is real, and it must be opposed. Beyond all differences of race or creed, we are one country, mourning together and facing danger together. Deep in the American character, there is honor, and it is stronger than cynicism. And many have discovered again that even in tragedy—especially in tragedy—God is near.

In a single instant, we realized that this will be a decisive decade in the history of liberty, that we've been called to a unique role in human events. Rarely has the world faced a choice more clear or consequential.

Our enemies send other people's children on missions of suicide and murder. They embrace tyranny and death as a cause and a creed. We stand for a different choice, made long ago, on the day of our founding. We affirm it again today. We choose freedom and the dignity of every life.

Steadfast in our purpose, we now press on. We have known freedom's price. We have shown freedom's power. And in this great conflict, my fellow Americans, we will see freedom's victory.

Thank you all. May God bless.

Source: Public Papers of the Presidents of the United States: George W. Bush, 2002, Book 1. Washington, D.C.: Government Printing Office, 2003, 129–136.

ANALYSIS

President Bush began the speech noting the considerable progress made in Afghanistan since the beginning of hostilities in October 2001 and also called out to two of his invited guests, President Hamid Karzai and Minister of Women's Affairs Dr. Sima Samar.

Yet, as he also described the discovery and destruction of terrorist training camps in Afghanistan by advancing Coalition forces, he used the speech to significantly broaden the scope of the Global War against Terrorism. Most important, in identifying the three "axis of evil" nations, he followed through on earlier statements that Afghanistan would be only the first battleground in this conflict. The Taliban had retreated from the Northern Alliance supported by NATO airpower and some Coalition ground forces, so the U.S. military footprint in Afghanistan remained limited. However, in labeling these new nations as possible threats, President Bush threatened to distract American and international attention away from the campaign in Afghanistan, which, while extraordinarily successful to date, remained incomplete.

- **Document 41: Remarks as Delivered by U.S. Secretary of Defense Donald Rumsfeld, National Defense University, Fort McNair, Washington, D.C.**
- **When:** January 31, 2002
- **Where:** Washington, D.C.
- **Significance:** Secretary of Defense Donald Rumsfeld's speech discussed the war in Afghanistan as well as efforts to "transform" the U.S. military into a faster, more technologically capable force to fight future conflicts.

DOCUMENT

. . .

So to the students and the faculty of our War College community, distinguished guests, and men and women of the armed forces, just before Christmas I traveled to Afghanistan and the neighboring countries, where I had an opportunity to spend time with our troops in the field. They are remarkable. They're brave, they're dedicated, they voluntarily risk their lives in a dangerous corner of the world to defend our freedom and our way of life, and I was grateful to be able to personally tell them that.

Among the many, I met with an extraordinary group of men, the Special Forces who'd been involved in the attack on Mazar-e Sharif. Now I've said on a number of occasions that the war on terrorism would likely be unlike any war we had fought before. These men surprised us all with their early requests for supplies. They asked for boots, ammunition . . . and horse feed.

From the moment they landed in Afghanistan, they began adapting to the circumstances on the ground. They sported beards and traditional scarves. They rode horses—horses that had been trained to run into machine-gun fire, atop saddles that had been fashioned from wood and saddle bags that had been crafted from Afghan carpets. They used pack mules to transport equipment along some of the roughest terrain in the world, riding at night, in darkness, often near mine fields and along narrow mountain trails with drops so sheer that, as one soldier put it, it took him a week to ease the death-grip on his saddle. Many had never been on horseback before.

As they linked up and trained with anti-Taliban forces, they learned from their new allies about the realities of war on Afghan soil, and they assisted the Afghans with weapons, with supplies, with food, with tactics and training. And they helped plan the attack on Mazar.

On the appointed day, one of their teams slipped in and hid well behind the lines, ready to call in airstrikes, and the bomb blasts would be the signal for others to charge. When the moment came, they signaled their targets to the coalition aircraft and looked at their watches. Two minutes and 15 seconds, 10 seconds—and then, out of nowhere, precision-guided bombs began to land on Taliban and al-Qaeda positions. The explosions were deafening, and the timing so precise that, as the soldiers described it, hundreds of Afghan horsemen literally came riding out of the smoke, coming down on the enemy in clouds of dust and flying shrapnel. A few carried RPGs. Some had as little as 10 rounds for their weapons. And they rode boldly—Americans, Afghans, towards the Taliban and al Qaeda fighters. It was the first cavalry attack of the 21st century.

After the battle one soldier described how he was called over by one of the Afghans who'd been with him, started to pull up his pant leg, and he thought he was going to see a wound. Instead, he looked down and saw a prosthetic limb. The Afghan had ridden into battle with only one good leg.

Now, what won the battle for Mazar and set in motion the Taliban's fall from power was a combination of ingenuity of the Special Forces, the most advanced precision-guided munitions in the U.S. arsenal delivered by U.S. Navy, Air Force and Marine crews, and the courage of the Afghan fighters, some with one leg. That day on the plains of Afghanistan, the 19th century met the 21st century, and they defeated a dangerous and determined adversary, a remarkable achievement.

When President Bush called me back to the Pentagon after a quarter of a century, he asked me to come up with a new defense strategy to work with the Department of Defense and the senior military to fashion a new approach. He knew I was an old-timer, but I'll bet he never imagined for a second that we'd bring back the cavalry.

DID YOU KNOW?

Provincial Reconstruction Teams

Provincial Reconstruction Teams (PRTs) were teams comprised of soldiers and personnel from other U.S. government agencies that sought to facilitate the rebuilding of Afghanistan's infrastructure and civil society. The concept originated in 2002 with small Army Civil Affairs units conducting small-scale reconstruction projects that soon added members from other agencies to allow them to take on more responsibilities. Eventually, U.S. PRTs incorporated between 500 and 1,000 personnel. Other nations, especially the United Kingdom and Germany, developed their own PRTs, although the exact responsibilities and size of PRTs varied from nation to nation. PRTs also worked closely with local Afghan authorities in order to link the activities of the teams with more effective governance. PRTs operated in nearly every Afghan province at the height of the war in Afghanistan. The concept proved so successful that it was exported to Iraq. PRTs were disbanded as the Coalition presence in Afghanistan withdrew in the mid-2010s.

But really, this is precisely what transformation is about. Here we are in the year 2002, fighting the first war of the 21st century, and the horse cavalry was back and being used, but being used in previously unimaginable ways. It showed that a revolution in military affairs is about more than building new high tech weapons, though that is certainly part of it. It's also about new ways of thinking, and new ways of fighting.

In World War II, the German blitzkrieg revolutionized warfare. But it was accomplished by a German military that was really only about 10 or 15 percent transformed. The Germans saw that the future of war lay not with massive armies and protracted trench warfare, but rather with its small, high quality, mobile shock forces supported by air power and coordinated with air power, capable of pulling off lightning strikes against the enemy. They developed the lethal combination of fast-moving tanks, mobilized infantry and artillery supported by dive bombers, all concentrated on one part of the enemy line. The effect was devastating on their adversary's capabilities, on their morale, and it was, for a period, on the cause of freedom in the world.

What was revolutionary and unprecedented about the blitzkrieg was not the new capabilities the Germans employed, but rather the unprecedented and revolutionary way that they mixed new and existing capabilities.

In a similar way, the battle for Mazar was a transformational battle. Coalition forces took existing military capabilities from the most advanced laser-guided weapons to antique, 40-year-old B-52s—actually, 40 years old doesn't sound antique to me—but the B-52s had been updated with modern electronics—and also to the most rudimentary, a man on horseback. And they used them together in unprecedented ways, with devastating effect on enemy positions, on enemy morale, and this time, on the cause of evil in the world.

Preparing for the future will require us to think differently and develop the kinds of forces and capabilities that can adapt quickly to new challenges and to unexpected circumstances. An ability to adapt will be critical in a world where surprise and uncertainty are the defining characteristics of our new security environment. During the Cold War, we faced a fairly predictable set of threats. We came to know a great deal about our adversary, because it was the same one for a long period. We knew many of the capabilities they possessed, and we fashioned strategies and capabilities that we believed we needed to deter them. And they were successful. It worked.

For almost a half a century, that mix of strategy, forces and capabilities allowed us to keep the peace and to defend freedom. But the Cold War is over. The Soviet Union is gone, and with it, the familiar security environment to which our nation had grown accustomed.

As we painfully learned on September 11th, the challenges of a new century are not nearly as predictable as they were during the Cold War. Who would have imagined only a few months ago that terrorists would take commercial airliners, turn them into missiles and use them to strike the Pentagon and the World Trade Towers, killing thousands? But it happened.

And let there be no doubt, in the years ahead, it is likely that we will be surprised again by new adversaries who may also strike in unexpected ways.

And as they gain access to weapons of increasing power—and let there be no doubt but that they are—these attacks will grow vastly more deadly than those we suffered several months ago.

. . .

Our experience on September 11th, and indeed in the Afghan campaign, have served to reinforce the importance of moving the U.S. defense posture in these directions. Our challenge in the 21st century is to defend our cities and our infrastructure from new forms of attack while projecting force over long distances to fight new and perhaps distant adversaries.

To do this, we need rapidly deployable, fully integrated joint forces capable of reaching distant theaters quickly and working with our air and sea forces to strike adversaries swiftly, successfully, and with devastating effect. We need improved intelligence, long-range precision strikes, sea-based platforms to help counter the access denial capabilities of adversaries.

Our goal is not simply to fight and win wars, it is to try to prevent wars. To do so, we need to find ways to influence the decision-makers of potential adversaries, to deter them not only from using existing weapons, but to the extent possible, try to dissuade them from building dangerous new capabilities in the first place.

. . .

For example, the experience in Afghanistan showed the effectiveness of unmanned aircraft. But it also revealed how few we have and what their weaknesses are. The department has known for some time that it does not have enough manned reconnaissance and surveillance aircraft, command-and-control aircraft, air-defense capabilities, chemical and biological defense units, as well as certain types of special operations forces.

But in spite of the shortages of these and other scarce systems, the United States postponed the needed investment while continuing to fund what were, in retrospect, less valuable programs. That needs to change.

Moreover, as we change investment priorities, we have to begin shifting the balance in our arsenal between manned and unmanned capabilities between short- and long-range systems, stealthy and non-stealthy systems, between shooters and sensors, and between vulnerable and hardened systems. And we need to make the leap into the information age, which is the critical foundation of our transformation efforts.

As we deployed forces and capabilities to defend U.S. territory after September 11th, we found that our new responsibilities in homeland defense have exacerbated these shortages. No U.S. president should be placed in the position where he must choose between protecting our citizens at home and protecting our interests and our forces overseas. We, as a country, must be able to do both.

The notion that we could transform while cutting the defense budget over the past decade was seductive, but false.

. . .

And we must transform not only our armed forces, but also the Department that serves them by encouraging a culture of creativity and intelligent risk taking. We must promote a more entrepreneurial approach to developing military capabilities, one that encourages people, all people, to be proactive and not reactive, to behave somewhat less like bureaucrats and more like venture capitalists; one that does not wait for threats to emerge and be "validated," but rather anticipates them before they emerge and develops new capabilities that can dissuade and deter those nascent threats.

We need to change not only the capabilities at our disposal, but also how we think about war. All the high-tech weapons in the world will not transform U.S. armed forces unless we also transform the way we think, the way we train, the way we exercise and the way we fight.

Some believe that, with the U.S. in the midst of a dangerous war on terrorism, now is not the time to transform our armed forces. I believe that quite the opposite is true. Now is precisely the time to make changes. The impetus and the urgency added by the events of September 11th powerfully make the case for action.

Every day, we are faced with urgent near-term requirements that create pressure to push the future off the table. But September 11th taught us that the future holds many unknown dangers and that we fail to prepare for them at our peril.

Our challenge is to make certain that, as time passes and the shock of what befell us that day wears off, we do not simply go back to doing things the way we did them before. The war on terrorism is a transformational event that cries out for us to rethink our activities, each of us to rethink our activities, and put that new thinking into action.

. . .

Of course, as we transform, we must not make the mistake of assuming that our experience in Afghanistan presents us with a model for the next military campaign.

Preparing to re-fight the last war is a mistake repeated throughout much of military history, and one we must avoid, and will. But we can glean important lessons from recent experiences that apply to the future. Here are a few worth considering:

First, wars in the 21st century will increasingly require all elements of national power: economic, diplomatic, financial, legal, law enforcement, intelligence, as well as overt and covert military operations. Clausewitz said "war is the continuation of politics by other means." In this new century, many of those means may not be military.

Second, the ability of forces to communicate and operate seamlessly on the battlefield will be critical to our success. In Afghanistan, we saw composite teams of U.S. special forces on the ground, working with Navy, Air Force and Marine pilots in the sky, to identify targets, communicate targeting information and coordinate the timing of strikes with devastating consequences for the enemy. The change between what we were able to do before U.S. forces, special forces, were on the ground and after they were on the ground was absolutely dramatic.

The lesson of this war is that effectiveness in combat will depend heavily on "jointness," how well the different branches of our military can communicate and coordinate their efforts on the battlefield. And achieving jointness in wartime requires building that jointness in peacetime. We need to train like we fight and fight like we train, and too often, we don't.

Third, our policy in this war of accepting help from any country on a basis that is comfortable for them and allowing them to characterize what it is they doing to help us instead of our characterizing if for them or our saying that we won't have a country participate unless they could participate in every single respect of this effort, is enabling us to maximize both their cooperation and our effectiveness against the enemy.

Fourth, wars can benefit from coalitions of the willing, to be sure. But they should not be fought by committee. The mission must determine the coalition, and the coalition must not determine the mission. If it does, the mission will be dumbed down to the lowest common denominator, and we can't afford that.

Fifth, defending the U.S. requires prevention, self-defense and sometimes preemption. It is not possible to defend against every conceivable kind of attack in every conceivable location at every minute of the day or night. Defending against terrorism and other emerging 21st century threats may well require that we take the war to the enemy. The best, and in some cases, the only defense, is a good offense.

Sixth, rule out nothing, including ground forces. The enemy must understand that we will use every means at our disposal to defeat them, and that we are prepared to make whatever sacrifices are necessary to achieve victory. To the extent the United States is seen as leaning back, we weaken the deterrent, we encourage people to engage in acts to our detriment. We need to be leaning forward as a country.

Seventh, getting U.S. special forces on the ground early dramatically increased the effectiveness of the air campaign. In Afghanistan, precision-guided bombs from the sky did not achieve their effectiveness until we had boots, and eyes, on the ground to tell the bombers exactly where to aim.

And finally, we need to be straight with the American people. We need to tell them the truth. And when you can't tell them something, we need to tell them that we can't tell them something. The American people understand what we're trying to accomplish, what is needed to get the job done, that it's not easy and that there will be casualties. And they must know that, good news or bad, we will tell it to them straight. Broad bipartisan public support must be rooted in a bond of trust, of understanding and of common purpose.

There is a great deal we can learn from this first war of the 21st century. But we cannot, and must not, make the mistake of assuming that terrorism is the only threat. The next threat we face may indeed be from terrorists, but it could also be a cyber-war, a traditional, state-on-state conflict or something entirely different.

And that's why, even as we prosecute this war on terrorism, we must be preparing for the next war. We need to transform our forces for new and unexpected challenges. We must be prepared for surprise. We must learn to live with little or no warning.

And as we do so, much will change about our armed forces—about the way they will think and fight in this new century.

. . .

Q Sir, Lieutenant Colonel Pete Mons [ph], ICAF. In regard to the war on terrorism, how do we know when we've won the war? What indicators are you looking for?

SEC. RUMSFELD: I'll let you know. No, that's not fair. It's a tough question. There will not be a signing ceremony on the USS Missouri—for several reasons, but ... The reality is that our goal is to be able to live as free people and to be able to get up in the morning and go out and know that our children can go to school and they'll come home safely, and that we don't have to carry weapons and hide and live underground and be fearful and acquiesce and give up our freedoms because some other group of people have imposed their will on us.

Now, what does that mean? It means that we have to go after the terrorist networks. It means that we have to deal with countries that harbor terrorists. And you are never going to solve every terrorist act. I mean, some people in Chicago terrorize their neighbors. But that's not what we're talking about here. We're talking about global terrorism. And I think we can do an effective job on that problem. I think it will take a period of years. It's not something that will be quick. It's not something that at the end of that that it will be over and then you can relax, because there will always be people who will attempt to work their will against their neighbors and against the United States.

But I think we'll know when we have been successful in for the most part dealing with the most serious global network threats and the countries that are harboring those. The real—the real concern at the present time is the nexus between terrorist networks and terrorist states that have weapons of mass destruction. And let there be no doubt, there is that nexus, and it must force people all across this globe to realize that what we're dealing with here is something that is totally different than existed in previous periods, and it poses risks of not thousands of lives, but hundreds of thousands of lives, when one thinks of the power and lethality of those weapons.

...

Q Joanne Callahan [sp], Central Intelligence Agency. Mr. Secretary, you have alluded to the fact that you need actionable intelligence and that there has to be a lot more flexibility, interoperability, elimination of stovepipes, and that sort of thing.

Since you are undergoing a period of transformation, one could argue that the intelligence community, in order to continue to provide relevant support, also has to change. I'm wondering if you can talk about briefly the type of intelligence that has worked for you and—without getting into specifics, of course—and what you might like to see, what you're looking for from the intelligence community in the future. Thank you.

SEC. RUMSFELD: We have developed a very close relationship between the CIA and the Department of Defense in the last 12 months. I think I probably have lunch with George Tenet about once a week, and I'm probably with him once a day, on the phone or in person. And I know Tom Franks has got—in fact, I'm going to have you come up here and comment on this, because here's a real-life example that's happening, where we have tried to connect and fuse the relationship between DOD and the agency. It's never perfect, but it has gotten better every single day since September 11th, I think it's fair to say.

Tom, do you want to comment?

GEN. FRANKS: Sure. I think that's exactly right. I think I'd probably character-ize it as the very best relationship that I've seen since I've been in this line of work—not as a CINC, but over 35 years.

And it's—as the secretary said, it's the agency. It's also other other [sic] intelli-gence capabilities that we have within our government.

And I look back five, six months ago, and I think about the characteristics that the vice chairman mentioned, and that is, we'll get together, we'll think our way through something, and then everyone goes back to his own stovepipe, and we begin to function as best we can. And to be sure, we started that way in our activities in Operation Enduring Freedom.

But what we have learned is the—what we've learned a lot about is the possibil-ities if you get together, create focus groups in order to think about a particular prob-lem. It sounds a bit "old think," but there is no excuse for putting people together to work on a problem—joint interagency intelligence groups, that sort of thing—and we have found them to be very, very effective.

We do it differently now than we did four months ago. I predict we'll probably do it differently four months from now than we did four months ago, but we started out being very slow in our ability to move information. We—and very slow in our ability to react to information, and it got better day by day by day.

And so I think we have a lot to be satisfied with at this point, but I don't think we need to be totally satisfied, because we're still in fact working around some impedi-ments, rather than removing the impediments.

And so we have work to do in the future, but I think we ought to feel okay with where we are now.

SEC. RUMSFELD: Admiral Gaffney has just given me the hook.

Colonel, congratulations again. General Pace, General Franks, thank you for assisting. And to all of you, thanks to you for what you do for our country. Good-bye.

Source: Air University. Available online at http://www.au.af.mil/au/awc/awcgate/dod/transformation-secdef-31jan02.htm.

ANALYSIS

Secretary Rumsfeld's speech and the answers to the students' questions that followed outlined the "lessons learned" from the invasion of Afghanistan. By inserting small teams of special operations forces who could identify targets and communicate with roving aircraft, Rumsfeld outlined how the invasion had been successfully executed and used this as a template for possible future conflicts. His speech, however, ignored the considerable contributions made by the Northern Alliance in fighting the Taliban and securing the country as the Coalition forces moved southward.

As will be discussed with later documents in this volume, Rumsfeld's efforts to transform the military into a lighter, faster force fell into disrepute as the Taliban reemerged in Afghanistan and the United States became embroiled in an insur-gency against the Sunni minority in Iraq. Unlike the quick invasions of both countries, successfully stamping out insurgencies required far more manpower than what Rumsfeld had originally envisioned necessary.

- **Document 42: George W. Bush, The President's News Conference with President Pervez Musharraf of Pakistan**
- **When:** February 13, 2002
- **Where:** Washington, D.C.
- **Significance:** A joint press conference between President Bush and President Musharraf that outlined the progress made in Afghanistan and in U.S.-Pakistani relations since the September 11 attacks.

DOCUMENT

President Bush. Good morning. It's my honor to welcome President Musharraf to the White House. President Musharraf is a leader with great courage and vision, and his nation is a key partner in the global coalition against terror. Pakistan's continuing support of Operation Enduring Freedom has been critical to our success so far in toppling the Taliban and routing out the Al Qaida network.

Yet President Musharraf has made an even broader commitment. He has declared that Pakistan will be an enemy of terrorism and extremism wherever it exists, including inside his own border. He understands that terrorism is wrong and destructive in any cause. He knows that his nation cannot grow peacefully if terrorists are tolerated or ignored in his country, in his region, or in the world. He is committed to banning the groups that practice terror, closing their offices and arresting the terrorists themselves.

Terrorists operating in Pakistan recently kidnaped American reporter Daniel Pearl. We spent a time today in the Oval Office talking about our mutual desire to see that Mr. Pearl is returned home safely. I want to thank the President for his assistance and work on securing Mr. Pearl's release.

I also applaud President Musharraf's clearly stated intention to work for peace in Kashmir and lower tensions with India. I'm particularly pleased to note that he is going to be holding elections later on this fall.

The President has articulated a vision of a Pakistan as a progressive, modern, and democratic Islamic society, determined and serious about seeking greater learning and greater prosperity for its citizens. The

DID YOU KNOW?

Operation Anaconda

Operation Anaconda was a Coalition military operation from March 2 to March 16, 2002, in the Shah-i-Kot Valley in Paktia Province in eastern Afghanistan. Designed to trap and destroy a force of up to 1,000 Taliban and al-Qaeda fighters, Anaconda was the first major operation of the war involving conventional U.S. forces since most of the early fighting had involved U.S. Special Forces units and the troops from the Northern Alliance. During Anaconda, forces from the 101st Airborne Division, 10th Mountain Division, and other U.S. and allied units sought to trap the enemy in the valley. This led to several heavy firefights that killed 15 Coalition personnel and wounded 82 more. The Coalition claimed that hundreds of Taliban and al-Qaeda died in the battle, but only 23 bodies were recovered. The battle provided many lessons learned for fighting in Afghanistan's rugged terrain and in coordinating units from different services and nations.

United States is committed to working in partnership with Pakistan to pursue these objectives.

Together, our nations will continue to cooperate against terror and trafficking in drugs. We will strengthen ties of trade and investment between our nations. We'll work to improve educational and economic opportunities for all Pakistanis, especially women and children. And my Government stands ready to work with all parties on the subcontinent to foster dialog to lower tensions and resolve outstanding issues.

The forces of history have accelerated the growth of friendship between the United States and Pakistan. I believe the pages of history will record that this friendship was hopeful and positive and will lead to peace.

Mr. President.

President Musharraf. Thank you very much, Mr. President, for your welcome and your kind words and sentiments expressed for me and for Pakistan and for my Government.

I recall with great pleasure our very productive meeting last November in New York. We have also spoken quite frequently on the telephone since then. I value most highly this opportunity to exchange views with you in person.

Our discussions this morning have been fruitful and constructive and will continue over the lunch. Our meetings and discussions with senior members of your administration continue as part of the ongoing dialog which characterizes our close and cooperative relations.

For more than half a century, the relations between Pakistan and the United States have been friendly, multifaceted, and enduring. They represent an important element of stability in our region and beyond. The criminal terrorist attacks of September 11th and the momentous events since then have demonstrated the depth and strength of this relationship between the United States and Pakistan.

Pakistan has a firm position of principle in the international battle against terrorism. We reject terrorism in all its forms and manifestations anywhere in the world. We will continue to fulfill our responsibilities flowing from our commitment.

I am gratified that my vision of Pakistan as a dynamic, liberal, progressive, peaceful, and genuinely democratic Muslim country and the decision I announced on 12 January have evoked a supportive response in the United States. I believe that Pakistan-United States relationship must draw strength from our past relationship as we move to a new century, a changed world and meet the challenges faced ahead.

. . .

The faithful implementation of the Bonn accord provides the best guarantee for the future of Afghanistan. The interim administration must be strengthened and its writ established over the entire country. Rehabilitation and reconstruction must begin in Afghanistan. The Tokyo donors conference has provided a forceful and timely impulse to this process, which will also accelerate the return of millions of Afghan refugees in Pakistan to their homeland.

Together, the United States and Pakistan can accomplish great things. We have embarked on a long-term partnership. We look forward to an era of robust collaboration. I look forward, Mr. President, to your visit to Pakistan, where a warm and cordial welcome awaits you from the people of Pakistan, who hold you in the highest of esteem.

I thank you, sir.

President Bush. Thank you, Mr. President; good job.

President Musharraf. Thank you.

. . .

Pakistan-U.S. Relations

Q. President Bush, you talked about history——

President Bush. Talked about—excuse me?

Q. You talked about history——

President Bush. Oh, history, yes. Getting a little hard of hearing.

Q. And history shows that the U.S. dumped Pakistan after the Afghan war in 1980. So a common Pakistani wants to know whether the U.S. will repeat the same history again, once again. And secondly, how do you plan to help Pakistan, the modernization of Pakistan in its struggle of survival against mighty and militarized India?

President Bush. Well, that's a very legitimate question. And it's—one of the reasons why President Musharraf and I are spending time together is, he has got to be confident in me and my Government willingness to stay supportive of Pakistan.

I think one of the things, in order for us to have a positive relationship, is that he realizes that when we say we're committed, we're committed. And we're committed to peace in the region. We're committed to fighting terror.

The President made a tough decision and a strong decision. It's not only a decision about fighting terror; it's a decision for the direction of his country. And we support that strongly.

So I can understand why some in Pakistan are saying, "Well, oh, this is just a short-term dance." But so long as we share the same ideals and values and common objectives, we'll work with Pakistan. And there are ways to help. The President is going to go see Secretary Rumsfeld today. We have—he negotiated and we willingly supported a strong aid package in the '02 budget. We're now discussing help in the '03 budget. We want to help facilitate the President's concerns about a debt burden on Pakistan. We want to talk about trade matters. We want to help him achieve his vision of elevating the average citizen by giving them a chance and a hopeful opportunity for life.

And so, I would suggest that people in Pakistan remember to think about the future and not dwell in the past. That's what the President has done with his vision, and I am proud to call him friend.

I want to remind people from Pakistan that I didn't mention many world leaders in my State of the Union. But I mentioned President Musharraf, for a reason. And hopefully, that's an indication of my sincerity of developing a strong and meaningful relationship.

Education Reform in Pakistan

Q. Mr. Bush and Mr. Musharraf, should secular schools be the standard in Islamic communities in Pakistan to prevent jihads and other terrorists attacks like 9/11?

President Bush. Let me first—and I'd like the President to speak on this, basically on the madrasa school issue in Pakistan. One of the things that most impressed me about President Musharraf, that gives me confidence in his vision, is that the last time we met in New York City, we spent a fair amount of time talking about education reform. And the President has placed a very intriguing and very interesting woman in charge of the education system in Pakistan. She used to work in rural areas, a rural province of the country. He's elevated her to Cabinet position because she's a reformer. She understands the modern world requires an education system that trains children in basic sciences and reading and math and the history of Pakistan.

And the President laid out to me a vision, which he can share with you, about how to encourage madrasas to adopt a curriculum that will actually—will work and will provide a workforce, a trained workforce, and will give people hope.

And so our Government is committed to working with the Pakistani Government on education reform. We had a—as I understand that of the $600 million, part of the aid package last year, 100 million of those dollars have gone into education reform. The President will make the decision as to how best to use that. There's 35 million— or 34 million additional dollars this year that will go help on education reform.

I shared with him my passion about education reform here in America, and I want to applaud him for making a visionary statement about education. He knows what I know: An educated child is one much more likely to be able to realize dreams and to be a productive citizen.

So, April [April Ryan, American Urban Radio Networks], I think—let the President speak to this issue, if you don't mind.

President Musharraf. Thank you. We are involved in Pakistan, as I laid out in the 12 January speech, in a jihad—*jihadi-e-akbar*, which I call a greater jihad, which is in our teaching in Islam, a jihad against illiteracy, a jihad against poverty, backwardness, hunger. This is the jihad that we are engaged now and we have initiated.

Now, within this jihad, education forms a focal area. And since the President wants me to focus particularly on madrasa, in education we are taking three areas of education. One is the madrasa education; the second is the primary and secondary education; and the third is higher education. I would just like to focus on the madrasa education. We have formulated strategies in each one of these three areas.

Madrasas, we must understand, are basically—there are about 600,000 to 800,000 students here in madrasas. Now, the positive aspect of the madrasa—which I did lay out in my speech also; I would like to highlight for everyone to hear—is that they are a welfare. They have a welfare and humanitarian aspect to them. They feed and house the poorest of the poor children. So this is the positive aspect of their providing free board and lodge to the poorest of the poor.

Now, the weaknesses of some of the madrasas only teaching religious—giving religious education to the children has to be removed. And the children in these madrasas need to be brought into the mainstream of life. And that is what we are doing.

We have asked the madrasas to introduce four subjects, and these are science, English, Pakistan studies, and mathematics. Now, with these four subjects introduced, we have also created a board for them to take their examinations from. And once they take their examinations through these boards, it will make them eligible to transfer to any other college or university, if I want to give them a scholarship and take them there, or to get them a job anywhere, in a banking area or in the military or anywhere, instead of focusing only into the religious field.

So this is the strategy that we have adopted to get these children into the mainstream of life in Pakistan. So the basic idea is, utilize their strength, the strength of their giving free board and lodge to such a vast population of the poorest of the poor, and eradicate their weakness so that they are drawn into the mainstream of life in Pakistan. This is the strategy we are following.

. . .

Source: Public Papers of the Presidents of the United States: George W. Bush, 2002, Book 1. Washington, D.C.: Government Printing Office, 2003, 220–226.

ANALYSIS

Dating back to the days of the Soviet occupation of Afghanistan, the security situation in that country remained intertwined with that of Pakistan's. Pakistan had helped the United States funnel weapons and men to the mujahedeen, and Pakistan had helped support the Taliban's rise to power. The madrasas in Pakistan, which were often funded by wealthy Saudi proponents of the conservative Wahabi sect of Islam, had helped fuel the Taliban and at times posed internal security problems in Pakistan. In pledging his support to radically overhaul his country's education system, President Musharraf indicated a complete reversal of his country's prior policies. Still, his country continued to support other insurgent groups in Kashmir, and Pakistan's internal security forces continued to assist the Taliban. Thus, by 2002, Pakistan was already seen as an inconsistent partner for the U.S. war effort in Afghanistan.

- **Document 43: UN Security Council Resolution 1401**
- **When:** March 28, 2002
- **Where:** New York, New York
- **Significance:** This UN Security Council resolution authorized the creation of the new UN Assistance Mission in Afghanistan to assist in the political development of the country.

DOCUMENT

Resolution 1401 (2002)
Adopted by the Security Council at its 4501st meeting, on 28 March 2002
The Security Council,
Reaffirming its previous resolutions on Afghanistan, in particular its resolutions 1378 (2001) of 14 November 2001, 1383 (2001) of 6 December 2001, and 1386 (2001) of 20 December 2001,
Recalling all relevant General Assembly resolutions, in particular resolution 56/220 (2001) of 21 December 2001,

Stressing the inalienable right of the Afghan people themselves freely to determine their own political future,

Reaffirming its strong commitment to the sovereignty, independence, territorial integrity and national unity of Afghanistan,

Reiterating its endorsement of the Agreement on provisional arrangements in Afghanistan pending the re-establishment of permanent government institutions, signed in Bonn on 5 December 2001 (S/2001/1154) (the Bonn Agreement), in particular its annex 2 regarding the role of the United Nations during the interim period,

Welcoming the establishment on 22 December 2001 of the Afghan interim authority and looking forward to the evolution of the process set out in the Bonn Agreement,

Stressing the vital importance of combating the cultivation and trafficking of illicit drugs and of eliminating the threat of landmines, as well as of curbing the illicit flow of small arms,

Having considered the report of the Secretary-General of 18 March 2002 (S/2002/278),

Encouraging donor countries that pledged financial aid at the Tokyo Conference on reconstruction assistance to Afghanistan to fulfill their commitments as soon as possible,

Commending the United Nations Special Mission in Afghanistan (UNSMA) for the determination shown in the implementation of its mandate in particularly difficult circumstances,

1. *Endorses* the establishment, for an initial period of 12 months from the date of adoption of this resolution, of a United Nations Assistance Mission in Afghanistan (UNAMA), with the mandate and structure laid out in the report of the Secretary-General of 18 March 2002 (S/2002/278);

2. *Reaffirms* its strong support for the Special Representative of the Secretary-General and endorses his full authority, in accordance with its relevant resolutions, over the planning and conduct of all United Nations activities in Afghanistan;

3. *Stresses* that the provision of focused recovery and reconstruction assistance can greatly assist in the implementation of the Bonn Agreement and, to this end, urges bilateral and multilateral donors, in particular through the Afghanistan Support Group and the Implementation Group, to coordinate very closely with the Special Representative of the Secretary-General, the Afghan Interim Administration and its successors;

4. *Stresses also*, in the context of paragraph 3 above, that while humanitarian assistance should be provided wherever there is a need, recovery or reconstruction assistance ought to be provided, through the Afghan Interim Administration and its

---

DID YOU KNOW?

The Economy of Afghanistan

Afghanistan has traditionally been a poor and underdeveloped country, and the four decades of conflict have certainly inhibited the development of a fully functioning economy. Throughout its history, Afghanistan has mostly been an agricultural economy, with the growth of fruits and grains and the raising of livestock bringing the most profit. In certain regions, forestry is also a major source of income. In recent decades, Afghans have increasingly grown poppy plants, which can be processed into opium, heroin, and other narcotics. The growth of poppies became a significant issue with the Taliban, who quietly encouraged its growth, and the new Afghan government continues to struggle with poppy growth. Afghanistan's mineral resources remain underdeveloped, and attempts to facilitate the extraction and movement of oil and natural gas have been inhibited by the lack of security. The Afghan economy fared well after 2001, but this was due to the large amount of Western aid supporting the economy. Unless the insurgency against the Kabul government is permanently suppressed, Afghanistan is likely to remain a poor nation.

successors, and implemented effectively, where local authorities contribute to the maintenance of a secure environment and demonstrate respect for human rights;

5. *Calls upon* all Afghan parties to cooperate with UNAMA in the implementation of its mandate and to ensure the security and freedom of movement of its staff throughout the country;

6. *Requests* the International Security Assistance Force, in implementing its mandate in accordance with resolution 1386 (2001), to continue to work in close consultation with the Secretary-General and his Special Representative;

7. *Requests* the Secretary-General to report to the Council every four months on the implementation of this resolution;

8. *Decides* to remain actively seized of the matter.

Source: United Nations. Available online at http://www.un.org/en/ga/search/view_doc.asp?symbol=S/RES/1401(2002).

ANALYSIS

Since 1993, the United Nations had maintained a Special Mission to Afghanistan that sought to facilitate reconstruction and reconciliation, but this group had little effect on the Afghan Civil War. This new resolution replaced the Special Mission with the Assistance Mission in Afghanistan that sought to facilitate the orderly transition and development of the Afghan government into one that could effectively govern the entire nation. The Assistance Mission also oversees all other UN activities in Afghanistan that cover human rights and aid missions. As of mid-2018, the Assistance Mission continues to operate in Afghanistan.

- **Document 44: Prague Summit Declaration**
- **When:** November 21, 2002
- **Where:** Prague, Czech Republic
- **Significance:** At the meeting of the heads of the NATO countries, the Alliance committed to the creation of the NATO Response Force on the basis of lessons learned in Afghanistan and to allow the Alliance to respond to future threats.

DOCUMENT

Prague Summit Declaration
issued by the Heads of State and Government participating in the meeting of the North Atlantic Council in Prague, Czech Republic

1. We, the Heads of State and Government of the member countries of the North Atlantic Alliance, met today to enlarge our Alliance and further

strengthen NATO to meet the grave new threats and profound security challenges of the 21st century. Bound by our common vision embodied in the Washington Treaty, we commit ourselves to transforming NATO with new members, new capabilities and new relationships with our partners. We are steadfast in our commitment to the transatlantic link; to NATO's fundamental security tasks including collective defence; to our shared democratic values; and to the United Nations Charter.

2. Today, we have decided to invite Bulgaria, Estonia, Latvia, Lithuania, Romania, Slovakia and Slovenia to begin accession talks to join our Alliance. We congratulate them on this historic occasion, which so fittingly takes place in Prague. The accession of these new members will strengthen security for all in the Euro-Atlantic area, and help achieve our common goal of a Europe whole and free, united in peace and by common values. NATO's door will remain open to European democracies willing and able to assume the responsibilities and obligations of membership, in accordance with Article 10 of the Washington Treaty.

3. Recalling the tragic events of 11 September 2001 and our subsequent decision to invoke Article 5 of the Washington Treaty, we have approved a comprehensive package of measures, based on NATO's Strategic Concept, to strengthen our ability to meet the challenges to the security of our forces, populations and territory, from wherever they may come. Today's decisions will provide for balanced and effective capabilities within the Alliance so that NATO can better carry out the full range of its missions and respond collectively to those challenges, including the threat posed by terrorism and by the proliferation of weapons of mass destruction and their means of delivery.

4. We underscore that our efforts to transform and adapt NATO should not be perceived as a threat by any country or organisation, but rather as a demonstration of our determination to protect our populations, territory and forces from any armed attack, including terrorist attack, directed from abroad. We are determined to deter, disrupt, defend and protect against any attacks on us, in accordance with the Washington Treaty and the Charter of the United Nations. In order to carry out the full range of its missions, NATO must be able to field forces that can move quickly to wherever they are needed, upon decision by the North Atlantic Council, to sustain operations over distance and time, including in an environment where they might be faced with nuclear, biological and chemical threats, and to achieve their objectives. Effective military forces, an essential part of our overall political strategy, are vital to safeguard the freedom and security of our populations and to contribute to peace and security in the Euro-Atlantic region. We have therefore decided to:

    a. Create a NATO Response Force (NRF) consisting of a technologically advanced, flexible, deployable, interoperable and sustainable force including land, sea, and air elements ready to move quickly to wherever needed, as decided by the Council. The NRF will also be a catalyst for focusing and promoting improvements in the Alliance's military capabilities. We gave directions for the development of a comprehensive concept for such a force, which will have its initial operational capability as soon as possible, but not later than October 2004 and its full operational capability not later than October 2006, and for a report to Defence Ministers in Spring 2003. The NRF and the related work of the EU Headline Goal should be mutually reinforcing while respecting the autonomy of both organisations.

b. Streamline NATO's military command arrangements. We have approved the Defence Ministers' report providing the outline of a leaner, more efficient, effective and deployable command structure, with a view to meeting the operational requirements for the full range of Alliance missions. It is based on the agreed Minimum Military Requirements document for the Alliance's command arrangements. The structure will enhance the transatlantic link, result in a significant reduction in headquarters and Combined Air Operations Centres, and promote the transformation of our military capabilities. There will be two strategic commands, one operational, and one functional. The strategic command for Operations, headquartered in Europe (Belgium), will be supported by two Joint Force Commands able to generate a land-based Combined Joint Task Force (CJTF) headquarters and a robust but more limited standing joint headquarters from which a sea-based CJTF headquarters capability can be drawn. There will also be land, sea and air components. The strategic command for Transformation, headquartered in the United States, and with a presence in Europe, will be responsible for the continuing transformation of military capabilities and for the promotion of interoperability of Alliance forces, in cooperation with the Allied Command Operations as appropriate. We have instructed the Council and Defence Planning Committee, taking into account the work of the NATO Military Authorities and objective military criteria, to finalise the details of the structure, including geographic locations of command structure headquarters and other elements, so that final decisions are taken by Defence Ministers in June 2003.

c. Approve the Prague Capabilities Commitment (PCC) as part of the continuing Alliance effort to improve and develop new military capabilities for modern warfare in a high threat environment. Individual Allies have made firm and specific political commitments to improve their capabilities in the areas of chemical, biological, radiological, and nuclear defence; intelligence, surveillance, and target acquisition; air-to-ground surveillance; command, control and communications; combat effectiveness, including precision guided munitions and suppression of enemy air defences; strategic air and sea lift; air-to-air refuelling; and deployable combat support and combat service support units. Our efforts to improve capabilities through the PCC and those of the European Union to enhance European capabilities through the European Capabilities Action Plan should be mutually reinforcing, while respecting the autonomy of both organisations, and in a spirit of openness.

We will implement all aspects of our Prague Capabilities Commitment as quickly as possible. We will take the necessary steps to improve capabilities in the identified areas of continuing capability shortfalls. Such steps could include multinational efforts, role specialisation and reprioritisation, noting that in many cases additional financial resources will be required, subject as appropriate to parliamentary approval. We are committed to pursuing vigorously capability improvements. We have directed the Council in Permanent Session to report on implementation to Defence Ministers.

d. Endorse the agreed military concept for defence against terrorism. The concept is part of a package of measures to strengthen NATO's capabilities in this area, which also includes improved intelligence sharing and crisis response arrangements.

Terrorism, which we categorically reject and condemn in all its forms and manifestations, poses a grave and growing threat to Alliance populations, forces and territory, as well as to international security. We are determined to combat this scourge for as long as necessary. To combat terrorism effectively, our response must be multi-faceted and comprehensive.

We are committed, in cooperation with our partners, to fully implement the Civil Emergency Planning (CEP) Action Plan for the improvement of civil preparedness against possible attacks against the civilian population with chemical, biological or radiological (CBR) agents. We will enhance our ability to provide support, when requested, to help national authorities to deal with the consequences of terrorist attacks, including attacks with CBRN against critical infrastructure, as foreseen in the CEP Action Plan.

. . .

We reaffirm that disarmament, arms control and non-proliferation make an essential contribution to preventing the spread and use of WMD and their means of delivery. We stress the importance of abiding by and strengthening existing multilateral non-proliferation and export control regimes and international arms control and disarmament accords.

. . .

14. NATO member countries have responded to the call of the UN Security Council to assist the Afghan government in restoring security in Kabul and its surroundings. Their forces constitute the backbone of the International Security Assistance Force (ISAF) in Afghanistan. We commend the United Kingdom and Turkey for their successive contributions as ISAF lead nations, and welcome the willingness of Germany and the Netherlands jointly to succeed them. NATO has agreed to provide support in selected areas for the next ISAF lead nations, showing our continued commitment. However, the responsibility for providing security and law and order throughout Afghanistan resides with the Afghans themselves.

. . .

Source: NATO. Available online at http://www.nato.int/cps/en/natohq/official_texts_19552.htm.

ANALYSIS

NATO had been created in 1949 to create a conventional military deterrent against the Soviet Union in Western Europe. Established prior to the destruction of the first Soviet atomic weapon, NATO's founders feared an invasion by the large Red Army supported by Soviet airpower. The collapse of the Soviet Union had not completely altered NATO's orientation toward conventional conflicts, but the September 11 attacks and the war in Afghanistan finally compelled significant changes to the Alliance. At the Prague Summit, the member nations agreed to develop a NATO Response Force that could execute counterterrorism or counterproliferation missions and to make a series of additional structural reforms to better accomplish this goal. It would take four more years before NATO declared this new Response Force operational.

- **Document 45: Statement of General Tommy Franks before the Senate Armed Services Committee**
- **When:** July 9, 2003
- **Where:** Washington, D.C.
- **Significance:** General Franks, the Commander of U.S. Central Command, which has responsibility for the Middle East, discussed the status of the war in Afghanistan.

DOCUMENT

Mr. Chairman and members of the Committee, I am honored to appear before you today. Since we last met here together, much has taken place in the Central Command area of responsibility. We have removed a brutal regime in Iraq and have begun to help Iraq build its new future. Our forces have continued to help Afghanistan make strides towards independence, and have continued to help the Afghan people develop their nation while continuing to seek and destroy terrorists and their networks all across the Central region. I look forward to discussing these important subjects with you and to your questions.

Let me begin by bringing you a message from the more than 281,000 US and Coalition troops that I have been privileged to command. That message is thank you. Throughout both Operation Iraqi Freedom and Operation Enduring Freedom, our forces in the field have been blessed to serve civilian leaders who set clear military objectives and then provide our men and women in uniform the tools they need to win. On their behalf, let me thank you for all that you continue to do for the troops.

As you know, earlier this week General John Abizaid took the reins of command at CENTCOM. He is a principled leader and soldier who has been tested under fire, and I am confident about the future of CENTCOM under his leadership.

I would like to begin today by recognizing the Coalition nations whose contributions of forces, equipment, and economic support have signaled a worldwide commitment to eradicate terrorism. Over the past twelve months, the Coalition has been steadfast. Today there are 63 nations represented at Central Command's Tampa headquarters.

We have built a force in the CENTCOM Area of Responsibility (AOR) to help achieve our objectives in Operation Iraqi Freedom and Operation Enduring Freedom—to deny terrorists the use of weapons of mass destruction (WMD), and to bring terrorists to justice and dismantle their terrorist networks. We have also established a more visible and viable presence in the Horn of Africa (HOA) in order to combat terrorism and promote stability. Work in the Central Region is underway, but as I will discuss in the sections ahead, the environment within the region remains challenging. Securing US interests and ensuring regional stability will involve risks and will require continuing commitment of resources.

. . .

OPERATION ENDURING FREEDOM—LESSONS LEARNED

In Afghanistan, Coalition forces continue to deny anti-coalition elements sanctuary while disrupting their ability to plan, target, rehearse and execute operations. This is accomplished through active combat patrolling from secure fire bases and forward operating bases (FOB) in order to promote stability, enhance the legitimacy of the Interim Transitional Government of Afghanistan (ITGA), and prevent the re-emergence of terrorism.

During OEF, we saw a number of functional areas and capabilities that reached new levels of performance. In some areas, improvements were made prior to Operation Iraqi Freedom. For example the DoD/CIA synergy which worked well during OEF was built upon the integration of liaison officers in each of our headquarters which facilitated teamwork and paid great dividends in Iraq.

Also, we continued to leverage coalition strengths as new Coalition members were added. "The mission determines the Coalition; the Coalition does not determine the mission."

Advanced technologies employed during OEF were also critical. The command and control of air, ground, naval, and SOF from 7,000 miles away was a unique experience in warfare as our forces achieved unprecedented real time situational awareness and C2 connectivity. We learned that precision-guided munitions represent a force multiplier. Low collateral damage during both OEF and OIF was a fundamental factor in achieving our objectives. Early in OEF we saw the need for an unmanned sensor-to-shooter capability to support time-sensitive targeting (TST). The armed Predator demonstrates great potential and will be a high payoff system in the future. Blue Force Tracking and enhanced C4I systems increase lethality and decrease response time, and also represent transformational technologies. We will continue with development of Global Hawk as an unmanned, high-altitude, long loiter time, beyond line-of-sight multi-sensor UAV, and will work to incorporate laser designation and delivery of precision weaponry from that platform.

The integrated common operating picture (COP) was a very powerful tool. Tracking systems were previously Service unique. Workarounds were developed for OIF, but there is a need to develop one integrated, user-friendly, C4I architecture that captures blue and red air, ground and maritime forces.

Strategic lift and tanker aircraft availability were stretched during OEF and OIF. These forces are critical to rapid future force projection and we must enhance this vital capability in the years ahead.

Combined and joint training of our forces was also a key factor during OEF and was carried over into OIF. Our military forces are the best-prepared forces in the world and I thank the members of Congress for providing assets and funding to train these wonderful fighting men and women to give them every possible advantage.

Finally, our ability to take action in OEF was predicated on "Strategic Anchors," one of which was "Cooperative Security" relationships, which paid high dividends in basing, staging and over flight rights during recent crisis.

Regional Concerns

. . .

Afghanistan

Our efforts in Afghanistan have given the Afghan people a chance to break the chain of violence, civil war, and poverty that many have endured their entire lives. Our Coalition has made considerable progress over the last 18 months, but much remains to be done. The average Afghan now enjoys basic freedoms, a higher quality of life, and prospects for a better future. A Loya Jirga to ratify a new Constitution will be held this fall and national elections are scheduled for next summer. President Karzai's transitional government continues to develop as he works to expand its authority beyond Kabul. Security and stability are the keys to President Karzai's success. Since 1 May, our primary focus has shifted to stability operations. A stable and secure environment enables reconstruction. U.S. Civil-Military Operations forces have completed more than 150 projects and nearly 300 more are underway. To date, these projects have improved drinking water, medical care, transportation, communications, irrigation, and agriculture throughout the country. To further our reconstruction efforts and to help foster stability, Provincial Reconstruction Teams (PRT) are working in Bamian, Konduz, and Gardez. A fourth U.K. led team will soon deploy to Mazar-e-Sharif, and other PRTs are being planned for future deployments to additional provinces.

A critical step toward stability in Afghanistan is building the Afghanistan National Army (ANA). The U.S. is leading this effort, supported by five Coalition partners. To date, three brigades of professional Afghan soldiers have been fielded; we project ANA strength of approximately 8,500 soldiers by Dec 03.

. . .

South and Central Asia

Pakistan's support has been fundamental to our success in Operation ENDURING FREEDOM. President Musharraf has committed substantial national resources against terrorism to include arresting a number of Al Qaida leaders, freezing the financial accounts of known terrorists and banning fundraising to support Kashmiri militancy. He has pursued these actions despite ongoing tensions with India and significant domestic pressure, and he continues on a path toward democracy and sustained economic development. The US has expressed gratitude and solidified his political position by lifting sanctions and granting economic assistance.

CENTCOM will continue to support our mil-to-mil relationship and build closer security cooperation with Pakistan.

The Central Asian States remain dedicated partners in the Global War on Terrorism. Each country declared its support for the US immediately after the attacks of 9/11. All offered to host U.S. personnel and equipment. Bases established in the Central Asian States have been critical to the success of our operations in Afghanistan. The defeat of the Taliban and the removal of Al Qaida from Afghanistan have enabled the Central Asian States to refocus their attention on internal development. We will continue working with our Central Asian partners to prevent the resurgence of terrorism, and the Department of State and the Bureau of Customs and Border Protection will continue to improve their capacity to secure their borders against the flow of illegal narcotics.

. . .

Terrorism and Counterterrorism

Over the past year, the Global War on Terrorism has been marked by major achievements. Multiple terrorist operations sponsored by al-Qaida and affiliated extremists have been disrupted; and many terrorists, including high-ranking operational planners, have been captured. Al-Qaida has proven unable to reestablish the extensive training infrastructure it had earlier instituted in Afghanistan. The dispersal of its leaders and cadre from Afghanistan continues to impede al-Qaida's ability to accomplish timely and secure communications exchanges.

Nevertheless, al-Qaida has responded to our counter-terrorism initiatives; in this context, several lesser-known personalities have emerged and this has translated into strikes such as the May 2003 bombings of multiple housing complexes in Riyadh. So far, these attacks have focused on "soft" targets; however, al-Qaida retains an interest in striking larger, more spectacular targets.

Counterterrorism operations against al-Qaida, U.S. victories in Iraq and Afghanistan, and the persistent conflict between Israel and the Palestinians have generated pressure throughout the USCENTCOM AOR. Jihadist groups and disgruntled individuals constitute another important source of potential terrorist threats. Given this setting, we are constantly working to identify vulnerabilities and refine our force protection measures.

Security Cooperation Overview

Our success in gaining basing, staging and over-flight rights for ENDURING FREEDOM and IRAQI FREEDOM and our influence in the region are directly related to an active security cooperation program.

USCENTCOM's program builds relationships that promote U.S. interests, build allied and friendly nations' military capabilities, and provide U.S. forces with access and en route infrastructure. Prosecution of the GWOT requires continued fiscal and political investment in these vital programs. I would like to highlight a few dividends of our approach.

The FY03 supplemental appropriation of $908M in FMF is currently enabling the training of a professional Afghan National Army and allowing Pakistan to restore its military forces. Additionally, longstanding partners such as Jordan are increasing their interoperability through FMF-funded purchases. Continued investment in security assistance allows USCENTCOM to improve the capabilities of friendly nations by enabling them to provide for their own security.

International Military Education and Training (IMET) remains a low-cost, high-pay off investment that helps shape the security environment. Courses offered under IMET provide military members of regional states an opportunity to attend courses in U.S. military institutions such as Command and Staff Colleges and Senior Service Schools. IMET participation by students from the Central Region supports Congressionally-mandated initiatives: providing exposure to the U.S. concepts of military professionalism, respect for human rights, and subordination to civilian authority. The Counter Terrorism Fellowship, a new DoD appropriation, enables us to provide flexible course offerings to several nations who are key partners in the GWOT.

Conclusion

The Global War on Terrorism is underway. The precision, determination, and expertise of our military forces and our Coalition partners brought about the liberation of Afghanistan and Iraq in lightning speed with minimum bloodshed. However, these two nations have only taken only the first steps toward freedom, and United States and our Coalition partners must be there to support the whole journey.

While we have accomplished much, the potential for terrorist acts and other setbacks remains very real. Afghanistan has a new government, a new army, and with Coalition support the nation is making great strides towards long term stability. In Iraq, Saddam Hussein's regime was destroyed and regime supporters are being rooted out. Our focus has changed from military destruction of a regime to providing security and humanitarian assistance to the Iraqi people, while helping to establish a representative form of Government. Decisive combat operations have been completed, but much work remains.

. . .

Source: Air University. Available online at http://www.au.af.mil/au/awc/awcgate/congress/franks_09july03.pdf.

ANALYSIS

In his opening statement to his testimony, General Franks echoed Secretary Rumsfeld's arguments at the National Defense University (Document 41) that suggested that the combination of better intelligence gathering and dissemination, unmanned aircraft, and special operations forces represented the future of the American military.

By the time of this statement, as General Franks noted, the United States had largely shifted its focus in Afghanistan toward stability operations that would maintain security so that the reconstruction of the country could continue free of interference. He also described how Afghanistan was one of many military fronts within the U.S. Central Command now that the United States had occupied Iraq and become involved in counterterrorism campaigns in northern Africa.

- **Document 46: UN Security Council Resolution 1510**
- **When:** October 13, 2003
- **Where:** New York, New York
- **Significance:** This UN Security Council resolution removed the restrictions on the ISAF so that it could operate in areas beyond Kabul.

DOCUMENT

Adopted by the Security Council at its 4840th meeting,
on 13 October 2003
The Security Council,

Reaffirming its previous resolutions on Afghanistan, in particular its resolutions 1386 (2001) of 20 December 2001, 1413 (2002) of 23 May 2002 and 1444 (2002) of 27 November 2002,

Reaffirming also its strong commitment to the sovereignty, independence, territorial integrity and national unity of Afghanistan,

Reaffirming also its resolutions 1368 (2001) of 12 September 2001 and 1373 (2001) of 28 September 2001 and reiterating its support for international efforts to root out terrorism in accordance with the Charter of the United Nations,

Recognizing that the responsibility for providing security and law and order throughout the country resides with the Afghans themselves and welcoming the continuing cooperation of the Afghan Transitional Authority with the International Security Assistance Force,

Reaffirming the importance of the Bonn Agreement and recalling in particular its annex 1 which, inter alia, provides for the progressive expansion of the International Security Assistance Force to other urban centres and other areas beyond Kabul,

Stressing also the importance of extending central government authority to all parts of Afghanistan, of comprehensive disarmament, demobilization and reintegration of all armed factions, and of security sector reform including reconstitution of the new Afghan National Army and Police,

Recognizing the constraints upon the full implementation of the Bonn Agreement resulting from concerns about the security situation in parts of Afghanistan,

Noting the letter dated 10 October 2003 from the Minister for Foreign Affairs of Afghanistan (S/2003/986, annex) requesting the assistance of the International Security Assistance Force outside Kabul,

Noting the letter dated 6 October 2003 from the Secretary-General of the North Atlantic Treaty Organization (NATO) to the Secretary-General (S/2003/970) regarding a possible expansion of the mission of the International Security Assistance Force,

Determining that the situation in Afghanistan still constitutes a threat to international peace and security,

Determined to ensure the full implementation of the mandate of the International Security Assistance Force, in consultation with the Afghan Transitional Authority and its successors,

Acting for these reasons under Chapter VII of the Charter of the United Nations,

1. *Authorizes* expansion of the mandate of the International Security Assistance Force to allow it, as resources permit, to support the Afghan Transitional Authority and its successors in the maintenance of security in areas of Afghanistan outside of Kabul and its environs, so that the Afghan Authorities as well as the personnel of the United Nations and other international civilian personnel engaged, in particular, in reconstruction and humanitarian efforts, can operate in a secure environment, and to provide security assistance for the performance of other tasks in support of the Bonn Agreement;

2. *Calls upon* the International Security Assistance Force to continue to work in close consultation with the Afghan Transitional Authority and its successors and the Special Representative of the Secretary-General as well as with the Operation Enduring Freedom Coalition in the implementation of the force mandate, and to report to the Security Council on the implementation of the measures set out in paragraph 1;

3. *Decides also* to extend the authorization of the International Security Assistance Force, as defined in resolution 1386 (2001) and this resolution, for a period of twelve months;

4. *Authorizes* the Member States participating in the International Security Assistance Force to take all necessary measures to fulfil its mandate;

5. *Requests* the leadership of the International Security Assistance Force to provide quarterly reports on the implementation of its mandate to the Security Council through the Secretary-General;

6. *Decides* to remain actively seized of the matter.

Source: United Nations. Available online at http://www.un.org/en/ga/search/view_doc.asp?symbol=S/RES/1510(2003).

ANALYSIS

Since the creation of ISAF in late 2001, it had remained limited to providing security in and around the capital of Kabul as delineated in UN Security Council Resolution 1386 (Document 37). NATO had taken command of ISAF in August 2003, and this resolution finally allowed those forces to operate throughout the entire country. This allowed ISAF to become more involved in the ongoing counterinsurgency operations as well as training the Afghan National Army and assisting both counternarcotics and humanitarian operations.

3

DOCUMENTS FROM THE RETURN OF THE TALIBAN AND COUNTERINSURGENCY, 2003–2009

- **Document 47: Lieutenant General David Barno Oral History**
- **When:** May 2006
- **Where:** Washington, D.C.
- **Significance:** From October 2003 to 2005, Major General Barno served as the Commander, Military Operations, Afghanistan, and was the senior American military officer in country. He later recounted his experiences to the U.S. Army's Center of Military History.

DOCUMENT

DR. HUGHES: There must have been different challenges in dealing with al Qaeda, Taliban, the warlords. Could you elaborate on what the different challenges were?

LT. GEN. BARNO: Well, I think one of the things that we did is we assessed—we, with our six people initially, and then about twenty-five, thirty, of us—assessed the overall environment that we were operating in. We decided very early on that this wasn't simply a counterterrorist environment. This was really a classic counterinsurgency campaign. We began to build the structural support to execute a classic counterinsurgency campaign. We had no U.S. military doctrine whatsoever at that point in time by which to guide us. In fact, as I was searching about in my own memory for things I knew about counterinsurgency, I actually took to Afghanistan three West Point textbooks that I had as a cadet, dated 1974, Department of History, "Counter-Revolutionary Warfare," and they were up on my bookshelf in the embassy in Kabul, because we really had nothing in the way of doctrine. None of us really had much of any training on the counterinsurgency business, so we were kind of scraping on how to think about this. I had, fortunately, a number of British officers there during my time, including my J-5 [staff officer for plans], who had had quite a bit of counterinsurgency experience of their own. Between us, we were able to think through what were some of the basic premises that we needed to put in place to execute a counterinsurgency campaign in Afghanistan. Among those—and this was the strategy we moved to in November–December '03, January '04, across the country—we laid out what

DID YOU KNOW?

Counterinsurgency

Counterinsurgency is a specific type of warfare designed to neutralize insurgencies, which are rebellions against the recognized legitimate authority of a territory or nation. Insurgencies have occurred throughout human history, but counterinsurgency as a distinct model evolved in the colonial era when Europe and the United States maintained colonies in overseas territories. Methods of counterinsurgency, especially those advocated by French officer David Galula on the basis of his experience in Algeria in the 1950s, involve a mix of improving the governance and living conditions of the rebelling populations while simultaneously neutralizing and destroying insurgent groups using military methods. The U.S. Marines developed counterinsurgency doctrine prior to World War II, but this experience largely dissipated during the Cold War. During the Vietnam War, the United States struggled with suppressing the insurgency in South Vietnam, but the continued competition with the Soviet Union meant that the U.S. military never truly integrated the lessons learned from that war.

we called the "Five Pillar" campaign strategy for our counterinsurgency in Afghanistan with the people of Afghanistan as the center of gravity of that effort, ensuring that how they decided ultimately would determine the outcome of that campaign, which is a pretty typical counterinsurgency outlook . . . trying to attain unity of effort in the interagency and international community in Afghanistan—not unity of command and not ownership or leadership of that effort, but just a unity of effort that moves all the players down the field and in the same direction, playing the same sport, as I used to say, but with different jerseys on.

We had basically five pillars of our effort, which was the counterterrorism, deny sanctuary, which was what had been the primary focus of effort until that point in time: to continue to put pressure on the enemy to keep offensive pressure on him. To build the Afghan security forces was the second pillar, which was the Afghan National Army, Afghan National Police, which was a program at about the sixty-five hundred mark for the army and probably a bit higher than that for the police, but it was a dysfunctional program on the police side. The third pillar was really to establish and create area ownership, which was a change in how our military units actually operated in Afghanistan. Prior to the fall of '03, units typically would operate out of bases, enclaves, small military locations—fortresses to a degree—where they would gather intelligence, plan and prepare operations, and then go up to some distant location, typically for two weeks, and conduct a main operation like a [Operation] Mountain Lion, whatever it might be to hunt down insurgents, and exploit intelligence they had gathered. Then they would return back to their base and do maintenance, debrief, plan for another operation, gather more intelligence, then go perhaps to a completely different province for another couple-week operation, kind of a "raid" strategy, if you will. We changed that to a different structure across the country, particularly in the south and the east, where we had most of our forces. Our units actually were assigned territory that they owned for their entire tour in Afghanistan. So if you were a battalion commander, you might have an area the size of Vermont or Rhode Island that would be your area of operation, but it was yours for your whole tour. You got to know the leaders, the mullahs, the key provincial officials; and your companies or platoons typically got areas they were assigned, became expert at, and worked closely with the key leadership in those areas. Again, basic counterinsurgency strategy, where units had territory for the first time since we'd been in Afghanistan, and they stayed with these areas for the whole time there. So that was a very important part of what we were trying to do.

We also worked on looking at how we could engage regional states [the fifth pillar]. That was part of my charter, particularly with the border of Pakistan. My area of operations assigned to me by General Abizaid had parts of four different countries in it: all of Afghanistan; all of Pakistan, except for Jammu and Kashmir; and the southern portions of Tajikistan; and Uzbekistan. So I had four countries that I interacted with military and senior security leadership on, particularly with Pakistan, where I could typically travel once, twice a month, meet with their senior military, senior intelligence, sometimes foreign ministry officials, to be able to work on maintaining pressure on the Pakistani side of the border and being able to minimize any border conflicts between friendly forces on both sides of the border as well. As part of that, we also hosted a, about every two months, tripartite conference. That was a meeting of the senior security leadership of Afghanistan, typically represented by their national security adviser; Pakistan, usually with their director general of military operations; and then me as the U.S. leg of that. We would rotate that typically between Kabul, Islamabad, and Bagram every two months to talk about various issues between the countries and the war and the strategic security relationships there. So, that was important.

And then the fourth pillar there in between, I didn't mention, which was essentially to build good governance, extend the reach of the Afghan government out into the provinces, which we did primarily through our provincial reconstruction teams out there. The base of all this is information operations, trying to win a war of ideas and continue to get the messages out through the Afghan government to their people to assist them in building for the future. So, that was a broad laydown of what the strategy was that we moved to, which was much more comprehensive and had a lot less kinetic and a lot less traditional military components than what we were doing prior to that time as we evolved into a new phase in Afghanistan in late '03.

. . .

DR. HUGHES: Okay. You mentioned that you gave units geographical responsibility. That had to change their tactical deployment—obviously, their entire way of operating. Would you elaborate on that?

LT. GEN. BARNO: Well, I think the best shorthand model I've seen is probably the Marine three-block war model, where you've got the description of an organizational company or platoon, whether it be doing kinetic force-on-force fighting in the morning, be doing peacekeeping operations in the afternoon, and you could be doing relief handout and supply operations and taking care of babies and sick people in the evening. That was not uncommon for our units out there as we shifted to a more counterinsurgency-based model.

DR. HUGHES: As opposed to counterterrorism.

LT. GEN. BARNO: Correct. As opposed to primarily focusing on kinetic operations to kill and capture bad guys wherever you find them. Now, they still did that, but they also did: "Okay, let's go to this village, do an assessment, and find out what the people's needs are, see what we can do." We had this Commander's Emergency Response Program, CERP, that was an incredibly powerful weapon in the toolbox to be able to deliver immediate aid, immediate dollars, through the Afghan government, typically local governments, to be able to trade quick-impact projects on the ground: build wells, repair schools, buy schoolbooks, in some cases buy tractors or seed—a wide variety of things, only limited by the imagination of the commanders in the field. But again, this was new territory for them to be surfing on. They did a tremendous job, and I give huge credit to our young commanders and young noncommissioned officers and platoon leaders out there for innovation and adaptability. A good friend of mine was one of the battalion commanders down at the border of Pakistan. He had been one of my company commanders when I was a battalion commander. I went down to visit him a number of times, and one of the things I asked him in early '04 was: "Mike, we just changed your mission here from counterterrorism, which it was when you first got here last summer, to now a broad-based counterinsurgency approach. How did you get your platoon leaders and company commanders and first sergeants and platoon sergeants to be able to shift gears here midstream and go from one to the other?" He goes, "Easy, sir: booksamillion.com."

He had actually ordered books on the Internet from Afghanistan on counterinsurgency warfare, had them shipped into his units, had his people read them as they were in the middle of this fight. So, it was, again, tuning the car while you're going down the highway, great adaptability by our young soldiers. It's also pointing out the fact that we were pretty bankrupt in our doctrinal process as we went into this war, and the units just responded magnificently well, and my feedback was that they very much appreciated having the flexibility to use a broader "hearts and minds" counterinsurgency strategy as opposed to a more narrow focus, and they loved the areas of responsibility they were given, because then they became expert in those areas, and they were able to hand those areas off to other units who would come into the same area. Barring tactical emergencies, we would not move them around.

. . .

DR. HUGHES: Okay. In the interview you gave with the press just after you got back, you indicated that there were some advantages in having a light footprint—that is, fewer visible soldiers in country. Would you please elaborate on your thoughts there?

LT. GEN. BARNO: Well, it was a fact-of-life issue as well, as we had twenty thousand or less troops there covering a huge amount of territory, so we had to operate in a way that leveraged Afghan forces as much as possible, and also recognize the fact that we didn't have an immense number of forces to cover every bit of the territory. So, we operated at a fairly low profile where, I think, in most cases, we were able to leverage our airpower very effectively. One of the things I've mentioned in other interviews is that we had the ability to operate throughout the country, essentially at platoon level, because we had pretty widespread knowledge that twenty minutes away from any contact there would be airpower overhead. I can get A–10s. I can get F–16s out there. I can get attack helicopters out there. So, our forces could operate fairly small-sized units on remote patrols for multiple days and have the confidence that if they got into a fight, they'd have very quick reactions from reinforcing forces and from tactical airpower, and they'd be able to deliver some ordnance on the target.

So, what that portrayed to the Afghans, though, is that you didn't have battalions of U.S. troops typically tromping around. You had small units coming out. They were operating and getting face to face with the Afghans; they were interacting with the local people; they were having tea with the mullahs; they were meeting with the elders; and we had the PRTs—which, again, were a very small footprint. PRTs were eighty to one hundred soldiers, mostly all U.S. military or Coalition military; always an Afghan Ministry of Interior official as part of the PRT; always a Department of State official; typically a USAID [United States Agency for International Development] official there; sometimes a U.S. agricultural [United States Department of Agriculture] official. But operating in a provincial capital, which is typically quite a small place, a long ways from any other American military power, unless it was really tough country; that projected a lot of confidence out there again that we could reinforce quickly. And so we talked "light footprint," which made in some ways virtue of necessity.

I've also been asked, "Did you have enough troops? Could you have used more troops? etc." I was very comfortable with the troops I got, and I asked for troops when I needed them. I asked for additional troops for the '04 election. I got a battalion from the 82d [Airborne Division] for a month and a half, which was just right at the right place at the right time. I got a marine expeditionary unit in at the spring of '04 for about seven or eight weeks. They ran some good disruptive operations up in Oruzgan Province. So, I had a lot of flexibility. General Abizaid responded very well to requests when I made a good case for them to bring in additional forces for specific operations for specific reasons. So, I felt very comfortable having that many forces in country and being able to accomplish the mission in the environment we had there—a very different environment, obviously, than Iraq, radically different. I think as an order of magnitude the number of attacks, typically when I was there, was about one-tenth the number of attacks I recall seeing in Iraq on a given day in the same period of time. I don't know if that's true or different or the same or anything else today, but when I was there, that was about the order of magnitude in terms of what we were dealing with for violence.

. . .

DR. HUGHES: Okay. What lessons should the United States and the U.S. Army learn from our experiences there? Your experiences there?

LT. GEN. BARNO: Well, I think one of our continuous challenges here is to understand the nature of the war that we're fighting in that part of the world, not just at the tactical level, but how does the strategic level of war apply in a counterinsurgency fight that reaches outside of a single country and to the region and perhaps globally, certainly, if you include al Qaeda? I don't know that we have, as an army, as a military at large, thought our way through the implications of that and how you fight, how you succeed, how you design a strategy in Afghanistan that isn't simply an Afghanistan-centric internal strategy but is a part of a global strategy—how those pieces all fit together. How does Pakistan fit into that? How do we look regionally, instead of simply at a single country? As many people have said—a few people have said, I guess, and I certainly say—this is not a war in Iraq and a war in Afghanistan. Those are parts of broader regional conflicts. They are part of a global war, and how you structure your long-term strategic approach in each one of those for a global war is not necessarily the same way you structure for a war inside a single country that hasn't got regional and global implications. So, I think that's a subtle but very important lesson yet to be learned on what we're doing and have been doing in Afghanistan. So, I think that's something we have to give some thought to.

Otherwise, I think we've had great success, and we've shown the adaptability of our units. We've been able to reinvent ourselves on the fly to do counterinsurgency operations after a long hiatus of not touching that at all and not getting exposed to it and not training our folks on it at all. We've now got a very experienced force, both from duty in Iraq and duty in Afghanistan and from thinking about different types of warfare. I still think that we've got to work our way through this strategic level and what this means, not simply the tactical level. The Army, in my view, is an area where it needs to be careful that it does not become too tactically focused, given the fact that just like with my headquarters, the operational level and strategic level weren't Army functions any longer; they are now joint functions. My headquarters was effectively an orphan headquarters. It didn't have a post, didn't have a flag, didn't have a patch, didn't have a museum, didn't have a World War II history; therefore, it didn't exist in the Army institutional hierarchy at all in any way, shape, or form. That also is true in terms of where the Army devotes its thinking about fighting. It no longer owns the headquarters and does those kinds of things. By and large, there's a risk that we're going to nosedive into only being experts at tactics, techniques, and procedures; and that's where our dollars are going, that's where an awful lot of our thinking is going, and that seems to be where a good bit of our writing is going. I have concerns about that, because I think the Army is an institution that does have enough depth to be able to talk, think, write, influence at the operational and strategic level, and to take some ownership of that once again. I think this trend is kind of the inadvertent second-order effect of the Goldwater-Nichols Act [which streamlined the military chain of command] because we don't operate at the operational headquarters level and the strategic headquarters level any more in the Army. All of a sudden, the Army is now simply train, organize, and equip as a force, and that does not leverage, in my opinion, the immense depth that the institution has on war fighting writ large, and we need to be careful about that.

Source: Koontz, Christopher, ed. *Enduring Voices: Oral Histories of the U.S. Army Experience in Afghanistan, 2003–2005*. Washington, D.C.: Center for Military History, 2008, 13–94. Available online at http://www.history.army.mil/html/books/enduring_voices/CMH_70-112-1.pdf.

ANALYSIS

General Barno's interview highlighted a number of challenges that he and the rest of the U.S. Army encountered while operating in Afghanistan. Even though most official statements by 2003 emphasized stability and counterterrorism operations as the primary missions, General Barno and his staff concluded that counterinsurgency—which, to be sure, has some overlap with both stability and counterterrorism operations—should be a core mission for his forces.

Unfortunately, for General Barno, he only had approximately 10,000 troops at his disposal when he arrived, although this force would double during his tenure. This small force, combined with a small International Security Assistance Force (ISAF) and the slowly expanding Afghan National Army, needed to protect the entire country just as the Taliban began to show signs of resurgence. General Barno does not openly bemoan the small size of his force and argues that it sometimes allowed for greater creativity, but it reflects the difficulty of operating in Afghanistan as the lion's share of attention was focused on the war in Iraq.

- **Document 48: The Constitution of Afghanistan**
- **When:** January 26, 2004
- **Where:** Kabul, Afghanistan
- **Significance:** Following a three-week deliberation by the Constitutional Loya Jirga, President Hamid Karzai ratified the new Constitution of Afghanistan on January 26, 2004.

DOCUMENT

Islamic Republic of Afghanistan
The Constitution of Afghanistan
(Ratified) January 26, 2004

The Constitution of the Islamic Republic of Afghanistan

The present Constitution of the Islamic Republic of Afghanistan was agreed upon by more than 500 delegates representing Afghan men and women from across the country at the Constitutional Loya Jirga (December 13, 2003–January 4, 2004). The Constitution was formally ratified by President Hamid Karzai at a ceremony in Kabul on January 26, 2004. The full text of the Constitution may be found below.

. . .

Preamble
In the name of Allah, the Most Beneficent, the Most Merciful
Praise be to Allah, the Cherisher and Sustainer of Worlds; and Praise and Peace be upon Mohammad,
His Last Messenger and his disciples and followers

We the people of Afghanistan:

- Believing firmly in Almighty God, relying on His divine will and adhering to the Holy religion of Islam;
- Realizing the previous injustices, miseries and innumerable disasters which have befallen our country;
- Appreciating the sacrifices, historical struggles, jihad and just resistance of all the peoples of Afghanistan, admiring the supreme position of the martyr's of the country's freedom;
- Comprehending that a united, indivisible Afghanistan belongs to all its tribes and peoples;
- Observing the United Nations Charter as well as the Universal Declaration of Human Rights;

And in order to:

- Strengthen national unity, safeguard independence, national sovereignty and territorial integrity of the country;

- Establish an order based on the peoples' will and democracy;
- Form a civil society void of oppression, atrocity, discrimination as well as violence, based on rule of law, social justice, protecting integrity and human rights, and attaining peoples' freedoms and fundamental rights;
- Strengthen political, social, economic as well as defense institutions;
- Attain a prosperous life and sound living environment for all inhabitants of this land;
- And, eventually, regain Afghanistan's appropriate place in the international family;

Have, herein, approved this constitution in accordance with the historical, cultural and social realities as well as requirements of time through our elected representatives in the Loya Jirga, dated January 3, 2004, held in the city of Kabul.

Chapter One: *State*
Article One
Afghanistan shall be an Islamic Republic, independent, unitary, and indivisible state.

Article Two
The sacred religion of Islam is the religion of the Islamic Republic of Afghanistan. Followers of other faiths shall be free within the bounds of law in the exercise and performance of their religious rituals.

Article Three
No law shall contravene the tenets and provisions of the holy religion of Islam in Afghanistan.

. . .

Article Six
The state shall be obligated to create a prosperous and progressive society based on social justice, preservation of human dignity, protection of human rights, realization of democracy, attainment of national unity as well as equality between all peoples and tribes and balance development of all areas of the country.

. . .

Chapter Two: *Fundamental Rights and Duties of Citizens*
Article Twenty-Two
Any kind of discrimination and distinction between citizens of Afghanistan shall be forbidden. The citizens of Afghanistan, man and woman, have equal rights and duties before the law.

Article Twenty-Three
Life is the gift of God as well as the natural right of human beings. No one shall be deprived of this except by legal provision.

Article Twenty-Four
Liberty is the natural right of human beings. This right has no limits unless affecting others freedoms as well as the public interest, which shall be regulated by law.

Liberty and human dignity are inviolable. The state shall respect and protect liberty as well as human dignity.

. . .

Article Thirty-Four

Freedom of expression shall be inviolable. Every Afghan shall have the right to express thoughts through speech, writing, illustrations as well as other means in accordance with provisions of this constitution. Every Afghan shall have the right, according to provisions of law, to print and publish on subjects without prior submission to state authorities. Directives related to the press, radio and television as well as publications and other mass media shall be regulated by law.

. . .

Chapter Three: *The President*
Article Sixty

The President shall be the head of state of the Islamic Republic of Afghanistan, executing his authorities in the executive, legislative and judiciary fields in accordance with the provisions of this Constitution. The President shall have two Vice-Presidents, first and second. The Presidential candidate shall declare to the nation names of both vice presidential running mates. In case of absence, resignation or death of the President, the first Vice-President shall act in accordance with the provisions of this Constitution. In the absence of the first Vice-President, the second Vice-President shall act in accordance with the provisions of this Constitution.

. . .

Chapter Five: *National Assembly*
Article Eighty-One

The National Assembly of the Islamic Republic of Afghanistan, as the highest legislative organ, shall manifest the will of its people as well as represent the entire nation.

Every member of the Assembly, when voting, shall judge according to the general interests as well as the supreme benefits of the people of Afghanistan.

Article Eighty-Two

The National Assembly consists of two houses: House of People and House of Elders.

No individual shall be a member of both houses at the same time.

. . .

Article Ninety

The National Assembly shall have the following duties:

1. Ratification, modification or abrogation of laws or legislative decrees;
2. Approval of social, cultural, economic as well as technological development programs;
3. Approval of the state budget as well as permission to obtain or grant loans;

4. Creation, modification and or abrogation of administrative units;

5. Ratification of international treaties and agreements, or abrogation of membership of Afghanistan in them;

6. Other authorities enshrined in this Constitution.

Article Ninety-One

The House of People shall have the following special authorities:

1. Decide about elucidation session from each Minister in accordance with Article Ninety-Two of this Constitution;

2. Decide on the development programs as well as the state budget;

3. Approve or reject appointments according to provisions of this Constitution.

. . .

Chapter Six: *Loya Jirga*
Article One Hundred Ten

The Loya Jirga is the highest manifestation of the will of the people of Afghanistan. The Loya Jirga consists of:

1. Members of the National Assembly;

2. Presidents of the provincial as well as district assemblies.

Ministers, Chief Justice and members of the Supreme Court as well as the attorney general shall participate in the Loya Jirga sessions without voting rights.

Article One Hundred Eleven

The Loya Jirga shall convene in the following situations:

1. To decide on issues related to independence, national sovereignty, territorial integrity as well as supreme national interests;

2. Amend provisions of this Constitution;

3. Impeach the President in accordance with the provisions of Article Sixty Nine of the Constitution.

. . .

Chapter Seven: *The Judiciary*
Article One Hundred Sixteen

The judiciary shall be an independent organ of the state of the Islamic Republic of Afghanistan. The judiciary shall be comprised of one Supreme Court, Courts of Appeal as well as Primary Courts whose organization and authority shall be regulated by law. The Supreme Court shall be the highest judicial organ, heading the judicial power of the Islamic Republic of Afghanistan.

. . .

Source: Embassy of the Islamic Republic of Afghanistan in Warsaw. Available online at http://www.afghanembassy.com.pl/afg/images/pliki/TheConstitution.pdf.

ANALYSIS

The new Constitution materialized from the process agreed upon at Bonn in 2001. The Loya Jirga, however, was very contentious and led to many heated debates. These included whether Afghanistan should have a presidential or parliamentary system and which languages the country should officially recognize in order to appease the ethnic divisions within the country. As a result, the Loya Jirga met for more than three weeks rather than the originally planned 10 days before reaching a consensus on the new Constitution. In Afghan fashion, the consensus of the document constituted passage; no formal vote was ever taken.

The Afghans chose a presidential system of government with a bicameral legislature and an independent judiciary system. The Constitution also codified a number of rights, including the freedom of speech and equality before the law. Crucially, however, the Constitution also identified Afghanistan as an Islamic republic with Article Three stating that "no law shall contravene the tenets and provisions of the holy religion of Islam in Afghanistan."

- **Document 49: Review of Matters Related to the Death of Corporal Patrick Tillman**
- **When:** March 26, 2007
- **Where:** Washington, D.C.
- **Significance:** This report concluded a multiyear investigation into the death of U.S. Army corporal Patrick Tillman that occurred in a friendly fire incident in 2004.

DOCUMENT

. . .

FOREWORD

The course of this review, in particular the central issues, was framed through a series of requests from the Army Inspector General, Members of Congress, and the family of Corporal Patrick Tillman concerning Corporal Tillman's death by friendly fire while participating in combat operations in Afghanistan on April 22, 2004.

Within 30 days thereafter, Corporal Tillman's death was investigated twice by Army officers under the provisions of Army Regulation 15-6, "Procedures for Investigating Officers and Boards of Officers." Because of unresolved concerns regarding the nature of Corporal Tillman's death and its aftermath, a third investigation was completed by general officer in January 2005. However, by letter dated April 21, 2005, Mr. [redacted], father of Corporal Tillman, raised significant issues with the results of that investigation.

By memorandum dated June 2, 2005, the Army Inspector General requested that this Office conduct an independent review of concerns expressed by Mr. [redacted].

After completing an initial assessment, we requested that the Army Criminal Investigation Command conduct a full investigation into the facts and circumstances of Corporal Tillman's death. Concurrently, we conducted a review of the three investigations noted above, the adequacy of Army notifications to the Tillman family in the weeks following his death, and the basis for the posthumous award of the Silver Star.

Several Members of Congress also questioned the series of events that led to Corporal Tillman's death, subsequent investigations, the need to establish accountability in matters concerning the death and its aftermath, and the possibility of an Army cover-up. Correspondence to this Office from Senator John McCain in July 2005 and Representative Michael M. Honda in August 2005 questioned specific findings of the investigations. Correspondence from Senator Charles Grassley, Representative Zoe Lofgren, and Representatives Honda, Ike Skelton, Christopher Shays, and Dennis Kucinich in March 2006 reiterated those concerns, requested further explanations regarding Army actions taken following Corporal Tillman's death, and asked for briefings after we completed our work.

In addition, the Senate Armed Services Committee, the House Armed Services Committee, and the Subcommittee on National Security, Emerging Threats, and International Relations (House Committee on Government Reform) requested the results of our review.

This report provides the results of our review and summarizes results of the concurrent investigation by the Army Criminal Investigation Command. The full Army Criminal Investigation Command report is being issued separately. We concur with the results of that investigation. Although some of the Army activities related to Corporal Tillman's death remain classified, this report is unclassified to promote maximum utility and avoid delays that would attend a classified issuance.

. . .

REVIEW OF MATTERS RELATED
TO THE DEATH OF
CORPORAL PATRICK TILLMAN, U.S. ARMY

I. INTRODUCTION AND SUMMARY

We initiated the review to address allegations that three sequential investigations into the "friendly fire" death of Corporal (CPL) Patrick Tillman, U.S. Army, on April 22, 2004, in Afghanistan, did not meet established investigative standards and, therefore, failed to disclose relevant facts of his death or assign requisite accountability. Additionally, our review sought to determine whether those investigations, as well as the delayed notifications to CPL Tillman's family members and the posthumous award of the Silver Star based on erroneous information, were indicative of an Army effort to conceal the circumstances of CPL Tillman's death of possible misconduct by those involved. In doing so, we focused our review on the following specific issues:

- Did responsible officials comply with applicable standards for investigating friendly fire deaths?
- Did responsible officials comply with applicable standards for notification of next of kin of CPL Tillman's death and related investigations?

- Did responsible officials comply with applicable standards for award of the Silver Star to CPL Tillman?

Apart from those issues, our initial assessment found that questions remained regarding the events that transpired during the course of the friendly fire incident itself, particularly with respect to conduct of the Service members involved. Because of its investigative capability and independence, we requested the Army Criminal Investigation Command (CID) to investigate the circumstances of CPL Tillman's death and the death of injuries to others in the incident. After conducting extensive investigative work, including restaging of the incident on-site, the Army CID found insufficient evidence to support any further action under the Uniform Code of Military Justice. We concur with that conclusion and have provided a summary of these investigative results at Appendix A to this report. The Army CID will issue its full report separately.

Our review concluded that CPL Tillman's chain of command made critical errors in reporting CPL Tillman's death and in assigning investigative jurisdiction in the days following his death, and bears ultimate responsibility for the inaccuracies, misunderstandings, and perceptions of concealment that led to our investigation. For example, CPL Tillman's chain of command failed to timely report suspected death by friendly fire. Established Army policy required notification of death by friendly fire, which was suspected the day following the incident, up through the chain of command as well as to the Army Safety Center. In turn, DoD guidance required that the Combatant Commander convene a legal investigation and authorized the cognizant Service to convene any safety investigation required by its regulations. The safety investigation required by Army regulations would have conducted by a board of trained, experienced investigators who would have collected, processed, and retained forensic evidence, and coordinated with criminal investigative authorities if warranted. Both legal and safety investigations would have been independent of CPL Tillman's immediate chain of command and, therefore, not vulnerable to accusations that command Service members were shielded from culpability.

None of CPL Tillman's superiors complied with these requirements. Instead, after clear evidence of fratricide emerged the day following the incident, CPL Tillman's battalion commander (a lieutenant colonel three levels below the Combatant Commander), with the concurrence of his regimental commander, appointed a subordinate Army captain to investigate. That investigation, completed in about 2 weeks, determined CPL Tillman's death was fratricide caused by leadership failures and tactical errors. Dissatisfied with the thoroughness of that investigation, CPL Tillman's regimental commander (a colonel) ordered his own executive officer (a lieutenant colonel) to conduct a second investigation. That investigation, building on the first, was completed in 9 days, confirmed death by friendly fire, and provided expanded findings on the contributing tactical errors. No independent investigator; that is, outside CPL Tillman's immediate chain of command, was appointed by the appropriate authority until 6 months after CPL Tillman's death. A safety investigation was initiated until nearly 6 months after the incident when most of the forensic evidence had been destroyed. Expertise available from the Army CID was not obtained until we initiated this review.

We concluded that the first two investigations, conducted by officers in CPL Tillman's battalion and regiment under Army Regulation (AR) 15-6, "Procedures for Investigating Officers and Boards of Officers," were tainted by the failure to preserve evidence, a lack of thoroughness, the failure to pursue logical investigative leads, and conclusions that were open to challenge based on the evidence provided. More significantly, neither investigator visited the site to visually reenact the incident, secure physical evidence, take photographs, or obtain accurate measurements. In addition, the first investigating officer, with advice from his legal advisor, withheld information concerning suspected fratricide from medical examiners who rained questions based on anomalies they discovered during the autopsy. As a result, the first two investigations lacked credibility and contributed to perceptions that Army officials were purposefully withholding key information concerning CPL Tillman's death.

In November 2004, because of the lingering concerns regarding CPL Tillman's death, the Acting Secretary of the Army directed that Lieutenant General (LTG) Phillip R. Kensinger, Jr., Commander, U.S. Army Special Operations Command (Airborne) (USASOC), conduct a third investigation. LTG Kensinger appointed a subordinate, Brigadier General (BG) Gary M. Jones, Commander, U.S. Army Special Forces Command (Airborne), to conduct the investigation. BG Jones' investigation was more thorough than the first two, included an on-site visit, and was pronounced legally sufficient by LTG Kensinger's Staff Judge Advocate in January 2005.

Subsequent review by the Army Inspector General raised concerns which caused BG Jones to conduct additional investigative work and file supplementary information. However, weaknesses remained. Like the first two investigators, he also failed to interview some witnesses who were part of the unit that fired on CPL Tillman's position. He did not assess accountability for failures by the chain of command (including LTG Kensinger) to comply with Army policy for reporting and investigating friendly fire incidents, to coordinate with other investigative authorities, to provide timely information concerning suspected friendly fire to CPL Tillman's next of kin, and to ensure accuracy in documentation submitted in support of the Silver Star.

Notwithstanding our conclusions with respect to these three investigations, we emphasize that all investigators established the basic facts of CPL Tillman's death—that it was caused by friendly fire, that occupants of one vehicle in CPL Tillman's platoon were responsible, and that circumstances on the ground at the time caused those occupants to misidentify friendly forces as hostile. None of the investigations suggested that CPL Tillman's death was other than accidental. Our review, as well as the investigation recently completed by the Army CID, obtained no evidence contrary to those key findings.

CPL Tillman's family members were not told of the investigations and subsequent fratricide determination until 35 days after CPL Tillman's death, despite Army regulations that require next of kin be advised of additional information concerning a Service member's death as that information becomes available. Because CPL Tillman's regimental commander desired to keep information concerning the death "close hold" until investigative results were finalized, no "supplemental reports" were issued to correct initial reports that CPL Tillman's death was caused by enemy fire.

Although LTG Kensinger knew friendly fire was suspected and under investigation before he served as the Army representative at CPL Tillman's memorial service on May 3, 2004, he decided to withhold notification from family members until all facts concerning the incident could be verified. Certain senior Army officials were aware of the friendly fire investigation in early May, but none took measures to ensure that family members were, at a minimum, advised that CPL Tillman's death was under review. We find no reasonable explanation for these failures to comply with Army regulations.

Finally, the citation and narrative justification submitted to support the Silver Star awarded to CPL Tillman contained inaccurate information—particularly with respect to descriptions that suggested CPL Tillman performed heroically in the face of, and was killed by, enemy fire. The two supporting valorous witness statements stamped "original signed" were attributed to two of CPL Tillman's platoon members, but were drafted by others and contained inaccurate information. The posthumous presentation of the Silver Star to CPL Tillman as if he had been killed by the enemy was ill-advised and contributed to continuing mistrust of Army representations to family members, especially since LTG Kensinger and other officials knew at the time that friendly fire was the likely cause of his death.

We recommend that the Acting Secretary of the Army take appropriate corrective action with respect to officials whom we identified as accountable for the regulatory violations and errors in judgment that are described in this review. Additionally, we recommend that the Acting Secretary initiate a review of the Silver Star award to ensure that it meets regulatory requirements. We note that the Army already has taken action to delay approval of posthumous valor awards until completion of pending investigations and has strengthened guidance concerning next of kin notifications.

This report sets forth our findings and conclusions based on a preponderance of the evidence.

. . .

Source: Department of Defense. Available online at http://archive.defense.gov/home/pdf/Tillman_Redacted_Web_0307.pdf.

ANALYSIS

Patrick Tillman enlisted in the U.S. Army in 2002 after a three-year career in the National Football League, where he had been regarded as one of the best strong safeties in the league and likely to receive a multimillion-dollar contract. Instead he, along with his brother Kevin, enlisted out of a sense of patriotism and duty.

Tillman's death while serving in the army's 2nd Ranger Battalion garnered much press coverage, and his high public profile likely contributed to the decision by his superiors to mask the nature of his death and mislead his next of kin. It took three years for this Inspector General investigation to conclude that Tillman had died in a friendly fire incident and to reveal the extent of the cover-up of the facts surrounding the incident.

- **Document 50: General Accountability Office Report "Afghanistan Reconstruction"**
- **When:** June 2, 2004
- **Where:** Washington, D.C.
- **Significance:** This report chronicled much waste and misuse of American aid provided to Afghanistan since late 2002.

DOCUMENT

June 2, 2004
The Honorable Richard G. Lugar
Chairman
The Honorable Joseph R. Biden
Ranking Minority Member
Committee on Foreign Relations
United States Senate
The Honorable Henry J. Hyde
Chairman
The Honorable Tom Lantos
Ranking Minority Member
Committee on International Relations
House of Representatives

. . .

Results in Brief

In fiscal years 2002–2003, the U.S. obligated $1.4 billion and spent $900 million, or more than half its obligations for nonsecurity-related assistance to Afghanistan. Of the $900 million that the U.S. government spent, over 75 percent supported short-term, humanitarian assistance, including emergency food and shelter, and over 20 percent supported longer-term reconstruction needs. USAID, the largest provider of nonsecurity-related assistance, spent about $508 million on both humanitarian and reconstruction projects. During the same period, the Department of State spent $254 million, mainly on refugee and humanitarian assistance, and the Department of Defense spent $64 million on food assistance and quick-impact projects. Most of the funding by USAID and Defense supported local projects in 31 of Afghanistan's 32 provinces, particularly in 4 of the most heavily populated. Overall, U.S. funding represented about 38 percent of the $3.7 billion disbursed by the international community for nonsecurity-related assistance to Afghanistan in fiscal years 2002–2003.

U.S. humanitarian and small-scale, quick-impact projects benefited Afghanistan in fiscal years 2002–2003, but longer-term reconstruction efforts had achieved limited results by the end of fiscal year 2003 due to delayed funding. USAID and the Departments of Agriculture and State provided humanitarian assistance, including emergency food, health care, sanitation, and shelter, which helped avert a famine and reintegrate returning refugees. In addition, to assist Afghanistan in its transition from humanitarian relief to reconstruction of its infrastructure and civil society, USAID and Defense implemented small-scale, quick-impact projects such as renovating or rebuilding schools, clinics, bridges, and irrigation canals. Further, under USAID's leadership, a number of longer-term reconstruction activities in a number of sectors achieved limited results. However, notable accomplishments include building a road from Kabul to Kandahar, establishing a democracy and governance program, and helping farmers reestablish farm production.

Although the U.S. government established coordination mechanisms for its assistance efforts in Afghanistan in fiscal years 2002–2003, it lacked a complete operational strategy; in addition, coordination of international assistance was weak. A number of mechanisms to coordinate U.S. assistance were established and, in general, U.S. officials believed that U.S. assistance was well coordinated. The United States did not have a comprehensive strategy to direct its assistance efforts until June 2003. In addition, USAID's operational strategy did not clearly articulate measurable goals or other details. U.S. officials responsible for coordinating assistance efforts also lacked financial data necessary for program oversight and coordination. Without a comprehensive strategy or adequate financial data, the ability of the U.S. government to ensure progress toward development goals and make informed resource allocation decisions was impaired. Further, international assistance was not well coordinated in 2002, and efforts by the Afghan government to improve coordination in 2003 had not succeeded.

In fiscal years 2002–2003, the postconflict environment in Afghanistan threatened progress toward U.S. policy goals, and poor security, increasing opium cultivation, and inadequate resources impeded U.S. reconstruction efforts. Afghanistan faces many of the same obstacles that other nations have faced after civil conflict, such as multiple competing parties. Throughout fiscal years 2002–2003, terrorists attacked U.S., international, and Afghan government targets, and criminal activity by warlords and clashes between rival factions increased the overall climate of insecurity. In addition, record levels of opium production and associated revenues threatened Afghanistan's stability by funding the activities of terrorists and warlords. Further, small staff size, inadequate working conditions, and the timing of funding for reconstruction impeded U.S. efforts. To increase funding and expedite progress, in September 2003, the U.S. government announced an initiative called "Accelerating Success" that would provide an additional $1.76 billion for reconstruction projects in Afghanistan in fiscal year 2004.

We are recommending that USAID revise its operational strategy for its assistance program in Afghanistan. The revised strategy should delineate measurable goals, specific time frames, resource levels, external factors that could significantly affect the achievement of goals, and a schedule for program evaluations that assess progress against the strategy's goals. To improve management and oversight of U.S. assistance to Afghanistan, we are also recommending that the Department of State produce an annual consolidated budget for all U.S. assistance to Afghanistan and report to Congress semiannually on obligations and expenditures for the assistance provided.

We provided a draft of this report to the Departments of State and Defense and to USAID. State and USAID commented that they concurred with much of the information presented on the situation in Afghanistan for the period covered by our review. They also provided additional information on more recent activities taken and progress made. USAID and the Department of Defense also provided technical comments, which we incorporated where appropriate.

In response to our recommendation that USAID revise its operational strategy for Afghanistan to include details such as measurable goals, timeframes, and required resources, USAID said that its less comprehensive "interim" strategy was appropriate given the situation in Afghanistan during the early phases of the ongoing efforts. Nonetheless, USAID said that it was committed to developing a standard strategic plan for Afghanistan during 2004, which is consistent with our recommendation. The Department of State disagreed with our finding that the United States lacks a complete and integrated assistance strategy, citing its December 15, 2003, report to Congress "Fiscal Year 2004 Strategic and Financial Plan for Reconstruction and Related Activities in Afghanistan" as meeting this need. We found that most of the strategies that were published during fiscal years 2002–2003 lacked details on funding and other resources, measurable goals, timeframes, as well as a means to measure progress. However, in the report, we cite the State Department's June 2003 Mission Performance Plan as meeting many of the requirements for a government-wide operational strategy. While the fiscal year 2004 plan cited by the State Department in its comments includes more details on the U.S. assistance budget for Afghanistan, it lacks operational details including time frames, measurable goals, and a means to measure progress towards those goals.

In response to our recommendation that State produce an annual consolidated budget for all U.S. assistance to Afghanistan and report to Congress semiannually on obligations and expenditures, State emphasized that policy makers are provided with information on U.S. obligations weekly and that there is close interagency collaboration on all funding issues. We disagree. As we reported, complete and readily accessible obligation and expenditure data was not available and consequently, it is difficult to determine the extent to which U.S. assistance dollars are being used to achieve measurable results on the ground in Afghanistan. Specifically, we found that (1) government-wide expenditure data on U.S. assistance to Afghanistan is not collected, (2) obligation data are collected on an ad hoc basis, and (3) the Coordinator's office experienced difficulty in consistently collecting complete and accurate obligation data from U.S. government agencies. Regular reporting of both obligations and expenditures for U.S. assistance to Afghanistan would provide the State Coordinator and Congress a more complete picture of what funds have been spent on the ground on visible projects.

Source: General Accounting Office. Available online at http://www.gao.gov/new.items/d04403.pdf.

ANALYSIS

The report, which did not allege any widespread fraud and abuse of funds, criticized the lack of a coherent strategy behind Afghan reconstruction. To be fair, it highlighted many of the problems that the United States encountered after entering Afghanistan, including the incredibly poor state of Afghan infrastructure, poor internal security, and the lack of effective international and interagency coordinating mechanisms that could make for a streamlined reconstruction program. Furthermore, the report praised the emphasis upon short-term projects and humanitarian aid that proved instrumental in avoiding a famine in Afghanistan during the time period covered by the report.

- **Document 51: George W. Bush, The President's News Conference with President Hamid Karzai of Afghanistan**
- **When:** June 15, 2004
- **Where:** Washington, D.C.
- **Significance:** President Bush held a joint press conference with President Karzai at the White House to discuss progress in Afghanistan.

DOCUMENT

President Bush. Good day. Laura and I are pleased to welcome President Karzai back to the White House—really glad you're here.

President Karzai. Thank you very much.

President Bush. Thanks for the good visit, and I'm looking forward to having a good lunch with you and your delegation.

President Karzai. Well, I'm looking forward to that.

President Bush. President Karzai recently visited Fort Drum and thanked American troops on behalf of the Afghan people—

President Karzai. Yes.

President Bush. —for their service and sacrifice. And Mr. President, that was a sign of a true friend. I want to thank you for doing that.

President Karzai. Thank you very much.

President Bush. I also appreciate your honor and your courage and your skill in helping to build a new and democratic Afghanistan. You've been instrumental in lifting your country from the ashes of two decades of war and oppression. Under your leadership, Afghanistan's progress has been dramatic.

Three years ago, the Taliban had granted Usama bin Laden and his terrorist Al Qaida organization a safe refuge. Today, the Taliban has been deposed; Al Qaida is in hiding; and coalition forces continue to hunt down the remnants and holdouts. Coalition forces, including many brave Afghans, have brought America, Afghanistan, and the free world its first victory in the war on terror. Afghanistan is no longer a terrorist factory sending thousands of killers into the world.

Three years ago, 70 percent of Afghans were malnourished, and one in four Afghan children never saw their 5th birthday.

President Karzai. Yes.

President Bush. Today, clean water is being provided throughout the country; hospitals and clinics have been rehabilitated; and millions of children have been vaccinated against measles and polio.

Three years ago, women were viciously oppressed and forbidden to work outside the home and even denied what little medical treatment was available. Today, women are going to school, and their rights are protected in Afghanistan's Constitution.

President Karzai. Yes.

President Bush. That document sets aside a certain number of seats for women in the National Assembly, and women will soon compete for those seats in open elections this September.

Three years ago, the smallest displays of joy were outlawed. Women were beaten for wearing brightly colored shoes. Even the playing of music and the flying of kites were outlawed. Today, we witness the rebirth of a vibrant Afghan culture. Music fills the marketplaces, and people are free to come together to celebrate in open.

Afghanistan's journey to democracy and peace deserves the support and respect of every nation, because free nations do not breed the ideology of terror. Last week, at the G-8 summit, President Karzai talked with world leaders about the challenges of building a secure and stable country.

My Government reaffirms its ironclad commitment to help Afghanistan succeed and prosper. Security is essential for steady progress and growth. The forces of many nations are working hard with Afghans to find and defeat Taliban remnants and eliminate Al Qaida terrorists. We're helping to build the new Afghan national army and to train new Afghan police and border patrol. Together, we will maintain the peace, secure Afghanistan's borders, and deny terrorists any foothold in that country.

I'm proud to call President Karzai a strong ally in the war on terror.

The United States is also joining with Afghanistan to announce five new initiatives that will help the Afghan people achieve the peace, stability, and prosperity they deserve. First, the United States pledges its full support as Afghans continue to build the institutions of democracy. America will launch an ambitious training program for newly elected Afghan politicians and help newly elected Assembly members better serve those who elected them.

Second, Afghanistan and America are working together to print millions of new textbooks and to build modern schools in every Afghan province. Girls as well as boys are going to school, and they are studying under a new curriculum that promotes religious and ethnic tolerance. We pledge to continue this progress through a new $4 million women's teacher training institute in Kabul. Graduates of this innovative program will return to their provinces and rural districts to train other teachers in the crusade against illiteracy.

Education can be nurtured in other ways as well. Cultural exchange programs help to foster understanding and respect as well as accelerate progress. Last year, close to 100 Afghans studied here in various training programs. More want to come to learn and to share their experiences, so our third initiative will expand these opportunities to include more than 250 qualified Afghans who will participate in Humphrey, Fulbright, Cochran, and other exchange programs.

Fourth, to promote bilateral economic ties, the United States and Afghanistan announced our intent to pursue a bilateral trade and investment framework agreement. Years of war and tyranny have eroded Afghanistan's economy and infrastructure, yet a revival is underway. Afghans are busy starting their own businesses. Some 15,000 licenses have already been issued for foreign businesses and investors to explore economic opportunities in Afghanistan. Working with Japan, we have rebuilt the Kandahar-Kabul highway, a vital commercial and transportation link between Afghanistan's two largest cities. A bilateral trade agreement will add new fuel to the economic revival.

And finally, we pledge to continue our efforts to create opportunities for women. The United States is dedicating $5 million to fund training programs and grants for small businesses. Under the Taliban, women were oppressed; their potential was ignored. Under President Karzai's leadership, that has changed dramatically. A number of innovative programs designed in collaboration with the Afghan Government are increasing the role of women in the private sector. The traditional funding we announce today—the additional funding we announce today will provide Afghan women with small-business grants and training in business management skills. As my wife, Laura, has said, no society can prosper when half of its population is not allowed to contribute to its progress.

The road ahead for Afghanistan is still long and difficult. Yet, the Afghan people can know that their country will never be abandoned to terrorists and killers. The world and the United States stands with them as partners in their quest for peace and prosperity and stability and democracy.

Welcome, President, glad you're here.

President Karzai. Thank you very much. Thank you. Mr. President, it's a tremendous privilege and honor for us to be invited again by you and the First Lady to the White House. It was a great honor for me today to be speaking to a joint meeting of the U.S. Congress. I will cherish that memory of talking to the representatives of the American people.

There, today I thanked America for the help that it gave us liberate ourselves and rebuild ourselves and prosper. That help has been the source of all growth in the past 2 years. Our economy in the year 2002 grew by 30 percent, in the year 2003 by 25 percent or more. In the year 2004, the growth is estimated to be 20 percent. And we are hoping, as some of the banks have predicted, that the Afghan economy will grow 'til 2008 by 15 percent, and beyond that, for another 5 years, by 10 percent.

Thank you very much. This could have not been possible without your help, without America's assistance.

We are sending today 5 million children to school. Almost half of those children are girls. Our universities are open. Our universities are coming up in all—all over the country, in all the provinces of the country.

We are building a national army, a vital institution for the defense of our country. You want us to stand on our own feet; you want us to defend our own sovereignty and provide security to our people; and you're helping us do that. The national army of Afghanistan is popular with the Afghan people. Wherever they go, people receive them with welcome. In Farah Province, where they went some months ago, school girls and boys gave them flowers. Thank you very much for that.

We are also building our police forces. We have a constitution that we have today which is the most enlightened in that part of the world. And that constitution has been made possible because of the liberation that you helped us gain and because of the stability that the United States helped us have in Afghanistan. As a result of that, we have a constitution that sets us as an example of an Islamic democratic state. Thank you very much, Mr. President, for that.

We are looking forward in this relationship to a stronger relationship, and I'm sure the United States will remain committed to Afghanistan. Afghanistan is, in the month of September, looking forward to elections—Presidential elections and elections of parliament and elections of the provincial assemblies and district assemblies. So far, we have registered 3.8 million voters, and out of the 3.8 million voters, Mr. President, 35.4 percent are, so far, women. And as the trend continues, as we move forward to the registration of more voters, the number of women registering will exceed, definitely, 40 percent. In certain parts of the country, in the central highlands, today I learned that the registration of women has exceeded that of men. They are more than 50 percent. This could not have not been achieved in Afghanistan without your help and that of the international community.

Afghanistan has problems too. Among the problems is the question of drugs. The Afghan Government is adamant, the Afghan people are adamant to fight this menace, to end it in Afghanistan, and we seek your help in that.

Thank you very much, Mr. President. It's been nice visiting the United States again. One likes to stay here and not go, it's such a good country. Thanks very much.

President Bush. Get home and get to work, will you?

President Karzai. Thank you, yes.

President Bush. We'll answer some questions, in the tradition of democratic societies. Are you ready?

President Karzai. I'm ready.

President Bush. We'll start with Hunt [Terence Hunt, Associated Press].

President Karzai. I now know, Mr. President, what the free press means. We have it in Afghanistan.

President Bush. That's good.

Hunt.

Saddam Hussein/Usama bin Laden and Mullah Omar

Q. . . .

And President Karzai, who will try Usama bin Laden and Mullah Omar when they're caught?

. . .

President Karzai. Usama and Mullah Omar have committed crimes against the Afghan people, against the people in the United States, and against the international community. They are international criminals. They are wanted by the international community. They are wanted by the world conscience. They have to be arrested and tried. And when they are arrested, we will consult the international community and find appropriate mechanism for their trial.

. . .

Wendell.

Reactions of Iraqis and Afghans to Coalition Presence

Q. Mr. President, how do you explain why the success we've had in Afghanistan appears to be eluding us in Iraq? Is it possible that the Afghan people objected to the Taliban more strongly than the Iraqi people objected to the reign of Saddam Hussein?

President Bush. No, that's not possible. The Iraqi people objected to the reign of Saddam Hussein, and you would, too, if you lived there, where you couldn't express yourself, where you got tortured, where there was mass graves.

This is hard work, and it wasn't easy work in Afghanistan, by the way. I mean, it seems easy now that we're standing here, Wendell, after several years of working together with this great leader, but it was hard work. And out of kind of the desperate straits that the Afghan people found themselves is now a welcoming society beginning to grow. And the same thing is going to happen in Iraq.

These aren't easy tasks. I mean, somehow there's this expectation, "Well, all this is supposed to have happened yesterday." That's just not the way it works when you go from a society that has—that was subjugated to a tyrant—by a tyrant to a free society. And the President will tell you, it's hard work. It may look easy in retrospect, but it's not easy. And that's why it's very important for us to speak clearly to the people of Afghanistan and in Iraq that the United States will help them, will stay and help them fulfill the mission, which is a free and peaceful Afghanistan, a free and peaceful Iraq, which are in our Nation's interests.

First, it's in our interests that we defeat terrorists there than fight them here. That's our short-term security interests. Secondly, it's in our long-term interests that we work for free societies in parts of the world that are desperate for freedom. And the reason I keep saying that, Wendell, is because I know that a free society is a peaceful society. And America is interested in working with friends to promote the peace, and that's what we're doing. The short-term solution for our security problem is to find the terrorists and bring them to justice before they hurt Americans again, is to deny them training bases, is to deny them affiliates and allies in the war on terror. That's what we have done in Afghanistan and Iraq. The long-term solution is to promote free societies that are able to defeat the forces of pessimism, darkness, intolerance, and hatred.

. . .

Richard [Richard Benedetto, *USA Today*].

Movement toward Democracy in Afghanistan

Q. Mr. President, there have been some reports that the Afghan Government has been cooperating with warlords, former warlords in Afghanistan, and I wondered if you talked about that with President Karzai today—

President Bush. Yes, I did.

Q. —and how you feel about it?

President Bush. I did, and he can answer the question, what he told me.

President Karzai. Yes. See, Afghanistan is emerging from years of oppression to a free, democratic society. And in democracy, you are supposed to be talking to each other. You are supposed to be preparing the country for a better future by negotiating and by understanding each other. And as the Afghan President, it's my job to take that nation, the Afghan people, into a better future, through stability and peace, to a higher degree of democracy, to the elections. It's my job to do that peacefully. It's my job to keep stability and peace in Afghanistan. And I will talk to anybody that comes to talk to me about stability and peace and about movement towards democracy.

No deals have been made. No coalitions have been made, and no coalition will be made. And they did not ask for it. First of all, we don't call them warlords. Some of those people are respected leaders of the Afghan resistance. Some of them are former Presidents, and we respect them in Afghanistan. Yes, there are bad people in the country as well with whom we're not making a deal, with whom we are not talking. This country is moving forward. It's a society now emerging with a strong civil society sense in institutions, and that's what we are doing there.

President Bush. Mr. President, thank you very much.

President Karzai. Thanks very much.

President Bush. Lunch awaits us.

President Karzai. Lunch awaits us, indeed. Thank you.

Source: Public Papers of the Presidents of the United States: George W. Bush, 2004, Book 1. Washington, D.C.: Government Printing Office, 2005, 1046–1055.

ANALYSIS

The opening statements and questions revealed that the combined efforts of the international community and the interim government of Afghanistan successfully alleviated the immediate humanitarian crisis in Afghanistan in 2001–2002 while also immediately easing the cultural restrictions that the Taliban had imposed over much of the country.

The press conference also brought to the fore problems that continued to dog Afghanistan nearly three years after the American invasion, most critically how to maintain stability and continue to build civil institutions even as a resurgent Taliban waged an insurgency in the southern and eastern provinces of the country.

- **Document 52: U.S. Embassy (Islamabad), Cable, "Impressions of Waziristan"**
- **When:** January 25, 2005
- **Where:** Islamabad, Pakistan
- **Significance:** An analysis of the political and social situation in the border regions of Pakistan where Taliban and al-Qaeda leaders sought refuge from ISAF forces in Afghanistan.

DOCUMENT

FM AMEMBASSY ISLAMABAD
TO SECSTATE WASHDC
. . .

1. Summary: As part of a Pakistan military sponsored trip for visiting Congressman Mark Kirk, POLOFF visited the capitals of North and South Waziristan on

DID YOU KNOW?

Afghan Star

Afghan Star is an Afghan television show inspired by the British program *Pop Idol*, the latter of which inspired *American Idol* and numerous other singing competition shows around the world. First broadcast in 2005, *Afghan Star* was especially significant because it signaled that the cultural restrictions that had marked the era of Taliban rule—including bans on public singing—had come to an end. The show continues to air in Afghanistan as of early 2018. In the United States, HBO released a documentary about the third season of the show, also titled *Afghan Star*, in 2009. One of the contestants from that season chronicled in the film, Setara Hussainzada, faced persecution because she appeared in the show singing and dancing without the traditional Muslim *hijab* over her head. Her ordeal signified the extent to which Afghanistan continued to struggle with finding a cultural balance between the West and the traditional, tribal cultures.

January 14. The visit brought home the extreme difficulties the GOP faces in trying to counter terrorist insurgents in these remote regions, the need for a continued political component to the FATA campaign, and the importance of development work as part of the counter-insurgency effort. GOP interlocutors stressed that the success of their efforts would require a joint political/military/development strategy that emphasizes reestablishing the authority of the maliks (traditional tribal leaders), winning the support of the local populace, and ultimately integrating FATA's political and legal system with the rest of Pakistan. End Summary.

2. On January 14, POLOFF accompanied Congressman Mark Kirk on a visit to Wana, South Waziristan and Miram Shah, North Waziristan [redacted]. In addition to briefings at the military headquarters in both locations, POLOFF visited a forward troop position overlooking Shakai Valley in South Waziristan. Briefings in South Waziristan were conducted by [redacted] and in North Waziristan by [redacted]. [Redacted] accompanied delegation to both locations. In North Waziristan, [redacted] met the delegation. In South Waziristan, the delegation met briefly with a group of local maliks.

The People

3. Lengthy discussions with military and GOP officials operating in the region offered some insight into local culture. The concepts of hospitality and refuge, often cited as traditions exploited by the terrorists, certainly appeared from conversations to be defining factors. However, our interlocutors stressed that there were very narrow parameters under which these were extended and very broad, and often unclear (to the outsider) parameters under which these could be withdrawn. [Redacted]

The Politics

4. Prior to the launch of jihad against the Soviet invasion of Afghanistan, GOP officials said the maliks were fully in control of their respective tribes and able to prevent influences from impacting the stability of the tribal areas. Cooperation between maliks and political agents was relatively good and contact between the FATA and the "settled areas" was largely curtailed. The decision by the GOP to actively recruit Waziris and Mehsuds for jihad in Soviet-occupied Afghanistan disrupted this balance. Deobandi and Jamaat-e-Islami religious leaders began recruitment in the tribal areas and ultimately usurped much of the authority of the maliks. Following the withdrawal of the Soviets, these religious leaders continued to recruit tribesmen to fight on the side of the Taliban in the Afghan civil war and encouraged contacts between the tribes and the religious, political, and military leadership of the Taliban largely against the wishes of the maliks. Relationships between the mullahs and the political agents were strained. Following the defeat

of the Taliban, religious leaders in the Waziristans convinced the tribes to open their territories to Taliban remnants and their foreign supporters. Maliks, our interlocutors argued, acquiesced only because they had no further authority to challenge the mullahs.

5. Since the military entrance to the Waziristans, the GOP has attempted to reestablish the maliks as the primary authority. Successful military actions against foreign fighters integrated with the tribes convinced tribesmen of the danger in confronting the military. By refusing to discuss cessation of hostilities with any parties other than the maliks, the military helped undermine the authority of problematic religious leaders. Active pursuit and arrest of maliks who continued support for terrorist elements resulted in a decision by the Waziri tribes to align with the GOP against the terrorists. Military officials were convinced that their new offensive in Mehsud areas would have a similar impact. Throughout this strategy, the military has relied on the provisions of the Frontier Crimes Regulation that allows for collective punishment, including economic blockades of tribes.

6. Over the long term GOP officials were convinced that development assistance was the only way to retain the loyalty of the maliks and endure maliks' authority in the tribes. If maliks' relationships with the army and the political agents were seen to produce tangible benefits, tribesmen would follow. If not, the military feared the pliable maliks might again be replaced. In this vein, the Army Corps of Engineers stressed the works it had already initiated in the Waziristans, including well, road, health clinic, and school construction. While pleased with the initial impact of these social development projects, officials stressed the need to develop sustainable income generating activities. Military officials, political leaders, and the maliks all stressed the need for international donors to assist in projects in the region. [Redacted]

The Military

7. Refs A and B provide an overview of military action and plans in both North and South Waziristan. The military strategy appeared to be extremely successful in destroying concentrations and positions of foreign fighters in South Waziristan and in driving a wedge between the terrorists and their former tribal hosts. [Redacted]

Comment

9. There is no question that the GOP faces a daunting military and political challenge in trying to drive foreign fighters from North and South Waziristan and an even greater challenge in integrating these isolated areas into Pakistan. The officials that we met on the ground were clearly committed to this challenge and willing to use all resources provided to ensure that it occurs. They were making unprecedented efforts in a difficult and unyielding environment and using an approach that appears to be slowly yielding results. The military leadership is aware that ultimate success in the FATA campaign depends on successful integration of this area into mainstream Pakistani society. [Redacted]

Crocker

Source: National Security Archive. Available online at http://nsarchive2 .gwu.edu/NSAEBB/NSAEBB325/doc13.pdf.

ANALYSIS

The political situation in Waziristan posed a major challenge to both the Coalition and the Pakistani government. The government did not fully control this rugged, isolated area along its own border, and the conservative, tribal societies that lived there represented natural havens for the Taliban and other insurgent groups seeking refuge beyond the reach of the Coalition. The difficulties in Waziristan served as yet another reminder that problems in Afghanistan required regional solutions that often eluded the United States and its allies.

- **Document 53: NATO SACEUR OPLAN 10302 Revise-1**
- **When:** December 8, 2005
- **Where:** Casteau, Belgium
- **Significance:** The NATO and Supreme Allied Command, Europe, plan outlining the goals for ISAF and the strategy to achieve those objectives.

DOCUMENT

OPLAN 10302 (REVISE 1)
SACEUR OPERATION PLAN FOR
THE INTERNATIONAL SECURITY ASSISTANCE
FORCE (ISAF) IN AFGHANISTAN

REFERENCES:

A. Bonn Agreement, dated 5 Dec 01.

B. United Nations Security Council Resolution (UNSCR) 1386(2001) and subsequent UNSCRs for Afghanistan.

C. Military Technical Agreement (MTA) between ISAF and the Interim Administration of Afghanistan, dated 4 Jan 02, and subsequent amendments.

1. **SITUATION.**

a. **Strategic Conditions.** NATO assumed the lead for ISAF on 11 Aug 03, drawing its authority from References A-C. The original operations plan foresaw five phases. Phase I was assessment and preparation and ISAF operations in Kabul. In Phase 2, ISAF is expanding its presence from Kabul into the northern, western, eastern and southern regions of the country. Coincident with the final stage of ISAF expansion in Phase 2, command and control structures will be adjusted to ensure greater synergy between ISAF and coalition forces, while respecting the two distinct missions/mandates. Phase 3 is "stabilisation". Phases 4 and 5 are "transition" and "redeployment" respectively. Coalition forces will continue to operate in Afghanistan, adjusting as ISAF expands.

b. **Strategic Environment.** In the fields of security and development, there are a considerable number of international actors assisting the Afghan government. An integrated and strategic approach is crucial to overall success. In the anticipated post-Bonn environment, primary responsibility for this coordination rests with the Afghan government, though in the mid-term it will require assistance from the UN and others. The NATO Senior Civilian Representative in Kabul is responsible for carrying forward political aspects of NATO's engagement in Afghanistan.

c. **Alliance Political Objective**. Full support for implementation of the Bonn and Kabul (ie post-Bonn) processes, as endorsed by UNSCR 1386 and subsequent UNSCRs for Afghanistan, in co-operation and coordination with key international organisations and the coalition, by assisting the Afghan government to meet its responsibilities to provide security, order, stability and reconstruction.

d. **Alliance Political End-State**. A self-sustaining, moderate and democratic Afghan government able to exercise its sovereign authority, independently, throughout Afghanistan.

e.–f. Reserved.

g. **Political Limitations**.

(1) ISAF military elements will engage in mine clearing and explosive ordnance disposal when essential for mission accomplishment.

(2) Counter terrorism operations will not be conducted by ISAF forces, or under ISAF command.

h. **Strategic Planning Assumptions**.

(1) Reserved.

(2) G8 lead nations will retain leadership for the designated pillars of security sector reform, the success of which will be of critical importance to the fulfilment of ISAF's objectives.

(3) Reserved.

(4) To support ISAF operations in Afghanistan, political arrangements will be made to facilitate effective NATO engagement and military liaison with neighbouring states.

2. **MISSION**. When authorized by the NAC, SACEUR will direct the Joint Force commander (JFC) to conduct military operations across Afghanistan, as appropriate and within the mandate, in cooperation and coordination with Afghan national security forces and in coordination with coalition forces, in order to assist the Afghan government in the maintenance of security; facilitate the development of government structures and extension of its control; and assist reconstruction/humanitarian efforts, through the implementation of the mandate provided by the relevant UNSCRs.

3. **EXECUTION**.

a. **Conduct of Operations**. After completing Phases 1 ("assessment and preparation") and 2 ("geographic expansion") of the five, partially overlapping, phases of

---

DID YOU KNOW?

Marcus Luttrell

Marcus Luttrell is a former Navy SEAL operator who received the Navy Cross and Purple Heart for his actions during Operation Red Wings that occurred in June and July 2005. The operation involved the 2nd Battalion, 3rd Marines, and Special Forces units attempting to locate and destroy a notorious insurgent, Ahmad Shah, in the Korengal Valley in eastern Afghanistan. Luttrell's small reconnaissance team was to locate Shah, but local herdsmen spotted them and notified insurgents who placed the team under heavy fire. The other three members of Luttrell's team died in the firefight, and only the hospitality of a local tribesman saved the badly wounded Luttrell. Insurgents shot down a helicopter carrying 16 men during the search for Luttrell, but he was eventually recovered. Ahmad Shah escaped the dragnet but was gunned down in a firefight three years later.

DID YOU KNOW?

CH-47 Chinook

The CH-47 is a transport helicopter designed by Boeing and first flown in 1961. The helicopter has a distinctive design with tandem rotors mounted atop pylons at the front and rear of the helicopter's long fuselage. The design appears ungainly, but the helicopter can carry heavy payloads, with modern versions capable of transporting more than 21,000 pounds of personnel and equipment. In addition, the helicopter can reach a top speed of more than 170 miles per hour, which is fast for a helicopter. Nicknamed the Chinook, the helicopter has served in American conflicts since Vietnam, but it assumed added importance in the rugged terrain of Afghanistan. The helicopter's powerful engines allow it to deliver payloads at higher elevations than the more numerous UH-60 Blackhawk. Unfortunately, its large size makes it a target for insurgents, who shot down fully loaded helicopters in 2005 and 2011, killing 16 and 38 personnel, respectively. The Army intends for the Chinook to remain in service until at least 2060, making it one of the longest-serving military aircraft in the world.

Operations Plan 10302, the focus of the third ("stabilisation") phase (and of this revise of the operations plan), will be to assist the Afghan government to extend and exercise its authority and influence. This phase will end, most likely at different intervals for each province (or groups of provinces), as a level of stability is achieved to allow the handover of ISAF military tasks to Afghan authorities. This incremental transition of security responsibilities will take place in Phase 4. Phase 4 ends when SACEUR confirms that the mission from the NAC extant at that time is accomplished. The fifth phase is redeployment.

b. **Strategic Commander's Intent**.

(1) **Main Effort**. Coincident with the expansion of ISAF, as described in the strategic transition plan at Annex A, we will continue to assist the Afghan government in establishing and maintaining security throughout Afghanistan, and creating the conditions for stabilisation and reconstruction in its country. At the strategic level, our Main Effort is to achieve our goals in Afghanistan by conducting stability and security operations in order to allow the Afghan government to assume control in the regions and provinces; and by helping the Afghan government to develop its security forces, in cooperation with the G8 lead nations and other international organisations as they intensify their efforts in the south and the east, to the extent that they can be effective without outside assistance.

(2) **Creating Effect—Expanding Afghan Authority**.

(a) **Context**. As directed by the NAC, I will empower COMJFC Brunssum, as the JFC, to conduct NATO-led operations across Afghanistan, and provide strategic guidance, derived from political direction from the NAC, and the necessary forces and resources for this task. The JFC will, as the overall operational commander, determine the effects required to achieve the military strategic objectives, provide campaign guidance and continuity and codify and maintain those agreements necessary with US CENTCOM (on behalf of the coalition) to maximise operational synergy. In turn, the JFC will direct COMISAF, as the in-theatre operational commander, to achieve the effects sought and the key military and supporting tasks mandated by the NAC. This will take place in an environment where ISAF has become the principal international military force in Afghanistan. The stability and security components of this ISAF operation are mutually supporting and linked elements that must be driven centrally through coherent and consistent command and control. Moreover, they must be taken forward with the cognisance of the Afghan government. While political direction for this mission comes from the NAC, there must be full consultation with appropriate Afghan political and military authorities over the prosecution of operations by ISAF. Enduring change can only be sustained with clear Afghan support for, and ownership of, initiatives and programmes, leading to the development of self-reliant partners. Although final decisions over ISAF rest with NATO authorities, a collaborative approach will engender indigenous involvement in shaping Afghanistan's destiny and create a shared view of ISAF's execution of its stability and security operations in support of Afghan authorities and forces.

(b) **Stability**. Expanding the government's authority and the rule of law countrywide, and building the indigenous capacity required to sustain them effectively, are critical to success in Afghanistan. Provincial reconstruction teams (PRTs) will be at the leading edge of NATO's effort.

Military support to them is one of NATO's major contributions to the success of ISAF in Afghanistan. Stability operations will be used to create an environment that generates the confidence and ambient security required to enable reconstruction and nation-building activities. They will also facilitate the continued physical and moral extension of Afghan government authority. Results will be achieved through presence and engagement. PRTs act as catalysts for change, while remaining sensitive to Afghan sovereignty and political primacy. Teams will have significant influence and a disproportionately positive impact on authorities within a province. Broadening the range of capabilities within a PRT will increase its ability to assist with the expansion of provincial authority and achieve local success. Similarly, while recognizing the different national characters of PRTs, increasing convergence between the activities of all PRTs, with synchronised movement towards a set of common objectives, will have the desired strategic impact. Stimulating economic growth, increasing the level of security, improving governance and public services and enhancing living conditions will satisfy basic human security needs, reduce the need for farmers to acquire income through poppy cultivation and create greater loyalty to legitimate authorities. Lacking a common cause, and without the likelihood of support, extremists will be less able to operate. In this setting, ISAF will work alongside others, supporting the Afghan government (and its forces and agencies) and overall development efforts, sharing information and harmonising its own activities with those of others to the fullest extent practical to create coherent effects. ISAF elements will operate with subtlety and a light touch, striking a careful balance between the traditionally active approach of military organisations and the requirement for other actors to conduct reconstruction operations.

(c) **Security**. Security operations will be required to allow PRTs to perform their tasks. Such security operations will range from local force protection in a permissive environment to decisive, pro-active military ground and air manoeuvre, thereby creating the environment for PRTs to flourish. ISAF will support the Afghan government by deterring and disrupting those who challenge the extension of government authority or prevent ISAF from operating freely. A robust approach will be necessary to maintain the initiative. In-place forces can be supported by the deployment of out of theatre reserves from those elements of the Strategic Reserve Force earmarked by providing nations for operations in Afghanistan. Operational activity will be closely coordinated with coalition forces, to secure the synergies available and manage the operating space. Increasing involvement of the Afghan National Army (ANA) and Afghan National Police (ANP) will be developed as the mission progresses.

(3) **Building Afghan National Capacity**. Development of effective Afghan national security forces, responsive to central authorities, is a particularly important step in extending government influence. Progress in this area also aids movement towards the NAC desired end state. Manning, training and equipping of the ANA and ANP remains the responsibility of respective G8 lead nations. ISAF's focus will be on the coherent employment of indigenous capability. ISAF will mentor, support and aid the training and operational employment of ANA units in order to increase their capability and reach. This will include the coordination of ANA operations with those of ISAF to achieve synergy, primarily through ISAF operational mentor and liaison teams that can support ANA operations and manage joint operating space and ISAF mission enabling or battle-winning support. It will be critical to establish close coordination, mutual trust, unit-to-unit, and commander-to-commander partnerships at every level, with a clear understanding of respective operating parameters. Accordingly, the operational mentor and liaison teams will operate in support of kandak activities: in barracks; on collective training; and closely mentoring kandak operational deployments where such activities are consistent with the ISAF mandate. Operational effect will be further enhanced through ISAF focusing on practical steps to involve the ANP in the overall security effort, in accordance with Appendix 2 to Annex B. ISAF will assist provincial security committees and help coordinate the various police elements internally and when working in the same operating space with the ANA and/or ISAF. Advice and practical support will also be offered to border police and supporting ANA units to enhance their capacity through the adoption of an integrated border security strategy that reduces illegitimate movement and increases central government revenues. Niche and professional development training will also be conducted for Afghan national security forces on an opportunity basis. In coordination with other forces, ISAF will support Afghan government efforts to disarm illegally armed groups. Given the threats to stability arising from the drugs trade, ISAF will also support Afghan government counter narcotics efforts, within agreed guidelines. Throughout, all ISAF support to security sector reform will be in full coordination with the Afghan government and the G8 lead nations and within means and capabilities.

(4) **Comprehensive Awareness**. While it is clear that ISAF has no responsibility for the delivery of effects by nations and other international organisations supporting the Afghan government, or for the coordination of those effects, ISAF could help. Analysing PRTs' work across the breadth of their engagement provides ISAF with an almost unique ability to observe a range of provincial development activities. Similarly, ISAF, operating countrywide, has a comprehensive view of progress in security sector reform. COMISAF, working in concert with the NATO Senior Civilian Representative and with both supported by appropriately skilled staff, can gauge the breadth and depth of stabilisation, reconstruction and reform, spotting gaps or duplication of effort for the benefit of the wider community. Through politically agreed and accepted coordinating mechanisms, considering civil and military effort, such assessments will assist the Afghan government, who have primacy in this area, in coordinating the wide range of international community activities in the country. It should also prove useful to those nations, organisations and agencies supporting Afghan government development efforts, helping them judge the effects of their programmes.

(5) **External Influences**. Under overall Afghan lead, developing relations with Afghanistan's neighbours will buttress NATO's efforts, thereby enhancing regional and border security. In accordance with NAC guidance, ISAF should promote regular Afghan/NATO military to military contact with key neighbours, supported by a responsive military liaison structure, to provide the primary tool for liaison on the military side and support ISAF's tactical efforts in support of an indigenous border security strategy to reduce illegitimate movement and increase revenue collection.

(6)–(7) Reserved.

(8) **Military Strategic Campaign Objectives**.

(a) The extension of Afghan government authority across the country.

(b) Development of the structures necessary to maintain security in Afghanistan, without the assistance of international forces.

(c) Development and maintenance of a countrywide stable and secure environment by Afghan authorities, in which sustainable reconstruction and developmental efforts have taken hold.

(9) **Desired Strategic Military End-State**. Afghan national security forces provide security and sustain stability in Afghanistan without NATO support.

c. Reserved.

d. **Mission Review and Exit**. Progress towards mission accomplishment will be kept under review. Recommendations will be made through the medium of the periodic mission review process. NATO's exit from Afghanistan is dependent on the successful development of credible, professional and legitimate Afghan security structures able to maintain a safe and secure environment in their own country, and on the desires of the Afghan government. Once Afghan national security forces are trained and effective, ISAF should be able to reduce its profile, as decided by the NAC. The first reductions are likely to be in combat forces, leading to PRTs providing the longer-term ISAF military presence. Once these are no longer required, on a province-by-province basis, the capabilities provided by a PRT should be taken on by Afghan structures and the team dissolved.

. . .

Source: Danish Parliament. Available online at http://www.ft.dk/samling/20051/UM-del/Bilag/44/242709.pdf.

ANALYSIS

The NATO OPLAN mostly framed the ISAF mission as support-stabilization operations that would develop Afghanistan's military and security capacity while creating stability in the countryside to allow economic life and civil society to flourish. In particular, the section on the Provincial Reconstruction Teams acknowledged that Afghanistan desperately needed development but that different parts of the country might require different assistance and resources.

Only briefly in section 3.b.1 did the plan mention the resurgence of the Taliban and the need to focus military efforts against this threat. This was perhaps surprising given that General Barno spoke of managing a counterinsurgency campaign during his tenure in Afghanistan that concluded several months before the creation of this plan.

- **Document 54: U.S. Department of State, Issue Paper for Vice President of the United States (VPOTUS), "Counterterrorism Activities (Neo-Taliban)"**
- **When:** December 9, 2005
- **Where:** Washington, D.C.
- **Significance:** A paper furnished to Vice President Dick Cheney that analyzed the political and military situation in Afghanistan.

DOCUMENT

Rise in Violence: The volume of violence in Afghanistan rose this year. Taliban tactics have shifted: the Taliban is making greater use of suicide bombings and IEDs and are trying to disrupt local governance by assassinating pro-GoA religious leaders, tribal elders, and local government officials. Persistent insurgent activity in the southern provinces (Helmand and Kandahar) will require a robust NATO role as it assumes responsibility for southern Afghanistan. The U.S. remains steadfast in its counterterrorism mission throughout Afghanistan. Afghan security forces—which are key to defeating the insurgency—are taking on increasing responsibilities.

Afghan-Pak Border: The Taliban continues to recruit fighters from its traditional support base among Pashtun tribesmen residing in Afghanistan and Pakistan. Taliban and Al Qaida leaders continue to provide guidance and support from Pakistan for cross-border operations. Some Taliban leaders operate with relative impunity in some Pakistani cities, and may still enjoy support from the lower echelons of Pakistan's ISI. Close cooperation between Afghanistan and Pakistan is critical to stamping out the flow of Taliban and other insurgents.

Reconciliation Program: The Afghan Government's program to reconcile lower and mid-level Taliban fighters has been moderately effective but has not yet realized its potential.

Talking Points

- The US remains committed to defeating insurgents in Afghanistan—as well as supporting the reconciliation process.
- As NATO assumes responsibility for the southern sector, the US will maintain the forces necessary to conduct counterterrorism activities throughout Afghanistan.
- We are encouraged by the increasing effectiveness of Afghan security forces.

2. Programs designed to combat terrorism and lawlessness have continued. The Program for Strengthening Peace (PTS), which reconciles former Taliban and Hizb-i-Islam (HiG) members, founded six regional offices and reported that over

800 former fighters had joined the program, as of December 2005. The Disarmament, Demobilization, and Reintegration (DDR) program has process over 63,000 former combatants. The Disarmament of Illegal Armed Groups (DIAG) process began work in June, focusing on vetting parliamentary candidates to ensure they had no ties to illegal armed groups (IAGs). The DIAG disqualified a number of candidates, [redacted] The programs next phase will be a province-by-province effort to disband the most notorious IAGs, but progress has been slowed by the search for a successor to the Afghan head of the program, who left his post in October, [redacted]

. . .

FIGHT VS. AL-QAEDA AND THE TALIBAN

7. Mr. Hadley asked [redacted] to clarify the GOA strategy for eliminating the Al-Qaeda and Taliban threat in the next two to three years. [redacted] said that GOA strategy is based first on military action, second, on the Taliban reconciliation process, and third, improving relations and security cooperation with Pakistan. The strategic partnership is a further element that supports Afghanistan in the region and internally.

8. The GOA supports restoration and reconciliation with former Taliban when possible. The Taliban Peace and Reconciliation Program (PTS) is a partnership between the GOA, [redacted] to determine which former Taliban can be reintegrated into Afghan society. [redacted]

8. The Afghan insurgency is not monolithic. The Taliban, HiG, al-Qaida, Haqqani network, Jaish-i-Muslimeen, and other extremists have varying agendas, and lack internal cohesion. For example, one of our veteran international contacts continues to hear of frictions between Kandahari and non-Kandahari elements of the Taliban. While these extremist elements may be able to agree on grand strategy this generally does not translate into operational coordination.

Source: National Security Archive. Available online at http://nsarchive2.gwu.edu/NSAEBB/NSAEBB325/doc14.pdf.

ANALYSIS

In stark contrast to the SACEUR NATO plan developed the previous day, this paper clearly defined the security challenges in Afghanistan as an insurgency waged by the Taliban against the Afghan government and its attempts to build legitimacy and stability outside of Kabul. Furthermore, the base for this renewed Taliban oftentimes lay over the border in Pakistan, thus further blurring the security issues between the two countries.

The document also noted the cleavages in the Taliban that had been present in some form or another since the group's inception. Given that the bulk of U.S. forces were in Iraq at the time, a strategy to reconcile with some members of the Taliban while attempting to drive wedges between the remaining factions did not require large deployments of new troops to Afghanistan.

- **Document 55: Afghanistan Compact**
- **When:** February 1, 2006
- **Where:** London, United Kingdom
- **Significance:** The Afghanistan Compact outlined a new phase of Afghan reconstruction to occur over the following five years.

DOCUMENT

THE LONDON CONFERENCE ON AFGHANISTAN
31 January–1 February 2006

THE AFGHANISTAN COMPACT

The Islamic Republic of Afghanistan and the international community:

Determined to strengthen their partnership to improve the lives of Afghan people, and to contribute to national, regional, and global peace and security;

Affirming their shared commitment to continue, in the spirit of the Bonn, Tokyo and Berlin conferences, to work toward a stable and prosperous Afghanistan, with good governance and human rights protection for all under the rule of law, and to maintain and strengthen that commitment over the term of this Compact and beyond;

Recognising the courage and determination of Afghans who, by defying violent extremism and hardship, have laid the foundations for a democratic, peaceful, pluralistic and prosperous state based on the principles of Islam;

Noting the full implementation of the Bonn Agreement through the adoption of a new constitution in January 2004, and the holding of presidential elections in October 2004 and National Assembly and Provincial Council elections in September 2005, which have enabled Afghanistan to regain its rightful place in the international community;

Mindful that Afghanistan's transition to peace and stability is not yet assured, and that strong international engagement will continue to be required to address remaining challenges;

Resolved to overcome the legacy of conflict in Afghanistan by setting conditions for sustainable economic growth and development; strengthening state institutions and civil society; removing remaining terrorist threats; meeting the challenge of counter-narcotics; rebuilding capacity and infrastructure; reducing poverty; and meeting basic human needs;

Have agreed to this Afghanistan Compact.

Purpose

The Afghan Government has articulated its overarching goals for the well-being of its people in the <u>Afghanistan Millennium Development Goals Country Report 2005—Vision 2020</u>. Consistent with those goals, this Compact identifies three critical and interdependent areas or pillars of activity for the five years from the adoption of this Compact:

1. Security;
2. Governance, Rule of Law and Human Rights; and
3. Economic and Social Development.

A further vital and cross-cutting area of work is eliminating the narcotics industry, which remains a formidable threat to the people and state of Afghanistan, the region and beyond.

The Afghan Government hereby commits itself to realising this shared vision of the future; the international community, in turn, commits itself to provide resources and support to realise that vision. Annex I of this Compact sets out detailed outcomes, benchmarks and timelines for delivery, consistent with the high-level goals set by the Afghanistan National Development Strategy (ANDS). The Government and international community also commit themselves to improve the effectiveness and accountability of international assistance as set forth in Annex II.

PRINCIPLES OF COOPERATION

As the Afghan Government and the international community embark on the implementation of this Compact, they will:

1. Respect the pluralistic culture, values and history of Afghanistan, based on Islam;
2. Work on the basis of partnership between the Afghan Government, with its sovereign responsibilities, and the international community, with a central and impartial coordinating role for the United Nations;
3. Engage further the deep-seated traditions of participation and aspiration to ownership of the Afghan people;
4. Pursue fiscal, institutional and environmental sustainability;
5. Build lasting Afghan capacity and effective state and civil society institutions, with particular emphasis on building up human capacities of men and women alike;
6. Ensure balanced and fair allocation of domestic and international resources in order to offer all parts of the country tangible prospects of well-being;
7. Recognise in all policies and programmes that men and women have equal rights and responsibilities;
8. Promote regional cooperation; and
9. Combat corruption and ensure public transparency and accountability.

SECURITY

Genuine security remains a fundamental prerequisite for achieving stability and development in Afghanistan. Security cannot be provided by military means alone. It requires good governance, justice and the rule of law, reinforced by reconstruction and development. With the support of the international community, the Afghan Government will consolidate peace by disbanding all illegal armed groups. The

Afghan Government and the international community will create a secure environment by strengthening Afghan institutions to meet the security needs of the country
in a fiscally sustainable manner.

To that end, the NATO-led International Security Assistance Force (ISAF),
the US-led Operation Enduring Freedom (OEF) and partner nations involved
in security sector reform will continue to provide strong support to the
Afghan Government in establishing and sustaining security and stability in
Afghanistan, subject to participating states' national approval procedures.
They will continue to strengthen and develop the capacity of the national security forces to ensure that they become fully functional. All OEF counterterrorism operations will be conducted in close coordination with the Afghan
Government and ISAF. ISAF will continue to expand its presence throughout
Afghanistan, including through Provincial Reconstruction Teams (PRTs), and
will continue to promote stability and support security sector reforms in its areas
of operation.

Full respect for Afghanistan's sovereignty and strengthening dialogue and cooperation between Afghanistan and its neighbours constitute an essential guarantee
of stability in Afghanistan and the region. The international community will support concrete confidence-building measures to this end.

GOVERNANCE, RULE OF LAW AND HUMAN RIGHTS

Democratic governance and the protection of human rights constitute the corner-
stone of sustainable political progress in Afghanistan. The Afghan Government will
rapidly expand its capacity to provide basic services to the population throughout the
country. It will recruit competent and credible professionals to public service on the
basis of merit; establish a more effective, accountable and transparent administration
at all levels of Government; and implement measurable improvements in fighting corruption, upholding justice and the rule of law and promoting respect for the human
rights of all Afghans.

The Afghan Government will give priority to the coordinated establishment in
each province of functional institutions—including civil administration, police,
prisons and judiciary. These institutions will have appropriate legal frameworks
and appointment procedures; trained staff; and adequate remuneration, infrastructure and auditing capacity. The Government will establish a fiscally and institution-
ally sustainable administration for future elections under the supervision of the
Afghanistan Independent Electoral Commission.

Reforming the justice system will be a priority for the Afghan Government and
the international community. The aim will be to ensure equal, fair and transparent access to justice for all based upon written codes with fair trials and enforce-
able verdicts. Measures will include: completing legislative reforms for the
public as well as the private sector; building the capacity of judicial institutions
and personnel; promoting human rights and legal awareness; and rehabilitating
judicial infrastructure.

The Afghan Government and the international community reaffirm their commitment to the protection and promotion of rights provided for in the Afghan
constitution and under applicable international law, including the international

human rights covenants and other instruments to which Afghanistan is party. With a view to rebuilding trust among those whose lives were shattered by war, reinforcing a shared sense of citizenship and a culture of tolerance, pluralism and observance of the rule of law, the Afghan Government with the support of the international community will implement the Action Plan on Peace, Justice and Reconciliation.

ECONOMIC AND SOCIAL DEVELOPMENT

The Afghan Government with the support of the international community will pursue high rates of sustainable economic growth with the aim of reducing hunger, poverty and unemployment. It will promote the role and potential of the private sector, alongside those of the public and non-profit sectors; curb the narcotics industry; ensure macroeconomic stability; restore and promote the development of the country's human, social and physical capital, thereby establishing a sound basis for a new generation of leaders and professionals; strengthen civil society; and complete the reintegration of returnees, internally displaced persons and ex-combatants.

Public investments will be structured around the six sectors of the pillar on economic and social development of the Afghanistan National Development Strategy:

1. Infrastructure and natural resources;
2. Education;
3. Health;
4. Agriculture and rural development;
5. Social protection; and
6. Economic governance and private sector development.

In each of these areas, the objective will be to achieve measurable results towards the goal of equitable economic growth that reduces poverty, expands employment and enterprise creation, enhances opportunities in the region and improves the well-being of all Afghans.

COUNTER-NARCOTICS—A CROSS-CUTTING PRIORITY

Meeting the threat that the narcotics industry poses to national, regional and international security as well as the development and governance of the country and the well-being of Afghans will be a priority for the Government and the international community. The aim will be to achieve a sustained and significant reduction in the production and trafficking of narcotics with a view to complete elimination. Essential elements include improved interdiction, law enforcement and judicial capacity building; enhanced cooperation among Afghanistan, neighbouring countries and the international community on disrupting the drugs trade; wider provision of economic alternatives for farmers and labourers in the context of comprehensive rural development; and building national and provincial counter-narcotics institutions. It will also be crucial to enforce a zero-tolerance policy towards official corruption; to pursue eradication as appropriate; to reinforce the message that producing or trading opiates is both immoral and a violation of Islamic law; and to reduce the demand for the illicit use of opiates.

COORDINATION AND MONITORING

The Afghan Government and the international community are establishing a Joint Coordination and Monitoring Board for the implementation of the political commitments that comprise this Compact. As detailed in Annex III, this Board will be co-chaired by the Afghan Government and the United Nations and will be supported by a small secretariat. It will ensure greater coherence of efforts by the Afghan Government and international community to implement the Compact and provide regular and timely public reports on its execution.

ANNEX I
BENCHMARKS AND TIMELINES

The Afghan Government, with the support of the international community, is committed to achieving the following benchmarks in accordance with the timelines specified.

. . .

Source: NATO. Available online http://www.nato.int/isaf/docu/epub/pdf/afghanistan_compact.pdf.

ANALYSIS

The Afghanistan Compact emerged from the London Conference between the Afghan government and series of international partner nations and organizations. Since Afghanistan had ratified a constitution and held national elections, it had essentially completed the political process outlined in Bonn in 2001. This new compact attempted to identify the next set of priorities for the government to accomplish and establish a series of goals to achieve by the end of 2010 when this next phase of nation building should be complete. Security, development, and human rights constituted the highest priority issues addressed and benchmarked in the Compact. Unfortunately, the resurgence of the Taliban and corruption would prevent the Afghan government from achieving many of its ambitious goals.

- **Document 56: U.S. Embassy (Kabul), Cable, "Policy on Track, but Violence Will Rise"**
- **When:** February 21, 2006
- **Where:** Kabul, Afghanistan
- **Significance:** The U.S. ambassador to Afghanistan warned the State Department that the Taliban would push back aggressively against efforts to extend reconstruction and security.

DOCUMENT

FM AMEMBASSY KABUL
TO SECSTATE WASHDC
...

SUBJECT: POLICY ON TRACK, BUT VIOLENCE WILL RISE

1. SUMMARY: I believe violence will rise through the next several months. It will likely be directed at ISAF as well as the Coalition in addition to more traditional targets such as pro-government officials and religious figures in the Provinces. We should anticipate more suicide bombs in Kabul and other major cities. As the troop density of NATO in the south increases and we conduct aggressive operations, the total number of incidents will also rise. We need to understand it analytically in a regional context. The violence does not indicate a failing policy; on the contrary we need to persevere in what we are doing. We will, however, need to anticipate and plan for increased media scrutiny and possibly increased concern from Europe, its Parliaments, and certainly its media. END SUMMARY.

WHY THE VIOLENCE WILL RISE

2. Several threads are coming together. NATO/ISAF is expanding its mandate. [redacted] Targeting of ISAR has already increased, with resulting casualties among the Germans, Poles, and Swedes, and it seems likely that the enemy will do its utmost to make the ISAF deployment politically costly. The increased use of IEDs and the suicide bombs is as much, perhaps even more the result of the failure of the Taliban's large-unit, force-on-force engagement tactics in the first part of 2005 as it is a sign of an increased threat. But the Taliban now seems to understand the propaganda value of the bomb and will use it to maximum advantage.

3. Additionally, [redacted] the Afghan government is more focused on narcotics extraction. [redacted] this will push them into areas of higher risk like Helmand province. Embassy and CFC-A are focusing maximum energy and attention on ensuring that the government gets the security fundamentals for these operations right; but incident levels will, nonetheless, rise. That said, the same strategic pressures will be on the Taliban; if it cannot resist in the high-threat areas it will lose some credibility and hence the Taliban may be forced to fight where it might otherwise prefer to dodge. Thus, both sides may find that the narcotics and strategic military imperatives intersect.

THE GOVERNANCE CHALLENGE

4. Afghanistan's notable success in the development of the elected government is apparent. Economic progress is beginning. It is very clear that the task now is to build governance in the provinces where Kabul's reach is still very limited. If this process works well over the next few years the government will be significantly stronger. But the Taliban need not be intellectual giants to understand that their long-term strategy depends on keeping the government weak in the provinces. The key will be to continue, aggressively, our work with the GOA to extend and deepen its reach nationwide and to counteract any Taliban strategy aimed at waiting us out while preventing NGO access to the countryside. This challenge will probably increase at the Taliban seeks to get ahead of our progress in deploying Afghan army and police in order to disrupt our

programmatic and development schedules. The Taliban will also look to contest GOA progress on disarmament and rural police deployments by increasing provincial violence. We anticipate, and are considering with the GOA, how best to balance calls for army and police deployments with the need to ensure that the forces sent are fully-manned, equipped, and trained.

THE REGIONAL CONTEXT

5. We tend to think in terms of Afghanistan and Pakistan. [redacted] In the wake of President Karzai's recent visit to Islamabad, there is a growing potential for working with both governments within this construct. We do not see intelligence indicating vast popular support for the Taliban or a large recruiting increase. Therefore, I believe that what we are seeing is largely the result of four years that the Taliban has had to reorganize and think about their approach in a sanctuary beyond the reach of either Government. This will lead to the increasing violence this summer; it will lead to a long-term continuation of the insurgency as long as they can re-supply from their current areas; and, if left unaddressed, it will also lead to the re-emergence of the same strategic threat to the United States that prompted our OEF intervention over 4 years ago.

6. There is more pressure—and intent—from Pakistan against the Taliban, and the Tripartite process is successfully building operational and strategic links between the Pakistan, Afghan, and US-led Coalition militaries. But there are concerns about Pakistani capabilities [redacted] action to date [redacted]. Better governance on the Afghan side of the border will steadily decrease the Taliban threat but achieving a cohesive government at the level required is a long term project. We will continue to do our utmost to show every-day Afghans tangible progress in their provinces to reinforce growing GOA authority.

POLICY CONTINUITY

7. Rising violence will spark some calls for policy evaluation. That is normal. There will certainly and always be something that can be adjusted at the margin. But we are on the right track. The combination of economic rehabilitation, narcotics confrontation, alternative livelihoods development and provincial governance support are all the correct policies. More money could drive reconstruction faster but the international community, not just the US, needs to do more. The lack of roads and energy will continue to delay our efforts and these are slow to build even when resources are available. Security and infrastructure development increasingly are two sides of the same coin here. We are building a better army and that takes time. We are reforming the police, but the comprehensive reform program was only approved and resourced six months ago. The Afghan National Security Forces will get there, but not this year.

8. We are expanding PRTs, [redacted]. The PRTs will make an important difference, but not one that will stem this year's violence.

9. [redacted] To avoid appearing to be playing catch-up to the violence, we must craft and quickly deploy, for Afghans as well for the international audience, a strategic overview that accommodates expanded violence with progress the GOA is making in creating a stable and viable state and lays out a vision for what lies beyond. We should consider working directly with NATO on this. There are plenty of positives to draw on, from the Parliament to the London Compact. [redacted]

NEUMANN

Source: National Security Archive. Available online at http://nsarchive2 .gwu.edu/NSAEBB/NSAEBB325/doc15.pdf.

ANALYSIS

The ambassador's analysis highlights the conundrum of conducting a large-scale reconstruction and counterinsurgency campaign: doing either or both of these activities means exposing personnel to risk, which inevitably leads to the incurrence of high casualties. While unstated, American sensitivity to losses and their possible political consequences could be heightened due to the mounting insurgency simultaneously occurring in Iraq.

The cable also ties together many issues discussed in other documents, including a strong emphasis upon reconstruction and the absolute necessity to link Afghan and Pakistani security issues together given the porous border and the large Pashtun population that lay on both sides of it.

- **Document 57: Statement of General John Abizaid before the Senate Armed Services Committee**
- **When:** March 16, 2006
- **Where:** Washington, D.C.
- **Significance:** General John Abizaid, Commander of U.S. Central Command, testified before Congress and provided a progress report on Operation Enduring Freedom.

DOCUMENT

UNITED STATES CENTRAL COMMAND POSTURE FOR 2006

. . .

VI. AFGHANISTAN
A. SITUATION OVERVIEW

1. Coalition Forces. There are approximately 20,000 U.S. and 4,500 Coalition forces from twenty-five nations deployed in Afghanistan as part of Operation Enduring Freedom (OEF). These forces are commanded by Combined Forces Command—Afghanistan (CFC-A), headquartered in Kabul, which assures unity of effort with the U.S. Ambassador in Kabul and the NATO International Security Assistance Force (ISAF). Combined Joint Task Force–76 (CJTF-76) is a division-level subordinate command. CJTF-76 directs major and routine combat operations throughout Afghanistan. Linked into CJTF-76 is a robust special operations capability from U.S. and Coalition nations. Additionally, NATO's ISAF contributes approximately 8,500 troops—over 150 of whom are American. These troops are primarily located in Kabul and northern and western Afghanistan.

2. The Enemy. Consistent with CENTCOM's primary goal of defeating al Qaida and its allies, CFC-A maintains an intense focus on any indications that al Qaida is attempting to reestablish a safe haven in Afghanistan. Al Qaida senior leaders operate in Pakistan's rugged and isolated Federally Administered Tribal Area (FATA) that borders eastern Afghanistan. In addition to al Qaida, three insurgent groups—all with al Qaida links—constitute the main enemy threat in Afghanistan: (1) the Taliban, (2) Haqqani Tribal Network, and (3) Hezb-i-Islami Gulbuddin (HIG).

The Taliban operates primarily in the southern and eastern provinces and Kabul. Its core supporters, mostly Pashtun, seek its return to power. The Taliban has demonstrated resilience after defeats. They appeared tactically stronger on the battlefield this year, and they demonstrated an increased willingness to use suicide bomber and IED tactics. While the Taliban remain very unpopular in most parts of the country, pockets of hardcore support remain. Taliban activities remain clearly linked to al Qaida funding, direction, and ideological thinking. The Taliban do not have the capability to exercise control over large areas of Afghanistan, but they are disruptive to reconstruction and reconciliation efforts. It is increasingly clear that Taliban leaders also use Pakistan's FATA to organize, plan, and rest. Pakistani efforts to deny this safe haven, while considerable, have yet to shut down this area to Taliban and al Qaida use.

The Haqqani Tribal Network operates primarily in eastern Afghanistan and the FATA region of Pakistan. Haqqani goals are limited primarily to obtaining autonomy in eastern Afghanistan and the FATA region. Although the most tactically proficient of the enemy we face in Afghanistan, they present a limited strategic threat.

The HIG, while remaining dangerous, similarly presents only a limited strategic threat. It operates primarily in eastern Afghanistan and is heavily involved in illicit activities such as narcotics and smuggling, resembling a Mafia-like organization more than an insurgent movement with national goals. Nevertheless, given its historical links with al Qaida, it can help facilitate al Qaida operations in Kabul and eastern Afghanistan if it finds that doing so enhances its interests. Some HIG operatives may be considering political reconciliation.

B. STRATEGIC FOCUS

In 2006, CFC-A will continue to focus on: killing and capturing terrorists and neutralizing the insurgency; providing the shield behind which economic and political progress can move forward and legitimate government institutions can form and take root; and training and building capable Afghan security forces. Additionally, CFC-A will work to ensure a smooth transition with NATO as NATO troops assume additional responsibilities and territory in Afghanistan and support counter-narcotics efforts throughout the country. Our goal, which we share with the people of Afghanistan, is a country at peace with its neighbors and an ally in the broader war against terror, with a representative government and security forces sufficient to maintain domestic order and deny Afghanistan as a safe haven for terrorists.

During the past year, CFC-A continued aggressive offensive military operations to kill and capture terrorists and insurgents and shut down the sanctuaries in which they operate. Given that the terrorists and insurgents that we are pursuing often operate in both Pakistan and Afghanistan, a key element of our strategy is deepening our cooperation with the Pakistani military operating on the Pakistan-Afghanistan border. The important work to de-legitimize Afghan warlords and disarm and demobilize irregular Afghan militias also continues. These efforts take time, rarely producing major breakthroughs, but incremental progress in this important area continues. U.S. and Coalition forces dominate the battlespace and are increasingly involving Afghan National Army units in military operations.

The continued insurgency in Afghanistan will not be defeated solely by military means. In fact, the center of gravity of CFC-A's campaign is decreasingly military and increasingly in the domain of governance and economic development. American, Coalition, and Afghan forces are continuing to provide the critical shield behind which progress in the political and economic realms can continue.

In 2005, there was noteworthy political progress in Afghanistan. The citizens of Afghanistan went to the polls in September to elect a Parliament, which was seated on December 19. Voter turnout was over 50%, with 6.2 million Afghans voting for over 5,800 national and provincial candidates. Extremists failed to make good on their threats of murder to disrupt the elections. Afghan security forces played their most visible and effective role to date in providing essential security to enable the election.

Reconstruction remains a critical way to isolate our enemies, depriving them of their support base and giving Afghans hope for a better future. Continuing and sustained development efforts will be critical to overall success. The United States and our allies will continue to work with the Afghan government in assisting Afghanistan in building the infrastructure needed for a functioning economy. The London Conference in January 2006 was an important step in this regard. More generally, Provincial Reconstruction Teams (PRTs), small civil-military affairs teams with civilian and interagency expertise, remain an important tool to achieve these results. This past year, CFC-A and its NATO-ISAF partners increased the number of PRTs to 24. Of these, 15 were directed by CFC-A, and nine others operated under the authority of NATO-ISAF. Over time, Afghan PRTs will transform from military to civilian-led organizations, and ultimately become provincial development authorities of the Afghan government.

A key strategic interest of both Afghanistan and the United States is to prevent Afghanistan from becoming a terrorist safe haven again. The most effective long-term way to achieve this end is to enable the institutions of the democratically-elected Afghan government to consolidate and extend their reach and legitimacy throughout the country. Coalition PRTs help do this by enhancing local security and extending the authority and visibility of the Afghan government into the provinces.

Training, building, and mentoring the Afghan National Army (ANA) remains a central pillar of our strategy to stabilize Afghanistan. The Afghan Army has suffered through thirty years of civil war, shattering the institutional structures of this force. Given the state of the ANA, our focus has been on quality—building from the ground up—not on quantity. There has been steady progress. The Afghan Army now numbers over 26,000 trained and equipped troops.

U.S. and Coalition forces support the training of fielded ANA battalions with Embedded Training Teams (ETT). There are over 650 military personnel serving in ETTs. These ETTs provide training, combat effects, and logistics support to ANA units. Additionally, ANA forces are now conducting combined operations with American and Coalition Forces. Most important in terms of progress, the citizens of Afghanistan are beginning to view the ANA as a truly national institution that is both trusted and respected. The ANA played a critical role in providing security for the September parliamentary elections, extending its reach to remote villages. Its performance was widely applauded by senior Afghan officials, U.S. commanders in the field, and, most importantly, the people of Afghanistan. As the ANA is fielded, CFC-A will continue initiatives to help the Afghans reform their Ministry of Defense, the Afghan General Staff, and the ANA Regional Military Commands. While the progress with the Army is remarkable, problems with recruiting, infrastructure, and organizational reach need continued attention.

Although the development of an effective Afghan National Army is proceeding on schedule, the Afghan National Police (ANP) force requires considerable work. In conjunction with Germany and other international partners, building a professional and competent ANP remains a top CFC-A priority. Over 58,000 police have been trained. However, the force is still hampered by irregular pay, corruption, and substandard leadership that is often unaccountable to a central ministry. CFC-A and the Department of State are focused on helping the leaders of Afghanistan address these problems with additional mentoring and an emphasis on building the institutional capacity and equipment of the police force. The Government of Afghanistan and the Ministry of Interior have begun reforms, including those that cover pay, rank structure, and curbing corruption. Ultimately, police provide the security backbone against any insurgency and criminal activity. Afghanistan is intensely tribal and lacks modern infrastructure. Loyal and competent police are essential to spreading the rule of law and good governance. A long, hard road is ahead to make the Afghan police what the nation needs.

2006 will be an important year in terms of transitioning additional responsibility and territory to NATO. Specifically, Stage III of the ISAF transition is scheduled for the late spring or summer of 2006 when Regional Command South (RC South) transfers to NATO command. NATO forces in this area will be primarily British, Canadian, and Dutch. They are prepared to aggressively address the threat situation in RC South, which remains high. CENTCOM continues to work closely with NATO to enable its command and control structures and to ensure a successful NATO transition in Afghanistan.

Having NATO, an organization consisting of 26 of the world's most powerful countries, committed to Afghanistan's future is good for Afghanistan. NATO-ISAF is already a major contributor to Afghanistan's security. As NATO eventually assumes control over all conventional U.S. and Coalition forces in Afghanistan, the United States will remain the single largest contributor of forces to this NATO effort, while also retaining a very robust counterterrorism force throughout the entire country. Deepening international commitment to Afghanistan's future will do much to assist the emerging Afghan government and diminish al Qaida's attractiveness to people in Central and South Asia.

The production and trafficking of illegal narcotics remain a significant threat not only to Afghanistan's long-term stability, but to the stability of the entire region. The United Kingdom has the overall lead, and the U.S. Department of State's Bureau of International Narcotics and Law Enforcement leads the U.S. effort. A

Counter Narcotics Branch in CENTCOM's Joint Interagency Coordination Group (JIACG) was established to better coordinate DoD's support for U.S. national efforts. During 2005, CENTCOM delivered $242 million in FY05 DoD supplemental funding in support of INL programs for the Afghan police, border security, and Counter-Narcotics Police (CNPA) equipment and training.

The campaign to stop narco-trafficking and eliminate poppy production is complex, requiring full interagency and international participation, particularly given the regional scope of the problem. The different elements of this campaign include law enforcement, judicial reform, poppy eradication, and alternative livelihood and public information programs. CENTCOM fully supports all of these programs. Our roles include intelligence support, helicopter transport, logistical and administrative assistance for counternarcotics operators in country, and *in extremis* rescue, to include MEDEVAC and close air support operations. Our PRTs also play a critical role developing viable economic alternatives to poppy production.

C. MUCH ACCOMPLISHED, MUCH MORE TO DO

Since September 2001, progress in Afghanistan has been remarkable: the al Qaida safe haven in Afghanistan was eliminated and the Taliban removed from power; security was established for a political process in which the people of the country have freely elected a president and parliament; military units spearheaded an effort to bring the significant resources and expertise of the international community to help Afghanistan begin to address many of its longstanding problems; and the United States, along with our international partners and the Afghan government, has begun the difficult work of helping the Afghan people build the institutions and infrastructure that are the key to the future of their country.

Given this progress, there is still a very strong notion of "consent" in this country—the Afghan people are very appreciative of the help they have received from international troops, especially those from the United States, and there is a strong, broad-based desire for such troops to remain in the country. But much work needs to be done and progress is not guaranteed. Helping Afghans build infrastructure, which in many regions is nonexistent, attack endemic corruption, address narco-trafficking, train their Army and police, all while fighting an insurgency that remains patient, hidden, and dangerous, are tasks that will require years. As in Iraq, an essential element of achieving overall success will depend on the leadership, character, and vision of Afghanistan's elected leaders.

Source: Department of Defense. Available online at www.globalsecurity.org/military/library/congress/2006_hr/060316-abizaid.pdf.

ANALYSIS

By 2006, concerns about the insurgency in Afghanistan had finally prompted General Abizaid from the U.S. Central Command to acknowledge that counterinsurgency was now coequal to counterterrorism as the biggest U.S. military priority in Afghanistan. U.S. military forces assumed most of the combat burden in Afghanistan in the southern and eastern provinces while the remainder of ISAF provided security in the less threatened northern and western provinces where the Taliban and other insurgents had minimal influence.

Still, much of the U.S. contingent remained focused on other missions, including building the Afghan National Army, counternarcotics, and supporting reconstruction through the Provincial Reconstruction Teams (PRTs). That these remained priorities even after more than four years speaks to how bereft Afghanistan had been of order and civil institutions under the Taliban and its predecessor regimes.

- **Document 58: Declaration by North Atlantic Treaty Organization and the Islamic Republic of Afghanistan**
- **When:** September 6, 2006
- **Where:** Lisbon, Portugal
- **Significance:** This declaration signed at a joint summit committed the Alliance to partnering with the Afghan government in continued development of Afghan military institutions.

DOCUMENT

I. Introduction: Framework for enduring co-operation in partnership

1. Building on the success of the National Assembly elections in 2005, the completion of the Bonn process and the results of the London Conference, in particular the Afghanistan Compact, NATO remains committed to working together with the Government of Afghanistan and other international organisations to help build a peaceful, stable and democratic Afghanistan. NATO acknowledges the importance of stability and security in Afghanistan to Central and South Asia and the wider international community, and the challenging nature of the security threats facing the Afghan Government. The Afghan Government's ultimate aim is to take full responsibility for its own security. To achieve this goal, strong and visible international commitment continues to be important to promote stability in Afghanistan, both through the deployment of international military forces and through support for the development of effective Afghan national security and defence institutions. Reaffirming NATO's determination in this regard, and in response to President Karzai's request for a broad and long-term relationship with NATO, Allied Foreign Ministers agreed in December 2005 to develop a programme of cooperation with Afghanistan. This programme builds on NATO's unique relationship with Afghanistan and reflects the Alliance's support for Afghanistan's national sovereignty, independence and territorial integrity. The relationship between NATO and Afghanistan is not limited to the provisions of this programme.

2. The Government of Afghanistan and Allies recognise that security cannot be provided by military means alone. Security requires good governance, justice and the rule of law, reinforced by reconstruction and development, as well as

international, and particularly regional co-operation. In this context, the Declaration on Good-neighbourly Relations signed in Kabul on 22 December 2002 between Afghanistan and its neighbours plays an important role. Afghanistan also considers terrorism, extremism and drug trafficking as major challenges to security, and is committed to taking full advantage of international support and assistance, and to cooperating with the international community to build capacity to eliminate these threats.

3. Afghanistan recognises that at present it is unable to fully meet its own security needs and highly appreciates NATO's contribution to providing security and stability in Afghanistan, Afghanistan is determined to develop rapidly the capabilities of its national security and defence institutions to meet national requirements, operate more effectively alongside ISAF and international military forces, and improve their capacity for independent action. Afghanistan stands ready to further broaden cooperation with the Alliance aimed at promoting interoperability with NATO member states' forces, as well as activities supporting defence reform, defence institution building and military aspects of security sector reform as well as other areas mutually agreed. Longer term, Afghanistan aspires to contribute to security and stability by taking part in NATO-led peacekeeping operations.

II. Main Principles of Cooperation

4. The programme will:

   a. Be realistic, both in terms of substance and available resources, and in those areas where NATO can substantially contribute and add value, within means and capabilities, if necessary through re-prioritisation under current budget ceilings;

   b. Be built on the principle of ownership by the Afghan authorities and reflect their capacities. To achieve this objective, such a programme should be tailored to the needs identified by, and implemented in close consultation with Afghan authorities, who will designate appropriate interlocutors;

   c. Complement ISAF's operational role and help consolidate the gains achieved through ISAF presence, in particular at the level of Afghanistan's central security and defence institutions in Kabul;

   d. Take into account the activities and cooperation programmes conducted by other actors, promoting possible collaboration and avoiding unnecessary duplication of efforts; it should also take into account the results of the London Conference, in particular the Afghan Compact between Afghanistan and the International Community, co-ordinated by the Joint Coordination and Monitoring Board

. . .

V. Forces and Assets

10. The Afghan authorities, NATO and Allies will consult together, using established Partnership tools, to identify the appropriate Afghan institutions, forces, assets and training facilities to take part in this cooperation. This will

include identifying those to take part in a systematic planning and assessment process aimed at promoting the required level of interoperability and developing the capabilities of the Afghan National Army. The desired end state is a credible, professional military force able to support Afghan authorities to maintain security and stability in the country, consistent with international norms and without external support.

VI. Main areas of cooperation

11. Subject to the principles outlined in paragraph 4, the programme will concentrate on defence reform, defence institution building and the military aspects of security sector reform, as well as on other areas mutually identified by both NATO and Afghanistan including promoting interoperability between the forces of the ANA and NATO members. Drawing on NATO's extensive experience in defence planning and reform, this programme may include support of the Afghan Government's efforts in the following areas:
    o Development of transparent, effective and democratically controlled Afghan national defence and appropriate security institutions, consistent with best practices and international norms, complementing lead nations' bilateral efforts in this area;
    o Creation of conceptual foundation of security and defence, including national security strategy and national military strategy, and related strategic planning systems and processes;
    o Development of effective national defence planning and budgeting processes under democratic control, including a transparent and effective personnel management and training system, as well as establishing plans for equipment acquisition/modernisation;
    o Promoting interoperability between NATO and the ANA, to allow them to take increasing responsibility for Afghanistan's national security; this will include designation of forces, assets and training facilities to take part in a systematic planning and assessment process, this will include the identification of equipment, logistic, training and education needs, including participation in selected NATO/PfP exercises, to meet interoperability objectives to be agreed;
    o Through bilateral programmes, assistance to enhance the capacity of the Afghan national defence forces to deploy in a timely manner across the country. Such assistance may include the provision of aircrew and technical training as well as the coordination by NATO members of bilateral assistance to address military equipment, infrastructure, technical support and sustainability requirements;
    o Creating adequate stockpile management of SALW, munitions, APLs and MANPADS including assessing requirements for safe destruction of surplus stocks and examining the possibility of establishing Trust Funds to decrease the threat from these stockpiles;
    o Facilitating contacts, co-operation and exchange of experience with Allies' national institutions to support monitoring and implementation of arms control agreements and treaties and adherence to multi-lateral

export control régime guidelines on military and dual-use goods and technology;

o In conformity with the OPLAN, support the Afghan Government's counter-narcotic efforts;

o Drawing on the NATO Policy on Combating Trafficking in Human Beings, relative to the conduct of the military, NATO will support and sustain development of practical cooperation and provide support to responsible authorities in their efforts to combat trafficking in human beings;

o Complementing and facilitating lead nations' efforts in the area of border security, promote civilian control and relevant mechanisms, such as effective and transparent legislative and judicial oversight of law enforcement organisations in charge of border security and control, identifying training needs;

o Develop cooperation in the area of civil emergency planning, in accordance with NATO procedures and drawing on Allies national institutions;

o Language training of defence and security institutions' personnel to support interoperability objectives to be agreed;

o Development of effective civil/military co-ordination of air traffic management;

o Enhancing public understanding, including by developing key messages for the public opinion, about defence and security issues, including defence reform, defence institution building and the military aspects of security sector reform, the role of the appropriate Afghan national security forces and NATO forces, taking into account Afghanistan's regional dimension; and

o Using the Virtual Silk Highway project in Afghanistan, to support access to information and contribute to successful implementation of this programme.

Jaap de Hoop Scheffer
Secretary General of the North
Atlantic Treaty Organisation

Hamid Karzai
President of the Islamic Republic
of Afghanistan

Source: NATO. Available online at http://www.nato.int/cps/en/natohq/official_texts_50575.htm.

ANALYSIS

This partnership agreement committed NATO to even closer cooperation with the Afghan government to rebuild its military and security institutions. Since ISAF had become a NATO mission in 2003 with the end of the UN mandate over the force, and concurrently, the construction of the Afghan National Army had been frustratingly slow, this partnership sought to deepen the relationship between both parties. By increasing the interoperability of NATO and Afghan forces, this agreement hoped to allow the Afghans to assume a larger degree of their security burden and professionalize their military.

- **Document 59:** George W. Bush, The President's News Conference with President Hamid Karzai of Afghanistan
- **When:** September 26, 2006
- **Where:** Washington, D.C.
- **Significance:** This joint press conference with President Bush and President Karzai addressed the state of Afghan reconstruction and many other topics.

DOCUMENT

President Bush. Thank you. Please be seated. It's my honor to welcome President Karzai back to the White House. Mr. President, Laura and I fondly remember your gracious hospitality when we met you in your capital. We had a chance today to reconfirm our strong commitment to work together for peace and freedom. And I'm proud of your leadership.

You've got a tough job—

President Karzai. Yes, sometimes it is.

President Bush. —and you're showing a lot of strength and character. And we're proud to call you ally and friend. I really am.

We discussed how the Government is building institutions necessary for Afghans to have a secure future. We talked about how America and our international partners can continue to help.

Our allies are working on initiatives to help the Afghan people in building a free Afghanistan. And we discussed those initiatives. We discussed whether or not they could be effective, and we discussed how to make them effective. We discussed our cooperation in defeating those who kill innocent life to achieve objectives, political objectives.

The Afghan people know firsthand the nature of the enemy that we face in the war on terror. After all, just yesterday, Taliban gunmen assassinated Safia Ama Jan—coldblooded kill—she got killed in cold blood. She was a leader who wanted to give young girls an education in Afghanistan. She was a person who served her Government. She was a person who cared deeply about the future of the country. And, Mr. President, Laura and I and the American people join you in mourning her loss.

And her loss shows the nature of this enemy we face. They have no conscience. Their objective is to create fear and create enough violence so we withdraw and let them have their way. And that's unacceptable. It's unacceptable behavior for the free world and the civilized world to accept, Mr. President.

I know that Taliban and Al Qaida remnants and others are trying to bring down your Government, because they know that as democratic institutions take root in your country, the terrorists will not be able to control your country or be able to use it to launch attacks on other nations. They see the threat of democratic progress.

In recent months, the Taliban and other extremists have tried to regain control, mostly in the south of Afghanistan. And so we've adjusted tactics, and we're on the offense to meet the threat and to defeat the threat. Forces from dozens of nations, including every member of NATO, are supporting the democratic Government of Afghanistan. The American people are providing money to help send our troops to your country, Mr. President, and so are a lot of other nations around the world. This is a multinational effort to help you succeed.

Your people have rejected extremism. Afghan forces are fighting bravely for the future of Afghanistan, and many of your forces have given their lives, and we send our deepest condolences to their families and their friends and their neighbors.

The fighting in Afghanistan is part of a global struggle. Recently British forces killed a long-time terrorist affiliated with Al Qaida named Omar Farouq. Farouq was active in Bosnia and Southeast Asia. He was captured in Indonesia; he escaped from prison in Afghanistan; he was killed hiding in Iraq. Every victory in the war on terror enhances the security of free peoples everywhere.

Mr. President, as I told you in the Oval Office, our country will stand with the free people of Afghanistan. I know there's some in your country who wonder or not—whether or not America has got the will to do the hard work necessary to help you succeed. We have got that will, and we're proud of you as a partner.

President Karzai. Wonderful. Great.

President Bush. We discussed our efforts to help the Government deliver a better life. President Karzai said this about his aspirations—he said he "wants to make Afghanistan a great success and an enduring example of a prosperous and democratic society."

We're helping you build effective and accountable Government agencies. We discussed different agencies in your Government and how best to make them accountable to the people. We're going to help you build roads. We understand that it's important for people to have access to markets. I thought our general had a pretty interesting statement; he said, "Where the road ends, the Taliban tries to begin." The President understands that.

We're helping you with a national literacy program.

President Karzai. Yes.

President Bush. We understand that a free society is one that counts upon a educated citizenry. The more educated a populace is, the more likely it is they'll be active participants in democratic forms of government. We're helping you build schools and medical centers.

We talked about the illegal drug trade. The President gave me a very direct assessment of successes in eradicating poppies and failures in eradicating poppies. It was a realistic assessment of the conditions on the ground. And he talked about his strategy, particularly in dealing in Helmand Province. And, Mr. President, we will support you on this strategy. We understand what you understand, and that is, we've got to eradicate drug trade for the good of the people of Afghanistan.

Tomorrow President Karzai and President Musharraf and I will have dinner. I'm looking forward to it. It's going to be an interesting discussion amongst three allies, three people who are concerned about the future of Pakistan and Afghanistan. It will be a chance for us to work on how to secure the border, how we can continue to work together and share information so we can defeat extremists, how we can work together to build a future of peace and democracy in your region, Mr. President.

I thank you for coming today. I'm looking forward to our discussion tomorrow evening. Welcome back to the White House. The podium is yours.

President Karzai. Thank you very much, Mr. President. It's a great honor to be in your very beautiful country once again, especially during fall with all the lovely leaves around. And thank you very much for the great hospitality that you and the First Lady are always giving to your guests, especially to me. And thanks also for your visit to Afghanistan and for seeing us in our country, for seeing from close as to who we are and how we may get to a better future.

I'm very grateful, Mr. President, to you and the American people for all that you have done for Afghanistan for the last $4\frac{1}{2}$ years, from roads to education to democracy to parliament to good governance effort to health and to all other good things that are happening in Afghanistan.

Mr. President, I was, the day before yesterday, in the Walter Reed Hospital. There I met wounded in Iraq and Afghanistan. And there also I met a woman soldier with six boys, from 7 to 21, that she had left behind in America in order to build us a road in a mountainous part of the country in Afghanistan. There's nothing more that any nation can do for another country, to send a woman with children to Afghanistan to help. We are very grateful. I'm glad I came to know that story, and I'll be repeating it to the Afghan people once I go back to Afghanistan.

We discussed today all matters that concern the two countries: the question of the reconstruction of Afghanistan, improvement for the reconstruction of Afghanistan, the equipping of the Afghan Army, the training of the Afghan Army, the police in Afghanistan, and all other aspects of reconstruction.

We also discussed the region around us, discussed our relations with Pakistan and the question of the joint fight that we have together against terrorism. And I am glad, Mr. President, that you are, tomorrow, hosting a dinner for me and President Musharraf. And I'm sure we'll come out of that meeting with a lot more to talk about to our nations in a very positive way for a better future.

Mr. President, we, the Afghan people, are grateful to you and the American people for all that you have done. I have things in mind to speak about, and you did that, so I'll stop short and let the questions come to us.

President Bush. Thanks. We'll have two questions a side. We'll start with Jennifer Loven [Associated Press].

National Intelligence Estimate/Situation in Afghanistan
Q . . .
And to President Karzai, if I might, what do you think of President Musharraf's comments that you need to get to know your own country better when you're talking about where terror threats and the Taliban threat is coming from?

        . . .

President Karzai. Ma'am, before I go to the remarks by my brother, President Musharraf, terrorism was hurting us way before Iraq or September 11th. The President mentioned some examples of it. These extremist forces were killing people in Afghanistan and around for years, closing schools, burning mosques, killing children, uprooting vineyards with vine trees, grapes hanging on them, forcing populations to poverty and misery.

They came to America on September 11th, but they were attacking you before September 11th in other parts of the world. We are a witness in Afghanistan to what they are and how they can hurt. You are a witness in New York. Do you forget people jumping off the 80th floor or 70th floor when the planes hit them? Can you imagine what it will be for a man or a woman to jump off that high? Who did that? And where are they now? And how do we fight them; how do we get rid of them, other than going after them? Should we wait for them to come and kill us again? That's why we need more action around the world, in Afghanistan and elsewhere, to get them defeated: extremism, their allies, terrorists and the like.

On the remarks of my brother, President Musharraf, Afghanistan is a country that is emerging out of so many years of war and destruction and occupation by terrorism and misery that they've brought to us. We lost almost two generations to the lack of education. And those who were educated before that are now older. We know our problems. We have difficulties. But Afghanistan also knows where the problem is— in extremism, in madrassas preaching hatred, preachers in the name of madrassas preaching hatred. That's what we should do together to stop.

The United States, as our ally, is helping both countries. And I think it is very important that we have more dedication and more intense work with sincerity, all of us, to get rid of the problems that we have around the world.

. . .

International Support for the War on Terror/Afghanistan-Pakistan Relations

Q. Thank you, sir. Mr. President, are you convinced, like President Bush, that the deal General Musharraf signed with the tribal leaders in Waziristan actually meant to fight the Taliban? And why are you convinced that Usama bin Laden is not in Afghanistan?

If I may, Mr. President, do you agree with the analysis from the counter chief European—counterterrorism chief European spokesman who said today that the international support for terrorism has receded? Do you agree with that? And do you see the tension between two important allies of yours, Pakistan and Afghanistan, undermining your effort to get Usama bin Laden? Thank you.

President Bush. It's a four-part question. First of all, I didn't—what was this person a spokesman for?

Q. Counterterrorism chief in Europe.

President Bush. Some obscure spokesman?

Q. No, actually, he has a name.

President Bush. Okay, he's a got a name. Well, no, I don't agree with the spokesman for the obscure organization that said that the international commitment to fighting terror is declining. It's quite the contrary, starting with the evidence that NATO has committed troops in Afghanistan. These are troops who are on the ground who are serving incredibly bravely to protect this country.

Secondly, when the Brits, along with our help, intercepted the plot to attack us, everybody started saying, "They're still there." They began to realize that their hopes that the terrorist threats were going away weren't true. Since September the 11th, it's important for the American people to remember, there have been a lot of attacks on a lot of nations by these jihadists. And some of them are Al Qaida and some of them are Al Qaida inspired. The NIE talked about how this group of folks are becoming more dispersed. That's what I've been saying as well. After all, look inside of Great Britain. These are people inspired by, perhaps trained by Al Qaida, but nevertheless plotted and planned attacks and conducted attacks in the summer of 2005, and then plotted attacks in the summer of 2006. See, they're dangerous, and the world knows that.

And so from my perspective, intelligence sharing is good, cooperation on the financial fronts is good, and that more and more nations are committing troops to the fight, in Afghanistan in particular.

Now, the other question—

Q. The tension between two allies—does this undermine the efforts of getting bin Laden?

President Bush. No. No, it doesn't. It's in President Karzai's interest to see bin Laden brought to justice. It is in President Musharraf's interest to see bin Laden brought to justice. Our interests coincide. It will be interesting for me to watch the body language of these two leaders to determine how tense things are.

President Karzai. I'll be good.

President Bush. Yes. From my discussions with President Karzai and President Musharraf, there is an understanding that by working together, it is more likely that all of us can achieve a common objective, which are stable societies that are hopeful societies, that prevent extremists from stopping progress and denying people a hopeful world.

I know that's what President Karzai thinks, and I know that's how President Musharraf thinks. And so—I'm kind of teasing about the body language for the dinner tomorrow night, but it's going to be a good dinner, and it's an important dinner.

So to answer your question, no. What you perceive as tension is stopping us from bringing high-value targets to justice, quite the contrary, we're working as hard as ever in doing that.

President Karzai. On the question of Waziristan, ma'am, President Musharraf, when he was in Kabul, explained what they had done there. My initial impression was that this was a deal signed by the Taliban, and then later I learned that they actually signed with the tribal chiefs. It will have a different meaning if it is that signed with the tribal chiefs—that for us, for the United States, for the allies against terror.

The most important element here is item number one in this agreement, that the terrorists will not be allowed to cross over into Afghanistan to attack the coalition against terror, that is, the international community and Afghanistan together. We will have to wait and see if that is going to be implemented exactly the way it is signed. So from our side, it's a wait-and-see attitude. But generally, we will back any move, any deal that will deny terrorism sanctuary in North Waziristan or in the tribal territories of Pakistan.

President Bush. Mr. President, thank you.

President Karzai. Thank you, sir.

President Bush. Well done.

Source: Public Papers of the Presidents of the United States: George W. Bush, 2006, Book 2. Washington, D.C.: Government Printing Office, 2007, 1700–1708.

ANALYSIS

This press conference noted the continued difficulties in building an Afghan government that could command the respect of its own citizens while remaining a reliable partner to the United States and other Western nations. Even though progress in human rights had been considerable since 2001, the recent assassination of a noted advocate for women's rights noted in President Bush's opening statement underscored the fragile nature of much of this progress.

The questions and answers directed to President Karzai also pointed to continued problems with the government maintaining effective control over the countryside as narcotics trafficking remained a serious problem, and President Musharraf even openly criticized President Karzai's knowledge of the security situation.

- **Document 60: Riga Summit Declaration**
- **When:** November 29, 2006
- **Where:** Riga, Latvia
- **Significance:** The Riga Summit Declaration formally announced the establishment of the NATO Response Force first proposed at the Prague Summit in 2002.

DOCUMENT

Issued by the Heads of State and Government participating in the meeting of the North Atlantic Council in Riga on 29 November 2006

1. We, the Heads of State and Government of the member countries of the North Atlantic Alliance, reaffirm today in Riga our resolve to meet the security challenges of the 21st century and defend our populations and common values, while maintaining a strong collective defence as the core purpose of our Alliance. Our 26 nations are united in democracy, individual liberty and the rule of law, and faithful to the purposes and principles of the United Nations Charter.

2. The principle of the indivisibility of Allied security is fundamental, and our solidarity gives us the strength to meet new challenges together. In today's evolving security environment, we confront complex, sometimes inter-related threats such as terrorism, increasingly global in scale and lethal in results, and the proliferation of Weapons of Mass Destruction and their means of delivery, as well as challenges from instability due to failed or failing states. This puts a premium on the vital role NATO plays as the essential forum for security consultation between North American and European Allies. It highlights the importance of common action against those threats, including in UN-mandated crisis response operations. It also underscores the importance of continuing transformation of NATO's capabilities and relationships, which

includes our operations and missions, strong investment in enhanced capabilities, and closer engagement with our partners, other nations and organisations. We have today endorsed our Comprehensive Political Guidance which provides a framework and political direction for NATO's continuing transformation, setting out, for the next 10–15 years, the priorities for all Alliance capability issues, planning disciplines and intelligence.

3. From Afghanistan to the Balkans and from the Mediterranean Sea to Darfur, in six challenging missions and operations in three geographic regions, we are advancing peace and security and standing shoulder-to-shoulder with those who defend our common values of democracy and freedom as embodied in the Washington Treaty. We are working closely with our partners and other nations in these endeavours. We pay tribute to the professionalism and dedication of the more than fifty thousand men and women from Allied and other nations dedicated to these tasks, and extend our deepest sympathies to the families and loved ones of the injured and the fallen.

4. We stand with the Government of President Karzai and the people of Afghanistan who seek to build a stable, democratic and prosperous society, free from terrorism, narcotics and fear, providing for its own security and at peace with its neighbours. Afghans have accomplished much in the last five years. Democratically elected institutions are in place, and the implementation of national reconstruction and development strategies is improving the lives of millions. We are committed to an enduring role to support the Afghan authorities, in cooperation with other international actors.

5. Contributing to peace and stability in Afghanistan is NATO's key priority. In cooperation with Afghan National Security Forces and in coordination with other international actors, we will continue to support the Afghan authorities in meeting their responsibilities to provide security, stability and reconstruction across Afghanistan through the UN-mandated NATO-led International Security Assistance Force (ISAF), respecting international law and making every effort to avoid harm to the civilian population. We reaffirm the strong solidarity of our Alliance, and pledge to ensure that ISAF has the forces, resources, and flexibility needed to ensure the mission's continued success. Moreover, the Afghan Government and NATO are working together to develop democratically-controlled defence institutions. We have agreed today to increase our support to the training and further development of the Afghan National Army, and decided to make stronger national contributions to Afghan National Police training. We welcome the continued contribution of partners and other nations to the ISAF mission and encourage all members of the international community to contribute to this essential effort.

6. There can be no security in Afghanistan without development, and no development without security. The Afghan people have set out their security, governance, and development goals in the Afghanistan Compact, concluded with the international community at the beginning of the year. Provincial Reconstruction Teams are increasingly at the leading edge of NATO's effort, supported by military forces capable of providing the security and stability

needed to foster civilian activity. Guided by the principle of local ownership, our nations will support the Afghan Government's National Development Strategy and its efforts to build civilian capacity and develop its institutions. We encourage other nations and international organisations, notably the UN and the World Bank, to do the same. NATO will play its full role, but cannot assume the entire burden. We welcome efforts by donor nations, the European Union (EU), and other international organisations to increase their support. We also welcome the steps already taken by the international community to improve the coordination of civilian and military activities, including dialogue between capitals and international organisations, and are convinced of the need to take this further. We encourage the UN to take a leading role in this regard in support of the Afghan Government.

7. We support the Government of Afghanistan's work to demonstrate decisive leadership, including reaching out to the provinces, strengthening the rule of law, tackling corruption and taking resolute measures against illegal narcotics. We further recognise the need to disrupt the networks that finance, supply and equip terrorists who threaten the government and people of Afghanistan. We recognise the linkage between narcotics and insurgents in Afghanistan and will continue to support the Afghan Government's counter-narcotics efforts, within ISAF's mandate.

8. We call on all Afghanistan's neighbours to act resolutely in support of the Afghan government's efforts to build a stable and democratic country within secure borders. We particularly encourage close cooperation between Afghanistan, Pakistan and NATO, including through the Tri-Partite Commission.
   . . .

10. Experience in Afghanistan and Kosovo demonstrates that today's challenges require a comprehensive approach by the international community involving a wide spectrum of civil and military instruments, while fully respecting mandates and autonomy of decisions of all actors, and provides precedents for this approach. To that end, while recognising that NATO has no requirement to develop capabilities strictly for civilian purposes, we have tasked today the Council in Permanent Session to develop pragmatic proposals in time for the meeting of Foreign Ministers in April 2007 and Defence Ministers in June 2007 to improve coherent application of NATO's own crisis management instruments as well as practical cooperation at all levels with partners, the UN and other relevant international organisations, Non-Governmental Organisations and local actors in the planning and conduct of ongoing and future operations wherever appropriate. These proposals should take into account emerging lessons learned and consider flexible options for the adjustment of NATO military and political planning procedures with a view to enhancing civil-military interface.
    . . .

22. Continuing defence transformation is essential to ensure that the Alliance remains able to perform its full range of missions, including collective defence and crisis response operations. Our operations in Afghanistan and the

Balkans confirm that NATO needs modern, highly capable forces—forces that can move quickly to wherever they are needed upon decision by the NAC. Building on our decisions at the Summits in Prague and Istanbul, much has already been done to make Alliance forces more capable and usable. We will strengthen capabilities further in accordance with the direction and priorities of the Comprehensive Political Guidance.

23. The establishment of the NATO Response Force (NRF) which today is at full operational capability has been a key development. It plays a vital part in the Alliance's response to a rapidly emerging crisis. It also serves as a catalyst for transformation and interoperability and will enhance the overall quality of our armed forces, not only for NATO, but also for EU, UN or national purposes. We support the improved implementation of the agreed NRF concept through mechanisms to enhance long term force generation, and steps to allow for a more sustainable and transparent approach to maintain the capability of the force in the future.

24. The adaptation of our forces must continue. We have endorsed a set of initiatives to increase the capacity of our forces to address contemporary threats and challenges.

These include:

- improving our ability to conduct and support multinational joint expeditionary operations far from home territory with little or no host nation support and to sustain them for extended periods. This requires forces that are fully deployable, sustainable and interoperable and the means to deploy them;
- commitments to increase strategic airlift, crucial to the rapid deployment of forces, to address identified persistent shortages. Multinational initiatives by NATO members and Partners include the already operational Strategic Airlift Interim Solution; the intent of a consortium to pool C-17 airlift assets, and offers to coordinate support structures for A-400M strategic airlift. Nationally, Allies have or plan to acquire a large number of C-17 and A-400M aircraft. There have also been significant developments in the collective provision of sealift since the Prague Summit;
- the launch of a special operations forces transformation initiative aimed at increasing their ability to train and operate together, including through improving equipment capabilities;
- ensuring the ability to bring military support to stabilisation operations and reconstruction efforts in all phases of a crisis, as required and as set out in the Comprehensive Political Guidance, drawing on lessons learned and emerging from current operations on the added value of such military support;
- work to develop a NATO Network Enabled Capability to share information, data and intelligence reliably, securely and without delay in Alliance operations, while improving protection of our key information systems against cyber attack;
- the activation of an Intelligence Fusion Centre to improve information and intelligence sharing for Alliance operations;

- continuing progress in the Alliance Ground Surveillance programme, with a view to achieving real capabilities to support Alliance forces;
- continuing efforts to develop capabilities to counter chemical, biological, radiological and nuclear threats;
- transforming the Alliance's approach to logistics, in part through greater reliance on multinational solutions;
- efforts to ensure that the command structure is lean, efficient and more effective; and
- the signature of the first major contract for a NATO Active Layered Theatre Ballistic Missile Defence system which is a major step towards improving the protection of deployed NATO forces.

. . .

Source: NATO. Available online at http://www.nato.int/docu/pr/2006/p06 -150e.htm.

ANALYSIS

In the four years since the Prague Summit (Document 44), the member nations of NATO established the NATO Response Force to better allow the Alliance to respond to crises like those seen in Afghanistan in the future. This public commitment, however, belied a number of significant disagreements in the direction of the Alliance, including low levels of defense spending by many of the member nations and a reluctance by many countries to allow the forces they contributed to ISAF to serve in combat roles. In practice, the United States and the United Kingdom constituted the bulk of ISAF's combat forces, while Germany and other nations limited their forces to development and other nonviolent missions in the more peaceful parts of Afghanistan.

- **Document 61: Field Manual 3-24, Counterinsurgency**
- **When:** December 15, 2006
- **Where:** Washington, D.C.
- **Significance:** Field Manual 3-24, collectively authored by a group of experienced military officers and analysts, established doctrine (best operating practices) for the U.S. military to wage population-centric counterinsurgency campaigns.

DOCUMENT

Foreword

This manual is designed to fill a doctrinal gap. It has been 20 years since the Army published a field manual devoted exclusively to counterinsurgency operations. For the Marine Corps it has been 25 years. With our Soldiers and Marines fighting

DID YOU KNOW?

Improvised Explosive Devices

Improvised explosive devices (IEDs) are weapons that are constructed and used in unconventional operations and intended to harass and destroy the enemy. IEDs are most often associated with insurgencies and have been used by many insurgent groups over the past several decades, including the mujahedeen. The term became more commonplace when Iraqi insurgents began using IEDs against U.S. troops and equipment in May 2003. Perhaps observing the success Iraqi insurgents had with IEDs from afar, the Taliban soon began to incorporate IEDs into their own attacks against the Coalition, becoming common in southern and some parts of eastern Afghanistan. IEDs posed the most danger to personnel and lightly armored vehicles, such as trucks and Humvees. The introduction of Mine Resistant Ambush Protected vehicles in 2007 as well as better tactics not only reduced the number of casualties but also caused more incidents of traumatic brain injury (TBI) from the concussive impact of IEDs. Coalition casualties from IEDs grew during the surge of 2010–2012 but then receded. In spite of countermeasures, IEDs continue to pose a threat to the security of Afghanistan.

insurgents in Afghanistan and Iraq, it is essential that we give them a manual that provides principles and guidelines for counterinsurgency operations. Such guidance must be grounded in historical studies. However, it also must be informed by contemporary experiences.

This manual takes a general approach to counterinsurgency operations. The Army and Marine Corps recognize that every insurgency is contextual and presents its own set of challenges. You cannot fight former Saddamists and Islamic extremists the same way you would have fought the Viet Cong, Moros, or Tupamaros; the application of principles and fundamentals to deal with each varies considerably. Nonetheless, all insurgencies, even today's highly adaptable strains, remain wars amongst the people. They use variations of standard themes and adhere to elements of a recognizable revolutionary campaign plan. This manual therefore addresses the common characteristics of insurgencies. It strives to provide those conducting counterinsurgency campaigns with a solid foundation for understanding and addressing specific insurgencies.

A counterinsurgency campaign is, as described in this manual, a mix of offensive, defensive, and stability operations conducted along multiple lines of operations. It requires Soldiers and Marines to employ a mix of familiar combat tasks and skills more often associated with nonmilitary agencies. The balance between them depends on the local situation. Achieving this balance is not easy. It requires leaders at all levels to adjust their approach constantly. They must ensure that their Soldiers and Marines are ready to be greeted with either a handshake or a hand grenade while taking on missions only infrequently practiced until recently at our combat training centers. Soldiers and Marines are expected to be nation builders as well as warriors. They must be prepared to help reestablish institutions and local security forces and assist in rebuilding infrastructure and basic services. They must be able to facilitate establishing local governance and the rule of law. The list of such tasks is long; performing them involves extensive coordination and cooperation with many intergovernmental, host-nation, and international agencies. Indeed, the responsibilities of leaders in a counterinsurgency campaign are daunting; however, the discussions in this manual alert leaders to the challenges of such campaigns and suggest general approaches for grappling with those challenges.

Conducting a successful counterinsurgency campaign requires a flexible, adaptive force led by agile, well-informed, culturally astute leaders. It is our hope that this manual provides the guidelines needed to succeed in operations that are exceedingly difficult and complex. Our Soldiers and Marines deserve nothing less.

DAVID H. PETRAEUS
Lieutenant General, U.S. Army Lieutenant General,

U.S. Army Combined Arms Center
JAMES F. AMOS
U.S. Marine Corps
Commander Deputy Commandant
Combat Development and Integration
. . .

Introduction

This is a game of wits and will. You've got to be learning and
adapting constantly to survive.
General Peter J. Schoomaker, USA, 2004

The United States possesses overwhelming conventional military superiority. This capability has pushed its enemies to fight U.S. forces unconventionally, mixing modern technology with ancient techniques of insurgency and terrorism. Most enemies either do not try to defeat the United States with conventional operations or do not limit themselves to purely military means. They know that they cannot compete with U.S. forces on those terms. Instead, they try to exhaust U.S. national will, aiming to win by undermining and outlasting public support. Defeating such enemies presents a huge challenge to the Army and Marine Corps. Meeting it requires creative efforts by every Soldier and Marine.

Throughout its history, the U.S. military has had to relearn the principles of counterinsurgency (COIN) while conducting operations against adaptive insurgent enemies. It is time to institutionalize Army and Marine Corps knowledge of this long-standing form of conflict. This publication's purpose is to help prepare Army and Marine Corps leaders to conduct COIN operations anywhere in the world. It provides a foundation for study before deployment and the basis for operations in theater. Perhaps more importantly, it provides techniques for generating and incorporating lessons learned during those operations—an essential requirement for success against today's adaptive foes. Using these techniques and processes can keep U.S. forces more agile and adaptive than their irregular enemies. Knowledge of the history and principles of insurgency and COIN provides a solid foundation that informed leaders can use to assess insurgencies. This knowledge can also help them make appropriate decisions on employing all instruments of national power against these threats.

All insurgencies are different; however, broad historical trends underlie the factors motivating insurgents. Most insurgencies follow a similar course of development. The tactics used to successfully defeat them are likewise similar in most cases. Similarly, history shows that some tactics that are usually successful against conventional foes may fail against insurgents.

One common feature of insurgencies is that the government that is being targeted generally takes awhile to recognize that an insurgency is occurring. Insurgents take advantage of that time to build strength and gather support. Thus, counterinsurgents often have to "come from behind" when fighting an insurgency. Another common feature is that forces conducting COIN operations usually begin poorly. Western militaries too often neglect the study of insurgency. They falsely believe that armies trained to win large conventional wars are automatically prepared to win small, unconventional ones. In fact, some capabilities required for conventional success—for example, the ability to execute operational maneuver and employ massive firepower—may be of limited utility or even counterproductive in COIN operations. Nonetheless, conventional forces beginning COIN operations often try to use these capabilities to defeat insurgents; they almost always fail.

The military forces that successfully defeat insurgencies are usually those able to overcome their institutional inclination to wage conventional war against insurgents. They learn how to practice COIN and apply that knowledge. This publication can help to compress the learning curve. It is a tool for planners, trainers, and field commanders. Using it can help leaders begin the learning process sooner and build it on a larger knowledge base. Learning done before deployment results in fewer lives lost and less national treasure spent relearning past lessons in combat.

In COIN, the side that learns faster and adapts more rapidly—the better learning organization—usually wins. Counterinsurgencies have been called learning competitions. Thus, this publication identifies "Learn and Adapt" as a modern COIN imperative for U.S. forces. However, Soldiers and Marines cannot wait until they are alerted to deploy to prepare for a COIN mission. Learning to conduct complex COIN operations begins with study beforehand. This publication is a good place to start. The annotated bibliography lists a number of other sources; however, these are only a sample of the vast amount of available information on this subject. Adapting occurs as Soldiers and Marines apply what they have learned through study and experience, assess the results of their actions, and continue to learn during operations.

As learning organizations, the Army and Marine Corps encourage Soldiers and Marines to pay attention to the rapidly changing situations that characterize COIN operations. Current tactics, techniques, and procedures sometimes do not achieve the desired results. When that happens, successful leaders engage in a directed search for better ways to defeat the enemy. To win, the Army and Marine Corps must rapidly develop an institutional consensus on new doctrine, publish it, and carefully observe its impact on mission accomplishment. This learning cycle should repeat continuously as U.S. counterinsurgents seek to learn faster than the insurgent enemy. The side that learns faster and adapts more rapidly wins.

Just as there are historical principles underlying success in COIN, there are organizational traits shared by most successful learning organizations. Forces that learn COIN effectively have generally—

- Developed COIN doctrine and practices locally.
- Established local training centers during COIN operations.
- Regularly challenged their assumptions, both formally and informally.
- Learned about the broader world outside the military and requested outside assistance in understanding foreign political, cultural, social and other situations beyond their experience.
- Promoted suggestions from the field.
- Fostered open communication between senior officers and their subordinates.
- Established rapid avenues of disseminating lessons learned.
- Coordinated closely with governmental and nongovernmental partners at all command levels.
- Proved open to soliciting and evaluating advice from the local people in the conflict zone.

These are not always easy practices for an organization to establish. Adopting them is particularly challenging for a military engaged in a conflict. However, these traits are essential for any military confronting an enemy who does not fight using conventional tactics and who adapts while waging irregular warfare. Learning organizations defeat insurgencies; bureaucratic hierarchies do not.

Promoting learning is a key responsibility of commanders at all levels. The U.S. military has developed first class lessons-learned systems that allow for collecting and rapidly disseminating information from the field. But these systems only work when commanders promote their use and create a command climate that encourages bottom-up learning. Junior leaders in the field often informally disseminate lessons based on their experiences. However, incorporating this information into institutional lessons learned, and then into doctrine, requires commanders to encourage subordinates to use institutional lessons-learned processes.

Ironically, the nature of counterinsurgency presents challenges to traditional lessons-learned systems; many nonmilitary aspects of COIN do not lend themselves to rapid tactical learning. As this publication explains, performing the many nonmilitary tasks in COIN requires knowledge of many diverse, complex subjects. These include governance, economic development, public administration, and the rule of law. Commanders with a deep-rooted knowledge of these subjects can help subordinates understand challenging, unfamiliar environments and adapt more rapidly to changing situations. Reading this publication is a first stop to developing this knowledge.

COIN campaigns are often long and difficult. Progress can be hard to measure, and the enemy may appear to have many advantages. Effective insurgents rapidly adapt to changing circumstances. They cleverly use the tools of the global information revolution to magnify the effects of their actions. They often carry out barbaric acts and do not observe accepted norms of behavior. However, by focusing on efforts to secure the safety and support of the local populace, and through a concerted effort to truly function as learning organizations, the Army and Marine Corps can defeat their insurgent enemies.

Source: U.S. Department of the Army. Counterinsurgency. Field Manual 3-24. Washington, D.C.: U.S. Department of the Army, December 15, 2006. Available online at http://usacac.army.mil/cac2/Repository/Materials/COIN-FM3-24.pdf.

ANALYSIS

The invasions of Afghanistan and Iraq had both been well suited to the strengths of the U.S. military by leveraging its superior training, technology, and logistics to defeat conventional forces that stood little chance of stopping the American onslaught. The insurgencies that developed in Iraq and Afghanistan during their respective U.S. occupations, however, had frustrated American attempts at nation building and led to increasing public disillusionment with both conflicts.

Field Manual (FM) 3-24 sought to distill the lessons learned from fighting in both Iraq and Afghanistan and guide the execution of future campaigns in both countries. It also advocated for a very different method of fighting than what U.S. forces were accustomed to by encouraging larger forces to make closer contact with civilians in order to help root out insurgencies. For General David Petraeus, one of the manual's authors, this helped him guide the "surge" of U.S. forces to Iraq to quell the insurgency there.

- **Document 62: President Bush Discusses Progress in Afghanistan, Global War on Terror**
- **When:** February 15, 2007
- **Where:** Washington, D.C.
- **Significance:** President Bush recounted the progress made in Afghan reconstruction since 2001 and outlined a series of new goals to be accomplished in the next two years.

DOCUMENT

. . .

As we implement a new strategy in Iraq, we are also taking new steps to defeat the terrorists and extremists in Afghanistan. My administration has just completed a top-to-bottom review of our strategy in that country, and today I want to talk to you about the progress we have made in Afghanistan, the challenges we face in Afghanistan, and the strategy we're pursuing to defeat the enemies of freedom in Afghanistan.

It wasn't all that long ago that we learned the lessons of how terrorists operate. It may seem like a long time ago—five years is a long time in this day and age of instant news cycles—but it really isn't all that long ago, when you think about the march of history. In Afghanistan, we saw how terrorists and extremists can use those safe havens, safe havens in a failed state, to bring death and destruction to our people here at home.

It was an amazing turning point in the history of our country, really, when you think about it. It was a defining moment for the 21st century. Think about what I just said, that in the remote reaches of the world, because there was a failed state, murderers were able to plot and plan and then execute a deadly attack that killed nearly 3,000 of our citizens. It's a lesson that we've got to remember. And one of the lessons of that September the 11th day is that we cannot allow terrorists to gain sanctuary anywhere, and we must not allow them to reestablish the safe haven they lost in Afghanistan.

Our goal in Afghanistan is to help the people of that country to defeat the terrorists and establish a stable, moderate, and democratic state that respects the rights of its citizens, governs its territory effectively, and is a reliable ally in this war against extremists and terrorists.

Oh, for some that may seem like an impossible task. But it's not impossible if you believe what Jeane Kirkpatrick said, and that freedom is universal; that we believe all human beings to live in freedom and peace.

Over the past five years, we've made real progress toward this goal I just described. In 2001, Afghanistan was a totalitarian nightmare—a land where girls could not go to school, where religious police roamed the streets, where women were publicly whipped, where there were summary executions in Kabul's soccer stadium, and terrorists operated freely—they ran camps where they planned and trained for horrific attacks that affected us and other nations.

Today, five short years later, the Taliban have been driven from power, al Qaeda has been driven from its camps, and Afghanistan is free. That's why I say we have made remarkable progress. Afghanistan has a democratically-elected President, named Hamid Karzai. I respect him. I appreciate his courage. Afghanistan has a National Assembly chosen by the Afghan people in free elections.

Under the Taliban, women were barred from public office. Today, Afghanistan's parliament includes 91 women—and President Karzai has appointed the first woman to serve as a provincial governor.

Under the Taliban, free enterprise was stifled. Today, the Afghan economy has doubled in size since liberation. Afghanistan has attracted $800 million in foreign investment during that time.

Under the Taliban, there were about 900,000 children in school. Today, more than 5 million children are in school—about 1.8 million of them are girls.

Under the Taliban, an estimated 8 percent of Afghans had access to basic health care. Today, the United States has built or renovated 681 health clinics across the country—now more than 80 percent of Afghans have access to basic health coverage—health care.

Under the Taliban, Afghans fled the country in large numbers, seeking safety abroad. Today, more than 4.6 million Afghan refugees have come home—one of the largest return movements in history.

In today's Afghanistan, people are free to speak their minds, they're free to begin to realize dreams. In today's Afghanistan there's a NATO Alliance is taking the lead to help provide security for the people of Afghanistan. In today's Afghanistan, the terrorists who once oppressed the Afghan people and threatened our country are being captured and killed by NATO forces and soldiers and police of a free Afghanistan. Times have changed. Our work is bringing freedom. A free Afghanistan helps make this country more secure.

We face a thinking enemy. And we face a tough enemy—they watch our actions, they adjust their tactics. And in 2006, this enemy struck back with vengeance. As freedom began to spread, an enemy that cannot stand the thought of a free society tried to do something about it, tried to stop the advance of this young democracy. It's not the only place in the world where the enemy struck back in 2006. They struck back in Iraq. They struck in Lebanon. This should be a lesson for our fellow

DID YOU KNOW?

Private Military Contractors

A recurring issue for the United States and the Coalition during the war in Afghanistan has been the use of private military contractors to provide security when military forces are otherwise unavailable. Mercenaries had operated during the Cold War, but some firms grew after the Cold War as many Western countries, including the United States, shrank their militaries after the collapse of the Soviet Union. In addition, since the United States and many of its allies rely solely on volunteers and no longer automatically conscript people into their armed forces, hiring personnel from private firms could fill any shortfalls in manpower. The practice first attracted much public notice after the U.S. invasion of Iraq in 2003, especially when the actions of members of the U.S. firm Blackwater led to the deaths of Iraqi civilians. The United States has also used contractors in Afghanistan, and while the Defense Department rarely systematically tracked the numbers of contractors, some estimates believe that contractors have almost always outnumbered U.S. troops in Afghanistan, even at the height of the surge in 2011. In addition to the public backlash against their use, the United Nations also frowns upon private military firms as existing beyond the norms of international law. Contractors still work in Afghanistan as of 2018, and it is unlikely they will leave the country anytime soon.

citizens to understand, where these group of people find freedom they're willing to resort to brutal tactics.

It's an interesting enemy, isn't it? An enemy that can't stand the thought of somebody being able to live a peaceful life, a life of hope, an optimistic life. And it's an enemy we've got to take seriously.

Across Afghanistan last year, the number of roadside bomb attacks almost doubled, direct fire attacks on international forces almost tripled, and suicide bombings grew nearly five-fold. These escalating attacks were part of a Taliban offensive that made 2006 the most violent year in Afghanistan since the liberation of the country.

And so the fundamental question is, how do you react? Do you say, maybe it's too tough? Let's just kind of let this young democracy wither and fade away. Do we forget the lessons of September the 11th? And the answer is absolutely not.

And so the Taliban offensive that was launched was turned back by incredible courage of the Afghan soldiers, and by NATO forces that stood strong. You see, I believe the Taliban felt that they could exploit weakness. I believe that they said to themselves, if we can—we'll test NATO and cause NATO leaders to turn their back on this young democracy.

After the fierce battles throughout the year 2006, the Taliban had failed in their objective of taking and holding new territory.

In recent months, the intensity of the fighting has died down—that's only natural. It does every year when the snow and ice set in there in Afghanistan. But even in these winter months, we stayed on the offensive against the Taliban and al Qaeda. This January, NATO reconnaissance units observed a major Taliban incursion from Pakistan—with about 150 Taliban fighters crossing the border into the Paktika province. So NATO and Afghan forces launched a coordinated air assault and ground assault, and we destroyed the Taliban force. A large number of enemy fighters were killed; they were forced to retreat, where they were engaged by Pakistani troops.

Just two weeks ago, NATO launched an air strike against Taliban fighters who had seized the town of Musa Qala in Helmand province—a key Taliban commander was brought to justice.

The snow is going to melt in the Hindu Kush Mountains, and when it does we can expect fierce fighting to continue. The Taliban and al Qaeda are preparing to launch new attacks. Our strategy is not to be on the defense, but to go on the offense. This spring there is going to be a new offensive in Afghanistan, and it's going to be a NATO offensive. And that's part of our strategy—relentless in our pressure. We will not give in to murderers and extremists.

And we're focused on five key goals that I want to share with you. First, the United States and our allies will help President Karzai increase the size and capabilities of the Afghan security forces. After all, for this young democracy to survive in the long term, they'll have their own security forces that are capable and trained. We don't have to teach them courage. These folks understand courage. They're willing to fight for their country. They're willing to defend this young democracy. And so it's in our interest and the interest of NATO countries to provide training so they have more, more strong fighters—so we're going to increase the size of the national police from 61,000 to 82,000 by the end of 2008. And we'll help them develop new specialties: new civil order brigades, counter-narcotics, and border surveillance.

We're going to increase the Afghanistan army. Today, it's 32,000—that's not enough to do the job in this vast country—to 70,000 by the end of 2008. It's one thing to get them trained and one thing to get them uniforms, but they're also going to have to have ways to move around their country. So we're going to add commando battalions, a helicopter unit, combat support units. In other words, we're going to help this young democracy have a fully integrated security force that will respond to the commands of the elected officials.

Capable troops need intelligence. This is a war that requires good intelligence on all fronts. So the United States and our allies will also work with Afghanistan's leaders to improve human intelligence networks, particularly in areas that are threatened by the Taliban. Together with the Afghan government and NATO, we created a new Joint Intelligence Operations Center in Kabul—so all the forces fighting the terrorists in Afghanistan have a common picture of the enemy. That may sound simple to those of us who have gotten used to sophisticated systems to protect ourselves. This is important innovation in Afghanistan.

America and our allies are going to stand with these folks. That's the message I want to deliver to the Afghanistan people today. Free debates are important. But our commitment is strong: we will train you, we will help you, and we will stand with you as you defend your new democracy.

The second part of our strategy is to work with our allies to strengthen the NATO force in Afghanistan. Today, Afghanistan is NATO's most important military operation. Isn't it interesting that NATO is now in Afghanistan? I suspect 20 years ago if a President stood in front of AEI and said, I'll make a prediction to you that NATO would be a force for freedom and peace outside of Europe—you probably never would have invited the person back. Today, NATO is in Afghanistan. And I thank the leaders of the NATO countries for recognizing the importance of Afghanistan in our own security and enhancing the security of our own countries.

For NATO to succeed, member nations must provide commanders on the ground with the troops and the equipment they need to do their jobs. Many allies have made commitments of additional forces and support—and I appreciate those commitments, but nearly as much as the people in Afghanistan appreciate them. Norway, Lithuania and the Czech Republic have all agreed to send special operation forces to Afghanistan. Britain, Poland, Turkey and Bulgaria have agreed to additional troops. Italy has agreed to send aircraft. Romania will contribute to the EU police mission. Denmark, Greece, Norway and Slovakia will provide funding for Afghan security forces. Iceland will provide airlift. The people of Afghanistan need to know that they've got a lot of friends in this world who want them to succeed.

For NATO to succeed, allies must make sure that we fill the security gaps. In other words, when there is a need, when our commanders on the ground say to our respective countries, we need additional help, our NATO countries must provide it in order to be successful in this mission.

As well, allies must lift restrictions on the forces they do provide so NATO commanders have the flexibility they need to defeat the enemy wherever the enemy may make a stand. The alliance was founded on this principle: An attack on one is an attack on all. That principle holds true whether the attack is on the home soil of a NATO nation, or on allied forces deployed on a NATO mission abroad. By standing together in Afghanistan, NATO forces protect our own people, and they must have the flexibility and rules of engagement to be able to do their job.

Third, the United States and our allies will help President Karzai improve provincial governance and develop Afghanistan's—and to help develop Afghanistan's rural economy. Many Afghans in remote regions fight with the Taliban simply because there are no other jobs available. The best way to dry up Taliban recruits is to help Afghanistan's government create jobs and opportunity. So NATO is operating 25 provincial reconstruction teams across the country. These teams are made up of civilian and military experts. They are helping the Afghan government extend its reach into distant regions, they're improving security, and they're helping to deliver reconstruction assistance. In other words, I just described military operations that are necessary, but in order for these young democracies to survive, there's got to be more than just military. There has to be political development, and tangible evidence that a government can provide opportunity and hope. And these provincial reconstruction teams do just that.

These teams will help build irrigation systems, improve power production, provide access to micro-credit. The idea is to encourage entrepreneurship, job formation, enterprise. These teams will undertake new efforts to train provincial and local leaders. We take democracy for granted. Democracy hasn't exactly been rooted deeply in Afghan history. It takes a while for people to understand how to function as an elected official. It takes help for people to understand the obligations to respond to the people, and these teams will change provincial and local leaders.

Another key element to bringing stability to Afghanistan is building roads. Lieutenant General Eikenberry, who served with distinction in Afghanistan, just finished his tour, he was the senior commander there, said really something very interesting that caught my attention. He said, "Where the roads end in Afghanistan, the Taliban begin." So in order to help the security of this country, the international community has stepped up its road-building campaign across Afghanistan. So far, the United States and other nations have completed construction of more than 4,000 miles of roads—that sounds like a lot, and it is a lot. We're also talking about a big country.

Much of the ring road—we call it the ring road—that links key provincial capitals to Kabul, is pretty well complete. And that's important, because, first of all, road building brings jobs to young men who might be recruited to the Taliban. But roads enable people to get commerce to centers of trade. In other words, roads promote enterprise. Enterprise provides hope. Hope is what defeats this ideology of darkness. And so we're going to build another 1,000 roads [sic] in 2007. It's an important effort, and our allies need to follow through on their commitments to help this young democracy have a road system that will enable it to flourish and survive.

Fourth, the United States and our allies will help President Karzai reverse the increase in poppy cultivation that is aiding the Taliban. After a decline in 2005, Afghanistan saw a marked increase in poppy cultivation last year. This is a direct threat to a free future for Afghanistan. I have made my concerns to President Karzai pretty clear—not pretty clear, very clear—and that in order for him to gain the confidence of his people, and the confidence of the world, he's got to do something about it, with our help.

The Taliban uses drug money to buy weapons—they benefit from this cultivation—and they pay Afghans to take up arms against the government. And so we're helping the President in a variety of ways to deal with the problem. First, he has established what's called a Central Narcotics Tribunal in Kabul. One way to deal with the drug problem is for there to be a push back to the drug dealers, and a good way to push back on the drug dealers is convict them and send them to prison. He has improved the Afghan Eradication Force this is mobile units that can deploy across the country to help governors in their eradication efforts.

We're supporting him. We're supporting him through direct aid on these mobile units, and we're supporting him to expand alternative livelihood programs. These poppy growers are trying to make a living. And the idea is to provide these farmers with credit, and seeds, and fertilizer, and assistance to bring their products to market. So the strategy to eliminate poppies is to encourage the government to eradicate, and to provide alternative means for a livelihood, and to help have the roads so that when somebody grows something somebody wants to buy in Kabul, there's a road to be able to take the product along to the markets.

It's important, and we're going to stay focused on the poppy issue. And when the President and his government is able to make progress on it, it will really inspire countries who want to help to do more.

Finally, we're going to help President Karzai fight corruption. And one place where he needs help is in the judicial system. There's nothing more discouraging when justice is not fair. And Afghans too often see their courts run by crooked judges. It's important to have the confidence of the people in a free society. Crooked judges make it hard to earn that confidence.

President Karzai, to his credit, has established a Criminal Justice Task Force that is now after public corruption. This task force has 400 prosecutors [sic] and there are ongoing investigations. The United States, Britain and Norway are providing full time prosecutors, judges, police, and defense attorneys to mentor their Afghan counterparts—and I appreciate our own citizens going over there. It is must be neat, really—I guess "neat" isn't a sophisticated word, but it must be heartening to be somebody who's helping this young democracy develop a judicial system that is worthy. And I cannot thank our citizens for taking time out of their lives to go.

The United States has built or renovated 40 judicial facilities; we've distributed more than 11,000 copies of the Afghan constitution; we've trained more than 750 Afghan judges and lawyers and prosecutors. The international community is helping this new government build a justice system so they can replace the rule of the Taliban with the rule of law.

Now, there's another part of our strategy I want to share with you, and that is to help President Musharraf defeat the terrorists and extremists who operate inside of Pakistan. We're going to work with Pakistan and Afghanistan to enhance cooperation to defeat what I would call a common enemy. Taliban and al Qaeda fighters do hide in remote regions of Pakistan—this is wild country; this is wilder than the Wild West. And these folks hide and recruit and launch attacks.

The President understands our desire to work with him to eliminate this kind of action. People say, well, do you think President Musharraf really understands the threat of extremists in his midst? I said, yes, I do. You know how I know? They've tried to kill him. Al Qaeda has launched attacks against the President of this country. He understands. He also understands that extremists can destabilize countries on the border, or destabilize countries from which they launch their attacks. And so he's launched what they call a frontier strategy, and that is to find and eliminate the extremists and deliver a better governance and economic opportunity.

We're helping him in these efforts. It's in our interest to help him. We provided him—we're helping him equip his security forces that are patrolling the border regions with Afghanistan. We're funding construction of more than 100 border outposts, which will provide their forces with better access to remote regions of this part of the country. We've given him high-tech equipment to help the Pakistani forces locate the terrorists attempting to cross the border. We're funding an air wing, with helicopters and fixed-wing aircraft, to give Pakistan better security, better swift response and better surveillance.

President Musharraf is going to better be able to now deal with this problem. Bob Gates went out and visited with him recently, had a good response. He's an ally in this war on terror and it's in our interest to support him in fighting the extremists.

I also had an interesting meeting at the White House last September—and that is, I hosted a private dinner with President Musharraf and President Karzai, right there in what's called the Family Dining Room. It was a fascinating discussion. Clearly there are different histories, different anxieties about the way forward. We did reach some agreements, however, that it's in all our interests for people to work together, for example, to improve intelligence sharing. It's in our interest to expand trade between these two countries. In other words, on the one hand it's in our interest to work closely on security for security operations, but it's also in our mutual interest—all three of our interests—to provide different alternatives for people to choose from.

Remember I said earlier that oftentimes people support the Taliban, or sometimes they support the Taliban in Afghanistan because it's the only job they can find. If that's the case—and I believe it's true—we need to help these folks provide an economy that gives hope. And so one way we can do this is what we call reconstruction opportunity zones that exist on both sides of the Pak and Afghan border. These zones will give residents the chance to export locally made products to the United States, duty free. That's our contribution. Got a vast market, wealthy country with a lot of consumers, and it's not going to take much to provide hope if we can get little manufacturing enterprises set up, local entrepreneurs to be able to manufacture goods and sell them here in our countries. It's a tiny contribution for us and a major contribution for providing the conditions necessary for stability.

I'm going to continue to work with both the leaders. It's a useful role for the President of the United States to be in constant contact with both Presidents, to remind them of the great obligations we have to fight the extremists and to help people realize dreams.

So our strategy in this country is robust and important. A lot of attention here in the United States is on Iraq. One reason I've come to address you is I want to make sure people's attention is also on Afghanistan. I'm asking Congress for $11.8 billion over the next two years to help this young democracy survive. I've ordered an increase in U.S. forces in Afghanistan. We've extended the stay of 3,200 troops now in the country, for four months, and we'll deploy a replacement force that will sustain this increase for the foreseeable future.

These forces and funds are going to help President Karzai defeat common enemies. Success in Afghanistan is important for our security. We are engaged in a long ideological struggle between the forces of moderation and liberty versus the forces of destruction and extremism. And a victory for the forces of liberty in Afghanistan will be a resounding defeat in this ideological struggle. It's in our national interest that we succeed, that we help President Karzai and the people of Afghanistan succeed. And I'm confident—I'm confident that with persistence and patience and determination, we will succeed.

And the biggest source for success is the Afghan people, themselves. They want their freedom. Freedom is universal. Jeane Kirkpatrick was right—people around the world, regardless of their faith, their background, or their gender, want to be free. There is tangible evidence in Afghanistan: 8 million people went to the polls to choose their President in a free election. We take it for granted. Eight million said we want to be free. Imagine how far that society has come from the days of the Taliban. There's courage in that country. People are showing faith and freedom and courage to defend that freedom.

I want to tell you an interesting story about an Afghan security office at Camp Phoenix near Kabul. This fellow has worked at this base for four years—nearly four years. His job was to guard the front gate and screen cars before they are allowed to approach a U.S. military checkpoint. He is very popular with our troops—people who have gotten to know him like him a lot. They appreciate his courage and his personality and they call him "Rambo." Must have been a lot for the Afghan citizen to be called "Rambo," but that's what they call him.

One day Rambo was on duty, a car loaded with explosives tried to crash through the front gate—they were attempting to get to our troops. This fellow did not hesitate, he jumped in the car and he prevented the terrorist from exploding the device. He saw somebody who was about to harm our citizens, our troops—he then jumps into the car and stops the attack. A U.S. Army sergeant then responded, helped him pull the guy out of the car.

One of our U.S. soldiers who was there said this, he said, "He saved our lives. I promised him I'd name my firstborn son after him." The guy is hoping for a boy.

It's a human story. It's a story that speaks of courage and alliance, respect for life. To me it's a story that says these people in Afghanistan want to do what is necessary to survive and succeed, and it's in our interest to help them.

I am really proud that our nation helped liberate the 25 million people of that country. We should be proud to stand alongside the people of Afghanistan, the newly liberated Afghanistan. And I know we're all proud of the men and women who have helped liberate that country—the men and women who wear our uniform who helped liberate that country and continue to make the sacrifices necessary.

I thank you for giving me a chance to come and talk about a strategy for success, a strategy that is part of our efforts to make sure that a generation of Americans, beyond our generation, will look back and say they did their duty to protect the homeland and, as a result, we can live in peace.

Source: Public Papers of the Presidents of the United States: George W. Bush, 2007, Book 1. Washington, D.C.: Government Printing Office, 2008, 146–155.

ANALYSIS

As he had in many of his previous public statements and speeches, President Bush described how much progress in Afghanistan had been made relative to the period of Taliban rule that ended in 2001. Yet, perhaps for the first time, he finally acknowledged that the resurgent Taliban posed a security threat to the government and that the group had killed more people than in any year since 2001.

These security problems stemmed from the inability of the Afghan government to control its territory. Among other initiatives, President Bush called for a doubling in the size of the Afghan National Army by 2008 and praised continued efforts by President Karzai to root out corruption. Unfortunately, this corruption—some of which was linked to Karzai himself—threatened the government's legitimacy. So long as all Afghans did not accept the government and its army, the violence would continue.

- **Document 63: Statement of Admiral William J. Fallon before the Senate Armed Services Committee**
- **When:** May 3, 2007
- **Where:** Washington, D.C.
- **Significance:** Admiral Fallon's opening statement to the Senate Armed Services Committee outlined the military situation in Afghanistan.

DOCUMENT

I. Introduction

. . .

In Afghanistan, I believe that the foundation of security and governance is in place. The vast majority of people are in favor of representative government and prosperity, not Taliban brutality, and they are standing up and fighting for their country's future. Capacity of the Afghan Security Forces, particularly the Afghan National Army (ANA), is growing and the ANA is eager and well led. However, many parts of the country have never known centralized governance, lack basic social services and infrastructure, and desperately require expanded capacity to meet the needs of a populace under pressure from the Taliban.

. . .

III. Expanding Governance and Security in Afghanistan

Afghanistan's primary insurgent threat, the Taliban, operate mostly in the southern and eastern provinces of the country. While they remain unpopular in most districts, small pockets of hard-core extremists are intent on asserting control and undermining the reform-minded government. As the NATO International Security Assistance Force (ISAF) expanded operations last year into previously uncontested areas, insurgent attacks increased to their highest levels since the fall of the Taliban in 2001. Violence did, however, level-off in October and remained lower throughout most of the winter.

We expect Taliban activities to increase from now through the summer but believe that predictions of a major Taliban offensive are overstated. Despite the ability to instigate increased levels of localized violence, they are not able to militarily defeat the Afghan National Army and Coalition forces. While continuing to counter the insurgent threat militarily, we will work with other agencies and a broadly based international effort to assist the Afghans to expand governance and promote economic development.

Improving Afghan governance, infrastructure, and the economy requires a concerted effort. The priorities are roads and electricity, followed by agricultural development, microcredit, job skills, and education. ISAF is actively pursuing initiatives in these areas, from building schools and providing them with supplies to encouraging and stimulating the growth of small businesses.

Until there are sustainable governmental institutions and a viable replacement for the Afghan poppy crop, opium trafficking will be a significant part of this country's future. In the interim, CENTCOM supports US government and United Kingdom lead nation counter-narcotics activities. These efforts include building infrastructure, training border forces and the Counter-Narcotics Police National Interdiction Unit (CNPA), and developing a CNPA aviation capability.

In addition to reconstruction and development activities, efforts have focused on the Afghan National Army. Now at fifty percent of desired end strength, its 35,000 soldiers enjoy a high level of support from the populace, and are growing steadily in competence, effectiveness, and professionalism. Though we have made progress in manning the Afghan National Police and Border Patrol, currently consisting of approximately 46,000 officers, these forces remain several steps behind the Army. As the Afghan Security Forces become capable of sustaining security and force development, we will hand responsibilities over to them and transition to a long-term security relationship.

Despite positive developments in the Afghan National Security Forces, long-term security requires the effective disruption of cross-border extremist operations. Essential security cooperation with Pakistan is increasing and more needs to be done. While the issues of border security and militant safe havens are difficult problems, coordination at tactical levels in both countries and with ISAF is increasing. This should lead to further confidence building measures and more robust joint

---

DID YOU KNOW?

Haqqani Network

Named for its founder, Jalaluddin Haqqani, the Haqqani Network is a quasi-independent terrorist group that works with both the Taliban and al-Qaeda in Afghanistan. Haqqani founded the group in 1973 in response to Mohammad Daoud Khan's coup against the king, Mohammad Zahir Shah. As early as 1975, the Haqqani Network launched attacks against the Afghan government from safe areas inside Pakistan, thus predating the rise of the mujahedeen. After the Soviet invasion, the Haqqani Network fought alongside other elements of the mujahedeen. Haqqani then backed the Taliban during its rise to power in the 1990s, and Haqqani himself took control of the Taliban military in 1996 as it fought the Northern Alliance north of Kabul. The Haqqani Network also worked closely with Osama bin Laden and al-Qaeda after the former's arrival in Afghanistan, and the Network likely escorted bin Laden away from Tora Bora in late 2001. During the 2000s, Jalaluddin's son Sirajuddin took control of the group as it attacked the Coalition and the Afghan government from its Pakistani sanctuaries. It remains an autonomous group and has been linked to several deadly attacks, including a 2011 attack against the U.S. Embassy in Kabul, although Sirajuddin was named a deputy to the Taliban leader, Mullah Akhundzada, in 2016.

DID YOU KNOW?

Salvatore Giunta

Born in Iowa in 1985, Salvatore Giunta enlisted in the Army in 2003 and reached the rank of specialist by October 2007. As part of the 1st Platoon, Bravo Company, 2nd Battalion of the 503rd Parachute Infantry Regiment, Giunta and his men were ambushed by insurgents as they returned to their combat outposts from an observation mission. Giunta's team used grenades to break up the attack, which allowed Giunta and another soldier to reach a wounded comrade. Soon afterward, Giunta spotted two insurgents attempting to drag away another wounded comrade, Sergeant Joshua Brennan. Giunta fired on them as he quickly advanced alone, killing one and wounding the other, which allowed him to rescue Brennan. The fight ended soon afterward, having lasted for only three brutal minutes. Brennan later succumbed to his wounds, but Giunta's bravery and selflessness eventually led him to being the first living recipient of the Medal of Honor since the Vietnam War. He eventually left the Army in 2011 after achieving the rank of staff sergeant, and then he authored a memoir.

efforts. Tri-lateral cooperation between ISAF, Pakistan and Afghanistan to improve governance, the rule of law, and trade in the border regions can also help eliminate extremist sanctuaries. Meanwhile, ISAF has retained the initiative, clearing and isolating enemy sanctuaries in places like Helmand Province since last autumn. In ongoing operations, MEDUSA and ACHILLES, ISAF forces have undertaken a multifaceted approach to clearing, holding, and building. They have killed and captured several hard core Taliban leaders and cut their lines of communications, while aggressively pursuing development projects in the surrounding districts. This not only encourages the population in these areas to reject the insurgents, it vividly demonstrates the contrast between the grim reality of Taliban rule and the health and prosperity of government-controlled areas.

There is a general sense of optimism and determination among the Afghan leaders and people. They regularly voice their appreciation for our assistance, and believe things have improved since last year. We must help them succeed.

. . .

V. Strengthening Relationships and Influencing States and Organizations

. . .

Pakistan. Pakistani security forces have captured and killed significant numbers of violent extremists, to include high-ranking leaders of al-Qaida and the Taliban. They have also suffered extensive casualties. Our long-term partnership with the Islamic Republic of Pakistan is central to defeating extremist groups in the region, and it is difficult to imagine success in that struggle without its support and cooperation. We are working together to reduce the tensions stemming from the radical and violent presence in the Federally Administered Tribal Areas (FATA). Useful initiatives include regular meetings with Pakistan's military leaders, and more robust liaison and communications among our units operating along the Afghanistan-Pakistan border. While President Musharraf is working to moderate groups within Pakistan and to prevent militants using the FATA for sanctuary, he is faced with a backdrop of potent political, social, and ethnic forces within his country.

Pakistan remains a strong partner of the United States, and our support for its counter-terror efforts will continue with a variety of focused programs. Our security cooperation funding and bilateral exercise programs help the country's government conduct counter-terror operations and enhance its internal stability. Our goal is for Pakistan to view the US as a long-term, preferred international partner, particularly in our efforts to defeat our common enemies.

. . .

VI. Posturing the Force to Build and Sustain Joint and Combined Warfighting Capabilities and Readiness

Joint and combined war fighting capability and readiness are fundamental in our ability to prosecute ongoing military operations, maintain a credible presence to deter aggression, and respond effectively to contingencies. Because we execute nearly all of our activities jointly and in concert with allies, we must cultivate effective inter-service and multinational ways of doing business. Additionally, because our region is filled with uncertainty, we must maintain a full spectrum of responsive capabilities through an effective forward deployed force structure, thorough planning, and realistic combined training exercises. Other critical capabilities include the following:

. . .

Interagency Coordination. Establishment of security and stability in our region requires the application of all elements of national power: military, diplomatic, economic, and information. The military instruments can set conditions for security but other agencies foster lasting change.

We are fortunate to have several US Government entities engaged in the Central Command AOR. The Departments of State, Treasury, Justice, and Homeland Security, as well as subordinate agencies including the US Agency for International Development, Diplomatic Security Service, Federal Bureau of Investigation, Drug Enforcement Administration, and United States Coast Guard, are actively engaged in our theater. Their efforts are helping to protect critical infrastructure, prevent terrorist attacks on our homeland, train fledgling law enforcement organizations, and rebuild damaged or aging infrastructure. There is clearly a need for better integration and more comprehensive application of all the elements of national power.

. . .

Responsive Counter Improvised Explosive Device Program. Insurgents' weapon of choice will likely continue to be the Improvised Explosive Device, or road-side bomb. They are cheap, effective, anonymous, and have been adapted to include toxic industrial chemicals such as chlorine. While some are crude, our adversaries increasingly use sophisticated technology, including Iranian-supplied Explosively Formed Penetrators. These weapons have killed or wounded 15,000 military and civilian personnel in Iraq, and IEDs are becoming increasingly prevalent in Afghanistan.

To counter this threat, and working with the interagency and our Coalition partners, we are fielding jammers, specialized route clearance vehicles and equipment, and improved vehicle and personnel protective armor. These initiatives have reduced IED effectiveness. We must continue to develop new technologies, tactics, techniques, and procedures. Of particular importance to CENTCOM is rapid fielding of Mine Resistant Armor Protected vehicles, and further research and development to improve the detection of mines, IEDs, and unexploded ordnance.

Personnel. Sustained operations in the CENTCOM Area of Responsibility depend on personnel who have foreign language proficiency and cultural awareness competency in addition to military skills. Retention is a critical issue, and we depend heavily on quality of life enhancements such as Combat Zone Tax Relief, Imminent Danger Pay, and Special Leave Accrual. The Rest and Recuperation program continues to be a success, serving more than 470,000 troops to date. Over the past year, we have conducted a comprehensive review of the manning of our headquarters, which, after five years of war, is still highly reliant on temporary individual augmentation personnel. My subordinate war fighting headquarters are also heavily manned with individual augmentees. I am committed to working with the Services and the Joint Staff to properly size and resource all of these headquarters.

CENTCOM is also working to address requirements for low density skills. Our present inventory of language and intelligence specialists (especially human intelligence) and counterintelligence agents does not support current requirements. Language expertise is crucial in counterinsurgency, counterterrorist, and counterintelligence operations, and will continue in high demand. Contracting language expertise provides interim capability, but in the long run, we need service members and career civilians with the requisite language and cultural skills.

. . .

Source: Department of Defense. Available online at http://ogc.osd.mil/olc/docs/ testFallon070503.pdf.

ANALYSIS

Admiral Fallon's opening statement listed many of the problems noted by President Bush in his speech (Document 62) and in several other previous documents that explain why the Taliban had been able to return from near extinction, including poor governance and the Taliban's ability to tap into the shadow economy created by opium production.

Of special interest in Admiral Fallon's statement was how the war in Afghanistan, as well as Iraq, had fundamentally altered the U.S. military. The insurgencies meant that the military now routinely partnered with dozens of other U.S. government agencies that had a mission to perform in Afghanistan and elsewhere. The insurgencies also forced the military to train and retain personnel with language skills more so than had been common in the immediate post–Cold War period. The wars had also compelled the Defense Department to create new pay and recreation incentives to maintain the all-volunteer military.

- **Document 64: Secretary of State Condoleeza Rice, Remarks at Air University**
- **When:** April 14, 2008
- **Where:** Montgomery, Alabama
- **Significance:** Secretary of State Rice spoke to the students and faculty at Air University about the war in Afghanistan.

DOCUMENT

SECRETARY RICE: ...

General Lorenz, General Trey Obering, Secretary Beth Chapman, Dr. Bruce Murphy, distinguished guests, faculty, again, members of the Board of Visitors, ladies and gentlemen, I'd like to speak with you today about one of our most important missions and, indeed, one of our strategic opportunities, and that's Afghanistan. But I want to thank all of you by helping to make possible what we are doing there. Much attention is paid to what is happening on the ground in Afghanistan and, of course, in Iraq. But we can never forget that our gains on the ground are possible because of our superiority in the sky. With our soldiers, sailors, and Marines, many of you, both active duty and reservists, have deployed to the Afghanistan theater, often for multiple tours. And we are winning in Afghanistan because of you.

Our Air Force is essential to that difficult form of warfare that we have had to learn, or perhaps I should say relearn, in recent years. We tend to think of counterinsurgency warfare as a ground-based activity. But again, our entire effort on the ground depends on the lift, precision strike, and reconnaissance that our Air Force provides. Furthermore, our Air Force is doing things to support our mission today that few people would have imagined in 2001. In Afghanistan, for example, six American airmen are leading Provincial Reconstruction Teams. And many more are on the ground helping to do things like build roads and guard facilities and support local agriculture.

You have been called to adapt to the demands of counterinsurgency. And I must say, the State Department has been called to adapt too. And it's been hard. We've had to work not only to engage with states, but to help post-conflict societies build states. Our diplomats and development workers have had to use—have had to get used to new and dangerous operating environments far beyond our embassy walls. American civilians are learning how to be effective partners to our men and women in uniform, and you to us.

In recent years, America has developed a counterinsurgency doctrine that fuses the tools of war with the instruments of peace to help countries in conflict shape a future of freedom and opportunity for themselves. Our armed forces can defeat any adversary, but our civilian agencies must shape the political and economic context in which our gains will endure. We're gaining the field experience to work with you to do this right.

There has been much talk, of late, about how we are doing in Afghanistan. Some of it has been positive, some of it has not. Today, I'd like to offer you my assessment. We now have a new strategic opportunity in Afghanistan, one that is a product of lessons learned from both successes and setbacks. So here is why we will win in Afghanistan.

Since 2001, there has been much that has been good and successful. First, and most importantly, we have seen that whenever the Afghan people have an opportunity to choose a course for their nation, they have voted overwhelmingly, and often at great personal risk and sacrifice, for a future of democracy and modernity and liberty under law, not for the medieval despotism of the Taliban. And we continue to have a strong partner in the elected government of President Karzai.

To support our Afghan partners, NATO is leading an International Assistance Force of 40 nations. The Afghan National Army, which we are training and equipping, is now at the forefront of many combat operations alongside international forces. Twenty-six Provincial Reconstruction Teams, including 14 led by allies, are helping our Afghan partners to turn improving security into better governance and development. The legitimate Afghan economy is now growing faster than any other in Central and South Asia, and it is benefiting more and more of Afghanistan's citizens.

America's commitment to Afghanistan is also bipartisan. Congress has played a leadership role in funding U.S. policy there. And thanks to the generosity of the American people, the United States has provided nearly $23 billion in assistance to Afghanistan, with our allies providing another 18 billion. This assistance has helped over 15—over 5 million Afghan refugees to return to their homes. It is supporting the construction of critical infrastructure, like the national ring road, which is nearly 75 percent complete. And it is enabling 5 million Afghan children to get an education, including, for the first time ever, 1.5 million girls.

Our mission in Afghanistan has led to substantial progress. But at times, our many good programs have amounted to less than the sum of their parts. We have grappled with a lack of coherence among a broad coalition of international partners with disparate capabilities. This partly reflects a learning curve, as we have re-engaged a nation that America and our allies had neglected for too long: a country of inhospitable terrain, many ungoverned spaces, and a long history of poverty, misrule, and weak civilian institutions and civil war. Indeed, much of the work in Afghanistan could be more properly described not as reconstruction, but as construction.

This challenge has been made more difficult too by a determined enemy, the Taliban that has regrouped after its initial defeat, and has now turned to the tactics of pure terror to further its intolerant goals. The Taliban has benefited from regional turmoil on Afghanistan's borders. And this has led many in Afghanistan and the region, some even in our alliance, maybe even some here at home in America, to question whether our coalition has what it takes to support Afghanistan's long-term success.

In recent months, our Administration has looked closely at our policy in Afghanistan, both what we're doing well, and what we can and should be doing better. We have studied the independent reports that have been issued. I went to Afghanistan myself in February, both to Kabul and out to Kandahar, to see the situation on the ground. And the President and I have recently conferred with our allies, at the NATO summit in Bucharest.

I am confident that we are now laying the foundation for a long-term commitment to the success of Afghanistan and this region. This commitment must be built on a bipartisan consensus that unites our Administration and the Congress today, but also future administrations and future congresses. This commitment must also be built on an international consensus among our allies and our Afghan partners. We must all understand and explain to our people that Afghanistan is not a peacekeeping operation. It is a hard counterinsurgency fight and the stakes could not be higher.

The United States and the entire free world have a vital interest in the victory of our Afghan partners over the Taliban, and the consolidation and empowerment of an effective democratic state. Successes in Afghanistan will roll back the drug trade in a country that produces 93 percent of the world's opium and a great deal of its heroin. Successes in Afghanistan will advance our broader regional interests in combating violent extremism, resisting the destabilizing behavior of Iran, and anchoring political and economic liberty in South and Central Asia. And success in Afghanistan is an important test for the credibility of NATO.

Let no one forget, Afghanistan is a mission of necessity, not a mission of choice. That country must never again become a haven for the kind of terrorists who attacked America on September 11th, who have attacked our friends and our allies repeatedly, and who seek to do us all even greater harm. We cannot afford, either, to think whether we will choose to succeed in Afghanistan or succeed in Iraq. That is a false choice.

In both countries, the stakes are too high, the potential benefits of success too great, and the real costs of failure too catastrophic for us to think that these missions are zero terms. The real choice, and it is a choice befitting a great people, a great power, and a great democracy, is how to forge long-term commitment to succeed both in Afghanistan and in Iraq.

This goal is not only essential, it is attainable. As in Iraq, our challenges in Afghanistan do not stem from a traditionally strong enemy. The Taliban does not offer a political vision that most Afghans embrace when free to choose. The Taliban's theory of victory is not to prevail on the battlefield, or to win hearts and minds. It is simply to undermine the elected Afghan government, fracture the international coalition, and outlast us.

Our theory of victory, and the counterinsurgency strategy that we are pursuing to achieve it, is far superior to the designs of our enemy. We can defeat the Taliban on the battlefield. But we will render the Taliban obsolete by supporting an effective, democratic Afghan state that can meet the needs of its people. Where we have been able to do this, for instance, in the east of Afghanistan, the Taliban is in retreat.

Earlier this month in Bucharest, we and our NATO allies renewed our commitment to Afghanistan. President Karzai announced that the Afghan National Army will assume responsibility for security in Kabul by August, and we are supporting our Afghan partners. The United States is deploying roughly 300–3,500 additional Marines. France is sending a battalion.

This has enabled Canada, whose service in Afghanistan is an inspiration for NATO, to extend its deployment through 2011. Our allies pledged to deploy additional forces, with some deciding to enter conflict zones in the south, where we are especially grateful to Canada, Britain, Denmark, the Netherlands, and Australia for shouldering most of the hardest fighting. We will continue to press our allies to lift the caveats on their military forces.

The international community is also taking new steps to increase the coherence of our assistance effort in Afghanistan, including appointing Kai Eide as the United Nations Secretary General's Special Representative. Our strategy directs resources toward the central pillars of counterinsurgency: protecting the people from the enemy by strengthening Afghan security institutions, connecting people to their government by improving governance and rule of law, and fueling economic and social opportunity through reconstruction and development.

On the security front, Afghans are eager to provide more of their own security, and our plan supports that. We and our allies must step up our efforts to train and equip the national army of Afghanistan. But we must also increase our efforts to help the Afghan National Police become a more professional force that can enforce the law and police the nation's now porous borders.

At the same time, we and our allies are helping the Afghan Government to marry these security gains with good governance and economic development. Success depends on expanding the good work of our Provincial Reconstruction Teams. These teams lead our growing effort to help Afghan leaders, both national and local, to promote the rule of law, to strengthen their ministries, to deliver essential services like health and education to the people, and to lay a foundation for long-term private investment. Just last week, I had the pleasure of meeting with eight Afghan governors who play an important role in these efforts. These are local leaders who are beginning to give Afghan—Afghanistan's government the means to deliver goods and services more directly to the people.

Within our counterinsurgency strategy, we and our Afghan partners must also expand our counternarcotics efforts. This has been one of the most difficult and vexing problems and, frankly, we've not found all the right answers. Yet, it is just as urgent as the fight against the insurgency, because the two are inextricably linked. There is an erroneous view that poppy in Afghanistan is mostly grown by poor farmers struggling to earn a living. In fact, over 70 percent of Afghanistan's poppy will likely be grown this year in the Taliban's stronghold, on vast narco-farms that benefit our enemies. These drug kingpins do not need alternative livelihoods; they need to be brought to justice.

We must step up our interdiction, eradication, and law enforcement campaign while helping those Afghan farmers who truly do need adjusting. In places where security and political will exist, this strategy has shown some promise. Two years ago, only six of Afghanistan's 34 provinces were nearly or completely poppy-free. This year, it will likely be 26.

In everything we do, we must encourage the Afghan people, empower the Afghan Government, bolster our allies, and demoralize our enemies. But success is only possible if Afghan ownership grows over time and with greater integrity. Afghanistan's democracy is already under attack from external enemies. It cannot allow corruption to undermine democracy from within. Institutions like the Independent Directorate for Local Governance are a good start and we are increasing our support for Afghan efforts to create a fair and functional system of justice.

Addressing Afghanistan's regional context is also crucial to success. A new strategic opportunity comes from the transition to democracy that is underway in Pakistan, a nation that, like Afghanistan, America had too long neglected. Pakistan has been an ally in the war on terror since September 11th and yes, this has necessitated a strong program of military assistance and cooperation. After 2001, we supported President Musharraf's efforts to chart a moderate, modern path for that nation.

Our engagement, however, has always been multidimensional. Since 2005, America has invested $300 million each year to help the Pakistani people by supporting health programs, educational reform, as well as the building of civil society. And when this progress was put at risk last November, we pushed hard, publicly and privately, for a return to civilian rule, an end to the state of emergency, and free and fair elections in February that were open to all of Pakistan's leaders.

To be sure, terrorists exacted a high toll in innocent life trying to stop this election, including the assassination of Benazir Bhutto. But not only did their violent efforts fail to disrupt the voting and plunge the country into chaos; the Pakistani people dealt the forces of political extremism a crushing defeat at the polls, including in the frontier province. Indeed, the election dispelled the myth of rising extremism in Pakistani politics, proving that a moderate, democratic center is the country's dominant political force. We salute the Pakistani people for courageously restoring their democracy.

Successful American engagement with a democratic Pakistan is vital to our national security and to the lasting success of South and Central Asia. In Pakistan, as in Afghanistan, we must help a democratic partner to meet the needs of its people and eliminate the conditions that feed continuing extremism. We will greatly expand our support for the efforts of Pakistani civilians to strengthen democratic institutions and the rule of law and to reinforce the foundation of every free society: good governance, judicial independence, a free media, health and education, good jobs and social justice. We will support Pakistan's efforts to secure all of its people, and to wage a counterinsurgency fight against the violent people who still threaten Pakistan's future.

Finally, the United States will support Pakistan's efforts to develop fruitful links with its neighbors and with the community of responsible nations. This includes intensified Pakistani-Afghan dialogue on regional security, continued efforts to reduce tensions and reconcile with India, and closer economic integration with the nations of South and Central Asia.

We have a unique opportunity to foster the lasting security of a troubled region, a region that is of vital interest to our nation. From our partnerships with the newly democratic Pakistan and a free Afghanistan that is fighting the Taliban, not governed by it, to our growing strategic partnership with India and our improved relationships all the way across South and Central Asia, the United States is in a dramatically different and better position in this region than we were in 2001.

Though we and our friends face savage and determined enemies, I am confident that we will prevail, not by force of arms alone, but by the power and the promise of the values we share: the conviction that parents everywhere want their children to grow up in dignity, in liberty, and with limitless horizons. Success in Afghanistan and Pakistan will demonstrate that these values are more compelling than the spiritual poverty of suicide bombing.

The journey ahead will be difficult and often winding. Most certainly, the path toward democracy is never a straight line. We have hard work to do. But I am confident that we will succeed because we have done hard work before. I was fortunate to be the White House Soviet Specialist from 1989 to 1991 at the end of the Cold War. It doesn't get much better than that. In fact, those were very heady days. But as we went through those extraordinary days, it was important to stop and to pay homage and to think about those who had set up the possibilities and laid the foundation for the victory of our values at the end of the Cold War.

. . .

And so, I know that some Secretary of State will stand here in 10 years or 20 or 30, but most certainly, will stand here to say, of course the people of Iraq have triumphed in democracy; of course, the people of Afghanistan have triumphed in democracy. What else would you expect? Because the power of our principles is that it makes those things that one day seemed impossible seem, after, to have been inevitable.

Thank you very much and God bless you.

. . .

QUESTION: Good morning, Dr. Rice. I am Group Captain, or Colonel, Iqbal, from Terminal 13 Air War College and Pakistan. Thank you very much for sharing your views about the region, especially Afghanistan and its neighbor, Pakistan. I just want to call your attention towards the recent developments which has happened in Pakistan; that means the country is getting back to the path of democracy. But traditionally, what we have seen, that U.S. is more—feels comfortable to engage with autocracy there. Because you know, about 30 years, in my country, the country has been ruled by the army. Now, you have a different stage. There is a broad-based government in Pakistan.

So I want to—I'd like to hear your views about it, because many of the intellectuals here has given their opinion that now the U.S. policy should be engaging both the political as well as the other half, that is, the army. So what are your shares? Thank you very much.

SECRETARY RICE: Thank you. And again, on Pakistan, you are absolutely right that the Pakistani people have made a transition. There is a broad-based Pakistani Government which we intend to engage, as the Government of Pakistan, as we would engage any other democratic government. In fact, Deputy Secretary Negroponte has already been to Pakistan to meet the new civilian leaders. I have spoken to a couple of them on the phone prior to the formation of the government. And we think this is a really terrific step for the people of Pakistan. They're to be congratulated for doing it, despite a lot of threats from extremists and efforts to disrupt the elections, starting, of course, first, with the assassination of Mrs. Benazir Bhutto.

Now, we will engage the armed forces in military training and in military cooperation in the way that we do militaries around the world, many of them from democratic countries. It is terrific that you are here. I think one of the most important things that we can do is to have military officers from countries like Pakistan here for international military education. We cut that off for a period of seven—let's see, four years, which really, I think, was a very, very bad thing to have done, frankly, because we need to engage with all of the institutions of Pakistan. And Pakistan now will need to find a way to have very solid civilian control of the armed forces. I believe that our tradition of that is a good one, in which Pakistani officers can come and be a part of a democratic state in which civilian control is really now taken for granted, but wasn't always taken for granted, so we've built the institutions of it.

So we will engage across a broad front. As I mentioned in my remarks, I believe that the coming of a democratic government in Pakistan is a new strategic opportunity. It is an opportunity for an ally in the war on terror. But remember that our answer to terrorism is not just to fight and defeat the terrorists; it is to deal with the conditions that produce terrorism, and the absence of freedom is one of the conditions that produces terrorism. Perhaps the most important condition is the absence of freedom.

And so when we see an ally in the war on terror makes a transition to democracy, it could not be more affirming of everything that President Bush believes about the power of democracy, the power of those principles, and their power to defeat terrorism long term.

. . .

Source: U.S. State Department. Available at https://2001-2009.state.gov/secretary/rm/2008/04/103539.htm.

ANALYSIS

In her speech, Secretary Rice noted that the war in Afghanistan had received nearly unanimous bipartisan support since it began. This was certainly not true of the war in Iraq, and, by 2008, Afghanistan had become a political issue. Democrats increasingly argued that Iraq had taken resources and attention away from the war in Afghanistan and that this inattention had failed to provide security for the populace and fueled the return of the Taliban. This debate would continue throughout the year during the presidential election.

- **Document 65: The Reinvestigation of Combat Action at Wanat Village**
- **When:** June 22, 2010
- **Where:** Washington, D.C.
- **Significance:** The results of the reinvestigation of the July 2008 Battle of Wanat, which reassigned blame for the deaths of 13 soldiers in the fight. (Footnotes have been removed.)

DOCUMENT

MEMORANDUM FOR INSPECTOR GENERAL
SUBJECT: Oversight Review of the Reinvestigation into the Combat Action at Wanat Village, Afghanistan

We have completed our oversight review of the reinvestigation conducted by Lieutenant General Richard Natonski, U. S. Marine Corps, into the Battle of Wanat at the direction of General David Petraeus, Commander, U.S. Central Command. The reinvestigation was completed on January 12, 2010, and approved with modification by General Petraeus on January 21, 2010.

We conclude that the reinvestigation sufficiently established the facts regarding the combat action at Wanat and reasonably assigned accountability by identifying those individuals whose acts or omissions could be characterized as dereliction in the performance of duties. It concluded that company, battalion, and brigade commanders were derelict in the performance of their duties through neglect or culpable inefficiency, but determined that Division staff exercised due care in the matter.

We concur with the findings and conclusions of the reinvestigation. Our determination in that regard is based on our review of the report of reinvestigation, its 78 enclosures, the initial commander's inquiry of the Battle at Wanat completed under Army Regulation 15-6, and applicable Army guidance/doctrine concerning command responsibility.

We recommend that you provide the attached report to the Secretary of Defense and to Members of Congress who have expressed interest in the matter.

Donald M. Horstman
Deputy Inspector General for Administrative
Investigations

OVERSIGHT REVIEW
REINVESTIGATION OF THE COMBAT ACTION
AT WANAT VILLAGE, AFGHANISTAN

I. INTRODUCTION AND SUMMARY

This summarizes the results of our oversight review of the reinvestigation directed by the Commander, U.S. Central Command (USCENTCOM), into the circumstances surrounding combat action at Wanat village, Wygal District, Nuristan Province, Afghanistan that occurred on July 13, 2008, and resulted in significant casualties to U.S. forces. The USCENTCOM appointing order, in part, directed that the investigating officer determine whether actions by commanders and staffs at the Battalion, Brigade, and Division levels relating to the initial occupation of Wanat and the establishment of a combat outpost constituted dereliction of duty. We focused our review on the adequacy of the reinvestigation, particularly with respect to its findings concerning senior officers at Division level. In that regard, we examined:

- The inherent responsibilities for Platoon-level tactical matters at Division level;
- Whether Division staff were sufficiently aggressive in monitoring the establishment of the combat outpost at Wanat; and
- Whether guidance at Division level of combat outpost establishment was sufficient.

We conclude that the USCENTCOM reinvestigation, completed on January 12, 2010, sufficiently established the facts regarding the combat action at Wanat and reasonably assigned accountability by identifying those individuals whose acts or omissions could be characterized as dereliction in the performance of duties. Notwithstanding the extraordinary courage, tenacity, and skill demonstrated by the Company

DID YOU KNOW?

Restrepo

Restrepo is a 2010 documentary film codirected by British-born photographer Tim Hetherington and American journalist Sebastian Junger. It chronicles a year that the two spent with a platoon manning the "KOP" or Combat Outpost Korengal as well as the smaller Outpost Restrepo. The outpost and film took their name from Private First Class Juan Restrepo, a member of the platoon killed on July 22, 2007, in a firefight in the Korengal Valley in eastern Afghanistan. The Korengalis come from the small Pashai tribe and are ethnically and linguistically different from the peoples in neighboring valleys, and this has led to their cultural isolation. The documentary showed the men from the platoon engaging with the local population, fighting against suspected insurgents, and staving off boredom while occupying these spartan outposts in an isolated corner of Afghanistan. Tim Hetherington later died while filming the civil war in Libya, but Junger released a book, *War*, based on his experiences, as well as a second film, *Korengal*, based upon unused footage from *Restrepo*.

Commander and all those who helped fight off the enemy attack at Wanat, we agree that the Company Commander, through neglect, was derelict in the performance of his duty to conduct detailed planning for his company's role in the establishment of the combat outpost at Wanat and in his duty to provide guidance, support, and supervision to his subordinates during the establishment of the combat outpost at Wanat. We also agree that the Battalion Commander, through neglect, was derelict in the performance of his duty to properly oversee the planning and execution of Operation Rock Move and the subsequent construction of the combat outpost at Wanat.

Additionally, we agree with the USCENTCOM endorsement dated January 21, 2010, that the Brigade Commander maintained overall command responsibility for the operation and should have known of its inadequacies with respect to planning, resourcing, and supervision; and therefore, the Brigade Commander's culpable inefficiency constituted dereliction of duty. Regarding Division Level, based on U.S. Army doctrine that commanders generally maintain information of friendly forces two levels down, we agree that Major General (MG) Jeffrey J. Schloesser, U.S. Army, and his Division staff exercised due care in the supervision of and support to Operation Rock Move and planned construction of combat outpost Wanat.

This report sets forth our findings and conclusions based on a preponderance of the evidence.

II. BACKGROUND

From November 2006 through July 2009 MG Schloesser was the Commanding General of the 101st Airborne Division (Air Assault), headquartered at Fort Campbell, Kentucky. The Brigade level commands of the Division consisted of the 1st, 2nd, 3rd, and 4th Brigade Combat Teams, the 101st Combat Aviation Brigade, and the 101st Sustainment Brigade. In late 2007, the Division's 1st, 2nd, and 3rd Brigade Combat Teams deployed independently to Iraq, where each served under the command of different Multinational Divisions conducting combat operations throughout Iraq. In December 2007, the 101st Combat Aviation Brigade deployed to Afghanistan in support of Operation Enduring Freedom. In March 2008, the Division Headquarters, the Division's 4th Brigade Combat Team, and the 101st Sustainment Brigade joined the 101st Combat Aviation Brigade in Afghanistan in support of Operation Enduring Freedom as Combined Joint Task Force 101 (CJTF-101).

In a transfer of authority ceremony on April 10, 2008, MG Schloesser assumed control of the Regional Command East sector of Afghanistan from MG David M. Rodriguez, U.S. Army, Commanding General of the 82nd Airborne Division (CJTF-82). The CJTF-101 Headquarters located at Bagram Air Base in Afghanistan was responsible for an area of operation approximately 46–48,000 square miles, including much of the volatile border region between Afghanistan and Pakistan. Prior to his actual arrival in Afghanistan on April 1, 2008, MG Schloesser had conducted pre-deployment site surveys in the spring of 2007 and again in the fall of 2007, which included visiting combat outposts in Regional Command East.

During the spring of 2008, CJTF-101, 173d Airborne Brigade Combat Team (hereinafter "Brigade"), and 2d Battalion, 503d Parachute Infantry Regiment (hereinafter "Battalion") undertook an effort to realign Coalition Forces in Regional Command East. The purpose of the realignment was to free-up maneuver elements and better support counterinsurgency operations by locating Coalition Forces near population/economic centers, local government officials, and Afghan National Security Forces.

The Battalion identified the village of Wanat as a location that would support the development of local governance, economics and security; would serve as a blocking position in the Wygal valley seven kilometers north of the Battalion's command post at Camp Blessing and eight kilometers south of a platoon-sized combat outpost (named Bella) that the Battalion wanted to close; and could be supported by a ground line of communication. In keeping with counterinsurgency doctrine, the Battalion negotiated with village elders at Wanat for use of land to build a combat outpost, as seizing the property would have alienated the local population. After several months of negotiations, a lease was signed in June 2008. The site selected for the combat outpost at Wanat was adjacent to the village's houses, mosque, bazaar, and hotel, and was near the local District Center and Afghan National police station. The site selected was on a plateau where two valleys met and was surrounded by mountains and low ground, resulting in extensive dead space (an area that cannot be visually observed) around the position.

The Battalion's plan to realign within the Wygal Valley and establish a combat outpost at Wanat was a two-part operation called Operation Rock Move. The Concept of Operations (CONOPS) covered a 3-day period from July 8–10, 2008, and addressed the simultaneous disestablishment of combat outpost Bella and the initial movement to and occupation of the site at Wanat, and included those assets external to the Battalion required to conduct the operation. The Battalion wanted to disestablish combat outpost Bella because Bella could only be reinforced/resupplied by air and was not associated with any local governance, Afghan National Security Forces, or population center.

The Battalion planned to occupy and secure the site at Wanat on July 8, 2008, with Coalition Forces consisting of a Battalion unit (the 2nd Platoon from Chosen Company) and an Afghan National Army platoon. The CONOPS directed the seizure of dominant terrain around Wanat and the emplacement of multiple observation posts. The plan called for construction of the combat outpost fortifications to begin July 9, 2008, using contracted Afghan heavy engineer equipment and labor. However, prior to briefing the CONOPS to higher headquarters for approval, the Battalion learned that the Afghan heavy engineer equipment would be delayed at least five days beyond the start of Operation Rock Move. The Battalion chose to execute the operation as scheduled, but made no adjustment to the number of forces in Wanat, even though soldiers would be required to simultaneously secure the site and construct defensive positions using soldier labor until the heavy engineer equipment arrived. Supplies needed to construct the combat outpost were scheduled to be delivered by ground convoy and aircraft on July 9, 2008.

On July 7, 2008, CONOPS Rock Move was briefed to and approved by Brigadier General (BG) Mark A. Milley, U.S. Army, Deputy Commanding General for Operations, CJTF-101. Operation Rock Move began on July 8, 2008, with 2d Platoon, Chosen Company occupying the position at Wanat with five up-armored vehicles. On July 9, 2008, additional U.S. and Afghan soldiers, construction supplies, and equipment were delivered by CH-47 Chinook helicopters. A ground convoy of five

Afghan supply trucks scheduled to deliver construction supplies to Wanat on July 9, 2008, did not depart Camp Blessing because of mechanical issues with a vehicle from the Route Clearance Package (vehicles/equipment used to detect, mark, report, and neutralize explosive hazards and other obstacles along a defined route).

From July 8–12, 2008, Coalition Forces at Wanat constructed defensive positions utilizing soldier labor, construction materials delivered by CH-47 helicopters, and a single U.S. Army Bobcat (small frontloader delivered by a CH-47 helicopter to fill HESCO barriers (large canvas and wire mesh containers filled with dirt, rocks, or other materials)) around a mortar pit and a latrine. By the evening of July 12, 2008, the Coalition Forces at Wanat had established individual defensive positions, a concertina wire perimeter (not all wire was anchored in the ground by metal pickets), and a single observation post (OP), named Topside. None of the positions had overhead protection.

OP Topside was located approximately 100 meters to the east of the main combat outpost. There were no observation posts established in the high ground surrounding the site. 2nd Platoon did not establish OP Topside along the most likely enemy avenues of approach into the position or into the area of operations; rather it was established based on constraints faced by 2nd Platoon, such as its proximity for reinforcement and the availability of existing cover (rock boulders). The dead space around OP Topside began approximately 10 meters to the north of the OP.

By the evening of July 12, 2008, the Coalition Force combat power at Wanat consisted of 76 personnel (49 U.S., consisting of 40 soldiers from 2nd Platoon, 6 combat engineer soldiers, and 3 Marines of an Embedded Training Team; 24 Afghan soldiers; and 3 interpreters), five up-armored vehicles; two .50 caliber machine guns; two grenade launchers; one TOW missile launcher with Improved Target Acquisition System (ITAS); one 120mm mortar and one 60mm mortar; one Long Range Scout Surveillance System (LRAS); and night vision capability throughout the Platoon.

At 4:00 a.m. on July 13, 2008, U.S. and Afghan forces at Wanat, to include OP Topside, conducted "stand-to" (the practice of ensuring all personnel are awake, alert, and manning their fighting positions) and were preparing for a joint U.S./Afghan patrol to reconnoiter locations for an Afghan observation post. At approximately 04:20 a.m., an estimated 120 Anti-Afghan Forces attacked Coalition Forces at Wanat (from positions in the mountains to the west, north, and east, as well as firing positions in the houses, mosque, hotel, and bazaar immediately adjacent to the combat outpost), using small arms, machine guns, and rocket propelled grenades. The ensuing battle lasted several hours, with Coalition Forces using artillery, AH-64 Apache gunships, and fixed wing close air support to defeat the attack. Coalition Forces fought valiantly throughout the battle, displaying courage, tenacity, and initiative. By the end of the battle, 9 U.S. soldiers had been killed in action, and 27 U.S. and 6 Afghan soldiers wounded.

Following the battle on July 13, 2008, MG Schloesser determined that Coalition Forces could no longer achieve their counterinsurgency objectives in Wanat, due to complicity in the attack by the local government officials, population, and Afghan National police. On July 15, 2008, Coalition Forces withdrew from Wanat.

In August 2009, we identified deficiencies in Army investigations into matters concerning the establishment of the combat outpost at Wanat on July 8, 2008, and the ensuing battle five days later. By Information Memorandum to the Secretary of Defense, dated September 4, 2009, the DoDIG advised that he and Admiral Michael G. Mullen, U.S. Navy, Chairman of the Joint Chiefs of Staff, agreed the Chairman's Office would initiate a reinvestigation.

By memorandum of September 24, 2009, General (GEN) David H. Petraeus, U.S. Army, Commander, USCENTCOM, appointed Lieutenant General (LtGen) Richard F. Natonski, U.S. Marine Corps, to conduct an investigation, pursuant to the Manual of the Judge Advocate General of the Navy, focusing on the accountability of commanders and staff at the Battalion, Brigade, and Division (CJTF 101) levels. MG Michael L. Oats, U.S. Army, was appointed as LtGen Natonski's deputy investigating officer.

LtGen Natonski completed the reinvestigation on January 12, 2010, finding the Battalion Commander and the Company Commander derelict, through neglect, in the performance of their duties.

By endorsement of January 21, 2010, GEN Petraeus modified the conclusions to hold the Brigade Commander derelict, through culpable inefficiency, in the performance of his duties.

GEN Petraeus concurred with findings concerning MG Schloesser and his division staff—that they reasonably relied on information provided from lower commands and exercised due care.

GEN Petraeus forwarded the report to the Army for action. GEN Charles C. Campbell, U.S. Army, Commanding General, U.S. Army Forces Command, was appointed to determine the nature of any disciplinary action taken against officers found derelict.

     . . .

Discussion

We conclude that the USCENTCOM reinvestigation of combat actions at Wanat was sufficiently thorough and rigorous, and in accordance with the JAG Manual. The investigative team conducted 48 sworn, recorded interviews of key participants at every level of command ranging from platoon members to the CJTF-101 Commander. The reinvestigation and subsequent USCENTCOM endorsement established 603 findings of fact that, through a preponderance of evidence, supported 61 opinions.

Further, we conclude that the USCENTCOM reinvestigation sufficiently established the facts regarding the combat action at Wanat, and reasonably assigned accountability by identifying those individuals whose acts or omissions could be characterized as dereliction in the performance of duties. Notwithstanding the extraordinary courage, tenacity, and skill demonstrated by the Company Commander and all those who helped fight off the enemy attack at Wanat, we agree that the Company Commander, through neglect, was derelict in the performance of his duty to conduct detailed planning for his company's role in the establishment of the combat outpost at Wanat and in his duty to provide guidance, support, and supervision to his subordinates during the establishment of the combat outpost at Wanat.

We also agree that the Battalion Commander, through neglect, was derelict in the performance of his duty to properly oversee the planning and execution of Operation Rock Move and the subsequent construction of the combat outpost at Wanat. Further, we agree with the USCENTCOM endorsement that the Brigade Commander maintained overall command responsibility for the operation and should have known of its inadequacies with respect to planning, resourcing, and supervision; and therefore, the Brigade Commander's culpable inefficiency constituted dereliction of duty.

We conclude that MG Schloesser and BG Milley were not derelict in the performance of their duties, in that they and the Division Staff exercised due care in the supervision of and support to Operation Rock Move and the planned construction of combat outpost Wanat. The UCMJ, Article 92, states that a person is derelict in the performance of duties when that person willfully or negligently fails to perform duties, or when that person performs them in a culpably inefficient manner. To constitute dereliction, three elements must be proven; i.e., that the accused: (1) had certain duties; (2) knew or reasonably should have known of the duties; and (3) was willfully or through neglect, or culpable inefficiency, derelict in the performance of those duties.

In MG Schloesser's role as CJTF-101 Commander, and in BG Milley's role as Deputy, both had a duty and reasonably knew of their duty as outlined in FM 71-100, "Division Operations," to provide purpose and direction to their subordinate units, to monitor their subordinate units' actions, and to obtain feedback from their subordinate units to assist in controlling an operation to its successful conclusion. Regarding combat outposts, FM 71-100 states that commanders augment combat outposts with substantial fire support and combat support forces to achieve desired results. Further, U.S. Army doctrine as provided in FM 6-0, "Mission Command: Command and Control of Army Forces," states that commanders should know the disposition and situation of their forces without having to visit each unit on the ground, and generally maintain information of friendly forces two levels down. Therefore, the analysis pivots on whether there was evidence that MG Schloesser or BG Milley willfully or through neglect or culpable inefficiency failed to exercise due care in the supervision of and support to Operation Rock Move and the planned construction of combat outpost Wanat which could have contributed to the large scale attack at Wanat.

. . .

V. CONCLUSIONS

We conclude that the USCENTOM reinvestigation sufficiently established the facts regarding the combat action at Wanat and appropriately assigned accountability.

VI. RECOMMENDATIONS

We have no recommendations in the matter.

We note that GEN Petraeus directed that the USCENTCOM Operations Directorate and the USCENTCOM major subordinate commands work together to prepare a Standard Operating Procedure (SOP) for the planning, resourcing, and supervision of the establishment, construction, and manning of fixed operating positions. Additionally, GEN Petraeus directed that a copy of the report and his endorsement be forwarded to the Commander, U.S. Joint Forces Command for the development of lessons learned and sharing of those lessons with the appropriate military service lessons learned organizations.

Source: Department of Defense. Available online at https://media.defense.gov /2010/Jun/22/2001712437/-1/-1/1/ROI-WANAT508.pdf.

ANALYSIS

The Battle of Wanat had been one of the costliest engagements of Operation Enduring Freedom to that time. The loss of 13 soldiers in the protracted firefight led to the investigation, and the original inquiry led by Lt. Gen. Richard Natonski had reprimanded the entire chain of command for failures of leadership leading up to and during the battle. Following this initial investigation, the reinvestigation cited here instead limited the blame to the company and battalion levels, a decision that prompted a strong public outcry. For several years afterward, the families of the soldiers killed at Wanat continued to press the Army to have the original reprimands against the more senior officers involved in the battle reinstated to no avail.

4

DOCUMENTS FROM THE SURGE, WITHDRAWAL, AND AN UNCERTAIN FUTURE, 2009–2017

- **Document 66: General Stanley McChrystal Initial Assessment**
- **When:** August 30, 2009
- **Where:** Kabul, Afghanistan
- **Significance:** This strategic review by General Stanley McChrystal, the new International Security Assistance Force (ISAF) commander, requested more men to fight a counterinsurgency campaign in Afghanistan.

DOCUMENT

Purpose

On 26 June 2009, the United States Secretary of Defense directed Commander, United States Central Command (CDRUSCENTCOM) to provide a multidisciplinary assessment of the situation in Afghanistan. On 02 July 2009, Commander, NATO International Security Assistance Force (COMISAF)/U.S. Forces-Afghanistan (USFOR-A) received direction from CDRUSCENTCOM to complete the overall review.

On 01 July 2009, the Supreme Allied Commander Europe and NATO Secretary General also issued a similar directive.

COMISAF subsequently issued an order to the ISAF staff and component commands to conduct a comprehensive review to assess the overall situation, review plans and ongoing efforts, and identify revisions to operational, tactical, and strategic guidance.

The following assessment is a report of COMISAF's findings and conclusions. In summary, this assessment sought to answer the following questions:

– Can ISAF achieve the mission?

– If so, how should ISAF go about achieving the mission?

– What is required to achieve the mission?

The assessment draws on both internal ISAF components, to include Regional Commands, and external agencies such as GIRoA ministries, International Governmental Organizations and Nongovernmental Organizations. It also draws on existing ISAF and USFOR-A plans and policy guidance, relevant reports and studies, and the consultation of external experts and advisors.

DID YOU KNOW?

Battle of Kamdesh

The Battle of Kamdesh occurred on October 3, 2009, at U.S. Combat Outpost (COP) Keating near the town of Kamdesh in Nuristan Province. Located at the juncture of three valleys near the Pakistani border, the United States had built up COP Keating to interdict the movement of men and illicit supplies while also supporting the efforts of the Provincial Reconstruction Team (PRT) operating in Nuristan Province. The COP was surrounded on three sides by mountains and a river on the fourth and had been slated for closure because of its vulnerability. Manned by Bravo Troop, 3rd Squadron, 61st Cavalry Regiment as well as two Latvian soldiers who led their Afghan National Army partner units, COP Keating came under heavy fire at 6:00 a.m. on October 3. An insurgent force of 300 quickly overwhelmed the observation post on one of the mountains and then streamed into the COP. Under heavy fire from all directions, the defenders formed a small perimeter around the COP's aid station and a few other structures. With heavy air support, the defenders rallied to force the insurgents out of the COP after a 12-hour battle. Eight U.S. soldiers were killed and 27 wounded, while the insurgents lost at least 150 men. Two men, Staff Sergeants Clint Romesha and Ty Carter, earned the Medal of Honor for their actions during the battle.

Commander's Summary

The stakes in Afghanistan are high. NATO's Comprehensive Strategic Political Military Plan and President Obama's strategy to disrupt, dismantle, and eventually defeat al Qaeda and prevent their return to Afghanistan have laid out a clear path of what we must do. Stability in Afghanistan is an imperative; if the Afghan government falls to the Taliban—or has insufficient capability to counter transnational forces—Afghanistan could again become a base for terrorism, with obvious implications for regional stability.

The situation in Afghanistan is serious; neither success nor failure can be taken for granted. Although considerable effort and sacrifice have resulted in some progress, many indicators suggest the overall situation is deteriorating. We face not only a resilient and growing insurgency; there is a crisis of confidence among Afghans—in both their government and the international community—that undermines our credibility and emboldens the insurgents. Further, a perception that our resolve is uncertain makes Afghans reluctant to align with us against the insurgents.

Success is achievable, but will not be attained simply by trying harder or "doubling down" on the previous strategy. Additional resources are required, but focusing on force or resource requirements misses the point entirely. The key take away from this assessment is the urgent need for significant change to our strategy and the way that we think and operate.

NATO's International Security Assistance Force (ISAF) requires a new strategy that is credible to, and sustainable by, the Afghans. This new strategy must also be properly resourced and executed through an integrated civilian-military counterinsurgency campaign that earns the support of the Afghan people and provides them with a secure environment.

To execute the strategy, we must grow and improve the effectiveness of the Afghan National Security Forces (ANSF) and elevate the importance of governance. We must also prioritize resources to those areas where the population is threatened, gain the initiative from the insurgency, and signal unwavering commitment to see it through to success. Finally, we must redefine the nature of the fight, clearly understand the impacts and importance of time, and change our operational culture.

Redefining the Fight

This is a different kind of fight. We must conduct classic counterinsurgency operations in an environment that is uniquely complex. Three regional insurgencies have intersected with a dynamic blend of local power struggles in a country damaged by 30 years of conflict. This makes for a situation that defies simple solutions or quick fixes. Success demands a comprehensive counterinsurgency (COIN) campaign.

Our strategy cannot be focused on seizing terrain or destroying insurgent forces; our objective must be the population. In the struggle to gain the support of the people, every action we take must enable this effort. The population also represents a powerful actor that can and must be leveraged in this complex system. Gaining their support will require a better understanding of the people's choices and needs. However, progress is hindered by the dual threat of a resilient insurgency and a crisis of confidence in the government and the international coalition. To win their support, we must protect the people from both of these threats.

Many describe the conflict in Afghanistan as a war of ideas, which believe to be true. However, this is a "'deeds-based'" information environment where perceptions derive from actions, such as how we interact with the population and how quickly things improve. The key to changing perceptions lies in changing the underlying truths. We must never confuse the situation as it stands with the one we desire, lest we risk our credibility.

The Criticality of Time

The impact of time on our effort in Afghanistan has been underappreciated and we require a new way of thinking about it.

First, the fight is not an annual cyclical campaign of kinetics driven by an insurgent "fighting season." Rather, it is year-round struggle, often conducted with little apparent violence, to win the support of the people. Protecting the population from insurgent coercion and intimidation demands a persistent presence and focus that cannot be interrupted without risking serious setback.

Second, and more importantly, we face both a short and long-term fight. The long-term fight will require patience and commitment, but I believe the short-term fight will be decisive. Failure to gain the initiative and reverse insurgent momentum in the near-term (next 12 months)—while Afghan security capacity matures—risks an outcome where defeating the insurgency is no longer possible.

Change the Operational Culture

As formidable as the threat may be, we make the problems harder. ISAF is conventional force that is poorly configured for COIN, inexperienced in local languages and culture, and struggling with challenges inherent to coalition warfare. These intrinsic disadvantages are exacerbated by our current operational culture and how we operate.

Pre-occupied with protection of our own forces, we have operated in a manner that distances us—physically and psychologically—from the people we seek to protect. In addition, we run the risk of strategic defeat by pursuing tactical wins that cause civilian casualties or unnecessary collateral damage. The insurgents cannot defeat us militarily, but we can defeat ourselves.

Accomplishing the mission demands a renewed emphasis on the basics through a dramatic change in how we operate, with specific focus in two principle areas:

1. **Change the operational culture to connect with the people.** I believe we must interact more closely with the population and focus on operations that bring stability, while shielding them from insurgent violence, corruption, and coercion.

2. **Improve unity of effort and command.** We must significantly modify organizational structure to achieve better unity of effort. We will continue to realign relationships to improve coordination within ISAF and the international community.

The New Strategy: Focus on the Population

Getting the basics right is necessary for success, but it is not enough. To accomplish the mission and defeat the insurgency we also require a properly resourced strategy built on four main pillars:

1. **Improve effectiveness through greater partnering with ANSF.** We will increase the size and accelerate the growth of the ANSF, with a radically improved partnership at every level, to improve effectiveness and prepare them to take the lead in security operations.
2. **Prioritize responsive and accountable governance.** We must assist in improving governance at all levels through both formal and informal mechanisms.
3. **Gain the initiative.** Our first imperative, in a series of operational stages, is to gain the initiative and reverse the insurgency's momentum.
4. **Focus Resources.** We will prioritize available resources to those critical areas where vulnerable populations are most threatened.

These concepts are not new. However, implemented aggressively, they will be revolutionary to our effectiveness. We must do things dramatically differently—even uncomfortably differently—to change how we operate, and also how we think. Our every action must reflect this change of mindset: how we traverse the country, how we use force, and how we partner with the Afghans. Conventional wisdom is not sacred; security may not come from the barrel of a gun. Better force protection may be counterintuitive; it might come from less armor and less distance from the population.

The Basis of Assessment: Analysis and Experience

My conclusions were informed through a rigorous multi-disciplinary assessment by a team of accomplished military personnel and civilians and my personal experience and core beliefs. Central to my analysis is a belief that we must respect the complexities of the operational environment and design our strategic approach accordingly. As we analyzed the situation, I became increasingly convinced of several themes: that the objective is the will of the people, our conventional warfare culture is part of the problem, the Afghans must ultimately defeat the insurgency, we cannot succeed without significantly improved unity of effort, and, finally, that protecting the people means shielding them from *all* threats.

A Strategy for Success: Balancing Resources and Risk

Our campaign in Afghanistan has been historically under-resourced and remains so today. Almost every aspect of our collective effort and associated resourcing has lagged a growing insurgency—historically a recipe for failure in COIN. Success will require a discrete "jump" to gain the initiative, demonstrate progress in the short term, and secure long-term support.

Resources will not win this war, but under-resourcing could lose it. Resourcing communicates commitment, but we must also balance force levels to enable effective ANSF partnering and provide population security, while avoiding perceptions of coalition dominance. Ideally, the ANSF must lead this fight, but they will not have enough capability in the near-term given the insurgency's growth rate. In the interim, coalition forces must provide a bridge capability to protect critical segments of the population. The status quo will lead to failure if we wait for the ANSF to grow.

The new strategy will improve effectiveness through better application of existing assets, but it also requires additional resources. Broadly speaking, we require more civilian and military resources, more ANSF, and more ISR and other enablers.

At the same time, we will find offsets as we reprogram other assets and improve efficiency. Overall, ISAF requires an increase in the total coalition force capability and end-strength. This "'properly resourced'" requirement will define the minimum force levels to accomplish the mission with an acceptable level of risk.

Unique Moment in Time

This is an important—and likely decisive—period of this war. Afghans are frustrated and weary after eight years without evidence of the progress they anticipated. Patience is understandably short, both in Afghanistan and in our own countries. Time matters; we must act now to reverse the negative trends and demonstrate progress.

I do not underestimate the enormous challenges in executing this new strategy; however, we have a key advantage; the majority of Afghans do not want a return of the Taliban. During consultations with Afghan Defense Minister Wardak, I found some of his writings insightful:

> "Victory is within our grasp, provided that we recommit ourselves based on lessons learned and provided that we fulfill the requirements needed to make success inevitable. . . . I reject the myth advanced in the media that Afghanistan is a 'graveyard of empires' and that the U.S. and NATO effort is destined to fail. Afghans have never seen you as occupiers, even though this has been the major focus of the enemy's propaganda campaign. Unlike the Russians, who imposed a government with an alien ideology, you enabled us to write a democratic constitution and choose our own government. Unlike the Russians, who destroyed our country, you came to rebuild."

Given that this conflict and country are his to win—not mine—Minister Wardak's assessment was part of my calculus. While the situation is serious, success is still achievable. This starts with redefining both the fight itself and what we need for the fight. It is then sustained through a fundamentally new way of doing business. Finally, it will be realized when our new operational culture connects with the powerful will of the Afghan people.

Source: Department of Defense. Available online at http://www.dtic.mil/get-tr-doc/pdf?AD=ADA602104.

ANALYSIS

As far back as General Barno's tenure in Afghanistan (2003–2005), the United States acknowledged the Taliban's insurgency against the Afghan government, but the priorities for those years remained reconstruction and counterterrorism missions that befitted the relatively small numbers of available forces.

General McChrystal's review took place in the wake of the seemingly successful "surge" of U.S. forces into Iraq in 2007 that, combined with a new counterinsurgency strategy and political rapprochements toward the disaffected Sunni population, finally stemmed the violence in that country. This review, in many respects, sought to transfer the lessons learned from Iraq into Afghanistan in spite of the very different social and political environments present in the two countries.

- **Document 67: Barack Obama, Remarks by the President in Address to the Nation on the Way Forward in Afghanistan and Pakistan**
- **When:** December 1, 2009
- **Where:** West Point, New York
- **Significance:** President Obama formally announced troop increases in Afghanistan to follow General McChrystal's recommendations.

DOCUMENT

Good evening. To the United States Corps of Cadets, to the men and women of our Armed Services, and to my fellow Americans: I want to speak to you tonight about our effort in Afghanistan—the nature of our commitment there, the scope of our interests, and the strategy that my administration will pursue to bring this war to a successful conclusion. It's an extraordinary honor for me to do so here at West Point—where so many men and women have prepared to stand up for our security, and to represent what is finest about our country.

To address these important issues, it's important to recall why America and our allies were compelled to fight a war in Afghanistan in the first place. We did not ask for this fight. On September 11, 2001, 19 men hijacked four airplanes and used them to murder nearly 3,000 people. They struck at our military and economic nerve centers. They took the lives of innocent men, women, and children without regard to their faith or race or station. Were it not for the heroic actions of passengers onboard one of those flights, they could have also struck at one of the great symbols of our democracy in Washington, and killed many more.

As we know, these men belonged to al Qaeda—a group of extremists who have distorted and defiled Islam, one of the world's great religions, to justify the slaughter of innocents. Al Qaeda's base of operations was in Afghanistan, where they were harbored by the Taliban—a ruthless, repressive and radical movement that seized control of that country after it was ravaged by years of Soviet occupation and civil war, and after the attention of America and our friends had turned elsewhere.

Just days after 9/11, Congress authorized the use of force against al Qaeda and those who harbored them—an authorization that continues to this day.

DID YOU KNOW?

FOB Chapman Attack

In 2001, the CIA established a small base in Khost Province in eastern Afghanistan during the southward retreat of the Taliban. Named in 2002 for Sergeant First Class Nathan Chapman, the first U.S. combat death in Afghanistan, Forward Operating Base Chapman grew in the following years as the CIA, special forces, and the Khost Provincial Reconstruction Team all operated from there. On December 30, 2009, the CIA detachment at FOB Chapman brought in Humam Khalil Abu-Mulal al-Balawi, a jihadi with suspected ties to al-Qaeda's deputy commander, Ayman al-Zawahiri. Al-Balawi represented a major intelligence coup, but he covertly carried a suicide bomb under his clothes as he was brought into FOB Chapman. He detonated the bomb in the presence of his hopeful CIA handlers, killing nine people—seven of whom worked for the CIA, including counterterrorism expert Jennifer Lynn Matthews, who had once hunted Osama bin Laden—and wounding six others. The attack was depicted in the 2012 film *Zero Dark Thirty*.

The vote in the Senate was 98 to nothing. The vote in the House was 420 to 1. For the first time in its history, the North Atlantic Treaty Organization invoked Article 5—the commitment that says an attack on one member nation is an attack on all. And the United Nations Security Council endorsed the use of all necessary steps to respond to the 9/11 attacks. America, our allies and the world were acting as one to destroy al Qaeda's terrorist network and to protect our common security.

Under the banner of this domestic unity and international legitimacy—and only after the Taliban refused to turn over Osama bin Laden—we sent our troops into Afghanistan. Within a matter of months, al Qaeda was scattered and many of its operatives were killed. The Taliban was driven from power and pushed back on its heels. A place that had known decades of fear now had reason to hope. At a conference convened by the U.N., a provisional government was established under President Hamid Karzai. And an International Security Assistance Force was established to help bring a lasting peace to a war-torn country.

Then, in early 2003, the decision was made to wage a second war, in Iraq. The wrenching debate over the Iraq war is well-known and need not be repeated here. It's enough to say that for the next six years, the Iraq war drew the dominant share of our troops, our resources, our diplomacy, and our national attention—and that the decision to go into Iraq caused substantial rifts between America and much of the world.

Today, after extraordinary costs, we are bringing the Iraq war to a responsible end. We will remove our combat brigades from Iraq by the end of next summer, and all of our troops by the end of 2011. That we are doing so is a testament to the character of the men and women in uniform. Thanks to their courage, grit and perseverance, we have given Iraqis a chance to shape their future, and we are successfully leaving Iraq to its people.

But while we've achieved hard-earned milestones in Iraq, the situation in Afghanistan has deteriorated. After escaping across the border into Pakistan in 2001 and 2002, al Qaeda's leadership established a safe haven there. Although a legitimate government was elected by the Afghan people, it's been hampered by corruption, the drug trade, an under-developed economy, and insufficient security forces.

Over the last several years, the Taliban has maintained common cause with al Qaeda, as they both seek an overthrow of the Afghan government. Gradually, the Taliban has begun to control additional swaths of territory in Afghanistan, while engaging in increasingly brazen and devastating attacks of terrorism against the Pakistani people.

Now, throughout this period, our troop levels in Afghanistan remained a fraction of what they were in Iraq. When I took office, we had just over 32,000 Americans serving in Afghanistan, compared to 160,000 in Iraq at the peak of the war. Commanders in Afghanistan repeatedly asked for support to deal with the reemergence of the Taliban, but these reinforcements did not arrive. And that's why, shortly after taking office, I approved a longstanding request for more troops. After consultations with our allies, I then announced a strategy recognizing the fundamental connection between our war effort in Afghanistan and the extremist safe havens in Pakistan. I set a goal that was narrowly defined as disrupting, dismantling, and defeating al Qaeda and its extremist allies, and pledged to better coordinate our military and civilian efforts.

Since then, we've made progress on some important objectives. High-ranking al Qaeda and Taliban leaders have been killed, and we've stepped up the pressure on al Qaeda worldwide. In Pakistan, that nation's army has gone on its largest offensive in years. In Afghanistan, we and our allies prevented the Taliban from stopping a presidential election, and—although it was marred by fraud—that election produced a government that is consistent with Afghanistan's laws and constitution.

Yet huge challenges remain. Afghanistan is not lost, but for several years it has moved backwards. There's no imminent threat of the government being overthrown, but the Taliban has gained momentum. Al Qaeda has not reemerged in Afghanistan in the same numbers as before 9/11, but they retain their safe havens along the border. And our forces lack the full support they need to effectively train and partner with Afghan security forces and better secure the population. Our new commander in Afghanistan—General McChrystal—has reported that the security situation is more serious than he anticipated. In short: The status quo is not sustainable.

As cadets, you volunteered for service during this time of danger. Some of you fought in Afghanistan. Some of you will deploy there. As your Commander-in-Chief, I owe you a mission that is clearly defined, and worthy of your service. And that's why, after the Afghan voting was completed, I insisted on a thorough review of our strategy. Now, let me be clear: There has never been an option before me that called for troop deployments before 2010, so there has been no delay or denial of resources necessary for the conduct of the war during this review period. Instead, the review has allowed me to ask the hard questions, and to explore all the different options, along with my national security team, our military and civilian leadership in Afghanistan, and our key partners. And given the stakes involved, I owed the American people—and our troops—no less.

This review is now complete. And as Commander-in-Chief, I have determined that it is in our vital national interest to send an additional 30,000 U.S. troops to Afghanistan. After 18 months, our troops will begin to come home. These are the resources that we need to seize the initiative, while building the Afghan capacity that can allow for a responsible transition of our forces out of Afghanistan.

I do not make this decision lightly. I opposed the war in Iraq precisely because I believe that we must exercise restraint in the use of military force, and always consider the long-term consequences of our actions. We have been at war now for eight years, at enormous cost in lives and resources. Years of debate over Iraq and terrorism have left our unity on national security issues in tatters, and created a highly polarized and partisan backdrop for this effort. And having just experienced the worst economic crisis since the Great Depression, the American people are understandably focused on rebuilding our economy and putting people to work here at home.

Most of all, I know that this decision asks even more of you—a military that, along with your families, has already borne the heaviest of all burdens. As President, I have signed a letter of condolence to the family of each American who gives their life in these wars. I have read the letters from the parents and spouses of those who deployed. I visited our courageous wounded warriors at Walter Reed. I've traveled to Dover to meet the flag-draped caskets of 18 Americans returning home to their final resting place. I see firsthand the terrible wages of war. If I did not think that the security of the United States and the safety of the American people were at stake in Afghanistan, I would gladly order every single one of our troops home tomorrow.

So, no, I do not make this decision lightly. I make this decision because I am convinced that our security is at stake in Afghanistan and Pakistan. This is the epicenter of violent extremism practiced by al Qaeda. It is from here that we were attacked on 9/11, and it is from here that new attacks are being plotted as I speak. This is no idle danger; no hypothetical threat. In the last few months alone, we have apprehended extremists within our borders who were sent here from the border region of Afghanistan and Pakistan to commit new acts of terror. And this danger will only grow if the region slides backwards, and al Qaeda can operate with impunity. We must keep the pressure on al Qaeda, and to do that, we must increase the stability and capacity of our partners in the region.

Of course, this burden is not ours alone to bear. This is not just America's war. Since 9/11, al Qaeda's safe havens have been the source of attacks against London and Amman and Bali. The people and governments of both Afghanistan and Pakistan are endangered. And the stakes are even higher within a nuclear-armed Pakistan, because we know that al Qaeda and other extremists seek nuclear weapons, and we have every reason to believe that they would use them.

These facts compel us to act along with our friends and allies. Our overarching goal remains the same: to disrupt, dismantle, and defeat al Qaeda in Afghanistan and Pakistan, and to prevent its capacity to threaten America and our allies in the future.

To meet that goal, we will pursue the following objectives within Afghanistan. We must deny al Qaeda a safe haven. We must reverse the Taliban's momentum and deny it the ability to overthrow the government. And we must strengthen the capacity of Afghanistan's security forces and government so that they can take lead responsibility for Afghanistan's future.

We will meet these objectives in three ways. First, we will pursue a military strategy that will break the Taliban's momentum and increase Afghanistan's capacity over the next 18 months.

The 30,000 additional troops that I'm announcing tonight will deploy in the first part of 2010—the fastest possible pace—so that they can target the insurgency and secure key population centers. They'll increase our ability to train competent Afghan security forces, and to partner with them so that more Afghans can get into the fight. And they will help create the conditions for the United States to transfer responsibility to the Afghans.

Because this is an international effort, I've asked that our commitment be joined by contributions from our allies. Some have already provided additional troops, and we're confident that there will be further contributions in the days and weeks ahead. Our friends have fought and bled and died alongside us in Afghanistan. And now, we must come together to end this war successfully. For what's at stake is not simply a test of NATO's credibility—what's at stake is the security of our allies, and the common security of the world.

But taken together, these additional American and international troops will allow us to accelerate handing over responsibility to Afghan forces, and allow us to begin the transfer of our forces out of Afghanistan in July of 2011. Just as we have done in Iraq, we will execute this transition responsibly, taking into account conditions on the ground. We'll continue to advise and assist Afghanistan's security forces to ensure that they can succeed over the long haul. But it will be clear to the Afghan government—and, more importantly, to the Afghan people—that they will ultimately be responsible for their own country.

Second, we will work with our partners, the United Nations, and the Afghan people to pursue a more effective civilian strategy, so that the government can take advantage of improved security.

This effort must be based on performance. The days of providing a blank check are over. President Karzai's inauguration speech sent the right message about moving in a new direction. And going forward, we will be clear about what we expect from those who receive our assistance. We'll support Afghan ministries, governors, and local leaders that combat corruption and deliver for the people. We expect those who are ineffective or corrupt to be held accountable. And we will also focus our assistance in areas—such as agriculture—that can make an immediate impact in the lives of the Afghan people.

The people of Afghanistan have endured violence for decades. They've been confronted with occupation—by the Soviet Union, and then by foreign al Qaeda fighters who used Afghan land for their own purposes. So tonight, I want the Afghan people to understand—America seeks an end to this era of war and suffering. We have no interest in occupying your country. We will support efforts by the Afghan government to open the door to those Taliban who abandon violence and respect the human rights of their fellow citizens. And we will seek a partnership with Afghanistan grounded in mutual respect—to isolate those who destroy; to strengthen those who build; to hasten the day when our troops will leave; and to forge a lasting friendship in which America is your partner, and never your patron.

Third, we will act with the full recognition that our success in Afghanistan is inextricably linked to our partnership with Pakistan.

We're in Afghanistan to prevent a cancer from once again spreading through that country. But this same cancer has also taken root in the border region of Pakistan. That's why we need a strategy that works on both sides of the border.

In the past, there have been those in Pakistan who've argued that the struggle against extremism is not their fight, and that Pakistan is better off doing little or seeking accommodation with those who use violence. But in recent years, as innocents have been killed from Karachi to Islamabad, it has become clear that it is the Pakistani people who are the most endangered by extremism. Public opinion has turned. The Pakistani army has waged an offensive in Swat and South Waziristan. And there is no doubt that the United States and Pakistan share a common enemy.

In the past, we too often defined our relationship with Pakistan narrowly. Those days are over. Moving forward, we are committed to a partnership with Pakistan that is built on a foundation of mutual interest, mutual respect, and mutual trust. We will strengthen Pakistan's capacity to target those groups that threaten our countries, and have made it clear that we cannot tolerate a safe haven for terrorists whose location is known and whose intentions are clear. America is also providing substantial resources to support Pakistan's democracy and development. We are the largest international supporter for those Pakistanis displaced by the fighting. And going forward, the Pakistan people must know America will remain a strong supporter of Pakistan's security and prosperity long after the guns have fallen silent, so that the great potential of its people can be unleashed.

These are the three core elements of our strategy: a military effort to create the conditions for a transition; a civilian surge that reinforces positive action; and an effective partnership with Pakistan.

I recognize there are a range of concerns about our approach. So let me briefly address a few of the more prominent arguments that I've heard, and which I take very seriously.

First, there are those who suggest that Afghanistan is another Vietnam. They argue that it cannot be stabilized, and we're better off cutting our losses and rapidly withdrawing. I believe this argument depends on a false reading of history. Unlike Vietnam, we are joined by a broad coalition of 43 nations that recognizes the legitimacy of our action. Unlike Vietnam, we are not facing a broad-based popular insurgency. And most importantly, unlike Vietnam, the American people were viciously attacked from Afghanistan, and remain a target for those same extremists who are plotting along its border. To abandon this area now—and to rely only on efforts against al Qaeda from a distance—would significantly hamper our ability to keep the pressure on al Qaeda, and create an unacceptable risk of additional attacks on our homeland and our allies.

Second, there are those who acknowledge that we can't leave Afghanistan in its current state, but suggest that we go forward with the troops that we already have. But this would simply maintain a status quo in which we muddle through, and permit a slow deterioration of conditions there. It would ultimately prove more costly and prolong our stay in Afghanistan, because we would never be able to generate the conditions needed to train Afghan security forces and give them the space to take over.

Finally, there are those who oppose identifying a time frame for our transition to Afghan responsibility. Indeed, some call for a more dramatic and open-ended escalation of our war effort—one that would commit us to a nation-building project of up to a decade. I reject this course because it sets goals that are beyond what can be achieved at a reasonable cost, and what we need to achieve to secure our interests. Furthermore, the absence of a time frame for transition would deny us any sense of urgency in working with the Afghan government. It must be clear that Afghans will have to take responsibility for their security, and that America has no interest in fighting an endless war in Afghanistan.

As President, I refuse to set goals that go beyond our responsibility, our means, or our interests. And I must weigh all of the challenges that our nation faces. I don't have the luxury of committing to just one. Indeed, I'm mindful of the words of President Eisenhower, who—in discussing our national security—said, "Each proposal must be weighed in the light of a broader consideration: the need to maintain balance in and among national programs."

Over the past several years, we have lost that balance. We've failed to appreciate the connection between our national security and our economy. In the wake of an economic crisis, too many of our neighbors and friends are out of work and struggle to pay the bills. Too many Americans are worried about the future facing our children. Meanwhile, competition within the global economy has grown more fierce. So we can't simply afford to ignore the price of these wars.

All told, by the time I took office the cost of the wars in Iraq and Afghanistan approached a trillion dollars. Going forward, I am committed to addressing these costs openly and honestly. Our new approach in Afghanistan is likely to cost us roughly $30 billion for the military this year, and I'll work closely with Congress to address these costs as we work to bring down our deficit.

But as we end the war in Iraq and transition to Afghan responsibility, we must rebuild our strength here at home. Our prosperity provides a foundation for our power. It pays for our military. It underwrites our diplomacy. It taps the potential of our people, and allows investment in new industry. And it will allow us to compete in this century as successfully as we did in the last. That's why our troop commitment in Afghanistan cannot be open-ended—because the nation that I'm most interested in building is our own.

Now, let me be clear: None of this will be easy. The struggle against violent extremism will not be finished quickly, and it extends well beyond Afghanistan and Pakistan. It will be an enduring test of our free society, and our leadership in the world. And unlike the great power conflicts and clear lines of division that defined the 20th century, our effort will involve disorderly regions, failed states, diffuse enemies.

So as a result, America will have to show our strength in the way that we end wars and prevent conflict—not just how we wage wars. We'll have to be nimble and precise in our use of military power. Where al Qaeda and its allies attempt to establish a foothold—whether in Somalia or Yemen or elsewhere—they must be confronted by growing pressure and strong partnerships.

And we can't count on military might alone. We have to invest in our homeland security, because we can't capture or kill every violent extremist abroad. We have to improve and better coordinate our intelligence, so that we stay one step ahead of shadowy networks.

We will have to take away the tools of mass destruction. And that's why I've made it a central pillar of my foreign policy to secure loose nuclear materials from terrorists, to stop the spread of nuclear weapons, and to pursue the goal of a world without them—because every nation must understand that true security will never come from an endless race for ever more destructive weapons; true security will come for those who reject them.

We'll have to use diplomacy, because no one nation can meet the challenges of an interconnected world acting alone. I've spent this year renewing our alliances and forging new partnerships. And we have forged a new beginning between America and the Muslim world—one that recognizes our mutual interest in breaking a cycle of conflict, and that promises a future in which those who kill innocents are isolated by those who stand up for peace and prosperity and human dignity.

And finally, we must draw on the strength of our values—for the challenges that we face may have changed, but the things that we believe in must not. That's why we must promote our values by living them at home—which is why I have prohibited torture and will close the prison at Guantanamo Bay. And we must make it clear to every man, woman and child around the world who lives under the dark cloud of tyranny that America will speak out on behalf of their human rights, and tend to the light of freedom and justice and opportunity and respect for the dignity of all peoples. That is who we are. That is the source, the moral source, of America's authority.

Since the days of Franklin Roosevelt, and the service and sacrifice of our grandparents and great-grandparents, our country has borne a special burden in global affairs. We have spilled American blood in many countries on multiple continents. We have spent our revenue to help others rebuild from rubble and develop their own economies. We have joined with others to develop an architecture of institutions—from the United Nations to NATO to the World Bank—that provide for the common security and prosperity of human beings.

We have not always been thanked for these efforts, and we have at times made mistakes. But more than any other nation, the United States of America has underwritten global security for over six decades—a time that, for all its problems, has seen walls come down, and markets open, and billions lifted from poverty, unparalleled scientific progress and advancing frontiers of human liberty.

For unlike the great powers of old, we have not sought world domination. Our union was founded in resistance to oppression. We do not seek to occupy other nations. We will not claim another nation's resources or target other peoples because their faith or ethnicity is different from ours. What we have fought for—what we continue to fight for—is a better future for our children and grandchildren. And we believe that their lives will be better if other peoples' children and grandchildren can live in freedom and access opportunity.

As a country, we're not as young—and perhaps not as innocent—as we were when Roosevelt was President. Yet we are still heirs to a noble struggle for freedom. And now we must summon all of our might and moral suasion to meet the challenges of a new age.

In the end, our security and leadership does not come solely from the strength of our arms. It derives from our people—from the workers and businesses who will rebuild our economy; from the entrepreneurs and researchers who will pioneer new industries; from the teachers that will educate our children, and the service of those who work in our communities at home; from the diplomats and Peace Corps volunteers who spread hope abroad; and from the men and women in uniform who are part of an unbroken line of sacrifice that has made government of the people, by the people, and for the people a reality on this Earth.

This vast and diverse citizenry will not always agree on every issue—nor should we. But I also know that we, as a country, cannot sustain our leadership, nor navigate the momentous challenges of our time, if we allow ourselves to be split asunder by the same rancor and cynicism and partisanship that has in recent times poisoned our national discourse.

It's easy to forget that when this war began, we were united—bound together by the fresh memory of a horrific attack, and by the determination to defend our homeland and the values we hold dear. I refuse to accept the notion that we cannot summon that unity again. I believe with every fiber of my being that we—as Americans—can still come together behind a common purpose. For our values are not simply words written into parchment—they are a creed that calls us together, and that has carried us through the darkest of storms as one nation, as one people.

America—we are passing through a time of great trial. And the message that we send in the midst of these storms must be clear: that our cause is just, our resolve unwavering. We will go forward with the confidence that right makes might, and with the commitment to forge an America that is safer, a world that is more secure, and a future that represents not the deepest of fears but the highest of hopes.

Source: Public Papers of the Presidents of the United States: Barack Obama, 2009, Book 2. Washington, D.C.: Government Printing Office, 2010, 1747–1754. Available online at https://obamawhitehouse.archives.gov/the-press-office/remarks-president-address-nation-way-forward-afghanistan-and-pakistan.

ANALYSIS

President Obama accepted some, though not all, of General McChrystal's recommendations and authorized a surge of U.S. forces into Afghanistan that would begin in mid-2010 and end in early 2012. U.S. troop strength had already nearly doubled during his time in office, and the surge would bring that number up to nearly 100,000. He argued that this was necessary and framed Afghanistan as the just, forgotten war relative to the war in Iraq that President Obama would draw to a close by the end of 2011. Some critics argued that placing the surge on a fixed timeline would allow the Taliban to withhold their strength until after the withdrawal had begun.

- **Document 68: Remarks by President Obama and President Karzai of Afghanistan in Joint Press Availability**
- **When:** May 12, 2010
- **Where:** Washington, D.C.
- **Significance:** President Obama and President Karzai held a joint press conference to discuss the war in Afghanistan.

DOCUMENT

Good morning, everybody. Please be seated. I am very pleased to welcome President Karzai back to the White House. And I also want to welcome the President's delegation—including ministers from across his government—whose presence speaks to the broad and deepening strategic partnership between the United States and Afghanistan.

This visit is an opportunity to return the hospitality that President Karzai showed me during my recent visit to Afghanistan. That included a wonderful Afghan dinner that the President shared with us, and where we were joined by members of his delegation. So, Mr. President, thank you and welcome to the United States.

DID YOU KNOW?

General Stanley McChrystal and *Rolling Stone*

In June 2010, an article by journalist Michael Hastings titled "The Runaway General" appeared in *Rolling Stone* magazine based on a series of conversations with General Stanley McChrystal and his staff during a visit to Paris in April 2010. The article quickly became controversial because Hastings anonymously quoted McChyrstal's aides reporting strong criticisms by McChyrstal of President Obama, Vice President Biden, and other top officials and policy makers. McChyrstal's staff argued that Hastings reported conversations intended to be off the record, but *Rolling Stone*'s editor insisted that they had fact-checked the article with the aides prior to publication. General McChrystal issued a public apology for the article, and he resigned from his post on June 23.

More importantly, this visit is an opportunity for us to assess the progress of our shared strategy in Afghanistan, and to advance the strong partnership between our two nations, one that's based on mutual interest and mutual respect.

I have reaffirmed the commitment of the United States to an Afghanistan that is stable, strong and prosperous. Afghans are a proud people who have suffered and sacrificed greatly because of their determination to shape their own destiny.

There is no denying the progress that the Afghan people have made in recent years—in education, in health care and economic development, as I saw in the lights across Kabul when I landed—lights that would not have been visible just a few years earlier.

Nor, however, can we deny the very serious challenges still facing Afghanistan. After 30 years of war, Afghanistan still faces daily challenges in delivering basic services and security to its people while confronting a brutal insurgency.

Whether Afghanistan succeeds in this effort will have consequences for the United States and consequences for the entire world. As we've seen in recent plots here in the United States, al Qaeda and its extremist allies continue to plot in the border regions between Afghanistan and Pakistan. And a growing Taliban insurgency could mean an even larger safe haven for al Qaeda and its affiliates.

So today, we are reaffirming our shared goal: to disrupt, dismantle and defeat al Qaeda and its extremist allies in Afghanistan and Pakistan, and to prevent its capacity to threaten America and our allies in the future. And we are reviewing the progress of our shared strategy and objectives: a military effort to reverse the Taliban's momentum and to strengthen Afghanistan's capacity to provide for their own security; a civilian effort to promote good governance and development; and regional cooperation, including with Pakistan, because our strategy has to succeed on both sides of the border.

Just over half of the additional military forces that I ordered to Afghanistan in December have now arrived, with the remainder due by this summer. As part of our 46-nation coalition, allies and partners have increased their commitments as well. We're partnering with Afghan and coalition forces, and we've begun to reverse the momentum of the insurgency. We have taken the fight to the Taliban in Helmand Province, pushed them out of their stronghold in Marja, and are working to give Afghans the opportunity to reclaim their communities.

We've taken extraordinary measures to avoid civilian casualties. And I reiterated in my meeting with President Karzai that the United States will continue to work with our Afghan and international partners to do everything in our power to avoid actions that harm the Afghan people. After all, it's the Afghan people we are working to protect from the Taliban, which is responsible for the vast majority of innocent civilian deaths.

Meanwhile, the training and development of Afghan security forces continues so that they can begin to take the lead in security next year. Towards this end, we're working with the Afghan government and our allies on a broader framework to guide the transition of responsibility for security, development and governance in Afghan provinces. I've also reaffirmed that the United States is committed to transferring responsibility for detention facilities to the Afghan government.

To support the second part of our strategy—the civilian effort—more American diplomats and experts are now on the ground and are partnering with their Afghan counterparts. In his inaugural address, and at the London Conference, President Karzai committed to making good governance a top priority. And I want to acknowledge the progress that has been made, including strengthening anti-corruption efforts, improving governance at provincial and district levels, and progress towards credible parliamentary elections later this year. Of course, President Karzai and I both acknowledge that much more work needs to be done.

I also welcomed President Karzai's commitment to take additional steps that can improve the lives of the Afghan people in concrete ways, especially with regard to the rule of law, agricultural production, economic growth, and the delivery of basic services. I pledged America's continued support for these efforts, and I've asked Secretary Clinton to lead an American delegation to this summer's Kabul Conference, where the Afghan government will be presenting concrete plans to implement the President's commitments.

On the related subject of Afghan-led peace and reconciliation efforts, I appreciated the President sharing his plans for the upcoming consultative peace jirga—an important milestone that America supports. In addition, the United States supports the efforts of the Afghan government to open the door to Taliban who cut their ties to al Qaeda, abandon violence, and accept the Afghan constitution, including respect for human rights. And I look forward to a continued dialogue with our Afghan partners on these efforts.

In support of the final part of our strategy—a regional approach—we discussed the importance of Afghanistan's neighbors supporting Afghan sovereignty and security. I was pleased to host President Karzai and President Zardari of Pakistan together here at the White House a year ago, and our trilateral cooperation will continue. Indeed, Pakistan's major offensive against extremist sanctuaries and our blows against the leadership of al Qaeda and its affiliates advance the security of Pakistanis, Afghans, and Americans alike.

Finally, as we pursue our shared strategy to defeat al Qaeda, I'm pleased that our two countries are working to broaden our strategic partnership over the long term. Even as we begin to transition security responsibility to Afghans over the next year, we will sustain a robust commitment in Afghanistan going forward. And the presence here today of so many leaders from both our governments underscores how we can partner across a full range of areas—including development and agriculture, education and health, rule of law and women's rights.

Together, we can unleash Afghanistan's vast potential. For example, I was pleased to welcome several remarkable Afghan women to our recent Entrepreneurship Summit here in Washington. And I look forward to formalizing a new strategic partnership between our countries later this year, and to deepening the lasting friendship between our people.

As I've said on numerous occasions, there are many difficult days ahead in Afghanistan. We face a determined and ruthless enemy. But we go forward with confidence because we have something that our adversaries do not—we have a commitment to seek a future of justice and peace and opportunity for the Afghan people. And we have the courage and resolve of men and women, from Afghanistan and our international coalition, who are determined to help Afghans realize that future.

And as I did at Bagram during my visit, I especially want to acknowledge the extraordinary sacrifices that are being made by American troops and civilians in Afghanistan every single day.

Our solidarity today sends a unmistakable message to those who would stand in the way of Afghanistan's progress. They may threaten and murder innocent people, but we will work to protect the Afghan people. They will try to destroy, but we will continue to help build Afghan capacity and allow Afghans to take responsibility for their country. They will try to drive us apart, but we will partner with the Afghan people for the long term—toward a future of greater security, prosperity, justice and progress. And I'm absolutely convinced we will succeed.

That is the work that we have advanced today. And I again want to thank our partners, President Karzai and his delegation, for the progress we have made and can continue to make in the months and years ahead.

President Karzai.

PRESIDENT KARZAI: . . .

We also discussed during our meeting this morning the Afghan-American strategic partnership and the relations towards the future beyond the successes that we will certainly gain against terrorism; the issues related to the region and Afghanistan; Afghanistan's difficulties and concerns with regard to capacity, institution building, the build-up of the Afghan security forces, the Afghan economy, the issues of agriculture and energy, and all those issues of developmental importance to Afghanistan, for which the United States is putting in considerable resources.

We also discussed the peace process and the upcoming peace consultative jirga in Kabul, for which, Mr. President, I am grateful to you for your support and very kind advice. We also discussed the parliamentary elections, the upcoming parliamentary elections in Afghanistan, and the Kabul Conference. We discussed in quite detail and in a very frank and productive manner the issues of protection of civilians and judicial—with respect to the judicial independence of Afghanistan.

I found it very happy for me to convey back to the Afghan people that I found a very supportive voice from President Obama on these accounts. And I'm very glad to report to you that we'll be setting up a team of our senior advisers to work out the exact timelines of the transfer of detention centers to the Afghan government, which I consider to be a major point of progress in our conversations.

. . .

Afghanistan is grateful. Afghanistan will definitely, with your help, succeed toward the future. There are of course issues that are still of concern to all of us. We have shortcomings in Afghanistan still. Afghanistan is still a very, very poor country. The work that we have done promises a better future for all of us, and

Afghanistan will assure you, Mr. President, that it will take the right steps in bringing a better government to Afghanistan for the benefit of the Afghan people and in partnership with the United States of America.

. . .

Q Thank you very much. First of all, thank you very much, Mr. President, to give this chance. There is a lot of issue in Afghanistan—first of all, I'm sorry, I should introduce myself. My name is Nazira Azim Karimi. I'm a correspondent for Ariana Television from Afghanistan.

Today, I'm not talking about as a journalist, as a woman in Afghanistan. As long as I remember, regarding Afghanistan's situation, the only reason that Afghanistan is not civilized—Pakistan. You mentioned, President Obama, about Pakistan. Pakistan has two faces regarding Afghanistan. That's why all the time we have problem. The Pakistan government is not really, really honest regarding—regard Afghanistan. I need your answer: What is the new policy of United States to solve this problem?

And next question for President Karzai, I want to ask—I want to ask my question in Dari, and I want to answer it in Dari, too. (Speaking Dari.) Thank you.

PRESIDENT OBAMA: I know you're going to translate that for us. He's very good at—President Karzai and I have, in the past, met with Pakistan's President, President Zardari, as well as their intelligence officers, their military, their teams, and emphasized to Pakistan the fact that our security is intertwined.

I think there has been in the past a view on the part of Pakistan that their primary rival, India, was their only concern. I think what you've seen over the last several months is a growing recognition that they have a cancer in their midst; that the extremist organizations that have been allowed to congregate and use as a base the frontier areas to then go into Afghanistan, that that now threatens Pakistan's sovereignty.

Our goal is to break down some of the old suspicions and the old bad habits and continue to work with the Pakistani government to see their interest in a stable Afghanistan which is free from foreign meddling—and that Afghanistan, Pakistan, the United States, the international community, should all be working to reduce the influence of extremists in those regions. And I am actually encouraged by what I've seen from the Pakistani government over the last several months.

But just as it's going to take some time for Afghanistan's economy, for example, to fully recover from 30 years of war, it's going to take some time for Pakistan, even where there is a will, to find a way in order to effectively deal with these extremists in areas that are fairly loosely governed from Islamabad.

Part of what I've been encouraged by is Pakistan's willingness to start asserting more control over some of these areas. But it's not going to happen overnight. And they have been taking enormous casualties; the Pakistani military has been going in fairly aggressively. But this will be a ongoing project.

And President Karzai and I both discussed the fact that the only way, ultimately, that Pakistan is secure is if Afghanistan is secure. And the only way that Afghanistan is secure is if the sovereignty, the territorial integrity, the Afghan constitution, the Afghan people are respected by their neighbors. We think that that message is starting to get through, but it's one that we have to continue to promote.

PRESIDENT KARZAI: Ma'am, we did discuss civilian casualties, the protection of civilians. I must report to you, ma'am, that since the arrival of General McChrystal in Afghanistan, there has been considerable progress achieved in this regard. There is a very open and frank attitude about that now.

The President expressed in fundamentally human terms his concern about civilian casualties, not only as a political issue, but as a human issue, that President Obama remarked about, to which I have my respect to the President on this issue.

We not only discussed the ways and means of how to reduce civilian casualties; rather not have them at all. Nitrates were discussed and detentions were discussed, the way I made a remark about in my opening remarks. And you will see the agreements between us on this reflected in the joint communiqué that I hope is coming up or is already issued.

. . .

Q I am Lina Rozbih, Afghanistan Service, Voice Of America. I will ask President Karzai a question and then President Obama. One of the—

PRESIDENT KARZAI: Voice of America's Afghanistan Service?

Q Yes.

PRESIDENT KARZAI: Good, good.

Q Thank you. One of the purposes of your trip here is to gain the support of U.S. government for reconciliation and reintegration of Taliban in Afghanistan. When you first initiated this strategy or plan, you were interested in talks with lower- to middle-level of Taliban. But you have increasingly shown interest into bringing Taliban leaders into the negotiations, while Taliban made it very clear that the only way for them to talk to the Afghan government is the complete withdrawal of foreign troops from Afghanistan and the creation of a sharia-based government in that country. Are you sure that this strategy, after all the support that you will gain from international community, will be a successful one and it will not be yet another failed strategy in Afghanistan?

And my question for President Obama would be that, Secretary Clinton yesterday mentioned in a gathering that U.S. support this initiative only if the Taliban put their weapons down, respect the Afghan constitution, and cut all ties with al Qaeda. And we all know that Taliban, al Qaeda, are pretty much fighting for the ideology, not material gains. And it's very hard to differentiate between the two in Pakistan and Afghanistan since they are fighting as a united force in those countries. Do you think it's a doable strategy for Afghanistan? Thank you.

PRESIDENT KARZAI: Ma'am, exactly the last part of your question is my answer. Afghanistan is seeking peace because through military means alone we are not going to get our objectives of bringing stability and peace to Afghanistan and the defeat of terrorism.

Now, there are thousands of the Taliban who are not ideologically oriented, who are not part of al Qaeda or other terrorist networks, or controlled from outside in any manner troublesome to us. There are thousands of them who are country boys who have been driven by intimidation or fear caused by at times misconduct by us, or circumstances beyond their control or our control.

It is these thousands of Taliban who are not against Afghanistan, or against the Afghan people, or their country—who are not against America either, or the rest of the world, and who want to come back to Afghanistan if given an opportunity and provided the political means. It's this group of the Taliban that we are addressing in the peace jirga. It is this group that has our intention.

Those within the Taliban leadership structure who, again, are not part of al Qaeda or the terrorist networks, or ideologically against Afghanistan's progress and rights and constitution, democracy, the place of women in the Afghan society, the progress that they've made—and are willing to march ahead with the rest of their people and their country towards a better future for Afghanistan, are welcome. And the jirga, the peace consultative jirga is intended for consulting the Afghan people, taking their advice on how and through which means and which speed should the Afghan government proceed in the quest for peace.

PRESIDENT OBAMA: Well, I think President Karzai summed it up well. We've been very clear that we need ultimately a political component to our overarching strategy in Afghanistan. And as President Karzai described, the Taliban is a loose term for a wide range of different networks, groups, fighters, with different motivations.

What we've said is that so long as there's a respect for the Afghan constitution, rule of law, human rights; so long as they are willing to renounce violence and ties to al Qaeda and other extremist networks; that President Karzai should be able to work to reintegrate those individuals into Afghan society.

This has to be an Afghan-led effort, though. It's not one that's dictated by the United States or any other outside power. And I think that the peace jirga will allow for a framework to then move forward.

One of the things I emphasized to President Karzai, however, is, is that the incentives for the Taliban to lay down arms, or at least portions of the Taliban to lay down arms, and make peace with the Afghan government in part depends on our effectiveness in breaking their momentum militarily. And that's why we put in the additional U.S. troops. That's why General McChrystal is working so hard to clear out key population centers from Taliban control.

And so the timing, how the reconciliation process works, at what point do the Taliban start making different calculations about what's in their interests, and how the Afghan people feel about these issues, is in part going to be dependent on our success in terms of carrying out our mission there. So we are a very I think important partner in facilitating this potential reconciliation and effectively empowering the Afghan government so that it is in the strongest possible position as these talks move forward.

Let me just say in conclusion, again, Mr. President, I am grateful for your visit. This is a reaffirmation of the friendship between the American people and the Afghan people.

When I came into office, I made it very clear that, after years of some drift in the relationship, that I saw this as a critical priority. I also said to the American people that this was going to take some time, and it was going to be hard, that we weren't going to see magical transformations immediately; but with slow, steady, persistent work on the part of both the United States and the Afghan government, that I was confident that, in fact, we could achieve peace and stability and security there, and that that ultimately would make the American people more safe and more secure.

I am more convinced than ever that we have found a difficult, but appropriate strategy for pursuing those goals. And I'm confident that we're going to be able to achieve our mission. There are going to be setbacks. There are going to be times where the Afghan government and the U.S. government disagree tactically. But I think our overarching approach is unified. And I think the visit by President Karzai to the United States and his willingness to listen to our concerns, even as we listen to his, as he indicated, only makes the relationship stronger.

Source: Public Papers of the Presidents of the United States: Barack Obama, 2010, Book 1. Washington, D.C.: Government Printing Office, 2011, 626–635. Available online at https://obamawhitehouse.archives.gov/realitycheck/photos-and-video/video/president-obama-and-president-karzai-press-conference#transcript.

ANALYSIS

As President Obama said in his opening statement, the surge of U.S. troops to Afghanistan was well underway by the time of this press conference. In addition, as discussed in a question to President Karzai, he had attempted to open negotiations with some members of the Taliban willing to reach a political compromise in hopes of splintering the insurgency. Finding common ground with some potential insurgents had been successful in Iraq, but the Taliban proved much more elusive negotiating partners.

Although not directly mentioned in this press conference, many began to raise doubts about President Karzai by 2010. Allegations of electoral fraud and financial improprieties by President Karzai and his brother, Mahmoud, caused concern that his government could not effectively root out corruption and create the stable, trustworthy institutions needed to persuade skeptical Afghans to support Kabul.

- **Document 69: General David Petraeus's Letter to ISAF Troops**
- **When:** July 4, 2010
- **Where:** Kabul, Afghanistan
- **Significance:** General David Petraeus's first message to the ISAF following his assumption of command.

DOCUMENT

To the Soldiers, Sailors, Airmen, Marines, and Civilians of NATO's International Security Assistance Force:

We serve in Afghanistan at a critical time. With the surge in ISAF strength and the growth of Afghan forces, we and other Afghan comrades have a new opportunity. Together, we can ensure that Afghanistan will not once again be ruled by those who embrace indiscriminate violence and transnational extremists, and we can ensure that Al Qaeda and other extremist elements cannot once again establish sanctuaries in Afghanistan from which they can launch attacks on our homelands and on the Afghan people.

This has been a hard fight. As you have soldiered together with our Afghan partners to reverse the Taliban momentum and to take away Taliban safe havens, the enemy has fought back ISAF and Afghan Forces sustained particularly tough losses last month. Nonetheless, in the face of an enemy willing to carry out the most barbaric of attacks, progress has been achieved in some critical areas, and we are poised to realize more.

This effort is a contest of wills. Our enemies will do all that they can to shake our confidence and the confidence of the Afghan people. In turn, we must continue to demonstrate our resolve to the enemy. We will do so through our relentless pursuit of the Taliban and others who mean Afghanistan harm, through our compassion for the Afghan people, and through our example and the values that we live.

Together with our Afghan partners, we must secure and serve the people of Afghanistan. We must help Afghan leaders develop their security forces and build their capacity to govern, so that they can increasingly take on the tasks of securing their country and seeing to the needs of the Afghan people.

This endeavour has to be a team effort. We must strive to contribute to the "Team of Teams" at work in Afghanistan and to achieve unity of effort with our diplomatic, international civilian and Afghan partners as we carry out a comprehensive, civil-military counterinsurgency campaign.

We must also continue our emphasis on reducing the loss of innocent civilian life to an absolute minimum. We must never forget that the decisive terrain in Afghanistan is the human terrain.

Protecting those we are here to help nonetheless does require killing, capturing, or turning the insurgents. We will not shrink from that, indeed, you have been taking the fight to the enemy and we will continue to do so. Beyond that, as you and our Afghan partners on the ground get into tough situations, we must employ all assets to ensure your safety, keeping in mind, again, the importance of avoiding civilian casualties.

I appreciate your sacrifices and those of your families as we serve in a mission of vital importance to the people of Afghanistan, to our nations, and to the world. And I pledge my total commitment to our mission as we work together to help achieve a brighter future for a new country in an ancient land.

Source: Central Command. Available online at https://www.scribd.com/doc/34003786/Letter-from-Gen-David-Petraeus.

DID YOU KNOW?

General David Petraeus

Born in 1952, David Petraeus first rose to fame in 2003 when, as a major general in command of the 101st Airborne Division, he used the counterinsurgency tactics he had once studied to pacify the city of Mosul in Iraq. Supporters argued that his engagement of the populace and rebuilding of civic institutions were highly successful, but other claimed his success was exaggerated. In any case, the Army assigned Petraeus to command the Combined Arms Center at Fort Leavenworth, where he continued to develop his ideas. In 2007, he returned to Iraq to command U.S. forces during the "surge," during which the violence in Iraq subsided. In 2008, he was promoted to run the U.S. Central Command, but he left this position in 2010 to command the U.S. "surge" in Afghanistan after the resignation of General Stanley McChrystal. He retired from the Army in 2011 to become the director of the CIA. In 2012, Petraeus unexpectedly resigned from the CIA, and news quickly broke that, while commander of ISAF, General Petraeus engaged in an extramarital affair with his biographer, Paula Broadwell, and shared classified information with her. He pled guilty to mishandling classified information and received probation. He remains an influential, even if highly controversial, thinker on defense and national security.

ANALYSIS

General Petraeus, who had previously served as the Commander, Central Command—the U.S. military command that oversees the Middle East—took command from General McChrystal following the latter's resignation. General Petraeus arrived in Afghanistan just as the "surge" in forces approved by President Obama began to materialize. The message implored the ISAF to work closely with their Afghan partners and to avoid civilian casualties, both of which are hallmarks of the counterinsurgency campaigns that General Petraeus had built his reputation upon.

- **Document 70: Report of the Afghanistan Study Group**
- **When:** August 16, 2010
- **Where:** Washington, D.C.
- **Significance:** A report from an independent group of scholars and analysts that argued for a radical change in strategy in Afghanistan that rejected "nation building" and instead favored a small, counterterror mission.

DOCUMENT

Summary

At nine years and counting, the U.S. war in Afghanistan is the longest in our history, surpassing even the Vietnam War, and it will shortly surpass the Soviet Union's own extended military campaign there. With the surge, it will cost the U.S. taxpayers nearly $100 billion per year, a sum roughly seven times larger than Afghanistan's annual gross national product (GNP) of $14 billion and greater than the total annual cost of the new U.S. health insurance program. Thousands of American and allied personnel have been killed or gravely wounded.

The U.S. interests at stake in Afghanistan do not warrant this level of sacrifice. President Obama justified expanding our commitment by saying the goal was eradicating Al Qaeda. Yet Al Qaeda is no longer a significant presence in Afghanistan, and there are only some 400 hard-core Al Qaeda members remaining in the entire Af/Pak theater, most of them hiding in Pakistan's northwest provinces.

America's armed forces have fought bravely and well, and their dedication is unquestioned. But we should not ask them to make sacrifices unnecessary to our core national interests, particularly when doing so threatens long-term needs and priorities both at home and abroad.

Instead of toppling terrorists, America's Afghan war has become an ambitious and fruitless effort at "nation-building." We are mired in a civil war in Afghanistan and are struggling to establish an effective central government in a country that has long been fragmented and decentralized.

No matter how desirable this objective might be in the abstract, it is not essential to U.S. security and it is not a goal for which the U.S. military is well suited. There is no clear definition of what would comprise "success" in this endeavor. Creating a unified Afghan state would require committing many more American lives and hundreds of billions of additional U.S. dollars for many years to come.

As the WikiLeaks war diary comprised of more than 91,000 secret reports on the Afghanistan War makes clear, any sense of American and allied progress in the conflict has been undermined by revelations that many more civilian deaths have occurred than have been officially acknowledged as the result of U.S. and allied strike accidents. The Pakistan Inter-Services Intelligence continued to provide logistics and financial support to the Afghan Taliban even as U.S. soldiers were fighting these units. It is clear that Karzai government affiliates and appointees in rural Afghanistan have often proven to be more corrupt and ruthless than the Taliban.

Prospects for success are dim. As former Secretary of State Henry Kissinger recently warned, "Afghanistan has never been pacified by foreign forces." The 2010 spring offensive in Marjah was inconclusive, and a supposedly "decisive" summer offensive in Kandahar has been delayed and the expectations downgraded. U.S. and allied casualties reached an all-time high in July, and several NATO allies have announced plans to withdraw their own forces.

The conflict in Afghanistan is commonly perceived as a struggle between the Karzai government and an insurgent Taliban movement, allied with international terrorists, that is seeking to overthrow that government. In fact, the conflict is a civil war about power-sharing with lines of contention that are 1) partly ethnic, chiefly, but not exclusively, between Pashtuns who dominate the south and other ethnicities such as Tajiks and Uzbeks who are more prevalent in the north, 2) partly rural vs. urban, particularly within the Pashtun community, and 3) partly sectarian.

The Afghanistan conflict also includes the influence of surrounding nations with a desire to advance their own interests—including India, Pakistan, Iran, Saudi Arabia and others. And with the U.S. intervention in force, the conflict includes resistance to what is seen as foreign military occupation.

Resolving the conflict in Afghanistan has primarily to do with resolving the distribution of power among these factions and between the central government and the provinces, and with appropriately decentralizing authority.

Negotiated resolution of these conflicts will reduce the influence of extremists more readily than military action will. The Taliban itself is not a unified movement but instead a label that is applied to many armed groups and individuals that are only loosely aligned and do not necessarily have a fondness for the fundamentalist ideology of the most prominent Taliban leaders.

The Study Group believes the war in Afghanistan has reached a critical crossroads. Our current path promises to have limited impact on the civil war while taking more American lives and contributing to skyrocketing taxpayer debt. We conclude that a fundamentally new direction is needed, one that recognizes the United States' legitimate interests in Central Asia and is fashioned to advance them. Far from admitting "defeat," the new way forward acknowledges the manifold limitations of a military solution in a region where our interests lie in political stability. Our recommended policy shifts our resources to focus on U.S. foreign policy strengths in concert with the international community to promote reconciliation among the warring parties, advance economic development, and encourage region-wide diplomatic engagement.

We base these conclusions on the following key points raised in the Study Group's research and discussions:

• *The United States has only two vital interests in the Af/Pak region: 1) preventing Afghanistan from being a "safe haven" from which Al Qaeda or other extremists can organize more effective attacks on the U.S. homeland; and 2) ensuring that Pakistan's nuclear arsenal does not fall into hostile hands.*

• *Protecting our interests does not require a U.S. military victory over the Taliban. A Taliban takeover is unlikely even if the United States reduces its military commitment. The Taliban is a rural insurgency rooted primarily in Afghanistan's Pashtun population, and succeeded due in some part to the disenfranchisement of rural Pashtuns. The Taliban's seizure of power in the 1990s was due to an unusual set of circumstances that no longer exist and are unlikely to be repeated.*

• *There is no significant Al Qaeda presence in Afghanistan today, and the risk of a new "safe haven" there under more "friendly" Taliban rule is overstated. Should an Al Qaeda cell regroup in Afghanistan, the U.S. would have residual military capability in the region sufficient to track and destroy it.*

• *Al Qaeda sympathizers are now present in many locations globally, and defeating the Taliban will have little effect on Al Qaeda's global reach. The ongoing threat from Al Qaeda is better met via specific counter-terrorism measures, a reduced U.S. military "footprint" in the Islamic world, and diplomatic efforts to improve America's overall image and undermine international support for militant extremism.*

• *Given our present economic circumstances, reducing the staggering costs of the Afghan war is an urgent priority. Maintaining the long-term health of the U.S. economy is just as important to American strength and security as protecting U.S. soil from enemy (including terrorist) attacks.*

• *The continuation of an ambitious U.S. military campaign in Afghanistan will likely work against U.S. interests. A large U.S. presence fosters local (especially Pashtun) resentment and aids Taliban recruiting. It also fosters dependence on the part of our Afghan partners and encourages closer cooperation among a disparate array of extremist groups in Afghanistan and Pakistan alike.*

• *Past efforts to centralize power in Afghanistan have provoked the same sort of local resistance that is convulsing Afghanistan today. There is ample evidence that this effort will join others in a long line of failed incursions.*

• *Although the United States should support democratic rule, human rights and economic development, its capacity to mold other societies is inherently limited. The costs of trying should be weighed against our need to counter global terrorist threats directly, reduce America's $1.4 trillion budget deficit, repair eroding U.S. infrastructure, and other critical national purposes. Our support of these issues will be better achieved as part of a coordinated international group with which expenses and burdens can be shared.*

The bottom line is clear: Our vital interests in Afghanistan are limited and military victory is not the key to achieving them.

On the contrary, waging a lengthy counterinsurgency war in Afghanistan may well do more to aid Taliban recruiting than to dismantle the group, help spread conflict further into Pakistan, unify radical groups that might otherwise be quarreling amongst themselves, threaten the long-term health of the U.S. economy, and prevent the U.S. government from turning its full attention to other pressing problems.

The more promising path for the U.S. in the Af/Pak region would reverse the recent escalation and move away from a counterinsurgency effort that is neither necessary nor likely to succeed. Instead, the U.S. should:

1. Emphasize power-sharing and political inclusion. The U.S. should fast-track a peace process designed to decentralize power within Afghanistan and encourage a power-sharing balance among the principal parties.

2. Downsize and eventually end military operations in southern Afghanistan, and reduce the U.S. military footprint. The U.S. should draw down its military presence, which radicalizes many Pashtuns and is an important aid to Taliban recruitment.

3. Focus security efforts on Al Qaeda and Domestic Security. Special forces, intelligence assets, and other U.S. capabilities should continue to seek out and target known Al Qaeda cells in the region. They can be ready to go after Al Qaeda should they attempt to relocate elsewhere or build new training facilities. In addition, part of the savings from our drawdown should be reallocated to bolster U.S. domestic security efforts and to track nuclear weapons globally.

4. Encourage economic development. Because destitute states can become incubators for terrorism, drug and human trafficking, and other illicit activities, efforts at reconciliation should be paired with an internationally-led effort to develop Afghanistan's economy.

5. Engage regional and global stakeholders in a diplomatic effort designed to guarantee Afghan neutrality and foster regional stability. Despite their considerable differences, neighboring states such as India, Pakistan, China, Iran and Saudi Arabia share a common interest in preventing Afghanistan from being dominated by any single power or being a permanently failed state that exports instability to others.

We believe this strategy will best serve the interests of women in Afghanistan as well. The worst thing for women is for Afghanistan to remain paralyzed in a civil war in which there evolves no organically rooted support for their social advancement.

The remainder of this report elaborates the logic behind these recommendations. It begins by summarizing U.S. vital interests, including our limited interests in Afghanistan itself and in the region more broadly. It then considers why the current strategy is failing and why the situation is unlikely to improve even under a new commander. The final section outlines "A New Way Forward" and explains how a radically different approach can achieve core U.S. goals at an acceptable cost.

Source: Afghanistan Study Group. Available online at http://www.afghanistan studygroup.org/NewWayForward_report.pdf.

ANALYSIS

The Afghanistan Study Group sought to mimic the impact that the congressionally sponsored Iraq Study Group had on that conflict. This report, endorsed by a number of conservative national security experts, sought to reframe the strategic situation in Afghanistan. Whereas President Obama's "surge" hoped to neutralize the Taliban insurgency and buy time to build up Afghan security forces, this strategy instead proposed to seek a political solution to the problem and limit American military forces to, at most, a counterterrorism mission. In many respects, this strategy echoes statements made by Vice President Joe Biden in the months leading up to President Obama's announcement of the surge. Ultimately, the recommendations of this report were not adopted, although one can see similarities with the postsurge strategy in Afghanistan.

- **Document 71: Lisbon Summit Declaration**
- **When:** November 20, 2010
- **Where:** Lisbon, Portugal
- **Significance:** At the annual NATO summit in Lisbon, the Alliance called for a continuation of the ISAF mission in Afghanistan and the planned turnover of security responsibilities to the Afghan government beginning at the end of 2011.

DID YOU KNOW?

Operation Dragon Strike

Operation Dragon Strike was a multiweek military operation that began in mid-September 2010 in Kandahar Province. Involving more than 8,000 troops from 101st Airborne Division with Canadian and Afghan units in support, the operation sought to clear multiple districts in the province of Taliban influence. Dragon Strike attracted much notice because the targeted districts included the areas where the Taliban had first emerged in late 1994. In addition, in the numbers of units and personnel involved, it was one of the largest operations conducted by the Coalition during the entire war in Afghanistan. Dragon Strike lasted for 10 weeks as U.S. forces, relying heavily on armored vehicles and air support to cover the movements through the relatively open terrain, gradually swept through southern Kandahar Province. The Taliban are believed to have suffered heavy losses, but the exact figure is unknown. Meanwhile, the Coalition lost 42 personnel during the operation.

DOCUMENT

Lisbon Summit Declaration
Issued by the Heads of State and Government participating in the meeting of the North Atlantic Council in Lisbon

. . .

4. As expressed in the Declaration by the Heads of State and Government of the nations contributing to the UN-mandated, NATO-led International Security Assistance Force (ISAF) in Afghanistan, our ISAF mission in Afghanistan remains the Alliance's key priority, and we welcome the important progress that has been made. Afghanistan's security and stability are directly linked with our own security. In meeting with President Karzai, all our 21 partners in ISAF, the United Nations, the European Union, the World Bank and Japan, we reaffirm our long-term commitment to Afghanistan, as set out in our strategic vision agreed at the Bucharest Summit and reaffirmed at the Strasbourg/Kehl Summit. We welcome the valuable and increased contributions made by our ISAF partners and would welcome further contributions. We are entering a new phase in our

mission. The process of transition to full Afghan security responsibility and leadership in some provinces and districts is on track to begin in early 2011, following a joint Afghan and NATO/ISAF assessment and decision. Transition will be conditions-based, not calendar-driven, and will not equate to withdrawal of ISAF-troops. Looking to the end of 2014, Afghan forces will be assuming full responsibility for security across the whole of Afghanistan. Through our enduring partnership with the Government of the Islamic Republic of Afghanistan, we reaffirm our long-term commitment to a better future for the Afghan people.

. . .

Source: NATO. Available online at http://www.nato.int/cps/en/natohq/official _texts_68828.htm.

ANALYSIS

By late 2010, NATO and Afghanistan had agreed upon a timeline whereby ISAF would gradually reduce its role until the end of 2014 when, it was hoped, Afghanistan's National Security Forces could fulfill the nation's security needs. The surge had allowed some American units such as the 101st Airborne Division to launch major operations to destroy insurgent networks so that Afghan security forces could maintain a more lasting peace in their wake.

- **Document 72: Remarks by President Obama on Osama bin Laden**
- **When:** May 2, 2011
- **Where:** Washington, D.C.
- **Significance:** In a televised address, President Barack Obama announced the death of al-Qaeda leader Osama bin Laden.

DOCUMENT

Good evening. Tonight, I can report to the American people and to the world that the United States has conducted an operation that killed Osama bin Laden, the leader of al Qaeda, and a terrorist who's responsible for the murder of thousands of innocent men, women, and children.

It was nearly 10 years ago that a bright September day was darkened by the worst attack on the American people in our history. The images of 9/11 are seared into our national memory—hijacked planes cutting through a cloudless September sky; the Twin Towers collapsing to the ground; black smoke billowing up from the Pentagon; the wreckage of Flight 93 in Shanksville, Pennsylvania, where the actions of heroic citizens saved even more heartbreak and destruction.

And yet we know that the worst images are those that were unseen to the world. The empty seat at the dinner table. Children who were forced to grow up without their mother or their father. Parents who would never know the feeling of their child's embrace. Nearly 3,000 citizens taken from us, leaving a gaping hole in our hearts.

On September 11, 2001, in our time of grief, the American people came together. We offered our neighbors a hand, and we offered the wounded our blood. We reaffirmed our ties to each other, and our love of community and country. On that day, no matter where we came from, what God we prayed to, or what race or ethnicity we were, we were united as one American family.

We were also united in our resolve to protect our nation and to bring those who committed this vicious attack to justice. We quickly learned that the 9/11 attacks were carried out by al Qaeda—an organization headed by Osama bin Laden, which had openly declared war on the United States and was committed to killing innocents in our country and around the globe. And so we went to war against al Qaeda to protect our citizens, our friends, and our allies.

Over the last 10 years, thanks to the tireless and heroic work of our military and our counterterrorism professionals, we've made great strides in that effort. We've disrupted terrorist attacks and strengthened our homeland defense. In Afghanistan, we removed the Taliban government, which had given bin Laden and al Qaeda safe haven and support. And around the globe, we worked with our friends and allies to capture or kill scores of al Qaeda terrorists, including several who were a part of the 9/11 plot.

Yet Osama bin Laden avoided capture and escaped across the Afghan border into Pakistan. Meanwhile, al Qaeda continued to operate from along that border and operate through its affiliates across the world.

And so shortly after taking office, I directed Leon Panetta, the director of the CIA, to make the killing or capture of bin Laden the top priority of our war against al Qaeda, even as we continued our broader efforts to disrupt, dismantle, and defeat his network.

Then, last August, after years of painstaking work by our intelligence community, I was briefed on a possible lead to bin Laden. It was far from certain, and it took many months to run this thread to ground. I met repeatedly with my national security team as we developed more information about the possibility that we had located bin Laden hiding within a compound deep inside of Pakistan. And finally, last week, I determined that we had enough intelligence to take action, and authorized an operation to get Osama bin Laden and bring him to justice.

Today, at my direction, the United States launched a targeted operation against that compound in Abbottabad, Pakistan. A small team of Americans carried out the operation with extraordinary courage and capability. No Americans were harmed. They took care to avoid civilian casualties. After a firefight, they killed Osama bin Laden and took custody of his body.

For over two decades, bin Laden has been al Qaeda's leader and symbol, and has continued to plot attacks against our country and our friends and allies. The death of bin Laden marks the most significant achievement to date in our nation's effort to defeat al Qaeda.

Yet his death does not mark the end of our effort. There's no doubt that al Qaeda will continue to pursue attacks against us. We must—and we will—remain vigilant at home and abroad.

As we do, we must also reaffirm that the United States is not—and never will be— at war with Islam. I've made clear, just as President Bush did shortly after 9/11, that our war is not against Islam. Bin Laden was not a Muslim leader; he was a mass murderer of Muslims. Indeed, al Qaeda has slaughtered scores of Muslims in many countries, including our own. So his demise should be welcomed by all who believe in peace and human dignity.

Over the years, I've repeatedly made clear that we would take action within Pakistan if we knew where bin Laden was. That is what we've done. But it's important to note that our counterterrorism cooperation with Pakistan helped lead us to bin Laden and the compound where he was hiding. Indeed, bin Laden had declared war against Pakistan as well, and ordered attacks against the Pakistani people.

Tonight, I called President Zardari, and my team has also spoken with their Pakistani counterparts. They agree that this is a good and historic day for both of our nations. And going forward, it is essential that Pakistan continue to join us in the fight against al Qaeda and its affiliates.

The American people did not choose this fight. It came to our shores, and started with the senseless slaughter of our citizens. After nearly 10 years of service, struggle, and sacrifice, we know well the costs of war. These efforts weigh on me every time I, as Commander-in-Chief, have to sign a letter to a family that has lost a loved one, or look into the eyes of a service member who's been gravely wounded.

So Americans understand the costs of war. Yet as a country, we will never tolerate our security being threatened, nor stand idly by when our people have been killed. We will be relentless in defense of our citizens and our friends and allies. We will be true to the values that make us who we are. And on nights like this one, we can say to those families who have lost loved ones to al Qaeda's terror: Justice has been done.

Tonight, we give thanks to the countless intelligence and counterterrorism professionals who've worked tirelessly to achieve this outcome. The American people do not see their work, nor know their names. But tonight, they feel the satisfaction of their work and the result of their pursuit of justice.

We give thanks for the men who carried out this operation, for they exemplify the professionalism, patriotism, and unparalleled courage of those who serve our country. And they are part of a generation that has borne the heaviest share of the burden since that September day.

Finally, let me say to the families who lost loved ones on 9/11 that we have never forgotten your loss, nor wavered in our commitment to see that we do whatever it takes to prevent another attack on our shores.

And tonight, let us think back to the sense of unity that prevailed on 9/11. I know that it has, at times, frayed. Yet today's achievement is a testament to the greatness of our country and the determination of the American people.

The cause of securing our country is not complete. But tonight, we are once again reminded that America can do whatever we set our mind to. That is the story of our history, whether it's the pursuit of prosperity for our people, or the struggle for equality for all our citizens; our commitment to stand up for our values abroad, and our sacrifices to make the world a safer place.

Let us remember that we can do these things not just because of wealth or power, but because of who we are: one nation, under God, indivisible, with liberty and justice for all.

Source: Public Papers of the Presidents of the United States: Barack Obama, 2011, Book 1. Washington, D.C.: Government Printing Office, 480–482. Available online at https://obamawhitehouse.archives.gov/blog/2011/05/02/osama-bin-laden-dead.

ANALYSIS

Following years of diligent effort, a team of CIA analysts traced Osama bin Laden's whereabouts to a compound in Abbottabad, Pakistan, approximately 160 miles east of the Afghan city of Jalalabad from which the U.S. Navy SEAL team launched their raid.

The successful mission had an almost immediate political effect on the war in Afghanistan. Given that bin Laden had been the primary perpetrator behind the September 11 attacks, and the U.S. invasion of Afghanistan had been a result of the Taliban's refusal to turn him over for trial, his death led some politicians and analysts to call for an accelerated U.S. withdrawal from the country.

- **Document 73: UN Security Council Resolution 1988**
- **When:** June 17, 2011
- **Where:** New York, New York
- **Significance:** This UN Security Council resolution placed new international sanctions on the Taliban.

DOCUMENT

Resolution 1988 (2011)
Adopted by the Security Council at its 6557th meeting, on 17 June 2011*

The Security Council,

Recalling its previous resolutions on international terrorism and the threat it poses to Afghanistan, in particular its resolutions 1267 (1999), 1333 (2000), 1363 (2001), 1373 (2001), 1390 (2002), 1452 (2002), 1455 (2003), 1526 (2004), 1566 (2004), 1617 (2005), 1624 (2005), 1699 (2006), 1730 (2006), 1735 (2006), 1822 (2008), 1904 (2009) and the relevant statements of its President,

Recalling its previous resolutions extending through March 22, 2012 the mandate of the United Nations Assistance Mission in Afghanistan (UNAMA) as established by resolution 1974 (2011),

Reaffirming that the situation in Afghanistan still constitutes a threat to international peace and security, and *expressing* its strong concern about the security situation in Afghanistan, in particular the ongoing violent and terrorist activities by the Taliban, Al-Qaida, illegal armed groups, criminals and those involved in the narcotics trade, and the strong links between terrorism activities and illicit drugs, resulting in threats to the local population, including children, national security forces and international military and civilian personnel,

Reaffirming its strong commitment to the sovereignty, independence, territorial integrity and national unity of Afghanistan,

Stressing the importance of a comprehensive political process in Afghanistan to support reconciliation among all Afghans, and *recognizing* there is no purely military solution that will ensure the stability of Afghanistan,

Recalling the Government of Afghanistan's strong desire to seek national reconciliation, as set forth in the Bonn Agreement (2001), the London Conference (2010), and the Kabul Conference (2010),

DID YOU KNOW?

August 2011 Chinook Shoot-down

On August 6, 2011, a group of nearly 50 U.S. Army Rangers entered the Tangi Valley in Wardak Province west of Kabul in search of a Taliban leader named Qari Tahir. When the Rangers reached the compound suspected of housing Tahir, supporting helicopters spotted a growing group of fighters several hundred meters away. Believing that the target Tahir might be among this group, the force commander called in their reserve force of 17 SEALs to engage the fighters. Unfortunately, as the CH-47 Chinook, call sign Extortion 17, carrying the SEAL team entered the valley, a group of Taliban armed with rocket-propelled grenades fired upon the large helicopter, with one rocket striking the aft rotor and assembly. This caused the helicopter to crash, killing the 17 SEALs, 16 other American and Afghan special forces, and the helicopter's 5 crew members. It was the single deadliest incident for the United States during the war in Afghanistan.

Recognizing that the security situation in Afghanistan has evolved and that some members of the Taliban have reconciled with the Government of Afghanistan, have rejected the terrorist ideology of Al-Qaida and its followers, and support a peaceful resolution to the continuing conflict in Afghanistan,

Recognizing that notwithstanding the evolution of the situation in Afghanistan and progress in reconciliation, the situation in Afghanistan remains a threat to international peace and security, and *reaffirming* the need to combat this threat by all means, in accordance with the Charter of the United Nations and international law, including applicable human rights, refugee and humanitarian law, stressing in this regard the important role the United Nations plays in this effort,

Recalling that the conditions for reconciliation, open to all Afghans, laid forth in the 20 July 2010 Kabul Communique, supported by the Government of Afghanistan and the international community, include the renunciation of violence, no links to international terrorist organizations, and respect for the Afghan Constitution, including the rights of women and persons belonging to minorities,

Stressing the importance of all individuals, groups, undertakings and entities participating, by any means, in the financing or support of acts or activities of those previously designated as the Taliban, as well as those individuals, groups, undertakings and entities associated with the Taliban in constituting a threat to the peace, stability and security of Afghanistan, accepting the Government of Afghanistan's offer of reconciliation,

Taking note of the Government of Afghanistan's request that the Security Council support national reconciliation by removing Afghan names from the UN sanctions lists for those who respect the conditions for reconciliation, and, there-fore, have ceased to engage in or support activities that threaten the peace, stability and security of Afghanistan,

Welcoming the results of the Consultative Peace Jirga held on 6 June 2010, in which 1,600 Afghan delegates, representing a broad cross-section of all Afghan eth-nic and religious groups, government officials, religious scholars, tribal leaders, civil society, and Afghan refugees residing in Iran and Pakistan, discussed an end to inse-curity and developed a plan for lasting peace in the country,

Welcoming the establishment of the High Peace Council and its outreach efforts both within and outside Afghanistan,

Stressing the central and impartial role that the United Nations continues to play in promoting peace, stability and security in Afghanistan, and *expressing* its appreci-ation and strong support for the ongoing efforts of the Secretary-General, his Special Representative for Afghanistan and the UNAMA Salaam Support Group to assist the High Peace Council's peace and reconciliation efforts,

Reiterating its support for the fight against illicit production and trafficking of drugs from, and chemical precursors to, Afghanistan, in neighbouring countries, countries on trafficking routes, drug destination countries and precursors producing countries,

Expressing concern at the increase in incidents of kidnapping and hostage-taking with the aim of raising funds, or gaining political concessions, and *expressing* the need for this issue to be addressed,

Reiterating the need to ensure that the present sanctions regime contributes effec-tively to ongoing efforts to combat the insurgency and support the Government of Afghanistan's work to advance reconciliation in order to bring about peace, stabil-ity, and security in Afghanistan, and *considering* the 1267 Committee's deliberations on the recommendation of the 1267 Monitoring Team in its Eleventh Report to the 1267 Committee that Member States treat listed Taliban and listed individuals and entities of Al-Qaida and its affiliates differently in promoting peace and stability in Afghanistan,

Reaffirming international support for Afghan-led reconciliation efforts, and express-ing its intention to give due regard to lifting sanctions on those who reconcile,

Acting under Chapter VII of the Charter of the United Nations,

Measures

1. *Decides* that all States shall take the following measures with respect to individ-uals and entities designated prior to this date as the Taliban, and other individuals, groups, undertakings and entities associated with them, as specified in section A ("Individuals associated with the Taliban") and section B ("entities and other groups and undertaking associated with the Taliban") of the Consolidated List of the Committee established pursuant to resolution 1267 (1999) and 1333 (2000) as of the date of adoption of this resolution, as well as other individuals, groups, under-takings and entities associated with the Taliban in constituting a threat to the peace, stability and security of Afghanistan as designated by the Committee estab-lished in paragraph 30, (hereafter known as "the List"):

(a) Freeze without delay the funds and other financial assets or economic resources of these individuals, groups, undertakings and entities, including funds derived from property owned or controlled directly or indirectly, by them or by persons acting on their behalf or at their direction, and ensure that neither these nor any other funds, financial assets or economic resources are made available, directly or indirectly for such persons' benefit, by their nationals or by persons within their territory;

(b) Prevent the entry into or transit through their territories of these individuals, provided that nothing in this paragraph shall oblige any State to deny entry or require the departure from its territories of its own nationals and this paragraph shall not apply where entry or transit is necessary for the fulfilment of a judicial process or the Committee determines on a case-by-case basis only that entry or transit is justified, including where this directly relates to supporting efforts by the Government of Afghanistan to promote reconciliation;

(c) Prevent the direct or indirect supply, sale, or transfer to these individuals, groups, undertakings and entities from their territories or by their nationals outside their territories, or using their flag vessels or aircraft, of arms and related materiel of all types including weapons and ammunition, military vehicles and equipment, paramilitary equipment, and spare parts for the aforementioned, and technical advice, assistance, or training related to military activities;

2. *Decides* that those previously designated as the Taliban, and other individuals, groups, undertakings and entities associated with them, whose names were inscribed in section A ("Individuals associated with the Taliban") and section B ("entities and other groups and undertakings associated with the Taliban") of the Consolidated List maintained by the Security Council Committee established pursuant to resolution 1267 (1999) concerning Al-Qaida and the Taliban and associated individuals and entities on the date of adoption of this resolution shall no longer be a part of the Consolidated List, but shall henceforth be on the List described in paragraph 1, and *decides further* that all States shall take the measures set forth in paragraph 1 against these listed individuals, groups, undertakings and entities;

3. *Decides* that the acts or activities indicating that an individual, group, undertaking or entity is eligible for designation under paragraph 1 include:

(a) Participating in the financing, planning, facilitating, preparing or perpetrating of acts or activities by, in conjunction with, under the name of, on behalf of, or in support of;

(b) Supplying, selling or transferring arms and related materiel to;

(c) Recruiting for; or

(d) Otherwise supporting acts or activities of those designated and other individuals, groups, undertakings and entities associated with the Taliban in constituting a threat to the peace, stability and security of Afghanistan;

4. *Affirms* that any undertaking or entity owned or controlled, directly or indirectly by, or otherwise supporting, such an individual, group, undertaking or entity on the List, shall be eligible for designation;

5. *Notes* that such means of financing or support include but are not limited to the use of proceeds derived from illicit cultivation, production and trafficking of narcotic drugs and their precursors originating in and transiting through Afghanistan;

6. *Confirms* that the requirements in paragraph 1 (a) above apply to financial and economic resources of every kind, including but not limited to those used for the provision of Internet hosting or related services, used for the support of the Taliban on this

List, and other individuals, groups, undertakings and entities associated with them, as well as other individuals, groups, undertakings and entities associated with the Taliban in constituting a threat to the peace, stability and security of Afghanistan and other individuals, groups, undertakings or entities associated with them;

7. *Confirms* further that the requirements in paragraph 1 (a) above shall also apply to the payment of ransoms to individuals, groups, undertakings or entities on the List;

8. *Decides* that Member States may permit the addition to accounts frozen pursuant to the provisions of paragraph 1 above of any payment in favour of listed individuals, groups, undertakings or entities, provided that any such payments continue to be subject to the provisions in paragraph 1 above and are frozen;

9. *Decides* that all Member States may make use of the provisions set out in paragraphs 1 and 2 of resolution 1452 (2002), as amended by resolution 1735 (2006) regarding available exemptions with regard to the measures in paragraph 1 (a), and *encourages* their use by Member States;

. . .

Reviews

34. *Decides* to review the implementation of the measures outlined in this resolution in eighteen months and make adjustments, as necessary, to support peace and stability in Afghanistan;

35. *Decides* to remain actively seized of the matter.

Source: United Nations. Available online at http://www.un.org/ga/search/view_doc.asp?symbol=S/RES/1988%20%282011%29.

ANALYSIS

Dating back to 1999, UN sanctions against al-Qaeda and the Taliban had been managed together because of the incredibly close ties between the two groups. By 2011, al-Qaeda remained an international threat, but some in the Taliban had expressed a willingness to negotiate with the Afghan government. As a result, this UN resolution split the sanctions between the two groups in order to allow greater flexibility on the part of the Afghan government to punish or reward the Taliban for negotiating with them.

- **Document 74: Conclusions of the International Afghanistan Conference in Bonn**
- **When:** December 5, 2011
- **Where:** Bonn, Germany
- **Significance:** This international conference sought to facilitate the transfer of power and responsibility to the Afghan government and to conclude Coalition involvement in the war by the end of 2014.

DOCUMENT

CONFERENCE CONCLUSIONS

1. We, the Islamic Republic of Afghanistan and the International Community, met today in Bonn to mark the 10th anniversary of the 2001 Bonn Conference, which laid the foundation of the ongoing partnership between Afghanistan and the International Community, and to renew our mutual commitment to a stable, democratic and prosperous future for the Afghan people. We honour all those, from Afghanistan and abroad, who have lost their lives for this noble cause. Afghanistan expressed its sincere gratitude for the steadfast commitment, solidarity and the immense sacrifices of its international partners.

2. Afghanistan and the International Community expressed deep appreciation to the Federal Republic of Germany for hosting this Conference. Germany is a long-standing friend of Afghanistan and, in particular over the past ten years, alongside other members of the International Community, has been a steadfast partner in Afghanistan's stabilization and development.

3. Ten years ago today at the Petersberg, Afghanistan charted a new path towards a sovereign, peaceful, prosperous and democratic future, and the International Community accepted the responsibility to help Afghanistan along that path. Together we have achieved substantial progress over these ten years, more than in any other period in Afghanistan's history. Never before have the Afghan people, and especially Afghan women, enjoyed comparable access to services, including education and health, or seen greater development of infrastructure across the country. Al Qaida has been disrupted, and Afghanistan's national security institutions are increasingly able to assume responsibility for a secure and independent Afghanistan.

4. However, our work is not yet done. Shortcomings must be addressed, achievements must be upheld. Our shared goal remains an Afghanistan that is a peaceful and promising home for all Afghans, at the centre of a secure and thriving region; an Afghanistan in which international terrorism does not again find sanctuary and that can assume its rightful place among sovereign nations.

5. In today's conference, chaired by Afghanistan, hosted by Germany and attended by 85 countries and 15 International Organisations, the International Community and Afghanistan solemnly dedicated themselves to deepening and broadening their historic partnership from Transition to the Transformation Decade of 2015–2024. Reaffirming our commitments as set out in the 2010 London Communiqué and the Kabul Process, this renewed partnership between Afghanistan and the International Community entails firm mutual commitments in the areas of governance, security, the peace process, economic and social development, and regional cooperation.

GOVERNANCE

6. Afghanistan reaffirms that the future of its political system will continue to reflect its pluralistic society and remain firmly founded on the Afghan Constitution. The Afghan people will continue to build a stable, democratic society, based on the rule of law, where the human rights and fundamental freedoms of its citizens, including the equality of men and women, are guaranteed under the Constitution.

Afghanistan recommits to upholding all of its international human rights obligations. Acknowledging that on this path Afghanistan will have its own lessons to learn, the International Community fully endorses this vision and commits to supporting Afghanistan's progress in that direction.

7. We have taken note of statements by Afghan civil society organisations, including today's statements by two of their delegates at this meeting. We all reaffirm that the human rights and fundamental freedoms enshrined in the Afghan Constitution, including the rights of women and children, as well as a thriving and free civil society are key for Afghanistan's future. Therefore, we underscore the further promotion of civil society participation, including both traditional civil society structures and modern manifestations of civic action, including the role of youth, in the country's democratic processes.

8. We recognise that building a democratic society above all entails enabling legitimate and effective civilian authority embodied in a democratically elected government and served by transparent and strong, functioning institutions. Despite significant achievements, Afghanistan needs to continue its work to strengthen state institutions and improve governance throughout the country, including through reforming the civil service and strengthening the linkage between justice reform and development of its security institutions, including an effective civilian police force. Strengthening and improving Afghanistan's electoral process will be a key step forward in the country's democratization. Afghan government institutions at all levels should increase their responsiveness to the civil and economic needs of the Afghan people and deliver key services to them. In this context, the protection of civilians, strengthening the rule of law and the fight against corruption in all its forms remain key priorities. We will move this agenda forward, in accordance with our commitments under the Kabul Process in line with the principle of mutual accountability.

9. Consistent with Transition, we reaffirm that the role of international actors will evolve further from direct service delivery to support and capacity-building for Afghan institutions, enabling the Government of Afghanistan to exercise its sovereign authority in all its functions. This process includes the phasing out of all Provincial Reconstruction Teams, as well as the dissolution of any structures duplicating the functions and authority of the Government of Afghanistan at the national and sub-national levels.

10. We support the crucial role of the United Nations in Afghanistan. We express our gratitude to the UN Secretary General's Special Representative Staffan de Mistura for his dedicated service, and welcome the Secretary General's decision to appoint Jan Kubis as his new Special Representative for Afghanistan. We note that the UNAMA mandate is currently under review in line with the increased capacity and ownership exercised by the Government of Afghanistan and consistent with the process of Transition that entails the assumption of leadership responsibility by the Afghan Government. We also take note with appreciation of the close collaboration of the International Contact Group with the Afghan Government and their work, and encourage them to continue their joint efforts.

SECURITY

11. We welcome the determination of the Afghan people to combat terrorism and extremism and take responsibility for their own security and for protecting their homeland. We share Afghanistan's vision for its national security forces to be built to modern standards and adequate capacity, so that they can effectively and independently defend Afghanistan.

12. We welcome the successful start of the Transition process. Afghan authorities are assuming full security responsibility for their country and will complete this process by the end of 2014. Correspondingly, the International Security Assistance Force (ISAF), authorized by the UN Security Council, has begun a gradual, responsible draw-down to be completed by that time. With the conclusion of the Transition process, our common responsibility for Afghanistan's future does not come to a close. The International Community, therefore, commits to remain strongly engaged in support of Afghanistan beyond 2014.

13. We underscore that the international support for sustainable Afghan National Security Forces (ANSF) needs to continue after 2014. In assistance to the ANSF, the International Community strongly commits to support their training and equipping, financing and development of capabilities beyond the end of the Transition period. It declares its intent to continue to assist in their financing, with the understanding that over the coming years this share will gradually be reduced, in a manner commensurate with Afghanistan's needs and its increasing domestic revenue generation capacity. In this context, we look forward to define a clear vision and appropriately funded plan for the ANSF, which should be developed before the forthcoming NATO summit in Chicago in May 2012.

14. We recognise that the main threat to Afghanistan's security and stability is terrorism, and that this threat also endangers regional and global peace and security. In this regard, we recognise the regional dimensions of terrorism and extremism, including terrorist safe havens, and emphasise the need for sincere and result-oriented regional cooperation towards a region free from terrorism in order to secure Afghanistan and safeguard our common security against the terrorist threat. We reiterate our common determination to never allow Afghanistan to once again become a haven for international terrorism.

15. The production, trafficking and consumption of narcotics equally pose a grave threat to Afghanistan's security and the growth of a legitimate economy as well as to international peace and stability. Recognizing their shared responsibility, Afghanistan and the International Community reiterate their determination to counter, in a comprehensive manner, including by crop eradication, interdiction and promoting alternative agriculture, the menace of illicit drugs, including drug precursors, which causes widespread harm and suffering. We recognise that the narcotics problem is a global challenge which also requires tackling the demand side.

PEACE PROCESS

16. We stress the need for a political solution in order to achieve peace and security in Afghanistan. To ensure enduring stability, in addition to building up Afghanistan's capacity to defend itself, a political process is necessary, of which negotiation and reconciliation are essential elements. In addition, the process of

reintegration will pave the way for postconflict rehabilitation of Afghan society through improvement of security, community development and local governance.

17. We condemn in the strongest terms the assassination of Professor Burhanuddin Rabbani, former President of Afghanistan and Chairman of the High Peace Council. The International Community welcomes and supports the undeterred peace efforts of the Afghan Government, particularly through the High Peace Council and the Afghanistan Peace and Reintegration Programme. We also take note of the recommendations of the consultative Traditional Loya Jirga of 16–19 November 2011, which provided a new impetus to the peace process.

18. Mindful of the relevant UN resolutions, the International Community concurs with Afghanistan that the peace and reconciliation process and its outcome must be based on the following principles:

(a) The process leading to reconciliation must be
• truly Afghan-led and Afghan-owned; as well as
• inclusive, representing the legitimate interests of all the people of Afghanistan, regardless of gender or social status.

(b) Reconciliation must contain
• the reaffirmation of a sovereign, stable and united Afghanistan;
• the renunciation of violence;
• the breaking of ties to international terrorism;
• respect for the Afghan Constitution, including its human rights provisions, notably the rights of women.

(c) The region must respect and support the peace process and its outcome.

An outcome of the peace process respecting the above principles will receive the full support of the International Community.

ECONOMIC AND SOCIAL DEVELOPMENT

19. The International Community shares Afghanistan's aim of achieving self-reliance and prosperity through developing its human and resource potential on its path towards sustainable and equitable growth and improved standards of living, and welcomes the Afghan Government's economic Transition strategy as elaborated in the document *Towards a Self-Sustaining Afghanistan*. Shifting the strategy from stabilisation to long-term development cooperation, the International Community will continue to support Afghanistan, including in the areas of rule of law, public administration, education, health, agriculture, energy, infrastructure development and job creation, in line with the Afghan Government's priorities as specified in the National Priority Programmes framework under the Kabul Process.

20. As the Afghan government sets priorities, embraces reform and meets its Kabul commitments, including strengthening transparent and accountable public financial management systems and improving budget execution capacity, its partners recommit to meeting the minimum targets set in London and Kabul for aligning international assistance with Afghanistan's priorities and channeling a growing share of development aid through the government budget. We welcome the Government of Japan's intention to host a ministerial conference in July 2012 in Tokyo, which will address, in addition to the coordination of international economic assistance through the Transition period, Afghanistan's strategy for

sustainable development, including aid effectiveness and regional economic co-operation.

21. As Transition gathers momentum, we recognise the economic risks identified by the World Bank and the International Monetary Fund, including the economic impact tied to the reduction of the international military presence. We intend to mitigate this effect, including by increasing aid effectiveness, consistent with the Kabul Process. The International Community shares Afghanistan's concern that a strategy to address the near-term effects of Transition must also facilitate the goal of attaining a sustainable market economy in line with the social needs of the population.

22. The intensive international effort in Afghanistan over the last decade represents a unique engagement. The International Community's commitment, both to Afghanistan and to its role in international security, lasts beyond Transition. Transition will reduce the international presence and the financial requirements associated with it. We recognize that the Government of Afghanistan will have special, significant and continuing fiscal requirements that cannot be met by domestic revenues in the years following Transition. Therefore, during the Transformation Decade, the International Community commits to directing financial support, consistent with the Kabul Process, towards Afghanistan's economic development and security-related costs, helping Afghanistan address its continuing budget shortfall to secure the gains of the last decade, make Transition irreversible, and become self-sustaining.

23. Afghanistan's long-term economic growth will, above all, depend on the development of its productive sectors, notably agriculture and mining. The International Community commits to supporting the development of an export-oriented agriculture-based economy, which is crucial for Afghanistan to achieve food security, poverty reduction, widespread farm-based job creation, and expanding the Government's revenue generation capacity. Concerning mining, we welcome the growing interest of international investors in Afghanistan's mineral wealth but emphasise the need for a regulatory framework to guarantee that this mineral wealth directly benefits the Afghan people. The International Community supports Afghanistan's efforts to develop a transparent and accountable regulatory regime, consistent with international best practices, for collecting and managing public resources and preserving the environment.

24. We recognise that a vibrant, private sector-led economy in Afghanistan will require the development of a competitive service industry and a stable financial system, and achieving regional integration through expanding Afghanistan's trade and transit networks, as well as its regional connectivity. The International Community commits to support Afghanistan's efforts to put in place and enhance the infrastructure and the relevant regulatory frameworks for the development of trade and transit.

25. We emphasize that attracting private investment, including from international sources, are key priorities for activating Afghanistan's economic potential. The Afghan Government commits to improving conditions conducive to international investments, inter alia, by implementing the recommendations of the EUROMINES International Investors Forum in Brussels on 26 October 2011.

REGIONAL COOPERATION

26. We believe that a stable and prosperous Afghanistan can only be envisioned in a stable and prosperous region. For the entire region, the rewards of peace and co-operation outweigh those of rivalry and isolation by far. We endorse Afghanistan's vision for building strong, sustainable bilateral and multilateral relationships with its near and extended neighbours. Such relationships should end external interference, reinforce the principles of good neighbourly relations, non-interference and sovereignty, and further Afghanistan's economic integration into the region.

27. We welcome the outcome of the "Istanbul Conference for Afghanistan: Security and Cooperation in the Heart of Asia" of 2 November 2011. In particular, we take note of the principles concerning territorial integrity, sovereignty, non-intervention and the peaceful settlement of disputes contained in the Istanbul Process, which we support as a valuable step towards building greater confidence and cooperation in the "Heart of Asia" region. We call for strict adherence by Afghanistan and its regional partners to these principles, and look forward to the follow-up Ministerial Conference in June 2012 in Kabul.

28. With a view to the long-term prospects for Afghanistan's development, we share Afghanistan's vision of a well-connected, economically integrated region, where Afghanistan can serve as a land-bridge connecting South Asia, Central Asia, Eurasia and the Middle East. We support enhanced trade connectivity along historical trade routes to utilize Afghanistan's economic potential at the regional level. In this context, we recognize the importance of early implementation of sustainable projects to promote regional connectivity, such as the TAPI gas pipeline, CASA-1000, railways and other projects. In this context, we look forward to the 5th RECCA conference to be hosted by the Republic of Tajikistan in Dushanbe in March 2012.

29. We acknowledge the burden of Afghanistan's neighbours, in particular Pakistan and Iran, in providing temporary refuge to millions of Afghans in difficult times and are committed to further work towards their voluntary, safe and orderly return.

THE WAY FORWARD

30. With a view to the future, we underscore that the process of Transition, which is currently underway and is to be completed by the end of 2014, should be followed by a decade of Transformation, in which Afghanistan consolidates its sovereignty through strengthening a fully functioning, sustainable state in the service of its people. This Transformation Decade will see the emergence of a new paradigm of partnership between Afghanistan and the International Community, whereby a sovereign Afghanistan engages with the International Community to secure its own future and continues to be a positive factor for peace and stability in the region.

31. At today's meeting, Afghanistan laid out its vision of the future: a country that is a stable and functioning democracy, a strong and sustainable state in the service of its people, and a prospering economy. Embedded in a region that is conducive to prosperity and peace, and enjoying friendly relations with all of its near and extended neighbours, Afghanistan aspires to becoming a contributor to international peace and security.

32. With a view to realizing the above vision, the International Community and Afghanistan make firm mutual commitments to continue to working together in a

spirit of partnership. Afghanistan reiterates its commitment to continue to improve governance, while the International Community commits to an enduring engagement with Afghanistan through and beyond 2014.

33. Today in Bonn, we solemnly declare a strategic consensus on deepening and broadening the partnership between Afghanistan and the International Community founded at the Petersberg ten years ago. Building on the shared achievements of the past ten years, and recognising that the security and well-being of Afghanistan continue to affect the security of the entire region and beyond, Afghanistan and the International Community strongly commit to this renewed partnership for the Transformation Decade.

Source: United Nations. Available online at http://afghanistan-un.org/wp-content/uploads/2011/12/Konferenzschlussfolgerung_engl.pdf.

ANALYSIS

The second Bonn Conference, coming a decade after the first Bonn Conference where the Interim Agreement was drafted and Hamid Karzai was chosen as the interim president, sought to advance the process of transferring security responsibilities from ISAF over to the Afghan military while also continuing the development of and support for the Afghan government.

Representatives from 85 nations and 15 international organizations attended the conference, but Pakistan withdrew their support for the meeting following a brief incident along its border where NATO forces killed and wounded 40 Pakistani soldiers at two border checkpoints. This was unfortunate as Pakistan could have played a major role in the projected plans for regional cooperation among Afghanistan and its neighbors and also in supporting the reconciliation process with current and former Taliban members seeking refuge inside its borders.

- **Document 75: Chicago Summit Declaration**
- **When:** May 20, 2012
- **Where:** Chicago, Illinois
- **Significance:** This summit of NATO leaders planned the withdrawal of NATO forces in Afghanistan in 2013 in advance of the 2014 deadline for the Afghan assumption of security responsibilities.

DOCUMENT

Chicago Summit Declaration

Issued by the Heads of State and Government participating in the meeting of the North Atlantic Council in Chicago on 20 May 2012

. . .

5. Today we have taken further important steps on the road to a stable and secure Afghanistan and to our goal of preventing Afghanistan from ever again becoming a safe haven for terrorists that threaten Afghanistan, the region, and the world. The irreversible transition of full security responsibility from the International Security Assistance Force (ISAF) to the Afghan National Security Forces (ANSF) is on track for completion by the end of 2014, as agreed at our Lisbon Summit. We also recognise in this context the importance of a comprehensive approach and continued improvements in governance and development, as well as a political process involving successful reconciliation and reintegration. We welcome the announcement by President Karzai on the third tranche of provinces that will start transition. This third tranche means that 75% of Afghanistan's population will live in areas where the ANSF have taken the lead for security. By mid-2013, when the fifth and final tranche of provinces starts transition, we will have reached an important milestone in our Lisbon roadmap, and the ANSF will be in the lead for security nationwide. At that milestone, as ISAF shifts from focusing primarily on combat increasingly to the provision of training, advice and assistance to the ANSF, ISAF will be able to ensure that the Afghans have the support they need as they adjust to their new increased responsibility. We are gradually and responsibly drawing down our forces to complete the ISAF mission by 31 December 2014.

6. By the end of 2014, when the Afghan Authorities will have full security responsibility, the NATO-led combat mission will end. We will, however, continue to provide strong and long-term political and practical support through our Enduring Partnership with Afghanistan. NATO is ready to work towards establishing, at the request of the Government of the Islamic Republic of Afghanistan, a new post-2014 mission of a different nature in Afghanistan, to train, advise and assist the ANSF, including the Afghan Special Operations Forces. This will not be a combat mission. We task the Council to begin immediately work on the military planning process for the post-ISAF mission.

7. At the International Conference on Afghanistan held in Bonn in December 2011, the international community made a commitment to support Afghanistan in its Transformation Decade beyond 2014. NATO will play its part alongside other actors in building sufficient and sustainable Afghan forces capable of providing security for their own country. In this context, Allies welcome contributions and reaffirm their strong commitment to contribute to the financial sustainment of the ANSF. We also call on the international community to commit to this long-term sustainment of the ANSF. Effective funding mechanisms and expenditure arrangements for all strands of the ANSF will build upon existing mechanisms, integrating the efforts of the Government of the Islamic Republic of Afghanistan and of the international community. They will be guided by the principles of flexibility, transparency, accountability, and cost effectiveness, and will include measures against corruption.

8. We reiterate the importance Allies attach to seeing tangible progress by the Government of the Islamic Republic of Afghanistan regarding its commitments made at the Bonn Conference on 5 December 2011 to a democratic society, based on the rule of law and good governance, including progress in the fight against corruption, where the human rights and fundamental freedoms of its citizens, including

the equality of men and women and the active participation of both in Afghan society, are respected. The forthcoming elections must be conducted with full respect for Afghan sovereignty and in accordance with the Afghan Constitution. Their transparency, inclusivity and credibility will also be of paramount importance. Continued progress towards these goals will encourage NATO nations to further provide their support up to and beyond 2014.

9. We also underscore the importance of our shared understanding with the Government of the Islamic Republic of Afghanistan regarding the full participation of all Afghan women in the reconstruction, political, peace and reconciliation processes in Afghanistan and the need to respect the institutional arrangements protecting their rights. We recognise also the need for the protection of children from the damaging effects of armed conflict.

10. We also recognise that security and stability in the "Heart of Asia" is interlinked across the region. The Istanbul Process on regional security and cooperation, which was launched in November 2011, reflects the commitment of Afghanistan and the countries in the region to jointly ensure security, stability and development in a regional context. The countries in the region, particularly Pakistan, have important roles in ensuring enduring peace, stability and security in Afghanistan and in facilitating the completion of the transition process. We stand ready to continue dialogue and practical cooperation with relevant regional actors in this regard. We welcome the progress on transit arrangements with our Central Asian partners and Russia. NATO continues to work with Pakistan to reopen the ground lines of communication as soon as possible.

. . .

17. We also remain committed to the implementation of UNSCR 1612 and related Resolutions on the protection of children affected by armed conflict. We note with concern the growing range of threats to children in armed conflict and strongly condemn that they are increasingly subject to recruitment, sexual violence and targeted attacks. NATO-led operations, such as ISAF in Afghanistan, are taking an active role in preventing, monitoring and responding to violations against children, including through pre-deployment training and a violations alert mechanism. This approach, based on practical, field-oriented measures, demonstrates NATO's firm commitment on this issue, as does the recent appointment of a NATO Focal Point for Children and Armed Conflict in charge of maintaining a close dialogue with the UN. NATO-UN cooperation in this field is creating a set of good practices to be integrated in NATO training modules and taken into account in possible future operations.

. . .

Source: NATO. Available online at http://www.nato.int/cps/en/natohq/official_-texts_87593.htm?selectedLocale=en.

ANALYSIS

In announcing the surge in 2009, President Obama had committed the United States to a timetable for drawing down its forces as the surge was completed. This

NATO summit further committed the Alliance to a timetable for withdrawal beginning in 2013 and to keep the original deadline of 2014 for Afghanistan to assume the combat burden. Some nations, such as France, had sought to speed up the deadline as well as the end of their own deployments to Afghanistan, but the Chicago Summit forestalled some of those plans. Once NATO combat forces left Afghanistan, the Alliance would continue to advise and train the Afghan military.

- **Document 76: Joint Press Conference by President Obama and President Karzai**
- **When:** January 11, 2013
- **Where:** Washington, D.C.
- **Significance:** President Obama and President Karzai held a joint press conference that discussed the end of the U.S. surge to Afghanistan and the projected end of U.S. forces in combat by the end of the following year.

DID YOU KNOW?

Unmanned Aerial Vehicle Strikes

Even before the September 11 attacks, the United States began using small unmanned aerial vehicles (UAVs) to monitor the movements of suspected terrorists, including Osama bin Laden. These early UAVs, however, carried no weapons. A test program successfully fitted MQ-1 Predator UAVs with a laser seeker and AGM-114 Hellfire missiles, thus giving them a precision strike capability by late 2001. The U.S. Air Force and the CIA employed armed UAVs in Afghanistan, but in 2004, President Bush directed their use against suspected Taliban insurgents and al-Qaeda fighters seeking sanctuary in Pakistan. The number of attacks increased during Bush's final year in office, but President Obama allowed the number of attacks to spike, reaching a reported 120 in 2010 alone. These attacks were launched from U.S. airbases in Afghanistan and were conducted without explicit permission from the Pakistani government. In addition to the issues of national sovereignty, the attacks sometimes led to civilian casualties that inflamed tensions in Pakistan. In addition, the attacks often raised legal questions about the due process of suspected militants. These difficult issues remain unresolved, however, and attacks directed by the Trump administration through mid-2018 show little sign that they will end soon.

DOCUMENT

PRESIDENT OBAMA: Good afternoon, everybody. Please have a seat.

It is my pleasure to welcome President Karzai back to the White House, as well as his delegation. We last saw each other during the NATO Summit, in my hometown of Chicago—a city that reflects the friendship between our peoples, including many Afghan-Americans, as well as the Karzai family. So, Mr. President, welcome.

We meet at a critical moment. The 33,000 additional forces that I ordered to Afghanistan have served with honor. They've completed their mission and, as promised, returned home this past fall. The transition is well underway, and soon nearly 90 percent of Afghans will live in areas where Afghan forces are in the lead for their own security.

This year, we'll mark another milestone—Afghan forces will take the lead for security across the entire country. And by the end of next year, 2014, the transition will be complete—Afghans will have full responsibility for their security, and this war will come to a responsible end.

This progress is only possible because of the incredible sacrifices of our troops and our diplomats, the forces of our many coalition partners, and the Afghan people who've endured extraordinary hardship. In this war, more than 2,000 of America's sons and daughters have given their lives. These are patriots that we honor today, tomorrow, and forever. And as we announced today, next month I will present our nation's highest military decoration, the Medal of Honor, to Staff Sergeant Clinton Romesha for his heroic service in Afghanistan.

Today, because of the courage of our citizens, President Karzai and I have been able to review our shared strategy. With the devastating blows we've struck against al Qaeda, our core objective—the reason we went to war in the first place—is now within reach: ensuring that al Qaeda can never again use Afghanistan to launch attacks against our country. At the same time, we pushed the Taliban out of their strongholds. Today, most major cities—and most Afghans—are more secure, and insurgents have continued to lose territory.

Meanwhile, Afghan forces continue to grow stronger. As planned, some 352,000 Afghan soldiers and police are now in training or on duty. Most missions are already being led by Afghan forces. And of all the men and women in uniform in Afghanistan, the vast majority are Afghans who are fighting and dying for their country every day.

We still face significant challenges. But because of this progress, our transition is on track. At the NATO Summit last year, we agreed with our coalition partners that Afghan forces will take the lead for security in mid-2013.

President Karzai and his team have been here for several days. We've shared a vision for how we're going to move ahead. We've consulted with our coalition partners, and we will continue to do so. And today, we agreed that as Afghan forces take the lead and as President Karzai announces the final phase of the transition, coalition forces will move to a support role this spring. Our troops will continue to fight alongside Afghans, when needed. But let me say it as plainly as I can: Starting this spring, our troops will have a different mission—training, advising, assisting Afghan forces. It will be an historic moment and another step toward full Afghan sovereignty—something I know that President Karzai cares deeply about, as do the Afghan people.

This sets the stage for the further reduction of coalition forces. We've already reduced our presence in Afghanistan to roughly 66,000 U.S. troops. I've pledged we'll continue to bring our forces home at a steady pace, and in the coming months I'll announce the next phase of our drawdown—a responsible drawdown that protects the gains our troops have made.

President Karzai and I also discussed the nature of our security cooperation after 2014. Our teams continue to work toward a security agreement. And as they do, they will be guided by our respect for Afghan sovereignty, and by our two long-term tasks, which will be very specific and very narrow—first, training and assisting Afghan forces and, second, targeting counterterrorism missions—targeted counterterrorism missions against al Qaeda and its affiliates. Our discussions will focus on how best to achieve these two tasks after 2014, and it's our hope that we can reach an agreement this year.

Ultimately, security gains must be matched by political progress. So we recommitted our nations to a reconciliation process between the Afghan government and the Taliban. President Karzai updated me on the Afghan government's road map to peace. And today, we agreed that this process should be advanced by the opening of a Taliban office to facilitate talks.

Reconciliation also requires constructive support from across the region, including Pakistan. We welcome recent steps that have been taken in that regard, and we'll look for more tangible steps—because a stable and secure Afghanistan is in the interest not only of the Afghan people and the United States, but of the entire region.

And finally, we reaffirmed the Strategic Partnership that we signed last year in Kabul—an enduring partnership between two sovereign nations. This includes deepening ties of trade, commerce, strengthening institutions, development, education and opportunities for all Afghans—men and women, boys and girls. And this sends a clear message to Afghans and to the region, as Afghans stand up, they will not stand alone; the United States, and the world, stands with them.

Now, let me close by saying that this continues to be a very difficult mission. Our forces continue to serve and make tremendous sacrifices every day. The Afghan people make significant sacrifices every day. Afghan forces still need to grow stronger. We remain vigilant against insider attacks. Lasting peace and security will require governance and development that delivers for the Afghan people and an end to safe havens for al Qaeda and its ilk. All this will continue to be our work.

But make no mistake—our path is clear and we are moving forward. Every day, more Afghans are stepping up and taking responsibility for their own security. And as they do, our troops will come home. And next year, this long war will come to a responsible end.

President Karzai, I thank you and your delegation for the progress we've made together and for your commitment to the goals that we share—a strong and sovereign Afghanistan where Afghans find security, peace, prosperity and dignity. And in pursuit of that future, Afghanistan will have a long-term partner in the United States of America.

Mr. President.

PRESIDENT KARZAI: Thank you. Thank you very much, Mr. President, for this very gracious and warm welcome to me and the Afghan delegation on this visit to Washington, and for bearing with us, as I mentioned during our talks in the Blair House, with all the crowds that we have there.

The President and I discussed today in great detail all the relevant issues between the two countries. I was happy to see that we have made progress on some of the important issues for Afghanistan. Concerning Afghan sovereignty, we agreed on the complete return of detention centers and detainees to Afghan sovereignty, and that this will be implemented soon after my return to Afghanistan. We also discussed all aspects of transition to Afghan governance and security.

I'm very happy to hear from the President, as we also discussed it earlier, that in spring this year the Afghan forces will be fully responsible for providing security and protection to the Afghan people, and that the international forces, the American forces will be no longer present in Afghan villages, that the task will be that of the Afghan forces to provide for the Afghan people in security and protection.

We also agreed on the steps that we should be taking in the peace process, which is of highest priority to Afghanistan. We agreed on allowing a Taliban office in

Qatar—in Doha, where the Taliban will engage in direct talks with the representatives of the Afghan High Council for Peace, where we will be seeking the help of relevant regional countries, including Pakistan—where we'll be trying our best, together with the United States and our other allies, to return peace and stability to Afghanistan as soon as possible, and employing all the means that we have within our power to do that, so the Afghan people can live in security and peace and work for their prosperity and educate their children.

The President and I also discussed the economic transition of Afghanistan and all that entails for Afghanistan. Once the transition to Afghan forces is completed, once the bulk of the international forces have withdrawn from Afghanistan, we hope that the dividends of that transition economically to Afghanistan will be beneficial to the Afghan people, and will not have adverse effects on Afghan economy and the prosperity that we have gained in the past many years.

We also discussed the issue of election in Afghanistan and the importance of election for the Afghan people, with the hope that we'll be conducting a free and fair election in Afghanistan where our friends in the international community—in particular, the United States—will be assisting in conducting those elections, of course; where Afghanistan will have the right environment for conducting elections without interference and without undue concern in that regard for the Afghan people.

We also discussed in a bit of detail, and in the environment that we have, all aspects of the bilateral security agreement between Afghanistan and the United States, and I informed the President that the Afghan people already in the Loya Jirga that we called for—the Strategic Partnership Agreement between us and the United States— have given their approval to this relationship and the value as one that is good for Afghanistan. So in that context, the bilateral security agreement is one that the Afghan people approve. And I'm sure we will conduct it in detail where both the interests of the United States and the interests of Afghanistan will be kept in mind.

We had a number of other issues also to talk about. During our conversations, and perhaps many times in that conversation, beginning with the conversation, of course, I thanked the President for the help that the United States has given to the Afghan people, for all that we have gained in the past 10 years, and that those gains will be kept by any standard while we are working for peace and stability in Afghanistan, including the respect for Afghan constitution.

I also thanked the President and endorsed with him the sacrifices of American men and women in uniform and those of other countries. Accordingly, I also informed President Obama of the sacrifices of the Afghan people—of the immense sacrifices of the Afghan people in the past 10 years, both for the servicemen and of the Afghan people.

I'll be going back to Afghanistan this evening to bring to the Afghan people the news of Afghanistan standing shoulder to shoulder with America as a sovereign, independent country, but in cooperation and in partnership.

Thank you, Mr. President, for the hospitality.

PRESIDENT OBAMA: Thank you very much, Mr. President.

. . .

Q I am Abdul Qadir, Kabul, Afghanistan. I prefer to ask my question to my own language.

(As interpreted.) Mr. President, the missions of—combat missions of United States after 2014—how this mission will be? Will it be resembling the same mission as it was during 11 years, or is there a difference, different kind of mission? Those who are in Pakistan, particularly the safe havens that are in Pakistan, what kind of policy will you have? Thank you.

PRESIDENT OBAMA: Just to repeat, our main reason should we have troops in Afghanistan post-2014 at the invitation of the Afghan government will be to make sure that we are training, assisting and advising Afghan security forces who have now taken the lead for and are responsible for security throughout Afghanistan, and an interest that the United States has—the very reason that we went to Afghanistan in the first place—and that is to make sure that al Qaeda and its affiliates cannot launch an attack against the United States or other countries from Afghan soil.

We believe that we can achieve that mission in a way that's very different from the very active presence that we've had in Afghanistan over the last 11 years. President Karzai has emphasized the strains that U.S. troop presences in Afghan villages, for example, have created. Well, that's not going to be a strain that exists if there is a follow-up operation because that will not be our responsibility; that will be the responsibility of the Afghan National Security Forces, to maintain peace and order and stability in Afghan villages, in Afghan territory.

So I think, although obviously we're still two years away, I can say with assurance that this is a very different mission and a very different task and a very different footprint for the U.S. if we are able to come to an appropriate agreement.

And with respect to Pakistan and safe havens there, Afghanistan and the United States and Pakistan all have an interest in reducing the threat of extremism in some of these border regions between Afghanistan and Pakistan. And that's going to require more than simply military actions. That's really going to require political and diplomatic work between Afghanistan and Pakistan. And the United States obviously will have an interest in facilitating and participating in cooperation between the two sovereign countries.

But as President Karzai I think has indicated, it's very hard to imagine stability and peace in the region if Pakistan and Afghanistan don't come to some basic agreement and understanding about the threat of extremism to both countries and both governments and both capitals. And I think you're starting to see a greater awareness of that on the part of the Pakistani government.

PRESIDENT KARZAI: (As interpreted.) The question that you have made about—we talked about this issue in detail today about the prisoners, about the detention centers. All of these will transfer to the Afghan sovereignty, and the U.S. forces will pull out from villages, will go to their bases, and Afghan sovereignty will be restored.

And after 2014, we are working on this relation. This relation will have a different nature and will be based on different principles. It will resemble probably Turkey-United States—Turkey or Germany. We are studying these relationships and we will do that.

Q Thank you, Mr. President. As you contemplate the end of this war, can you say as Commander-in-Chief that the huge human and financial costs that this has entailed can be justified, given the fact that the Afghanistan that the world will leave behind is somewhat diminished from the visions of reconstruction and democracy that were kind of prevalent at the beginning of the war?

And, President Karzai, many independent studies have criticized Afghanistan for corruption and poor governance. Do you stand by your assertion last month that much of this is due to the influence of foreigners? And are you completely committed to stepping down as President after the elections next year?

PRESIDENT OBAMA: I want us to remember why we went to Afghanistan. We went into Afghanistan because 3,000 Americans were viciously murdered by a terrorist organization that was operating openly and at the invitation of those who were then ruling Afghanistan.

It was absolutely the right thing to do for us to go after that organization; to go after the host government that had aided and abetted, or at least allowed for these attacks to take place. And because of the heroic work of our men and women in uniform, and because of the cooperation and sacrifices of Afghans who had also been brutalized by that then-host government, we achieved our central goal, which is—or have come very close to achieving our central goal—which is to de-capacitate al Qaeda; to dismantle them; to make sure that they can't attack us again.

And everything that we've done over the last 10 years from the perspective of the U.S. national security interests have been focused on that aim. And at the end of this conflict, we are going to be able to say that the sacrifices that were made by those men and women in uniform has brought about the goal that we sought.

Now, what we also recognized very early on was that it was in our national security interest to have a stable, sovereign Afghanistan that was a responsible international actor, that was in partnership with us, and that that required Afghanistan to have its own security capacity and to be on a path that was more likely to achieve prosperity and peace for its own people. And I think President Karzai would be the first to acknowledge that Afghanistan still has work to do to accomplish those goals, but there's no doubt that the possibility of peace and prosperity in Afghanistan today is higher than before we went in. And that is also in part because of the sacrifices that the American people have made during this long conflict.

So I think that—have we achieved everything that some might have imagined us achieving in the best of scenarios? Probably not. This is a human enterprise and you fall short of the ideal. Did we achieve our central goal, and have we been able I think to shape a strong relationship with a responsible Afghan government that is willing to cooperate with us to make sure that it is not a launching pad for future attacks against the United States? We have achieved that goal. We are in the process of achieving that goal. And for that, I think we have to thank our extraordinary military, intelligence, and diplomatic teams, as well as the cooperation of the Afghan government and the Afghan people.

PRESIDENT KARZAI: Sir, on the question of corruption, whether it has a foreign element to it, if I have correct understanding of your question, there is corruption in Afghanistan. There is corruption in the Afghan government that we are fighting against, employing various means and methods. We have succeeded in certain ways. But if your question is whether we are satisfied—of course not.

And on the corruption that is foreign in origin but occurring in Afghanistan, I have been very clear and explicit, and I don't think that Afghanistan can see this corruption unless there is cooperation between us and our international partners on correcting some of the methods or applications of delivery of assistance to Afghanistan—without cooperation and with recognition of the problems.

On elections, for me, the greatest of my achievements, eventually, seen by the Afghan people will be a proper, well-organized, interference-free election in which the Afghan people can elect their next president. Certainly, I would be a retired President, and very happily, a retired President.

. . .

Source: White House. Available online at https://obamawhitehouse.archives.gov /the-press-office/2013/01/11/joint-press-conference-president-obama-and-president -karzai.

ANALYSIS

Given the allegations of corruption swirling around him and his inner circle, President Karzai assuaged some concerns by announcing that he would retire from the presidency when his term ended in 2014. But his country continued to face major challenges, and reports of high rates of desertion dashed optimism that the homegrown Afghan National Army could assume the security burden by the end of 2014 as had been agreed upon by Afghanistan and NATO.

Both presidents also discussed their intention to recast the U.S.-Afghan relationship once the withdrawal of combat forces ended, with President Karzai suggesting that Germany or Turkey might serve as a useful model for the bilateral relationship. President Obama also intended the United States to continue to play a role in facilitating discussions between Afghanistan and Pakistan to ensure a smooth security relationship between the two neighbors.

- **Document 77: Barack Obama, Statement by the President on Afghanistan**
- **When:** May 27, 2014
- **Where:** Washington, D.C.
- **Significance:** President Obama announced the intention to keep 9,800 U.S. troops in Afghanistan past the end of 2014 for training and counterterrorism missions pending the ratification of a status of forces agreement.

DOCUMENT

THE PRESIDENT: Good afternoon, everybody. As you know, this weekend, I traveled to Afghanistan to thank our men and women in uniform and our deployed civilians, on behalf of a grateful nation, for the extraordinary sacrifices they make on behalf of our security. I was also able to meet with our commanding General and Ambassador to review the progress that we've made. And today, I'd like to update the American people on the way forward in Afghanistan and how, this year, we will bring America's longest war to a responsible end.

The United States did not seek this fight. We went into Afghanistan out of necessity, after our nation was attacked by al Qaeda on September 11th, 2001. We went to war against al Qaeda and its extremist allies with the strong support of the American people and their representatives in Congress; with the international community and our NATO allies; and with the Afghan people, who welcomed the opportunity of a life free from the dark tyranny of extremism.

We have now been in Afghanistan longer than many Americans expected. But make no mistake—thanks to the skill and sacrifice of our troops, diplomats, and intelligence professionals, we have struck significant blows against al Qaeda's leadership, we have eliminated Osama bin Laden, and we have

DID YOU KNOW?

Green-on-Blue Incidents

Green-on-blue incidents are the U.S. military terminology for when friendly (green) forces intentionally harm one's own forces (blue). Many, but not all, of the "green" attackers are insurgent sympathizers who have infiltrated the Afghan National Security Forces. For the first seven years of the U.S. involvement in Afghanistan, such incidents were extremely rare and caused less than 1 percent of Coalition casualties. Beginning in 2011, however, the number of these incidents began to rise sharply; 6 percent of Coalition deaths occurred at the hands of "friendly" Afghan forces. In 2012, this number rose to a remarkable 15 percent of Coalition deaths. In 2014, a green-on-blue attack at the Marshal Fahim National Defense University led to the death of Major General Harold Greene, by far the highest ranking U.S. officer killed in Afghanistan. Countermeasures, including posting guards on Afghan units and counterintelligence, have reduced the number of attacks, but this reduction also occurred as the Coalition presence in Afghanistan shrank.

prevented Afghanistan from being used to launch attacks against our homeland. We have also supported the Afghan people as they continue the hard work of building a democracy. We've extended more opportunities to their people, including women and girls. And we've helped train and equip their own security forces.

Now we're finishing the job we started. Over the last several years, we've worked to transition security responsibilities to the Afghans. One year ago, Afghan forces assumed the lead for combat operations. Since then, they've continued to grow in size and in strength, while making huge sacrifices for their country. This transition has allowed us to steadily draw down our own forces—from a peak of 100,000 U.S. troops, to roughly 32,000 today.

2014, therefore, is a pivotal year. Together with our allies and the Afghan government, we have agreed that this is the year we will conclude our combat mission in Afghanistan. This is also a year of political transition in Afghanistan. Earlier this spring, Afghans turned out in the millions to vote in the first round of their presidential election—defying threats in order to determine their own destiny. And in just over two weeks, they will vote for their next President, and Afghanistan will see its first democratic transfer of power in history.

In the context of this progress, having consulted with Congress and my national security team, I've determined the nature of the commitment that America is prepared to make beyond 2014. Our objectives are clear: Disrupting threats posed by al Qaeda; supporting Afghan security forces; and giving the Afghan people the opportunity to succeed as they stand on their own.

Here's how we will pursue those objectives. First, America's combat mission will be over by the end of this year. Starting next year, Afghans will be fully responsible for securing their country. American personnel will be in an advisory role. We will no longer patrol Afghan cities or towns, mountains or valleys. That is a task for the Afghan people.

Second, I've made it clear that we're open to cooperating with Afghans on two narrow missions after 2014: training Afghan forces and supporting counterterrorism operations against the remnants of al Qaeda.

Today, I want to be clear about how the United States is prepared to advance those missions. At the beginning of 2015, we will have approximately 98,000 U.S.—let me start that over, just because I want to make sure we don't get this written wrong. At the beginning of 2015, we will have approximately 9,800 U.S. servicemembers in different parts of the country, together with our NATO allies and other partners. By the end of 2015, we will have reduced that presence by roughly half, and we will have consolidated our troops in Kabul and on Bagram Airfield. One year later, by the end of 2016, our military will draw down to a normal embassy presence in Kabul, with a security assistance component, just as we've done in Iraq.

Now, even as our troops come home, the international community will continue to support Afghans as they build their country for years to come. But our relationship will not be defined by war—it will be shaped by our financial and development assistance, as well as our diplomatic support. Our commitment to Afghanistan is rooted in the strategic partnership that we agreed to in 2012. And this plan remains consistent with discussions we've had with our NATO allies. Just as our allies have been with us every step of the way in Afghanistan, we expect that our allies will be with us going forward.

Third, we will only sustain this military presence after 2014 if the Afghan government signs the Bilateral Security Agreement that our two governments have already negotiated. This Agreement is essential to give our troops the authorities they need to fulfill their mission, while respecting Afghan sovereignty. The two final Afghan candidates in the run-off election for President have each indicated that they would sign this agreement promptly after taking office. So I'm hopeful that we can get this done.

The bottom line is, it's time to turn the page on more than a decade in which so much of our foreign policy was focused on the wars in Afghanistan and Iraq. When I took office, we had nearly 180,000 troops in harm's way. By the end of this year, we will have less than 10,000. In addition to bringing our troops home, this new chapter in American foreign policy will allow us to redirect some of the resources saved by ending these wars to respond more nimbly to the changing threat of terrorism, while addressing a broader set of priorities around the globe.

I think Americans have learned that it's harder to end wars than it is to begin them. Yet this is how wars end in the 21st century—not through signing ceremonies, but through decisive blows against our adversaries, transitions to elected governments, security forces who take the lead and ultimately full responsibility. We remain committed to a sovereign, secure, stable, and unified Afghanistan. And toward that end, we will continue to support Afghan-led efforts to promote peace in their country through reconciliation. We have to recognize that Afghanistan will not be a perfect place, and it is not America's responsibility to make it one. The future of Afghanistan must be decided by Afghans. But what the United States can do—what we will do—is secure our interests and help give the Afghans a chance, an opportunity to seek a long, overdue and hard-earned peace.

America will always keep our commitments to friends and partners who step up, and we will never waver in our determination to deny al Qaeda the safe haven that they had before 9/11. That commitment is embodied by the men and women in and out of uniform who serve in Afghanistan today and who have served in the past. In their eyes, I see the character that sustains American security and our leadership abroad. These are mostly young people who did not hesitate to volunteer in a time of war. And as many of them begin to transition to civilian life, we will keep the promise we make to them and to all veterans, and make sure they get the care and benefits that they have earned and deserve.

This 9/11 Generation is part of an unbroken line of heroes who give up the comfort of the familiar to serve a half a world away—to protect their families and communities back home, and to give people they never thought they'd meet the chance to live a better life. It's an extraordinary sacrifice for them and for their families. But we shouldn't be surprised that they're willing to make it. That's who we are as Americans. That's what we do.

Tomorrow, I will travel to West Point and speak to America's newest class of military officers to discuss how Afghanistan fits into our broader strategy going forward. And I'm confident that if we carry out this approach, we can not only responsibly end our war in Afghanistan and achieve the objectives that took us to war in the first place, we'll also be able to begin a new chapter in the story of American leadership around the world.

Source: White House. Available online at https://obamawhitehouse.archives.gov/the-press-office/2014/05/27/statement-president-afghanistan.

ANALYSIS

President Obama's statement clarified the numbers of U.S. forces that he intended to keep in Afghanistan past the formal end of the U.S. combat presence at the end of the year. This commitment, however, hinged upon the signing of the Bilateral Security Agreement first discussed at the Chicago Summit in May 2012. The Obama administration had argued that the withdrawal of U.S. forces in Iraq occurred because the Iraqi government refused to sign a status of forces agreement that would have given U.S. forces legal protections during their deployment, so securing such protections from Afghanistan constituted a major hurdle.

- **Document 78: Agreement between the North Atlantic Treaty Organization and the Islamic Republic of Afghanistan on the Status of NATO Forces and NATO Personnel Conducting Mutually Agreed NATO-Led Activities in Afghanistan**

- **When:** September 30, 2014
- **Where:** Kabul, Afghanistan
- **Significance:** After two years of negotiations, Afghanistan and NATO formally concluded a status of forces agreement that outlined specific duties and legal terms for the continued operation of NATO forces in Afghanistan.

DOCUMENT

The North Atlantic Treaty Organization, hereinafter NATO
represented by His Excellency Mr. Maurits R. Jochems
NATO Senior Civilian Representative in Afghanistan,
and
the Islamic Republic of Afghanistan, hereinafter Afghanistan
represented by His Excellency Mr. Mohammed Haneef Atmar
National Security Advisor,

hereinafter referred to as the "Parties",

Considering that, in the 2012 Chicago Summit Declaration on Afghanistan, the Heads of State and Government of the Islamic Republic of Afghanistan and the nations contributing to the International Security Assistance Force (ISAF) renewed their firm and shared commitment to a sovereign, secure and democratic Afghanistan;

Confirming the shared understanding of the Parties of the threat to the international community posed by terrorism and their shared commitment to taking effective action to counter that threat and to ensuring that Afghanistan never again becomes a safe haven for terrorists;

Recognizing that the mission of the ISAF will be concluded by the end of 2014;

Recalling the commitment of NATO and other members of the international community to standing with Afghanistan and the Parties' agreement at the NATO Summit in Lisbon to renewing and building a robust Enduring Partnership complementing their past security cooperation and continuing beyond it;

Affirming the Parties' intention that this Enduring Partnership include an individual programme of co-operation activities with security ministries and other national institutions and on enhancing the capabilities and skill levels in the Afghan security forces, including their ability to tackle the

DID YOU KNOW?

Bowe Bergdahl

Bowe Bergdahl is a former U.S. Army private who was held captive by the Haqqani Network from 2009 until 2014. Born in 1986, Bergdahl enlisted in the U.S. Army and deployed to Paktika Province in Afghanistan the following year as a member of the 1st Battalion, 501st Infantry Regiment of the 25th Infantry Division. On June 30, 2009, under disputed circumstances, members of the Haqqani Network captured Bergdahl. Bergdahl has claimed that the incident occurred while on patrol, while the military instead argued that he simply abandoned his post. His captors released a video of Bergdahl a few weeks later, and several more videos followed over the next year. Some have claimed that several soldiers died searching for Bergdahl, although this, too, is disputed. Through his captivity, the Army continued to promote Bergdahl, first to specialist in 2010 and then to sergeant in 2011. By 2012, the United States began negotiating for his release, finally succeeding in 2014 in exchange for transferring some suspected terrorists detained at Guantanamo Bay to Qatari custody. After his release, the Army investigated Bergdahl for the next three years, but Bergdahl eventually pled guilty in October 2017 to desertion. He was dishonorably discharged from the Army the following month as a private, his original rank. He served no jail time.

threats of terrorism, through training and supporting specialised Afghan units and appropriate access to NATO courses, institutions and military and civilian expertise; and

Reaffirming, finally, the Parties' agreement on the value of NATO leading a non-combat, training, advising and assisting mission in Afghanistan beginning after 2014;

Have agreed as follows:

. . .

ARTICLE 2—Activities

1. In acknowledgement of the Parties' shared desire to develop an enduring partnership complementing their past and current security cooperation, the Parties mutually agree upon the importance of NATO's continuing engagement in support of Afghanistan's security.

2. The Parties hereby agree to the presence of NATO Forces in Afghanistan for the purpose of the post-2014 NATO non-combat training, advising and assistance mission, as well as for the purpose of all other mutually agreed NATO-led activities. It is envisioned that the focus of the training, advising and assistance delivered by this mission would be at the security ministry and national institutional level. Afghan National Defense and Security Force (ANDSF) advising would be extended only to the Corps and Corps-equivalent Police headquarters. The non-combat training, advising and assistance by NATO forces could be extended to the tactical level in the case of Afghan Special Operations Forces by the request and invitation of the Afghan Government.

3. The following provisions will govern the presence of any NATO Forces carrying out activities under this agreement in Afghanistan. The parties agree that these provisions will also apply to any NATO Forces that for any reason are required to redeploy out of Afghanistan, as well as personnel and equipment formerly involved in ISAF that may remain in Afghanistan after 31 December 2014, as long as necessary to complete their redeployment out of Afghanistan.

ARTICLE 3—Purpose and Scope

1. In furtherance of the non-combat train, advise, and assist mission, and other mutually agreed activities and consistent with the authorizations as detailed in this Agreement, NATO Forces may undertake transit, support, and related activities, including as may be necessary to support themselves while they are present in Afghanistan, and such other activities as may be mutually agreed.

2. This Agreement, including any Annexes and any implementing agreements or arrangements, provides the necessary authorizations for the presence and activities of NATO Forces in Afghanistan and defines the terms and conditions that describe that presence, and in the specific situations indicated herein, the presence and activities of NATO Contractors and NATO Contractor Employees in Afghanistan.

ARTICLE 4—Laws

1. It is the duty of Members of the Force and Members of the Civilian Component and NATO Personnel to respect the Constitution and laws of Afghanistan and to abstain from any activity inconsistent with the spirit of this Agreement and, in particular, from any political activity in the territory of Afghanistan. It is the duty of NATO Forces Authorities to take necessary measures to that end.

2. The Parties' respective obligations under this Agreement, and any subsequent arrangements, are without prejudice to Afghan sovereignty over its territory, and the right of self-defense, consistent with international law. Cooperation and activities relating to implementation of this Agreement shall be consistent with any applicable commitments and obligations under international law.

3. NATO Forces shall not arrest or imprison Afghan nationals, nor maintain or operate detention facilities in Afghanistan.

. . .

ARTICLE 11—Status of Personnel

1. Afghanistan, while retaining its sovereignty, recognizes the particular importance of disciplinary control, including judicial and non-judicial measures, by NATO Forces Authorities over Members of the Force and Members of the Civilian Component and NATO Personnel. Afghanistan therefore agrees that the State to which the Member of the Force or Members of the Civilian Component concerned belongs, or the State of which the person is a national, as appropriate, shall have the exclusive right to exercise jurisdiction over such persons in respect of any criminal or civil offenses committed in the territory of Afghanistan. Afghanistan authorizes such States to hold trial in such cases, or take other disciplinary action, as appropriate, in the territory of Afghanistan.

2. If requested by Afghanistan, NATO shall inform Afghanistan of the status of any criminal proceedings regarding offenses allegedly committed in Afghanistan by the Members of the Force or Members of the Civilian Component or by NATO Personnel involving Afghan nationals, including the final disposition of the investigations or prosecution. If so requested, NATO shall also undertake efforts to permit and facilitate the attendance and observation of such proceedings by representatives of Afghanistan.

3. In the interests of justice, the Parties shall assist each other in investigation of incidents, including the collection of evidence. In investigating offenses, NATO Forces Authorities shall take into account any report of investigations by Afghan authorities.

4. NATO recognizes the critical role that Afghan law enforcement officials play in the enforcement of Afghan law and order and the protection of the Afghan people. Relevant Afghan authorities shall immediately notify NATO Forces Authorities if they suspect a Member of the Force or a Member of the Civilian Component or NATO Personnel is engaged in the commission of a

crime so that NATO Forces Authorities can take immediate action. Members of the Force and Members of the Civilian Component and NATO Personnel shall not be arrested or detained by Afghan authorities. Members of the Force and Members of the Civilian Component and NATO Personnel arrested or detained by Afghan authorities for any reason, including by Afghan law enforcement authorities, shall be immediately handed over to the appropriate NATO Forces Authorities.

5. Afghanistan maintains the right to exercise jurisdiction over NATO Contractors and NATO Contractor Employees.

. . .

ARTICLE 25—Entry into Force, Amendment, and Termination

1. This Agreement shall enter into force on 1 January, 2015, after the Parties notify one another through diplomatic channels of the completion of their respective internal legal requirements necessary for the entry into force of this Agreement. It shall remain in force until the end of 2024 and beyond, unless terminated pursuant to paragraph 4 of this Article.

2. This Agreement, upon its entry into force, shall supersede the Afghanistan-NATO Exchange of Letters dated 5 September and 22 November 2004. This Agreement shall supersede any prior agreements and understandings which the Parties mutually determine, through a subsequent exchange of diplomatic notes, to be contrary to the provisions of this Agreement.

3. This Agreement may be amended by written agreement of the Parties through the exchange of diplomatic notes.

4. This Agreement may be terminated by mutual written agreement or by either Party upon two years' written notice to the other Party through diplomatic channels. Termination of any Annex to or Implementing Arrangement under this Agreement does not result in termination of this Agreement. Termination of this Agreement in accordance with this paragraph shall, without further action, result in termination of all Annexes and Implementing Arrangements.

IN WITNESS WHEREOF, the undersigned, being duly authorized thereto, have signed this Agreement.

DONE in Kabul on this Thirtieth day of September 2014 in duplicate, in the English, French, Pashto, and Dari languages, each text being equally authentic.

FOR THE NORTH ATLANTIC TREATY ORGANIZATION	FOR THE ISLAMIC REPUBLIC OF AFGHANISTAN
His Excellency	His Excellency
Mr. Maurits R. Jochems	Mr. Mohammed Haneef Atmar
NATO Senior Civilian Representative	National Security Advisor

Source: NATO. Available online at http://www.nato.int/cps/en/natohq/official _texts_116072.htm?selectedLocale=en.

ANALYSIS

Securing this agreement took more than two years of negotiations. It had been ratified by the Loya Jirga in 2013. President Karzai, however, refused to formally sign the agreement until after the 2014 elections had passed. The agreement allowed 9,800 U.S. troops as well as more than 2,000 troops from other NATO countries to remain in Afghanistan until 2024 to continue training and advising the Afghan military.

In addition, it allowed the United States to continue operating unmanned aerial vehicles from the airfield at Jalalabad that could be used to strike terrorists and insurgents across the border in Pakistan. By 2014, this practice had become extremely controversial and had led to numerous protests in Pakistan, but the Pakistani government often appeared to reluctantly allow the continued assassinations to occur on their territory.

- **Document 79: Barack Obama, Statement by the President on the End of the Combat Mission in Afghanistan**
- **When:** December 28, 2014
- **Where:** Washington, D.C.
- **Significance:** President Obama formally announced the end of the U.S. combat mission in Afghanistan after more than 13 years of fighting.

DOCUMENT

Today's ceremony in Kabul marks a milestone for our country. For more than 13 years, ever since nearly 3,000 innocent lives were taken from us on 9/11, our nation has been at war in Afghanistan. Now, thanks to the extraordinary sacrifices of our men and women in uniform, our combat mission in Afghanistan is ending, and the longest war in American history is coming to a responsible conclusion.

On this day we give thanks to our troops and intelligence personnel who have been relentless against the terrorists responsible for 9/11—devastating the core al Qaeda leadership, delivering justice to Osama bin Laden, disrupting terrorist plots and saving countless American lives. We are safer, and our nation is more secure, because of their service. At the same time, our courageous military and diplomatic personnel in Afghanistan—along with our NATO allies and coalition partners—have helped the Afghan people reclaim their communities, take the lead for their own security, hold historic elections and complete the first democratic transfer of power in their country's history.

We honor the profound sacrifices that have made this progress possible. We salute every American—military and civilian, including our dedicated diplomats and development workers—who have served in Afghanistan, many on multiple tours, just as their families have sacrificed at home. We pledge to give our many wounded warriors, with wounds seen and unseen, the world-class care and treatment they have earned. Most of all, we remember the more than 2,200 American patriots who made the ultimate sacrifice in Afghanistan, and we pledge to stand with their Gold Star families who need the everlasting love and support of a grateful nation.

Afghanistan remains a dangerous place, and the Afghan people and their security forces continue to make tremendous sacrifices in defense of their country. At the invitation of the Afghan government, and to preserve the gains we have made together, the United States—along with our allies and partners—will maintain a limited military presence in Afghanistan to train, advise and assist Afghan forces and to conduct counterterrorism operations against the remnants of al Qaeda. Our personnel will continue to face risks, but this reflects the enduring commitment of the United States to the Afghan people and to a united, secure and sovereign Afghanistan that is never again used as a source of attacks against our nation.

These past 13 years have tested our nation and our military. But compared to the nearly 180,000 American troops in Iraq and Afghanistan when I took office, we now have fewer than 15,000 in those countries. Some 90 percent of our troops are home. Our military remains the finest in the world, and we will remain vigilant against terrorist attacks and in defense of the freedoms and values we hold dear. And with growing prosperity here at home, we enter a new year with new confidence, indebted to our fellow Americans in uniform who keep us safe and free.

Source: White House. Available online at https://obamawhitehouse.archives.gov/the-press-office/2014/12/28/statement-president-end-combat-mission-afghanistan.

ANALYSIS

As had been scheduled for four years, the United States formally ended its part of the hostilities in Afghanistan at the end of 2014. This ended Operation Enduring Freedom as the war had been officially named and began Operation Resolute Support. To that point, more than 2,200 U.S. servicemen and women had been killed in Afghanistan, and the cost to U.S. taxpayers had reached nearly $1 billion. Unfortunately, while the surge had degraded the Taliban, insurgent attacks on government and security facilities rebounded and inflicted the highest numbers of casualties among Afghan personnel in 2014 as U.S. forces left. This left Afghanistan to an uncertain future after some years of optimism.

- **Document 80: Remarks by President Obama and President Ghani of Afghanistan in Joint Press Conference**
- **When:** March 24, 2015

- **Where:** Washington, D.C.
- **Significance:** President Obama's first joint press conference with new Afghan president Ashraf Ghani, which occurred after the formal end of the U.S. combat mission in Afghanistan.

DOCUMENT

PRESIDENT OBAMA: Good afternoon, everybody. Please have a seat. Before I begin, I want to say that our thoughts and prayers are with our friends in Europe, especially the people of Germany and Spain, following a terrible airplane crash in France. It's particularly heartbreaking because it apparently includes the loss of so many children, some of them infants.

I called German Chancellor Merkel—and I hope to speak with President Rajoy of Spain later today—to express the condolences of the American people and to offer whatever assistance that we can as they investigate what has proven to be an awful tragedy. Our teams are in close contact, and we're working to confirm how many Americans may have been onboard. Germany and Spain are among our strongest allies in the world, and our message to them is that, as their steadfast friend and ally, America stands with them at this moment of sorrow.

Now, it is a great pleasure to welcome President Ghani to the White House. As many of you know, President Ghani spent time here in the United States, as a student and as a scholar. He happened to go to Columbia University, where we both studied, and then spent time at the World Bank just down the street from here. And so his life reflects, in many ways, the friendship and mutual respect between Americans and Afghans. And in that spirit, Mr. President, I want to extend to you the warmest of welcomes.

President Ghani's presence here today, along with Chief Executive Abdullah, underscores Afghanistan's progress. In last year's election, millions of Afghans defied the threats from the Taliban and bravely cast their ballots. In the spirit of compromise and putting their interests behind the interests of the nation, President Ghani and Dr. Abdullah ensured the first peaceful and democratic transfer of power in Afghanistan's history. And together they now lead a national unity government that reflects the diversity, the strength and the determination of the Afghan people.

Their government signed the Bilateral Security Agreement between our two countries, and on December 31st, after more than 13 years, America's combat mission in Afghanistan came to a responsible end. Afghan forces now have full responsibility for security across their country. Some 330,000 Afghans serve in the police and security forces, and they are making extraordinary sacrifices—fighting and often dying for their country, and they continue to grow stronger month by month.

Today, we honor the many Afghans—men, women and children—who have given their lives for their country. We salute the more than 2,200 Americans, patriots who made the ultimate sacrifice in Afghanistan, and the many more who were wounded. This morning, President Ghani and Dr. Abdullah visited Arlington National Cemetery to pay their respects to our fallen heroes. We are grateful for that gesture of gratitude, and we know it meant a lot to the families as well. We'll see the bonds again between our people on display when President Ghani has an opportunity to address Congress tomorrow.

So with a new government in Afghanistan and with the end of our combat mission, this visit is an opportunity to begin a new chapter between our two nations. President Ghani and Dr. Abdullah, I thank you both for your strong support of the partnership between our two nations. And yesterday, they had a chance to spend time at Camp David with our respective teams, and had excellent discussions on how we can move forward together. Today, guided by our Strategic Partnership, we focused on several areas.

First, we agreed to continue to keep in place our close security cooperation. Afghanistan remains a very dangerous place, and insurgents still launch attacks, including cowardly suicide bombings against civilians. President Ghani is pursuing reforms to further strengthen Afghan security forces, including respect for human rights. And as part of the ongoing NATO mission, the United States will continue to train, advise and assist Afghan security forces.

As we announced yesterday, we'll work with Congress on funding to sustain 352,000 Afghan police and troops through 2017. At the same time, we'll continue to conduct targeted counterterrorism operations, and we agreed to maintain a dialogue on our counterterrorism partnership in the years ahead.

At our peak four years ago, the United States had more than 100,000 troops in Afghanistan. In support of today's narrow missions, we have just under 10,000 troops there. Last year, I announced a timeline for drawing down our forces further, and I've made it clear that we're determined to preserve the gains our troops have won. President Ghani has requested some flexibility on our drawdown timelines. I've consulted with General Campbell in Afghanistan and my national security team, and I've decided that we will maintain our current posture of 9,800 troops through the end of this year.

The specific trajectory of the 2016 drawdown will be established later this year to enable our final consolidation to a Kabul-based embassy presence by the end of 2016. This flexibility reflects our reinvigorated partnership with Afghanistan, which is aimed at making Afghanistan secure and preventing it from being used to launch terrorist attacks. Reconciliation and a political settlement remain the surest way to achieve the full drawdown of U.S. and foreign troops from Afghanistan in a way that safeguards international interests and peace in Afghanistan, as well as U.S. national security interests.

Second—and since the best way to ensure Afghanistan's progress is a political settlement—we're going to continue to support an Afghan-led reconciliation process. President Ghani, you've shown bold leadership in reaching out to Pakistan, which is critical to the pursuit of peace. Afghanistan and the United States agree on what the Taliban must do, which is break with al Qaeda, renounce violence, and abide by Afghan laws, including protections for women and minorities.

Third, we'll continue to support the national unity government in its efforts to truly serve the Afghan people. We discussed the urgent need, with parliament's support, to seat a full cabinet. President Ghani, in your inaugural address you spoke forcefully about the need to combat corruption, uphold rule of law, and strengthen democratic institutions—and the United States very much commends you for those efforts. And you moved many Afghans with your eloquent tribute to your wife and partner, First Lady Rula Ghani. America will continue to be your partner in advancing the rights and dignity of all Afghans, including women and girls.

And, finally, we'll continue to support the development that underpins stability and improves the lives of the Afghan people. Over the years, there have been major gains—dramatic improvements in public health, life expectancy, literacy, including for millions of girls who are in school. President Ghani is a leading expert on development, and I've been impressed by the reforms that he's pursuing to make Afghanistan more self-reliant. He wants to empower Afghans in these efforts, and that's why, under the new development partnership that we announced yesterday, U.S. economic assistance will increasingly go through Afghan institutions, in support of Afghan priorities, with an emphasis on accountability, performance and achieving results.

In closing, I'd note that, as many of you know, President Ghani is, by training, an anthropologist—as was my mother. It's been said that, "The purpose of anthropology is to make the world safe for human differences." Afghanistan, and our world, is marked by incredible diversity and differences of history, and culture and faiths. But I believe that the progress that we've made on this visit will advance the goal for which so many of your citizens, Mr. President, have sacrificed over the years—the goal of making our two countries, and the world, safer.

President Ghani, Chief Executive Abdullah, thank you both for your leadership and your partnership. America's combat mission in Afghanistan may be over, but our commitment to the Afghanistan people—that will endure.

President Ghani.

PRESIDENT GHANI: President Obama, first of all, I'd like to express the deep sympathies of the government and the people of Afghanistan to German and Spanish families and governments. Both of these countries took part in the ISAF coalition. They have made major commitments and they've sacrificed in Afghanistan.

I'd like to take this opportunity to pay tribute to those common sacrifices and, simultaneously, take the opportunity to pay tribute to the 2,215 American servicemen and women who paid the ultimate sacrifice; more than 22,000 American soldiers who have been wounded in action; civilians, numerous contractors and others. You stood shoulder-to-shoulder with us, and I'd like to say thank you.

I would also like to thank the American taxpayer for his and her hard-earned dollars that have enabled us. Yesterday at the Pentagon, I saw a young girl; her name is Reese. And her father came out of retirement, out of reserve, to serve again in Afghanistan. She is sending a care package every week to her father. And I want to thank her and the fathers of all other American children who are making sure that their parents are helping us and standing next to us.

Reese, I promised, now has 3 million Afghan sisters in school. And those sisters are dreaming of achievements that whatever career path, and hopefully one day we'll see an Afghan woman president. It should not be soon—it should not be too far, because we soon—we now have four women in the cabinet. That's 20 percent of our cabinet are women. I hope that some other countries will match us. That we are intent.

And thank you for the reference to Afghanistan's First Lady. She was delighted to have an opportunity to speak to Mrs. Obama. She's devoted her life to the most underprivileged of Afghans, and all of us are committed to make sure that 36 percent of Afghans that live below poverty will have—will live with dignity and one day not in the distant future see prosperity.

Dr. Abdullah and I are grateful for the reception that you've accorded us, Mr. President. Your national security team has gone out of its way to engage in intensive, comprehensive discussion, and both of us would like to thank Secretary Kerry for the loss of hours of sleep we caused you, and for your very able diplomacy and catalyzing the unity that today is on display. The government of national unity is going to be an enduring phenomena, and both of us stand for the unity against the divisions that our opponents and enemies had hoped for.

This unity is a reflection of the desire of the Afghan public to overcome the last 200 years of our political history where rarely public figures have chosen the country before themselves. We are committed in this regard to emulate the founding fathers and mothers of the United States, where national interest would stand above personal or factional interests.

I'm glad that the security transition is completed. You fulfilled your promise to your people, and we fulfilled our promise to our people.

Afghans, for millennia, they've guarded our homeland and have a reputation for serving. The last years were an exception when we needed help, and we're grateful that help was provided, but we are pleased that the security transition has been met according to the timeline that you set. Today the combat role of the United States and Afghanistan is over.

But the train, advise and assist mission is a vital part of our collective interests and collective endeavors. Tragedy brought us together; interests now unite us. And we can assure you that the government of national unity has revitalized the partnership, and looks at this partnership with the United States as foundational not just for Afghanistan's stability but for regional and global stability.

Much binds us together, and the flexibility that has been provided for 2015 will be used to accelerate reforms, to ensure that the Afghan National Security Forces are much better led, equipped, trained, and are focused on their fundamental mission.

I'm pleased to say that the departure of 120,000 international troops has not brought about the security gap or the collapse that was often anticipated. I'd like to pay tribute at this moment to the continuous sacrifice of the Afghan security forces, civilians, and a patriotic nation.

Our patriotism is part of, simultaneously, our internationalism. We are unique in that we have embraced democratic ways. We are very proud of our Islamic civilization that is in Islam. That is truly in dialogue with the word, and we have the capacity to speak truth to terror. They do not speak for Islam—we do. And it's the genuine Islam that is interested in dialogue between civilizations and cooperation and endeavor forward.

On regional cooperation, we have taken both in novel steps—we do hope that these steps would be reciprocated, because the threats that exist, the changing ecology of terror, are making it imperative that all governments cooperate with each other.

Today, the state system as we have known it is under attack. These are not classic national liberation movements; these are destructive, nihilistic movements. And it's essential that we confront them with vigor and determination. But we must differentiate between those and Afghan citizens who desire peace.

Any political difference, anything that defines us must be resolved politically, and we have shown the wisdom and determination that we can arrive at unity of purpose. So our commitment to peace is clear. What we require is reciprocity so that Afghan patriots will choose the country over themselves and unite in resolving whatever might be that divides us.

But we will not have peace with those who use our territory as a proxy for other purposes, as a battleground for alien forces, or as a launching pad for global terrorism.

This trip has provided us an opportunity to have a comprehensive overview, and I again want to express thank you for your commitment to submit a bill to Congress for support of our security forces 2017.

There's much work that lies ahead of us. And the flexibility that has been provided will be used to maximum effect to accelerate reforms to ensure that our security forces honor human rights; that they internalize the practices that binds an army, a police force, a secret service to the people. Violence against our people has no place within our security culture, and we will overcome those types of legacies.

It's again a pleasure to be standing next to a graduate of Columbia University. There's much that unites us. And your mother was an inspiration to us. I understand that the president of the World Bank actually got the job because he invoked your mother's teachings to convince you that an anthropologist could lead the World Bank. So thank you for according him that rare opportunity.

PRESIDENT OBAMA: He's doing a great job.

. . .

Source: White House. Available online at https://obamawhitehouse.archives.gov/the-press-office/2015/03/24/remarks-president-obama-and-president-ghani-afghanistan-joint-press-conf.

ANALYSIS

President Ghani, an ethnic Pashtun and Afghanistan's former finance minister, made his first visit to the United States after winning a hotly contested election against Abdullah Abdullah in September 2014. The two agreed to form a unity government, hence Abdullah's presence at this joint press conference too.

President Obama and President Ghani committed themselves to furthering the strategic partnership between the United States and Afghanistan in spite of the change in mission for U.S. forces. Although not mentioned at this press conference, the United States had quietly decided not to withdraw more than half of the 9,800 troops that remained in Afghanistan because of a recent upturn in attacks by the Taliban.

- **Document 81: Introduction of the Newly Appointed Leader of Islamic Emirate, Mullah Akhtar Mohammad**
- **When:** September 2, 2015
- **Where:** Unknown

- **Significance:** This Taliban press release announced the appointment of Mullah Akhtar Mohammad as their new leader and also formally announced the death of Mullah Omar nearly two years earlier.

DOCUMENT

The prominent figureheads of Jihad generally possess distinct leadership qualities. They are usually either naturally gifted with these capabilities or they master them through learning and studying other Jihadi leaders. Due to their deep sincerity and devotion, these Jihadi leaders are granted with exceptional divine generosity, support and benevolence as Almighty Allah says:

(And as for those who strive to meet Us—We will surely guide them in Our ways. And verily, ALLAH is with those who do good.) [Al-Ankaboot:69]

The Islamic Emirate of Afghanistan is considered an impregnable front of Jihad and struggle against international infidelity and tyranny whose founding founders are by the grace of Almighty Allah bequeathed with extraordinary proficiency and skills as leaders and guides.

The founder of Islamic Emirate of Afghanistan himself, the late Mullah Mohammad Umar Mujahid (may his soul rest in peace) was a living anthology of such leadership qualities. Amidst the battlefield of Jihad and combating international infidelity, he successfully managed to transfer these lofty aptitudes of Muslim leadership qualities to several of his Mujahidin brothers who were his intimate colleagues, struggling together in the thorny path of establishing the sacred and sovereign system of Allah, the Almighty.

His Excellency, the late Amir-ul-Momineen Mullah Mohammad Umar Mujahid (may his soul rest in peace) was the spiritual and moral guide of new students of the Jihadi madrassa [Mujahidin] as well as being their military leader. The Umari Jihadi Madrassa trained and graduated many high caliber personalities during his lifetime and under his leadership, each one perfectly capable of guiding the Muslim masses in the most critical junctures of this era.

It is established religious foundations rather than particular personalities which play a pivotal role in ideological and Jihadi movements. Everything here is organized on the basis of Jihad and ideology. Teachings of the Holy Quran and noble deeds of our Holy Prophet (peace be upon him) and his rightly guided Caliphs (may Allah be pleased with all of them) are the role models for the followers of these movements.

The core responsibility of the leadership in such ideological movements is merely to educate its members and followers both morally and ideologically and to impart them with spiritual passion and commitment.

Upon founding the Taliban Islamic Movement and establishment of the Islamic Emirate, his Excellency late Amir-ul-Momineen Mullah Mohammad Umar Mujahid (may his soul rest in peace) mentored for future leadership several Mujahidin who displayed foresight and leadership traits, capable of leading this Jihadi caravan to its goal and destination even in the most critical circumstances of Jihad and persistent struggle. Such fearless and courageous personalities who were undaunted by the most difficult of conditions nor influenced by dangerous temporal or spatial circumstances.

Among these foresighted vigilant personalities and pupils of the enduring Umari Madrassa is the newly selected leader of the Islamic Emirate, His Excellency Mullah Akhtar Mohammad Mansur (may Allah safeguard him) who practically handled leadership affairs of the Islamic Emirate during the lifetime of late Amir-ul-Momineen (may his soul rest in peace) and was appointed as the new head (leader) of the Islamic Emirate by Ahl hal wal Aqd dignitaries of the Islamic Emirate, religious scholars, Jihadi leaders and various other public figures after the announcement of his (RA) passing away.

Although the new leader of the Islamic Emirate is a well-recognized figure in all Jihadi spheres whoever to better acquaint his Excellency Mullah Akhtar Mohammad Mansur to all the Mujahidin of the Islamic Emirate and the general masses of the Muslim world having affection with the Islamic Emirate, it is deemed appropriate to write down a few lines about his life and personality.

. . .

His foundational role in the Islamic Movement of Taliban:

After the collapse of communist regime inside Afghanistan and the outbreak of civil war in 1992, Mansur Sahib laid down his arms just like all the sincere Mujahidin and did not support any party in the illegitimate war for power.

His Excellency Mansur Sahib, who was a renowned Mujahid at the time, abandoned all factional activities resembling other well-known local Jihadi and military personalities like the late Mullah Mohammad Rabbani, late Haji Mullah Mohammad and late Mullah Bor Jan. He started living an ordinary life and began engaging in various educational and training activities.

In 1994 when the Islamic Movement of Taliban was founded by His Excellency Amir-ul-Momineen late Mullah Mohammad Umar Mujahid (may his soul rest in peace), Mansur Sahib played a crucial role in the organization and development of this movement. Due to his Jihadi and administrative proficiencies, he was tasked major responsibilities by the then head of the Islamic Movement of Taliban which are as following:

1. After the conquest of Kandahar province and subsequent successes of Taliban Islamic Movement in south western zone, His Excellency Amir-ul-Momineen late Mullah Mohammad Umar Mujahid (may his soul rest in peace) appointed Mansur Sahib as the director general of Kandahar Airport due to the trust he placed in the administrative and Jihadi talents displayed by him.

2. When Kandahar province fell to the Taliban, he was given the responsibility of air force and air defense system of Kandahar.

3. After the conquest of the capital Kabul in 1996, he was appointed as the minister of aviation and tourism.

4. Simultaneously with heading the ministry, he was placed in charge of the Emirate's air-force and air-defense in the ministry of defense on the basis of a special decree of late Amir-ul-Momineen.

. . .

On top of several reconstructive services in various civil and military fields of the Islamic Emirate, his biggest accomplishment was his repairing a great asset of Afghanistan (the air force), its damaged planes and mostly destroyed airports.

. . .

Armed resistance against the American invasion:

After the American invasion of Afghanistan on 7 October 2001, Mansur Sahib began his armed resistance against them. In his Jihadi lifetime, this period was fraught with difficulties and challenges for Mansur Sahib.

Besides being a member of the supreme leading council of Islamic Emirate, he was given the additional responsibility of Jihadi in-charge of Kandahar province by the late Amir-ul-Momineen (may his soul rest in peace).

Like other provinces of Afghanistan, Kandahar was in need of a strong, experienced and sincere Jihadi commander because the Americans planned and launched all their military strategies against Mujahidin for the entire south west zone from Kandahar. This was the reason that following Helmand, the second largest contingent of American, Canadian and other foreign troops were based in Kandahar and the second largest base after Bagram airbase was also built here.

But due to his Jihadi acumen, Mansur Sahib managed to sketch successful Jihadi plans against the foreign invading troops in Kandahar, rendering their well-known generals and distinguished military planners of the time inept in its combat and prevention.

Mansur Sahib's Jihadi ingenuity saw him take charge in drawing and managing Jihadi plans for the entire south-western zone of Afghanistan after due consultations with the Jihadi in-charges of neighboring provinces, carrying out successful fatal attacks against the invading crusaders in Kandahar as well as in Uruzgan, Zabul and Helmand provinces.

Mujahidin of the Islamic Emirate extraordinarily managed to break the heavily fortified Kandahar central prison in the years 2003 and 2008, freeing over one thousand and five hundred captive Mujahidin each time from the brutal hands of the enemy. These events also took place when Mansur Sahib was the in-charge of Kandahar.

As the Deputy Head of the Islamic Emirate:

In 2007 when the former deputy head of the Islamic Emirate Alhaj Mullah Obaidullah Akhund was arrested, the late Amir-ul-Momineen (may his soul rest in peace) appointed Mullah Akhtar Mohammad Mansur as the second deputy alongside Mullah Baradar Akhond, the deputy head of the Islamic Emirate, and instructed him to concurrently continue his responsibility as the Jihadi in-charge of Kandahar province as it was a central fighting front against the foreign invaders.

In 2010 when the deputy head of Islamic Emirate Alhaj Mullah Obaidullah Akhund was martyred in the detention of Pakistani forces and Mullah Abdul Ghani Baradar, second deputy head of the Islamic Emirate was arrested by joint American and Pakistani forces in the city of Karachi, the late Amir-ul-Momineen Mullah Mohammad Umar Mujahid (may his soul rest in peace) appointed Mansur Sahib as the deputy head and general in-charge of all operational activities of the Islamic Emirate.

It was a time when the Jihadi resistance was facing tough challenges in Afghanistan as 30,000 extra troops were deployed by the Obama administration and over a hundred thousand foreign invading forces equipped with state-of-the-art technology and supported by 350,000 internal mercenary forces were actively fighting Mujahidin in each and every corner of our country.

On the one hand, it was nearly impossible for the leader of the Islamic Emirate, late Mullah Mohammad Umar Mujahid (may his soul rest in peace) to appear and guide the resistance militarily due to the critical security situation and on the other hand, the military and administrative vacuum in Jihadi fronts tipped the balance of resistance in the favor of the enemy.

There was huge military pressure on the Mujahidin on top of the increasing political and propaganda pressures. Many Jihadi in-charges were martyred on the battle field and a number of them were arrested. In those most daunting circumstances, the late Amir-ul-Momineen Mullah Mohammad Umar Mujahid (may his soul rest in peace) placed the enormous task of managing Mujahidin against the invading crusaders on the shoulders of Mansur Sahib and appointed no other deputy to support him.

Respected Mansur Sahib, with the divine help of Almighty Allah and aid of the leading council of the Islamic Emirate, successfully managed to control and lead the ongoing armed resistance in such an admirable way that no leadership vacuum was ever felt by the Mujahidin.

It was the year 2010 which would prove to be the most fatal and costly year for foreign crusading forces inside Afghanistan. Mujahidin managed to carry out their most fatal campaign against the enemy during the span of that year, forcing them to confess to the deaths of 770 foreign soldiers.

Similarly under the successful leadership of Mansur Sahib, Mujahidin managed to liberate vast areas of our beloved homeland from the enemy and establish an organized Islamic system of life in them.

After the passing away of Amir-ul-Momineen Mohammad Umar Mujahid (may his soul rest in peace):

On 23 April 2013, when Amir-ul-Momineen Mullah Mohammad Umar Mujahid passed away, some members of the leading council of the Islamic Emirate, authentic scholars, envoys and messengers of late Mullah Mohammad Umar Mujahid and his permanent colleagues who lived with him till the last moments of his life pledged their allegiance to Mansur Sahib and appointed him as the new leader of the Islamic Emirate.

Since 2013 was considered the last year of resistance and struggle for Mujahidin against the foreign invading crusaders therefore several key members of the supreme leading council of the Islamic Emirate and authentic religious scholars together decided on concealing the tragic news of passing away of His Excellency, late Amir-ul-Momineen Mullah Mohammad Umar Mujahid (may his soul rest in peace) and keep this secret limited to the very few colleagues who were already informed of this incorrigible loss. One of the main reasons behind this decision was due to the fact that 2013 was considered the final year of power testing between the Mujahidin and foreign invaders who in turn had announced that at the end of 2014, all military operations by foreign troops would be concluded.

It was for these Jihadi Masaleh (interests/considerations) that this depressing news was concealed in an extraordinary way up until 30 July 2015.

. . .

His appointment as new leader from Shariah point of view:

. . .

It can confidently be proclaimed that his appointment took place in full compliance with Islamic Shariah law therefore hundreds of thousands of other ordinary people from all parts of the country and hundreds of authentic scholars of the Holy Quran and the Traditions of the Holy Prophet (peace be upon him) accepted his leadership, labeled it totally legitimate and pledged their allegiances accordingly.

His leading and charismatic personality:

The newly appointed leader of the Islamic Emirate, His Excellency Amir-ul-Mumineen Mullah Akhtar Mohammad (Mansur), may Allah safeguard him, is considered an effective, influential and dominant personality from among the foundational members of the Islamic Emirate.

He is naturally bequeathed with unique leading and guiding capabilities.

Piety, sincerity, Jihadi vision, political acumen and administrative qualities in implementing various tasks are characteristics which individuate him.

His Excellency, Mullah Akhtar Mohammad Mansur thoroughly follows the footsteps of his predecessor and Jihadi leader, late Mulla Mohammad Umar Mujahid (may his soul rest in peace) in implementing all the Jihadi activities of the Islamic Emirate. Safeguarding lofty Jihadi ideals, liberation of our beloved homeland from foreign occupation and the implementation of Shariah system therein are the main objectives of his Jihad and struggle. According to the teachings of the Holy Quran, he carefully listens to all the useful and constructive advices and suggestions of all colleagues in executing all minor and major tasks. He tries to assign duties to competent people and subsequently trusts them thoroughly. He always recommends to the responsible people to have mercy and pity on the ordinary masses.

He greatly emphasizes on this point, "The Islamic Emirate is a common abode of all Afghans therefore all should be reflected herein."

His vision and ideological perspectives:

His Excellency, Mullah Akhtar Mohammad Mansur belongs to people of Ahl Sunnah wal Jama'ah (Sunnah and Consensus) and follows the path of the great Imam (jurist) Hazrat Abu Hanifa (may Allah bless him).

He is fully conscious of the delicacy and complexity of all contemporary regional and international politics.

While facing him, one can easily discern his serenity, gravity and dignity. Simplicity and straightforwardness are his common companions.

He has special interest in studying the role model of our Holy Prophet (peace be upon him) as well as the lives of his lofty companions (may Allah be pleased with them). He is always eager and interested to hear about the military situations of battlefields whenever meeting Mujahidin of the Islamic Emirate.

Despite all his many Jihadi and administrative activities and responsibilities, he regularly and keenly follows the media and subsequently gives distinct meaningful recommendations to Jihadi writers, particularly to the workers of the cultural and publication department of the Islamic Emirate of Afghanistan.

His routine life and some of his characteristics:

His Excellency, Mullah Mohammad Mansur assumes his day with the recitation of the Holy Quran. He remains in regular contact with Jihadi fronts and the military in-charges. He thoroughly checks all the military planning against the enemy and fully stresses upon all Jihadi commanders to protect the lives and properties of all civilian masses and to deal with them in sympathetic and dignified manner.

As a dominant military commander, he treats his Jihadi colleagues, Mujahidin and ordinary masses in respectful and compassionate manner. He pays full attention and renders due respect to the words and advices of scholars, teachers and all elderly people in public and private meetings. He gives special attention to looking after the orphans and families of Mujahidin who have laid down their lives in the path of Jihad. He takes due care in all political matters and carefully listens to views and suggestions of all discerning people in this regard.

He particularly loves and has interest in marksmanship. He considers the implementation of Jihadi exercises the most suitable and required sport of our time.

He speaks less and tries to listen more to other people. He likes and wears loose, neat and clean clothes. He dislikes and avoids extravagance and prodigality in dressing, eating and all other needs of everyday life.

The main and foremost purpose of his life is the well-organization of Jihadi activities and their subsequent follow-up. In this fashion he remains busy from dawn to dust.

May Almighty Allah safeguard him! Amin!

Source: Wayback Machine. Available online at https://web.archive.org/web/20150902153835/http://shahamat-english.com:80/introduction-of-the-newly-appointed-leader-of-islamic-emirate-mullah-akhtar-mohammad-mansur-may-allah-safeguard-hi/.

ANALYSIS

Mullah Omar had led the Taliban since its birth and, like most of the group's leadership, went into hiding—most likely in Pakistan—after the U.S. invasion in 2001. Rumors of ill health occasionally circulated, but he died of tuberculosis in 2013 in secret. As this press release related, the Taliban elected to not reveal his death because they did not want to distract from their final year of jihad against the United States prior to its withdrawal in 2014.

Mullah Mansour had fought the Soviets and the Americans while also showing some skill as an administrator during Taliban rule in the 1990s. Like many in the Taliban, he had a primarily religious education prior to earning respect on the battlefield. The press release noted that his selection complied with Sharia law and was strongly supported by the Taliban's leadership, but rumors circulated that many viewed his accession to power as illegitimate.

- **Document 82: Barack Obama, Statement by the President on Afghanistan**
- **When:** October 15, 2015
- **Where:** Washington, D.C.
- **Significance:** President Obama announced that U.S. troop strength would remain unchanged for the next year and that the United States would continue to operate from several Afghan bases.

DOCUMENT

Good morning. Last December—more than 13 years after our nation was attacked by al Qaeda on 9/11—America's combat mission in Afghanistan came to a responsible end. That milestone was achieved thanks to the courage and the skill of our military, our intelligence, and civilian personnel. They served there with extraordinary skill and valor, and it's worth remembering especially the more than 2,200 American patriots who made the ultimate sacrifice in Afghanistan.

I visited our troops in Afghanistan last year to thank them on behalf of a grateful nation. I told them they could take great pride in the progress that they helped achieve. They struck devastating blows against the al Qaeda leadership in the tribal regions, delivered justice to Osama bin Laden, prevented terrorist attacks, and saved American lives. They pushed the Taliban back so the Afghan people could reclaim their communities, send their daughters to school, and improve their lives. Our troops trained Afghan forces so they could take the lead for their own security and protect Afghans as they voted in historic elections, leading to the first democratic transfer of power in their country's history.

Today, American forces no longer patrol Afghan villages or valleys. Our troops are not engaged in major ground combat against the Taliban. Those missions now belong to Afghans, who are fully responsible for securing their country.

But as I've said before, while America's combat mission in Afghanistan may be over, our commitment to Afghanistan and its people endures. As Commander-in-Chief, I will not allow Afghanistan to be used as safe haven for terrorists to attack our nation again. Our forces therefore remain engaged in two narrow but critical missions—training Afghan forces, and supporting counterterrorism operations against the remnants of al Qaeda. Of course, compared to the 100,000 troops we once had in Afghanistan, today fewer than 10,000 remain, in support of these very focused missions.

I meet regularly with my national security team, including commanders in Afghanistan, to continually assess, honestly, the situation on the ground—to determine where our strategy is working and where we may need greater flexibility. I have insisted, consistently, that our strategy focus on the development of a sustainable

Afghan capacity and self-sufficiency. And when we've needed additional forces to advance that goal, or we've needed to make adjustments in terms of our timetables, then we've made those adjustments. Today, I want to update the American people on our efforts.

Since taking the lead for security earlier this year, Afghan forces have continued to step up. This has been the first fighting season where Afghans have largely been on their own. And they are fighting for their country bravely and tenaciously. Afghan forces continue to hold most urban areas. And when the Taliban has made gains, as in Kunduz, Afghan forces backed by coalition support have been able to push them back. This has come at a very heavy price. This year alone, thousands of Afghan troops and police have lost their lives, as have many Afghan civilians.

At the same time, Afghan forces are still not as strong as they need to be. They're developing critical capabilities—intelligence, logistics, aviation, command and control. And meanwhile, the Taliban has made gains, particularly in rural areas, and can still launch deadly attacks in cities, including Kabul. Much of this was predictable. We understood that as we transitioned, that the Taliban would try to exploit some of our movements out of particular areas, and that it would take time for Afghan security forces to strengthen. Pressure from Pakistan has resulted in more al Qaeda coming into Afghanistan, and we've seen the emergence of an ISIL presence. The bottom line is, in key areas of the country, the security situation is still very fragile, and in some places there is risk of deterioration.

Fortunately, in President Ghani and Chief Executive Abdullah there is a national unity government that supports a strong partnership with the United States. During their visit earlier this year, President Ghani and I agreed to continue our counterterrorism cooperation, and he has asked for continued support as Afghan forces grow stronger.

Following consultations with my entire national security team, as well as our international partners and members of Congress, President Ghani and Chief Executive Abdullah, I'm therefore announcing the following steps, which I am convinced offer the best possibility for lasting progress in Afghanistan.

First, I've decided to maintain our current posture of 9,800 troops in Afghanistan through most of next year, 2016. Their mission will not change. Our troops will continue to pursue those two narrow tasks that I outlined earlier—training Afghan forces and going after al Qaeda. But maintaining our current posture through most of next year, rather than a more rapid drawdown, will allow us to sustain our efforts to train and assist Afghan forces as they grow stronger—not only during this fighting season, but into the next one.

Second, I have decided that instead of going down to a normal embassy presence in Kabul by the end of 2016, we will maintain 5,500 troops at a small number of bases, including at Bagram, Jalalabad in the east, and Kandahar in the south.

Again, the mission will not change. Our troops will focus on training Afghans and counterterrorism operations. But these bases will give us the presence and the reach our forces require to achieve their mission. In this sense, Afghanistan is a key piece of the network of counterterrorism partnerships that we need, from South Asia to Africa, to deal more broadly with terrorist threats quickly and prevent attacks against our homeland.

Third, we will work with allies and partners to align the steps I am announcing today with their own presence in Afghanistan after 2016. In Afghanistan, we are part of a 42-nation coalition, and our NATO allies and partners can continue to play an indispensable role in helping Afghanistan strengthen its security forces, including respect for human rights.

And finally, because governance and development remain the foundation for stability and progress in Afghanistan, we will continue to support President Ghani and the national unity government as they pursue critical reforms. New provincial governors have been appointed, and President Ghani is working to combat corruption, strengthen institutions, and uphold rule of law. As I told President Ghani and Chief Executive Abdullah yesterday, efforts that deliver progress and justice for the Afghan people will continue to have the strong support of the United States. And we cannot separate the importance of governance with the issues of security. The more effective these reforms happen, the better off the security situation is going to be.

We also discussed American support of an Afghan-led reconciliation process. By now it should be clear to the Taliban and all who oppose Afghanistan's progress the only real way to achieve the full drawdown of U.S. and foreign troops from Afghanistan is through a lasting political settlement with the Afghan government. Likewise, sanctuaries for the Taliban and other terrorists must end. Next week, I'll host Prime Minister Sharif of Pakistan, and I will continue to urge all parties in the region to press the Taliban to return to peace talks and to do their part in pursuit of the peace that Afghans deserve.

In closing, I want to speak directly to those whose lives are most directly affected most by the decisions I'm announcing today. To the Afghan people, who have suffered so much—Americans' commitment to you and to a secure, stable and unified Afghanistan, that remains firm. Our two nations have forged a strategic partnership for the long term. And as you defend and build your country, today is a reminder that the United States keeps our commitments.

And to our men and women in uniform—I know this means that some of you will rotate back into Afghanistan. With the end of our combat mission, this is not like 2010, when nearly 500 Americans were killed and many more were injured. But still, Afghanistan remains dangerous; 25 brave Americans have given their lives there this year.

I do not send you into harm's way lightly. It's the most solemn decision I make. I know the wages of war in the wounded warriors I visit in the hospital and in the grief of Gold Star families. But as your Commander-in-Chief, I believe this mission is vital to our national security interests in preventing terrorist attacks against our citizens and our nation.

And to the American people—I know that many of you have grown weary of this conflict. As you are well aware, I do not support the idea of endless war, and I have repeatedly argued against marching into open-ended military conflicts that do not serve our core security interests.

Yet given what's at stake in Afghanistan, and the opportunity for a stable and committed ally that can partner with us in preventing the emergence of future threats, and the fact that we have an international coalition, I am firmly convinced that we should make this extra effort. In the Afghan government, we have a serious partner who wants our help. And the majority of the Afghan people share our goals. We have a bilateral security agreement to guide our cooperation. And every single day, Afghan forces are out there fighting and dying to protect their country. They're not looking for us to do it for them.

I'm speaking of the Afghan army cadet who grew up seeing bombings and attacks on innocent civilians who said, "because of this, I took the decision to join the army, to try and save innocent people's lives." Or the police officer training to defuse explosives. "I know it's dangerous work," he says, but "I have always had a dream of wearing the uniform of Afghanistan, serving my people and defending my country."

Or the Afghan commando, a hardened veteran of many missions, who said, "If I start telling you the stories of my life, I might start crying." He serves, he said, because, "the faster we bring peace, the faster we can bring education, and the stronger our unity will grow. Only if these things happen will Afghanistan be able to stand up for itself."

My fellow Americans, after so many years of war, Afghanistan will not be a perfect place. It's a poor country that will have to work hard on its development. There will continue to be contested areas. But Afghans like these are standing up for their country. If they were to fail, it would endanger the security of us all. And we've made an enormous investment in a stable Afghanistan. Afghans are making difficult but genuine progress. This modest but meaningful extension of our presence—while sticking to our current, narrow missions—can make a real difference. It's the right thing to do.

Source: White House. Available online at https://obamawhitehouse.archives.gov/the-press-office/2015/10/15/statement-president-afghanistan.

ANALYSIS

By October 2015, it seemed clear that Afghan security forces—even after receiving U.S. training and support—could not effectively neutralize the Taliban. In fact, many of the Pashtun-dominated provinces showed heavy Taliban activity. Furthermore, ISIS had sought to expand its presence in Afghanistan through an affiliated group, Wilayat Khorasan, although the Taliban challenged the group's presence.

This degraded security environment left President Obama no choice but to leave U.S. troop levels at 9,800. Furthermore, he canceled plans to limit U.S. forces to those linked to the U.S. Embassy in Kabul and instead allowed U.S. forces to operate from the major airbases where they had operated since the war began. This would allow the United States to continue training and advising Afghan forces for the tough fighting that continued.

- **Document 83: Statement by the Leadership Council of Islamic Emirate Regarding the Martyrdom of Amir ul Mumineen Mullah Akhtar Muhammad Mansour and the Election of the New Leader**

- **When:** June 13, 2016
- **Where:** Unknown
- **Significance:** Only three years after taking power and less than a year since his formal introduction, the Taliban announced the death of Mullah Mansour and introduced his successor, Mullah Haibatullah Akhundzada.

DOCUMENT

Translation: *No calamity befalls, but with the Leave of Allah, and whosoever believes in Allah, He guides his heart, and Allah is the All-Knower of everything. Obey Allah, and obey the Messenger (Muhammad), but if you turn away, then the duty of Our Messenger is only to convey (the Message) clearly. Allah! La ilaha illa Huwa (none has the right to be worshipped but He), and in Allah (Alone), therefore, let the believers put their trust. (At-Taghabun, 11–13)*

We accept and are pleased with Allah SWT as our Lord, and with Islam as our faith, and with Muhammad PBUH as a Prophet and a Messenger.

The Islamic Emirate of Afghanistan, with submission to divine providence and unwavering faith announces that the leader of the Islamic Emirate—Amir ul Mumineen Mullah Akhtar Muhammad Mansour (may Allah Almighty accept him)—was martyred by the American tyrant's unmanned drone aircraft in the border area between Kandahar's Registan and Balochistan's Nushki on 14 Shaban 1437 Lunar Hijri (corresponding with 1 Jawza 1395 Solar Hijri), *surely to Allah we belong and to Him we must return.*

The Leadership Council of the Islamic Emirate of Afghanistan forwards to our sympathizers, Mujahideen, the Afghan nation, the Islamic Ummah and particularly to the martyred Amir ul Mumineen's bereaved family its deepest condolences and prays to Allah Almighty for the acceptance of Amir ul Mumineen's martyrdom and bestowment of Jannat ul Firdous. May Allah Almighty have mercy on Shaheed Mansour Saheb and give his family, relatives, Mujahideen and the Islamic Emirate patience, reward and a befitting replacement in this time of great tragedy. *Ameen Ya Rabbal Aalameen*

Muslim Brothers!

History bears witness that the Islamic Ummah's virtuous movements have always been faced with the martyrdom or death of its leaders or other similar calamities. Yet such afflictions have never shaken the feet of righteous Muslims and instead have strengthened their faith and with great determination and strong faith they have continued their righteous campaign.

"And many a Prophet (i.e. many from amongst the Prophets) fought (in Allah's Cause) and along with him (fought) large bands of religious learned men. But they never lost heart for that which did befall them in Allah's Way, nor did they weaken nor degrade themselves. And Allah loves As-Sabirin (the patient ones)."

(Al Imran :146)

The martyred Amir ul Mumineen (may Allah accept him) was a servant of Allah and a Mujahid of the righteous path. He fulfilled his responsibilities with judicious and proud manner and remained steadfast in his determinations till his last breath. In his brief period of leadership he left examples of faith, determination and pride which the campaigners of justice and the Mujahideen will forever recall with pride.

The deceased—despite the difficulties of time and space—refused to submit to the Global Tyrant's demands and threats, neither did he accept anyone's imposed or false proposals, nor was he scared of their threats and no foreign and internal conspiracies and political pressures wavered his determination.

The martyred Mansour Saheb fulfilled the Islamic Emirate's leadership role in the footsteps of his predecessor Mullah Muhammad Omar Mujahid (may Allah have Mercy on him) until—with proud stance, strong faith and complete reliance on Allah—he met his Lord while in the process of a Jihadi journey.

Since it is a religious duty to install another leader for the Muslims with the martyrdom or passing away of an Imam or Amir, the Islamic Emirate's Leadership Council—composed of numerous Islamic scholars, teachers of Quran and Ahadeeth, righteous politicians and experts of Jihad—called a council of Ahl Hal wal Aqd and after deep contemplation, thought and consultation elected the esteemed **Sheikhul Hadith Maulawi Haibatullah Akhundzada Saheb** as the new leader of the Islamic Emirate and with full their full consensus the Council swore its allegiance to him. Similarly the esteemed **Alhaj Mullah Sirajjuddin Haqqani Saheb** and the son of the deceased Amir ul Mumineen Mullah Muhammad Omar, the esteemed **Maulawi Muhammad Yaqoub Saheb** were elected as his deputies.

The Islamic Emirate's Leadership Council invites all its Mujahideen and our nation towards unity and trust in Allah Almighty. Mujahideen should feel no anxiety. *Alhamdulillah* we have a patronizing Lord. The light of Islam and Jihad has continued to shine these past fourteen hundred years and will guide our path till the Day of Judgement. We must give thanks to our Lord that the Islamic Emirate has a functioning and prosperous governance system. For the continuity and strength of our Islamic system it is therefore the religious duty of all Mujahideen to swear their allegiance to the new Amir ul Mumineen, the esteemed *Sheikhul Hadith Maulawi Haibatullah Akhundzada Saheb* and continue their rightful campaign under his leadership.

Similarly the Leadership and the Leadership Council hopes that all the Islamic Ummah starting from tomorrow—for three days—will fulfill the religious rites for the martyred Amir ul Mumineen Mullah Akhtar Muhammad Mansour (may Allah Almighty have mercy on him) by recitations of the Holy Quran.

Wassalam

The Islamic Emirate of Afghanistan's Leadership Council

18 Shaban 1437 Lunar Hijri

5 Jawza 1395 Solar Hijri

25 May 2016 Gregorian

Source: Islamic Emirate of Afghanistan. Available online at https://alemarah-english.com/?p=52.

ANALYSIS

Mullah Mansour enjoyed a brief public tenure as the Taliban's leader, but this ended on May 21, 2016, when a U.S. Predator drone operating in Pakistan attacked his vehicle, killing him.

His successor, Mullah Akhundzada, is a religious scholar and rumored to have spent much of the war in Afghanistan and not in Pakistan with most of the Taliban's leadership. He also spent time as Mullah Mansour's deputy during his nearly three-year reign. Still, this sudden change in leadership temporarily halted the Taliban's stated plans to launch offensives against the Afghan government in the summer of 2016.

- **Document 84: Barack Obama, Statement by the President on Afghanistan**
- **When:** July 6, 2016
- **Where:** Washington, D.C.
- **Significance:** For the second time, President Obama publicly announced that the United States would maintain higher troop levels in Afghanistan than previously planned.

DOCUMENT

. . .

More than 14 years ago, after al Qaida attacked our nation on 9/11, the United States went to war in Afghanistan against these terrorists and the Taliban that harbored them. Over the years—and thanks to heroic efforts by our military, our intelligence community, our diplomats and our development professionals—we pushed al Qaida out of its camps, helped the Afghan people topple the Taliban and helped them establish a democratic government. We dealt crippling blows to the al Qaida leadership. We delivered justice to Osama bin Laden. And we trained Afghan forces to take responsibility for their own security.

And given that progress, a year and a half ago—in December 2014—America's combat mission in Afghanistan came to a responsible end. Compared to the 100,000 troops we once had there, today, fewer than 10,000 remain. And compared to their previous mission—helping to lead the fight—our forces are now focused on two narrow missions: training and advising Afghan forces, and supporting counterterrorist operations against the remnants of al Qaida as well as other terrorist groups, including ISIL. In short, even as we've maintained a relentless case against those who are threatening us, we are no longer engaged in a major ground war in Afghanistan.

But even these narrow missions continue to be dangerous. Over the past year and a half, 38 Americans—military and civilian—have lost their lives in Afghanistan on behalf of our security. And we honor their sacrifice. We stand with their families in their grief and in their pride. And we resolve to carry on the mission for which they gave their last full measure of devotion.

This is also not America's mission alone. In Afghanistan, we're joined by 41 allies and partners—a coalition that contributes more than 6,000 troops of their own. We have a partner in the Afghan government and the Afghan people, who support a long-term strategic partnership with the United States. And, in fact, Afghans continue to step up. For the second year now, Afghan forces are fully responsible for their own security. Every day, nearly 320,000 Afghan soldiers and police are serving and fighting, and many are giving their lives to defend their country.

To their credit—and in the face of a continued Taliban insurgency and terrorist networks—Afghan forces remain in control of all the major population centers, provincial capitals, major transit routes and most district centers. Afghan forces have beaten back attacks and they've pushed the Taliban out of some areas. Meanwhile, in another milestone, we recently removed the leader of the Taliban, Akhtar Mohammad Mansur.

Nevertheless, the security situation in Afghanistan remains precarious. Even as they improve, Afghan security forces are still not as strong as they need to be. With our help, they're still working to improve critical capabilities such as intelligence, logistics, aviation and command and control. At the same time, the Taliban remains a threat. They have gained ground in some cases. They've continued attacks and suicide bombings, including in Kabul. Because the Taliban deliberately target innocent civilians, more Afghan men, women and children are dying. And often overlooked in the global refugee crisis, millions of Afghans have fled their homes and many have been fleeing their country.

Now, as President and Commander-in-Chief, I've made it clear that I will not allow Afghanistan to be used as safe haven for terrorists to attack our nation again. That's why I constantly review our strategy with my national security team, including our commanders in Afghanistan. In all these reviews, we're guided by the facts, what's happening on the ground, to determine what's working and what needs to be changed. And that's why, at times, I've made adjustments—for example, by slowing the drawdown of our forces and, more recently, by giving U.S. forces more flexibility to support Afghan forces on the ground and in the air. And I strongly believe that it is in our national security interest—especially after all the blood and treasure we've invested in Afghanistan over the years—that we give our Afghan partners the very best opportunity to succeed.

Upon taking command of coalition forces this spring, General Nicholson conducted a review of the security situation in Afghanistan and our military posture. It was good to get a fresh set of eyes. And based on the recommendation of General Nicholson, as well as Secretary Carter and Chairman Dunford, and following extensive consultations with my national security team, as well as Congress and the Afghan government and our international partners, I'm announcing an additional adjustment to our posture.

Instead of going down to 5,500 troops by the end of this year, the United States will maintain approximately 8,400 troops in Afghanistan into next year, through the end of my administration. The narrow missions assigned to our forces will not change. They remain focused on supporting Afghan forces and going after terrorists. But maintaining our forces at this specific level—based on our assessment of the security conditions and the strength of Afghan forces—will allow us to continue to provide tailored support to help Afghan forces continue to improve. From coalition bases in Jalalabad and Kandahar, we'll be able to continue supporting Afghan forces on the ground and in the air. And we continue supporting critical counterterrorism operations.

And in reaffirming the enduring commitment of the United States to Afghanistan and its people, the decision I'm making today can help our allies and partners align their own commitments. As you know, tomorrow, I depart for the NATO Summit in Warsaw, where I'll meet with our coalition partners and Afghan President Ghani and Chief Executive Abdullah. Many of our allies and partners have already stepped forward with commitments of troops and funding so we can keep strengthening Afghan forces through the end of this decade. The NATO Summit will be an opportunity for more allies and partners to affirm their contributions—and I'm confident they will, because all of us have a vital interest in the security and stability of Afghanistan.

My decision today also sends a message to the Taliban and all those who have opposed Afghanistan's progress. You have now been waging war against the Afghan people for many years. You've been unable to prevail. Afghan security forces continue to grow stronger. And the commitment of the international community, including the United States, to Afghanistan and its people will endure. I will say it again—the only way to end this conflict and to achieve a full drawdown of foreign forces from Afghanistan is through a lasting political settlement between the Afghan government and the Taliban. That's the only way. And that is why the United States will continue to strongly support an Afghan-led reconciliation process, and why we call on all countries in the region to end safe havens for militants and terrorists.

Finally, today's decision best positions my successor to make future decisions about our presence in Afghanistan. In January, the next U.S. president will assume the most solemn responsibility of the Commander-in-Chief—the security of the United States and the safety of the American people. The decision I'm making today ensures that my successor has a solid foundation for continued progress in Afghanistan as well as the flexibility to address the threat of terrorism as it evolves.

So, in closing, I want to address directly what I know is on the minds of many Americans—especially our troops and their families who've borne a heavy burden for our security. When we first sent our forces into Afghanistan 14 years ago, few Americans imagined we'd be there—in any capacity—this long. As President, I focused our strategy on training and building up Afghan forces. It has been continually my belief that it is up to Afghans to defend their country. Because we have emphasized training and their capabilities, we've been able to end our major ground war there and bring 90 percent of our troops back home.

But even as we work for peace, we have to deal with the realities of the world as it is. And we can't forget what's at stake in Afghanistan. This is where al Qaida is trying to regroup. This is where ISIL continues to try to expand its presence. If these terrorists succeed in regaining areas and camps where they can train and plot, they will attempt more attacks against us. We cannot allow that to happen. I will not allow that to happen.

This September will mark 15 years since the attacks of 9/11. And once more, we'll pause to remember the lives we lost—Americans and peoples from around the world. We'll stand with their families, who still grieve. We'll stand with survivors, who still bear the scars of that day. We'll thank the first responders who rushed to save others. And perhaps, most importantly, we'll salute our men and women in uniform—our 9/11 Generation—who have served in Afghanistan and beyond for our security. We'll honor the memory of all those who've made the ultimate sacrifice, including more than 2,200 American patriots who have given their lives in Afghanistan. As we do, let's never forget the progress their service has made possible.

Afghanistan is not a perfect place. It remains one of the poorest countries in the world. It is going to continue to take time for them to build up military capacity that we sometimes take for granted. And given the enormous challenges they face, the Afghan people will need the partnership of the world—led by the United States— for many years to come. But with our support, Afghanistan is a better place than it once was. Millions of Afghan children—boys and girls—are in school. Dramatic improvements in public health have saved the lives of mothers and children. Afghans have cast their ballots in democratic elections and seen the first democratic transfer of power in their country's history. The current National Unity Government continues to pursue reforms—including record revenues last year—to strengthen their country and, over time, help decrease the need for international support.

That government is a strong partner with us in combatting terrorism. That's the progress we've helped make possible. That's the progress that our troops have helped make possible, and our diplomats, and our development personnel. That's the progress we can help sustain, in partnership with the Afghan people and our coalition partners. And so I firmly believe the decision I'm announcing today is the right thing to do—for Afghanistan, for the United States, and for the world.

Source: White House. Available online at https://obamawhitehouse.archives.gov/ the-press-office/2016/07/06/statement-president-afghanistan.

ANALYSIS

The security situation in Afghanistan had remained somewhat stable into the summer of 2016 in the wake of the death of Mullah Mansour, but many provinces remained under threat from the Taliban, and the Afghan military was often too weak and disorganized to mount a concerted challenge. Therefore, President Obama announced that U.S. troop strength would fall only to 8,400 rather than the original goal of 5,500. These troops would continue to operate from the same bases and continue to advise and train Afghan forces.

- **Document 85: Open Letter of Islamic Emirate to the American President Donald Trump**
- **When:** August 15, 2017
- **Where:** Unknown

- **Significance:** The Taliban sent an open letter to the newly elected President Trump and attempted to persuade him to withdraw all American forces from Afghanistan.

DOCUMENT

Open letter of Islamic Emirate to the American President Donald Trump

To Donald Trump, the President of the United States of America

Peace be upon those who follow the guidance!

Your forces have spent 16 years in our country Afghanistan and have used every means to win this war. Despite the fact that the former administration officials created a large coalition to attack our country, your 16 year military presence in Afghanistan has resulted in Afghanistan becoming the most unstable country security wise, the most corrupt administrative wise and the poorest country economically.

The reason behind all this is because foreign invasion is being used to subdue the will of our proud Afghan nation, our national integrity is stripped and keys to power have been handed to individuals who are the most repulsive, wretched and hated faces in the Afghan society due to their servitude to foreigners.

President Trump!

It is entirely possible that you are being provided rosy pictures about Afghanistan by the stooges you have installed and they are showering you will titles "allies of the Afghans" in their ceremonial addresses but understand that the Afghans possess sound intellect. They judge you by the results of your 16 year presence in Afghanistan and not by the slogans of the lying corrupt rulers under your control.

You must realize that these repulsive sellouts neither care about your interests nor that of their own nation, rather the only thing they hold dear is retaining their seat of power and securing their personal interests.

They are not solely subservient to you either but will eagerly be the puppet of any foreign backer to retain their illegitimate grip on power. Even in the current government that you have built, they maintain illicit contacts with tens of other foreign powers.

President of America!

The government which you tried to establish over the past 16 years by spending billions of dollars, sacrificing thousands of soldiers and losing tens of thousands to injuries and mental illness is in a condition where its leader cannot accept his own deputy. You

DID YOU KNOW?

Sexual Abuse by Afghan National Army Soldiers

In 2015, news reports surfaced about a number of incidents, dating back to 2011, where U.S. military personnel witnessed abuses perpetrated by members of the Afghan National Security Forces against children. An Afghan term, *bachah bazi*, translates to "boy play," and refers to the physical and sexual abuse of boys by much older men. Several current and former U.S. military personnel claimed that they had been disciplined for intervening on behalf of the abuse victims, even when such incidents reportedly occurred on installations manned by both American and Afghan personnel. One allegation claimed that Abdur Rashid Dostum's personnel engaged in sexual assaults. A Department of Defense investigation into whether these abuses violated the "Leahy Laws" that banned the United States from supporting foreign militaries committing human rights violations commenced in early 2016, but the final report released in late 2017 remained classified. The Afghan government has since passed some laws restricting human trafficking, but it is unclear whether those laws will stem the systemic abuses noted by critics.

are witnessing that at this very moment the First Vice President—the war criminal and warlord—General Dostum is creating an opposition coalition outside the country against Ashraf Ghani, provincial governors have begun rising against him and Members of Parliament are demanding his resignation.

President Trump!

If you glance over history you will come to know that the Afghans have done you the biggest favor internationally. They rescued you and the entire world from the Red Communist Plague with their immeasurable sacrifices. Do you wish to repay this historical favor of the valiant Afghan nation by forcing upon them such incompetent, corrupt, immoral and criminal officials?

A sound mind and healthy conscience dictates that the monumental actions and international favor of this persecuted nation should be repaid by dealing and interacting with them generously and not through invasions, throwing them into the fire of imposed wars, trampling upon their religious and national values and installing the most corrupt officials as custodians of their affairs.

President of America!

Your previous officials decided to invade Afghanistan without weighing its consequences. They occupied Afghanistan under irrational arguments which had nothing to do with the Afghans. The Afghans who rose against your forces in defense of their land, creed and people did so as a legitimate struggle that is why the fully armed forces of 48 nations under your leadership were unable to pacify and eliminate them.

The Afghans have no ill-intention towards the Americans or any other nation around the world but if anyone violates their sanctums then they are mighty proficient at beating and defeating the transgressors.

The religious and national struggle of our people is not some illegitimate or proxy war rather it takes root from a pure spiritual and national fervor. Your intelligence agencies admit that our Mujahideen are not being supported by any country and neither can they produce any proof in the contrary. After repeated invasions, our nation understands well how to wage long wars with invaders and force them out of their homeland with their traditional weapons and equipment paired with towering resolve and zeal.

Mr. President!

American youth are not born to be killed in the deserts and mountains of Afghanistan in order to establish the writ of thieves and corrupt officials and neither would their parents approve of them killing civilians in Afghanistan. Rather you and American officials have the grave responsibility of protecting the lives of American youth which is your indispensable human resource. It seems to be a historical mistake on part of the previous administrations to have dispatched American youth for the slaughter of Afghans however as a responsible American President, you need to study the mistakes of your predecessors and prevent death and injury to American forces in Afghanistan.

Generals are concealing the real statistics of your dead and crippled however the Afghans can easily count the coffins being sent your way on a daily basis.

President Trump!

We have noticed that you have understood the errors of your predecessors and have resolved to thoroughly rethinking your new strategy in Afghanistan. A number of warmongering congressmen and Generals in Afghanistan are pressing you to protract the war in Afghanistan because they seek to preserve their military privileges but instead you must act responsibly as the fate of many Americans and Afghans alike is tied to this issue and as is often said "War is imperative politics which cannot be left alone to the whims of fighters". You must also not handover the Afghan issue to warmongering Generals but must make a decision where history shall remember you as an advocate of peace.

The war situation in Afghanistan is far worse than you realize! You are witnessing that Mujahideen are wresting control of several districts from the corrupt regime in a one week span and are seizing so much equipment that they can continue fighting for a long time. They can easily take control of all major highways of the country and if it were not for fear of civilian casualties, they would conquer many provincial capitals currently under sieges.

Here every Afghan views your soldiers as invaders and transgressors and even the soldiers who you spend a lot of treasure upon frequently open fire on your troops with the same weapon you have provided. Here every parent teaches his offspring about emancipating his country from invaders. In a land where every child is raised with a spirit of vengeance and holds the historic honor of defeating three Empires before you, how will you achieve a stable condition for permanent presence?

President of America!

Everyone now understands that the main driver of war in Afghanistan is foreign occupation. The fire of war has been lit due to foreign occupation and everyone is utilizing these war conditions for their self-interests. If there was no war here, a responsible assertive government could have prevented anarchy and lawlessness. You have understood through your experience in the Middle East that kindling the fire of war is not in the interest of any country around the world.

Previous experiences have shown that sending more troops to Afghanistan will not result in anything other than further destruction of American military and economical might therefore it would be wise if you adopt the strategy of a complete withdrawal from Afghanistan instead of a troops increase. On the one hand, this strategy will truly deliver American troops from harm's way and on the other, it will bring to an end an inherited war by rectifying the mistakes of former American officials.

Final Words

President of the United States! The uprising of the people of Afghanistan under the leadership of Islamic Emirate is an organized and accountable national, political and regional military force which has prevented many calamities from taking root. If it were not for the responsible policies and organized movement of the Islamic Emirate, such disorder would arise that its flames shall reach the neighbors, region and the entire world. If someone were to understand this reality, they would truly consider the Islamic Emirate as mercy for Afghanistan, region and the world because the Islamic Emirate does not have any intention or policy of causing harm to anyone and neither will it allow others to use the Afghan soil against anyone. It would be a grave mistake on your part to force the Afghan Muslim nation—who have so far fought you with their meager tools—to reach out to your foes in order to gain their independence and free themselves from your oppression. Therefore it would be better for you to understand the realities as a responsible President of the United States and then make decisions based upon them. And understand this with an open heart that if you failed to win the Afghan war with professional US and NATO troops, advanced technology, experienced military Generals, consecutive strategies and mighty economy, you shall never be able to win it with mercenaries, notorious contractor firms and immoral stooges.

Islamic Emirate of Afghanistan
23/11/1438 Hijri Lunar
24/05/1396 Hijri Solar 15/08/2017 Gregorian

Source: Islamic Emirate of Afghanistan. Available online at https://alemarah -english.com/?p=18529.

ANALYSIS

In a rare public appeal to an American president, the Taliban painted a dim picture of American success in Afghanistan and argued that the United States cannot win this war so long as they ally with "immoral stooges." The forceful language and direct appeal seem tailored specifically for President Trump, who had built a base of support largely through his own incredibly blunt and inflammatory statements through his Twitter social media account. The timing of this appeal also was not accidental as it was well known that President Trump was reviewing U.S. options for continuing to maintain forces in Afghanistan.

- **Document 86: Remarks by President Trump on the Strategy in Afghanistan and South Asia**
- **When:** August 21, 2017
- **Where:** Fort Myer, Virginia
- **Significance:** Seven months into his presidency, Donald Trump announced his intention to continue the U.S. presence in Afghanistan and to alter the strategic approach to the conflict.

DOCUMENT

. . .

Vice President Pence, Secretary of State Tillerson, members of the Cabinet, General Dunford, Deputy Secretary Shanahan, and Colonel Duggan. Most especially, thank you to the men and women of Fort Myer and every member of the United States military at home and abroad.

We send our thoughts and prayers to the families of our brave sailors who were injured and lost after a tragic collision at sea, as well as to those conducting the search and recovery efforts.

I am here tonight to lay out our path forward in Afghanistan and South Asia. But before I provide the details of our new strategy, I want to say a few words to the servicemembers here with us tonight, to those watching from their posts, and to all Americans listening at home.

Since the founding of our republic, our country has produced a special class of heroes whose selflessness, courage, and resolve is unmatched in human history.

American patriots from every generation have given their last breath on the battlefield for our nation and for our freedom. Through their lives—and though their lives were cut short, in their deeds they achieved total immortality.

By following the heroic example of those who fought to preserve our republic, we can find the inspiration our country needs to unify, to heal, and to remain one nation under God. The men and women of our military operate as one team, with one shared mission, and one shared sense of purpose.

They transcend every line of race, ethnicity, creed, and color to serve together—and sacrifice together—in absolutely perfect cohesion. That is because all servicemembers are brothers and sisters. They're all part of the same family; it's called the American family. They take the same oath, fight for the same flag, and live according to the same law. They are bound together by common purpose, mutual trust, and selfless devotion to our nation and to each other.

The soldier understands what we, as a nation, too often forget that a wound inflicted upon a single member of our community is a wound inflicted upon us all. When one part of America hurts, we all hurt. And when one citizen suffers an injustice, we all suffer together.

Loyalty to our nation demands loyalty to one another. Love for America requires love for all of its people. When we open our hearts to patriotism, there is no room for prejudice, no place for bigotry, and no tolerance for hate.

The young men and women we send to fight our wars abroad deserve to return to a country that is not at war with itself at home. We cannot remain a force for peace in the world if we are not at peace with each other.

As we send our bravest to defeat our enemies overseas—and we will always win—let us find the courage to heal our divisions within. Let us make a simple promise to the men and women we ask to fight in our name that, when they return home from battle, they will find a country that has renewed the sacred bonds of love and loyalty that unite us together as one.

Thanks to the vigilance and skill of the American military and of our many allies throughout the world, horrors on the scale of September 11th—and nobody can ever forget that—have not been repeated on our shores.

But we must also acknowledge the reality I am here to talk about tonight: that nearly 16 years after September 11th attacks, after the extraordinary sacrifice of blood and treasure, the American people are weary of war without victory. Nowhere is this more evident than with the war in Afghanistan, the longest war in American history—17 years.

I share the American people's frustration. I also share their frustration over a foreign policy that has spent too much time, energy, money, and most importantly lives, trying to rebuild countries in our own image, instead of pursuing our security interests above all other considerations.

That is why, shortly after my inauguration, I directed Secretary of Defense Mattis and my national security team to undertake a comprehensive review of all strategic options in Afghanistan and South Asia.

My original instinct was to pull out—and, historically, I like following my instincts. But all my life I've heard that decisions are much different when you sit behind the desk in the Oval Office; in other words, when you're President of the United States. So I studied Afghanistan in great detail and from every conceivable angle. After many meetings, over many months, we held our final meeting last Friday at Camp David, with my Cabinet and generals, to complete our strategy. I arrived at three fundamental conclusions about America's core interests in Afghanistan.

First, our nation must seek an honorable and enduring outcome worthy of the tremendous sacrifices that have been made, especially the sacrifices of lives. The men and women who serve our nation in combat deserve a plan for victory. They deserve the tools they need, and the trust they have earned, to fight and to win.

Second, the consequences of a rapid exit are both predictable and unacceptable. 9/11, the worst terrorist attack in our history, was planned and directed from Afghanistan because that country was ruled by a government that gave comfort and shelter to terrorists. A hasty withdrawal would create a vacuum that terrorists, including ISIS and al Qaeda, would instantly fill, just as happened before September 11th.

And, as we know, in 2011, America hastily and mistakenly withdrew from Iraq. As a result, our hard-won gains slipped back into the hands of terrorist enemies. Our soldiers watched as cities they had fought for, and bled to liberate, and won, were occupied by a terrorist group called ISIS. The vacuum we created by leaving too soon gave safe haven for ISIS to spread, to grow, recruit, and launch attacks. We cannot repeat in Afghanistan the mistake our leaders made in Iraq.

Third and finally, I concluded that the security threats we face in Afghanistan and the broader region are immense. Today, 20 U.S.-designated foreign terrorist organizations are active in Afghanistan and Pakistan—the highest concentration in any region anywhere in the world.

For its part, Pakistan often gives safe haven to agents of chaos, violence, and terror. The threat is worse because Pakistan and India are two nuclear-armed states whose tense relations threaten to spiral into conflict. And that could happen.

No one denies that we have inherited a challenging and troubling situation in Afghanistan and South Asia, but we do not have the luxury of going back in time and making different or better decisions. When I became President, I was given a bad and very complex hand, but I fully knew what I was getting into: big and intricate problems. But, one way or another, these problems will be solved—I'm a problem solver—and, in the end, we will win.

We must address the reality of the world as it exists right now—the threats we face, and the confronting of all of the problems of today, and extremely predictable consequences of a hasty withdrawal.

We need look no further than last week's vile, vicious attack in Barcelona to understand that terror groups will stop at nothing to commit the mass murder of innocent men, women and children. You saw it for yourself. Horrible.

As I outlined in my speech in Saudi Arabia three months ago, America and our partners are committed to stripping terrorists of their territory, cutting off their funding, and exposing the false allure of their evil ideology.

Terrorists who slaughter innocent people will find no glory in this life or the next. They are nothing but thugs, and criminals, and predators, and—that's right—losers. Working alongside our allies, we will break their will, dry up their recruitment, keep them from crossing our borders, and yes, we will defeat them, and we will defeat them handily.

In Afghanistan and Pakistan, America's interests are clear: We must stop the resurgence of safe havens that enable terrorists to threaten America, and we must prevent nuclear weapons and materials from coming into the hands of terrorists and being used against us, or anywhere in the world for that matter.

But to prosecute this war, we will learn from history. As a result of our comprehensive review, American strategy in Afghanistan and South Asia will change dramatically in the following ways:

A core pillar of our new strategy is a shift from a time-based approach to one based on conditions. I've said it many times how counterproductive it is for the United States to announce in advance the dates we intend to begin, or end, military options. We will not talk about numbers of troops or our plans for further military activities.

Conditions on the ground—not arbitrary timetables—will guide our strategy from now on. America's enemies must never know our plans or believe they can wait us out. I will not say when we are going to attack, but attack we will.

Another fundamental pillar of our new strategy is the integration of all instruments of American power—diplomatic, economic, and military—toward a successful outcome.

Someday, after an effective military effort, perhaps it will be possible to have a political settlement that includes elements of the Taliban in Afghanistan, but nobody knows if or when that will ever happen. America will continue its support for the Afghan government and the Afghan military as they confront the Taliban in the field.

Ultimately, it is up to the people of Afghanistan to take ownership of their future, to govern their society, and to achieve an everlasting peace. We are a partner and a friend, but we will not dictate to the Afghan people how to live, or how to govern their own complex society. We are not nation-building again. We are killing terrorists.

The next pillar of our new strategy is to change the approach and how to deal with Pakistan. We can no longer be silent about Pakistan's safe havens for terrorist organizations, the Taliban, and other groups that pose a threat to the region and beyond. Pakistan has much to gain from partnering with our effort in Afghanistan. It has much to lose by continuing to harbor criminals and terrorists.

In the past, Pakistan has been a valued partner. Our militaries have worked together against common enemies. The Pakistani people have suffered greatly from terrorism and extremism. We recognize those contributions and those sacrifices.

But Pakistan has also sheltered the same organizations that try every single day to kill our people. We have been paying Pakistan billions and billions of dollars at the same time they are housing the very terrorists that we are fighting. But that will have to change, and that will change immediately. No partnership can survive a country's harboring of militants and terrorists who target U.S. servicemembers and officials. It is time for Pakistan to demonstrate its commitment to civilization, order, and to peace.

Another critical part of the South Asia strategy for America is to further develop its strategic partnership with India—the world's largest democracy and a key security and economic partner of the United States. We appreciate India's important contributions to stability in Afghanistan, but India makes billions of dollars in trade with the United States, and we want them to help us more with Afghanistan, especially in the area of economic assistance and development. We are committed to pursuing our shared objectives for peace and security in South Asia and the broader Indo-Pacific region.

Finally, my administration will ensure that you, the brave defenders of the American people, will have the necessary tools and rules of engagement to make this strategy work, and work effectively and work quickly.

I have already lifted restrictions the previous administration placed on our war-fighters that prevented the Secretary of Defense and our commanders in the field from fully and swiftly waging battle against the enemy. Micromanagement from Washington, D.C. does not win battles. They are won in the field drawing upon the judgment and expertise of wartime commanders and frontline soldiers acting in real time, with real authority, and with a clear mission to defeat the enemy.

That's why we will also expand authority for American armed forces to target the terrorist and criminal networks that sow violence and chaos throughout Afghanistan. These killers need to know they have nowhere to hide; that no place is beyond the reach of American might and Americans arms. Retribution will be fast and powerful.

As we lift restrictions and expand authorities in the field, we are already seeing dramatic results in the campaign to defeat ISIS, including the liberation of Mosul in Iraq.

Since my inauguration, we have achieved record-breaking success in that regard. We will also maximize sanctions and other financial and law enforcement actions against these networks to eliminate their ability to export terror. When America commits its warriors to battle, we must ensure they have every weapon to apply swift, decisive, and overwhelming force.

Our troops will fight to win. We will fight to win. From now on, victory will have a clear definition: attacking our enemies, obliterating ISIS, crushing al Qaeda, preventing the Taliban from taking over Afghanistan, and stopping mass terror attacks against America before they emerge.

We will ask our NATO allies and global partners to support our new strategy with additional troop and funding increases in line with our own. We are confident they will. Since taking office, I have made clear that our allies and partners must contribute much more money to our collective defense, and they have done so.

In this struggle, the heaviest burden will continue to be borne by the good people of Afghanistan and their courageous armed forces. As the prime minister of

Afghanistan has promised, we are going to participate in economic development to help defray the cost of this war to us.

Afghanistan is fighting to defend and secure their country against the same enemies who threaten us. The stronger the Afghan security forces become, the less we will have to do. Afghans will secure and build their own nation and define their own future. We want them to succeed.

But we will no longer use American military might to construct democracies in faraway lands, or try to rebuild other countries in our own image. Those days are now over. Instead, we will work with allies and partners to protect our shared interests. We are not asking others to change their way of life, but to pursue common goals that allow our children to live better and safer lives. This principled realism will guide our decisions moving forward.

Military power alone will not bring peace to Afghanistan or stop the terrorist threat arising in that country. But strategically applied force aims to create the conditions for a political process to achieve a lasting peace.

America will work with the Afghan government as long as we see determination and progress. However, our commitment is not unlimited, and our support is not a blank check. The government of Afghanistan must carry their share of the military, political, and economic burden. The American people expect to see real reforms, real progress, and real results. Our patience is not unlimited. We will keep our eyes wide open.

In abiding by the oath I took on January 20th, I will remain steadfast in protecting American lives and American interests. In this effort, we will make common cause with any nation that chooses to stand and fight alongside us against this global threat. Terrorists take heed: America will never let up until you are dealt a lasting defeat.

Under my administration, many billions of dollars more is being spent on our military. And this includes vast amounts being spent on our nuclear arsenal and missile defense.

In every generation, we have faced down evil, and we have always prevailed. We prevailed because we know who we are and what we are fighting for.

Not far from where we are gathered tonight, hundreds of thousands of America's greatest patriots lay in eternal rest at Arlington National Cemetery. There is more courage, sacrifice, and love in those hallowed grounds than in any other spot on the face of the Earth.

Many of those who have fought and died in Afghanistan enlisted in the months after September 11th, 2001. They volunteered for a simple reason: They loved America, and they were determined to protect her.

Now we must secure the cause for which they gave their lives. We must unite to defend America from its enemies abroad. We must restore the bonds of loyalty among our citizens at home, and we must achieve an honorable and enduring outcome worthy of the enormous price that so many have paid.

Our actions, and in the months to come, all of them will honor the sacrifice of every fallen hero, every family who lost a loved one, and every wounded warrior who shed their blood in defense of our great nation. With our resolve, we will ensure that your service and that your families will bring about the defeat of our enemies and the arrival of peace.

We will push onward to victory with power in our hearts, courage in our souls, and everlasting pride in each and every one of you.

. . .

Source: White House. Available online at https://www.whitehouse.gov/the-press -office/2017/08/21/remarks-president-trump-strategy-afghanistan-and-south-asia.

ANALYSIS

President Trump often criticized the U.S. presence in Afghanistan and the rest of the Middle East during his campaign but, once in office, largely perpetuated the policies started by his predecessors. He argued in this speech that the United States could not abandon Afghanistan because of the sacrifice of U.S. troops to protect the nation over the previous 16 years and because of lessons learned from the "hasty" withdrawal in Iraq. In addition, he announced his intent to ease the "rules of engagement" for U.S. forces in Afghanistan, although it was unclear what this might entail.

Perhaps most important, he strongly criticized Pakistan for its continued inability to control Islamic militant groups inside its own borders. Presidents Bush and Obama had sought to maintain strong ties with Pakistan in spite of these internal difficulties, but President Trump instead denounced Pakistan in especially harsh terms.

With this statement, President Trump committed the United States to an indefinite presence in Afghanistan. He would increase the number of troops in the country to 15,000 by the end of 2017. Despite efforts to end U.S. participation in the war in Afghanistan, it is unclear when it will end.

CHRONOLOGY

April 28, 1978	President Mohammed Daoud Khan is assassinated by military officers loyal to the People's Democratic Party of Afghanistan. The resulting communist reforms lead to unrest in the countryside against the government.
December 12, 1979	The Soviet Union authorizes the introduction of Soviet troops into Afghanistan. Soviet troops enter Afghanistan 12 days later.
January 8, 1980	U.S. president Jimmy Carter issues a statement calling the Soviet invasion of Afghanistan "the greatest threat to peace since the Second World War."
November 20, 1980	The United Nations issues Resolution 35/37 calling for the withdrawal of foreign troops from Afghanistan.
April 14, 1988	Afghanistan and Pakistan sign the Geneva Accords, which also include a timetable for the end of the Soviet occupation of Afghanistan that occurs on February 15, 1989.
April 23–25, 1992	Various *mujahedeen* factions enter the Afghan capital Kabul and depose the communist government of Mohammad Najibullah.
February 26, 1993	Islamic extremists, financed by the al-Qaeda terrorist group, detonate a car bomb in a basement garage of New York City's World Trade Center, killing 6 and injuring 1,042 people.
March 7, 1993	The various factions vying for control of Afghanistan sign the Islamabad Accord, also known as the Afghan Peace Accord, in an attempt to form a unified national government.
January 1994	Afghan warlord Rashid Dostum revokes his allegiance to Ahmad Shah Massoud and allies himself with Gulbuddin Hekmatyar.
November 4, 1994	The Taliban capture Kandahar.
September 5, 1995	Taliban fighters capture Herat.

May 18, 1996	The Sudanese government deports al-Qaeda terrorist leader Osama bin Laden, who goes to Afghanistan, where he is welcomed by the coalescing Taliban regime.
June 25, 1996	Al-Qaeda operatives detonate a truck bomb in Dhahran, Saudi Arabia, at the Khobar Towers, the main military barracks for U.S. service members, killing 19 Americans and wounding 500.
September 26, 1996	The Taliban capture Kabul with minimal resistance, executing former Afghan president Mohammad Najibullah and others and forcing many to flee.
May 19, 1997	Taliban fighters take Mazar-i-Sharif, but on May 23 a spontaneous uprising kills up to 3,000 fighters and forces the Taliban to withdraw.
February 23, 1998	Bin Laden publishes a fatwa declaring jihad (holy war) on all "nonbelieving crusaders" and Jews.
August 7, 1998	In Dar es Salaam, Tanzania, and Nairobi, Kenya, al-Qaeda operatives nearly simultaneously detonate two truck bombs in front of the U.S. embassies, killing 224 people and injuring more than 5,000.
August 8, 1998	The Taliban recapture the city of Mazar-i-Sharif from the Northern Alliance and kill as many as 6,000 civilians in retribution for the massacre of some 3,000 Taliban fighters in May 1997.
August 20, 1998	In retaliation for the deadly embassy bombings on August 7, the United States launches 75 cruise missiles against targets in Afghanistan and northern Khartoum, Sudan.
January 19, 2001	The UN Security Council passes Resolution 1333, imposing punitive economic sanctions and an arms embargo against the Taliban regime in Afghanistan and calling for the Taliban to hand over bin Laden.
September 9, 2001	Northern Alliance leader Ahmad Shah Massoud is mortally wounded by a bomb detonated by al-Qaeda operatives posing as journalists.
September 11, 2001	Nineteen al-Qaeda operatives hijack four airliners in the United States. Two crash into the twin towers of New York City's World Trade Center, killing 2,900 people, including all aboard both jetliners. A third plane crashes into the Pentagon in northern Virginia less than an hour later, killing 189 people, including all on board. A fourth flight is also hijacked by terrorists, allegedly intended for the Capitol or White House, but the passengers fight back, and the plane crashes into a field near Stony Creek, Pennsylvania, killing all 45 people on board.
September 14, 2001	Congress authorizes the use of force in retaliation for the attacks of September 11.
September 20, 2001	President George W. Bush demands that the Taliban turn Osama bin Laden over to the United States for trial.

October 2, 2001	NATO invokes Article 5, declaring the September 11 attacks on the United States as an attack against all NATO member states.
October 7, 2001	After the Taliban fail to turn bin Laden over to the United States, U.S. forces, assisted by the British, commence air attacks against Afghanistan.
November 11, 2001	The U.S.-supported Northern Alliance, fighting against the Taliban, captures Mazar-i-Sharif.
November 13, 2001	Coalition forces capture Kabul. On the same day, the Bush administration authorizes the creation of military tribunals, which will be used to try non-Americans suspected of planning or fomenting acts of terrorism against the United States.
December 5, 2001	Meeting in Bonn, Germany, Afghan leaders form a new interim government under the leadership of Hamid Karzai. He will be sworn in as president on December 22.
December 6, 2001	Kandahar, Afghanistan, the Taliban's last stronghold, falls to Coalition forces. The 11-day siege of Tora Bora also begins, but the Coalition fails to capture Osama bin Laden and other Taliban leaders before they escape into Pakistan.
December 20, 2001	UN Resolution 1386 creates the International Security Assistance Force (ISAF) to provide security in Kabul.
January 16, 2002	The UN Security Council votes unanimously to freeze all assets of the Taliban, al-Qaeda, and bin Laden. The same resolution also invokes a full arms embargo on the three entities.
March 1–18, 2002	Operation Anaconda neutralizes the Taliban threat in the Shah-i-Kot Valley.
September 5, 2002	A car bomb kills more than 30 people in Afghanistan, and an assassination attempt against Karzai fails. He will survive five more attempts during his two terms as president.
August 11, 2003	NATO assumes control of ISAF, marking the first time NATO assumed operational control of military operations outside of Europe in its history. On October 13, UN Security Council Resolution 1510 changes the mandate for ISAF, allowing it to operate throughout Afghanistan.
January 26, 2004	The Loya Jirga ratifies the Constitution of Afghanistan by consensus.
April 22, 2004	Corporal Patrick Tillman, a former National Football League star, is killed in a friendly-fire incident while serving as a member of the 2nd Ranger Battalion.
October 9, 2004	Hamid Karzai, Afghanistan's interim president, wins the nation's first presidential election.
February 1, 2006	The Afghanistan Compact is agreed to at the London Conference. It outlines a series of reconstruction targets to occur over the following five years.

December 15, 2006	The U.S. Department of Defense issues a new Field Manual 3-24, Counterinsurgency, based upon lessons learned in countering the Taliban and the Sunni insurgencies in Afghanistan and Iraq.
May 3, 2007	In testimony to the Senate Armed Services Committee, Admiral William J. Fallon states that the frequency of Taliban attacks had reached their highest levels since 2001.
June 13, 2008	More than 900 prisoners, 350 of them Taliban, escape from a prison in Kandahar when Taliban operatives explode a fuel truck adjacent to the prison using a rocket-propelled grenade. Similar incidents will occur in later years.
July 13, 2008	Thirteen U.S. soldiers are killed in an attack by more than 200 insurgents on an unfinished outpost in Wanat in the Waygal River Valley in Kunar Province.
February 2009	The administration of President Barack Obama announces that 17,000 additional troops will be sent to Afghanistan.
April 7, 2009	A joint German Afghan force, later dubbed Operation EAGLE, steps up efforts to combat the rising insurgency in Kunduz Province. Major fighting continues until July.
June 30, 2009	Private Bowe Bergdahl leaves his unit in Paktika Province and is captured by insurgents. He will remain in captivity until May 2014 when he is traded for five Taliban prisoners. He will later be convicted of desertion.
July 2, 2009	Operation Strike of the Sword (also known as Operation Khanjar), the largest airlift offensive since the Vietnam War, begins in southern Afghanistan.
August 20, 2009	Hamid Karzai wins reelection in a vote marred by fraud and low turnout.
August 30, 2009	General Stanley McChrystal, the new ISAF commander, completes a major strategic review that calls for significant troop increases in Afghanistan.
October 3, 2009	An estimated force of 300 insurgents nearly overwhelms Combat Outpost Keating near Kamdesh in Nuristan Province. Eight U.S. soldiers are killed and 27 wounded in the 12-hour firefight, in addition to approximately 150 insurgents.
December 1, 2009	In an address at the U.S. Military Academy, West Point, President Barack Obama announces that he will send 30,000 additional U.S. forces to Afghanistan in a "surge" beginning in 2010 and lasting into 2012. During the surge, nearly 100,000 U.S. troops will be in Afghanistan.
February 13, 2010	Operation Moshtarak, an offensive involving more than 6,000 Coalition troops against a Taliban stronghold in the town of Marja, begins.

June 24, 2010	U.S. president Barack Obama removes Stanley A. McChrystal from command of U.S. and NATO forces in Afghanistan following critical comments made by McChrystal and members of his staff against President Obama and others that appeared in *Rolling Stone* magazine. His replacement is Central Command Commander General David H. Petraeus.
July 25, 2010	WikiLeaks, an Internet organization dedicated to the public dissemination of government secrets, releases more than 91,000 documents, collectively called the Afghan War Diary, covering the Afghanistan War from 2004 to 2010. These reports by U.S. military personnel not only describe military actions but also detail the role of the Pakistani intelligence service in supporting Taliban activities in Afghanistan. These leaks will eventually be traced to U.S. Army Private Bradley Manning.
September 21, 2010	Operation Dragon Strike, an attack by more than 8,000 Coalition forces against Taliban strongholds in Kandahar Province, begins.
Mid-October 2010	U.S. and Afghan officials confirm that the Afghan government has been negotiating secretly with Taliban leaders and that NATO and U.S. forces have facilitated the transportation of Taliban leaders from Pakistan to the peace talks.
November 20, 2010	At the Lisbon Summit, NATO members announce their intent to gradually disengage from Afghanistan by the end of 2014.
April 27, 2011	Hamid Gul, an Afghan Air Corps officer who had been trained by the Soviets 30 years before, shoots and kills eight American service members and a military contractor in a meeting of foreign and Afghan military officers at Kabul International Airport before he himself is shot and killed. This is the first of several "green on blue" incidents that occur in succeeding years.
May 1, 2011	U.S. Navy SEALs kill Osama bin Laden in a raid on his compound in Abbottabad, Pakistan. President Obama announces the news in a televised address.
June 22, 2011	President Barack Obama, in a televised address to the American people concerning the Afghanistan War, announces that 10,000 troops will be withdrawn by the end of 2011, with the remainder of the so-called surge troops (about 23,000) to depart by the end of the summer of 2012. This would still leave some 70,000 American troops in Afghanistan until the end of 2014.
August 6, 2011	Taliban forces in Wardak Province shoot down a U.S. Army Boeing CH-47 Chinook helicopter, killing all 38 U.S. and Afghan passengers and crew on board.
October 29, 2011	In the Afghan capital of Kabul, a Taliban suicide bomber rams his vehicle loaded with 1,540 pounds of explosives into an armored NATO bus, killing 17 people, including 12 Americans. It is the deadliest attack on the U.S.-led coalition in Kabul since the beginning of the Afghanistan War.

November 26, 2011	A NATO attack on two Pakistani border bases kills 24 Pakistani soldiers. This is the deadliest incident by NATO forces against Pakistan since the beginning of the Afghanistan War, and it plunges already fragile U.S.-Pakistani relations into crisis.
January 27, 2012	Following an increase in casualties, French president Nicolas Sarkozy announces the withdrawal of remaining French forces from Afghanistan by the end of the year, a year earlier than anticipated.
February 1, 2012	The Obama administration announces a timetable for U.S. troop withdrawals from Afghanistan. By mid-2013, the Americans plan to cease combat operations and withdraw nearly all troops by the end of 2014.
February 23, 2012	Afghans begin demonstrating in response to news reports that U.S. military personnel burned copies of the Koran that Taliban prisoners used to pass messages to each other. Four Americans are killed in the demonstrations along with dozens of Afghans.
March 11, 2012	U.S. Army Staff Sergeant Robert Bales leaves a U.S. military base in Afghanistan under cover of darkness and murders 16 Afghan civilians, 9 of whom are children, in a nearby village. He will later be convicted and sentenced to life imprisonment.
May 1, 2012	While visiting Afghanistan, President Obama announces the U.S. intent to keep forces in Afghanistan past the scheduled end of the combat mission in 2014.
May 22, 2012	At the Chicago Summit, NATO member states agree on a withdrawal plan beginning in 2013 and to turn over all security responsibilities to Afghanistan by the end of 2014.
January 11, 2013	President Obama announces that U.S. troops in Afghanistan will begin the transition from combat to support in the spring of 2013.
April 23, 2013	Taliban leader Mullah Mohammad Omar dies in Pakistan, although it will not be formally announced until the Taliban unveil his successor, Mullah Akhtar Mohammad, in September 2015.
June 18, 2013	The Afghan military formally assumes complete responsibility for maintaining security throughout Afghanistan.
November 23, 2013	Afghanistan's Loya Jirga overwhelmingly approves the post-2014 security agreement with the U.S. government.
May 27, 2014	President Obama announces the end of the U.S. combat mission in Afghanistan by December, but 9,800 U.S. troops will remain in Afghanistan to conduct training and counterterrorism missions.
June 14, 2014	Presidential elections are held in Afghanistan. In September, Ashraf Ghani will be declared the winner, while the runner-up, Abdullah Abdullah, assumes the new position of chief executive officer.
June 15, 2014	Pakistani military aircraft target 8 militant hideouts in the area of North Waziristan, bordering Afghanistan, killing as many as 100 militants in the second strike on the region since a deadly Taliban attack on Karachi airport a week before.

August 5, 2014	A rogue Afghan soldier at Marshal Fahim National Defense University in Kabul opens fire, killing Army Major General Harold Greene, deputy commander of U.S. forces in Afghanistan, and wounding 15 Coalition soldiers, including a German general and two Afghan generals. Greene is the highest ranking U.S. military officer to be killed since September 11, 2001.
September 29, 2014	After his inauguration ceremony, President Ghani signs a new status of forces agreement with the United States and NATO.
October 26, 2014	The last U.S. Marines and British forces in Afghanistan both end their combat missions and hand over control of the massive Bastion-Leatherneck military complex that once housed 40,000 Coalition personnel to Afghan forces.
December 16, 2014	In retaliation for recent attacks by the government, Pakistani Taliban gunmen storm a school in the city of Peshawar, killing 145, including 132 children aged 10–18, 10 members of the school's staff, and 3 soldiers.
December 28, 2014	After more than 13 years, Operation Enduring Freedom–Afghanistan officially ends. ISAF is also formally disbanded on this date. Nine thousand and eight hundred U.S. troops and more than 2,000 NATO forces remain in Afghanistan.
March 24, 2015	The U.S. government confirms that it will maintain 9,800 troops in Afghanistan through at least the end of the year.
September 28 to October 13, 2015	In Afghanistan, Taliban insurgents capture the strategic city of Kanduz on September 28. Aided by U.S. air strikes, Afghan forces retake the city on October 13. During the battle on October 3, a U.S.-piloted AC-130 gunship mistakenly fires on a hospital run by Doctors without Borders. Nineteen people are killed and another 37 are wounded.
October 15, 2015	President Barack Obama announces that the 9,800 U.S. troops will remain in Afghanistan through the end of 2016 with a reduction to 5,500 in 2017.
May 21, 2016	Taliban leader Mullah Akhtar Mohammad is killed in Pakistan by a missile fired from a U.S. Predator unmanned aircraft. He is replaced by Mullah Akhundzada.
July 7, 2016	Owing to continued instability, President Obama announces that 8,400 U.S. troops (not the 5,500 number previously announced) will remain in Afghanistan through the end of January 2017.
July 24, 2016	A terrorist bombing in Kabul, Afghanistan, kills 80 and wounds more than 230 others. A branch of ISIS claims responsibility.
August 21, 2017	President Donald Trump announces that the United States will send more than 5,000 troops to Afghanistan with no timetable for reductions and openly criticizes Pakistan's lack of assistance in fighting the insurgency.

BIBLIOGRAPHY

Auerswald, David P., and Stephen M. Saideman. *NATO in Afghanistan: Fighting Together, Fighting Alone*. Princeton, NJ: Princeton University Press, 2014.

Bacevich, Andrew J. *America's War for the Greater Middle East: A Military History*. New York: Random House, 2016.

Barfield, Thomas. *Afghanistan: A Cultural and Political History*. Princeton, NJ: Princeton University Press, 2010.

Bergen, Peter L. *Manhunt: The Ten-Year Search for bin Laden from 9/11 to Abbottabad*. New York: Crown, 2012.

Berger, Peter L., and Daniel Rothenberg, eds. *Drone Wars: Transforming Conflict, Law, and Policy*. New York: Cambridge University Press, 2014.

Berger, Peter L., and Katherine Tiedemann, eds. *Talibanistan: Negotiating the Borders between Terror, Politics, and Religion*. New York: Oxford University Press, 2013.

Biddle, Stephen D. "Allies, Airpower, and Modern Warfare: The Afghan Model in Afghanistan and Iraq." *International Security* 30, no. 3 (Winter 2005/2006): 161–176.

Bolger, Daniel P. *Why We Lost: A General's Inside Account of Iraq and Afghanistan Wars*. New York: Houghton Mifflin Harcourt, 2014.

Call, Steve. *Danger Close: Tactical Air Controllers in Afghanistan and Iraq*. College Station: Texas A&M University Press, 2007.

Carafano, James Jay. *Private Sector, Public Wars: Contractors in Combat—Afghanistan, Iraq, and Future Conflicts*. Westport, CT: Praeger Security International, 2008.

Chandrasekaran, Rajiv. *Little America: The War within the War for Afghanistan*. New York: Knopf, 2012.

Coll, Steve. *Ghost Wars: The Secret History of the CIA, Afghanistan, and Bin Laden, from the Soviet Invasion to September 10, 2001*. New York: Penguin Books, 2004.

Combat Studies Institute. *Wanat: Combat Action in Afghanistan, 2008*. Fort Leavenworth, KS: Combat Studies Institute Press, 2010.

Crane, Conrad C. *Cassandra in Oz: Counterinsurgency and Future War*. Annapolis, MD: Naval Institute Press, 2016.

Crile, George. *Charlie Wilson's War: The Extraordinary Story of the Largest Covert Operation in History*. New York: Atlantic Monthly Press, 2003.

Dalrymple, William. *Return of a King: The Battle for Afghanistan, 1839–42*. New York: Knopf, 2013.

Darack, Edward. *Victory Point: Operations Red Wings and Whalers—The Marine Corps Battle for Freedom in Afghanistan*. New York: Berkley Caliber, 2009.

De Graaf, Beatrice, George Dimitriu, and Jens Ringsmose, eds. *Strategic Narratives, Public Opinion, and War: Winning Domestic Support for the Afghan War*. New York: Routledge, 2015.

Edwards, David B. *Before Taliban: Genealogies of the Afghan Jihad*. Berkeley: University of California Press, 2002.

Farrell, Theo. *Unwinnable: Britain's War in Afghanistan, 2001–2014*. London: Bodley Head, 2017.

Feifer, Gregory. *Great Gamble: The Soviet War in Afghanistan*. New York: Harper, 2009.

Galula, David. *Counterinsurgency Warfare: Theory and Practice*. New Edition. Westport, CT: Praeger Security International, 2006.

Gates, Robert M. *Duty: Memoirs of a Secretary at War*. New York: Knopf, 2014.

Gentile, Gian. *Wrong Turn: America's Deadly Embrace of Counterinsurgency*. New York: The New Press, 2013.

Goodson, Larry P. *Afghanistan's Endless War: State Failure, Regional Politics, and the Rise of the Taliban*. Seattle: University of Washington Press, 2011.

Grau, Lester W., ed. *The Bear Went over the Mountain: Soviet Combat Tactics in Afghanistan*. Washington, DC: National Defense University Press, 1996.

Grau, Lester W., and Ali A. Jalali, eds. *The Other Side of the Mountain: Mujahideen Tactics in the Soviet-Afghan War*. Quantico, VA: The U.S. Marine Corps Studies and Analysis Division, 1995.

Hastings, Max. *The Operators: The Wild and Terrifying Inside Story of America's War in Afghanistan*. New York: Blue Rider Press, 2012.

Immerman, Richard H., and Beth Bailey, eds. *Understanding the U.S. Wars in Iraq and Afghanistan*. New York: New York University Press, 2016.

Jalali, Ali Ahmad. *A Military History of Afghanistan: From the Great Game to the Global War on Terror*. Lawrence: University of Kansas Press, 2017.

Johnson, Robert. *The Afghan Way of War: How and Why They Fight*. New York: Oxford University Press, 2012.

Jones, Seth G. *In the Graveyard of Empires: America's War in Afghanistan*. New York: W.W. Norton and Company, 2009.

Junger, Sebastian. *War*. New York: Twelve, 2010.

Kaplan, Fred. *The Insurgents: David Petraeus and the Plot to Change the American Way of War*. New York: Simon and Schuster, 2013.

Kilcullen, David. *The Accidental Guerrilla: Fighting Small Wars in the Midst of a Big One*. New York: Oxford University Press, 2009.

Klassen, David, and Greg Albo, eds. *Empire's Ally: Canada and the War in Afghanistan*. Toronto: University of Toronto Press, 2013.

Leake, Elisabeth. *The Defiant Border: The Afghan-Pakistan Borderlands in the Era of Decolonization, 1936–1965*. New York: Cambridge University Press, 2016.

Luttrell, Marcus. *Lone Survivor: The Eyewitness Account of Operation Red Wings and the Lost Heroes of SEAL Team 10*. New York: Little, Brown, and Company, 2007.

McChrystal, Stanley. *My Share of the Task: A Memoir*. New York: Portfolio, 2013.

McFate, Montgomery, and Janet Laurence, eds. *Social Science Goes to War: The Human Terrain System in Iraq and Afghanistan*. New York: Oxford University Press, 2015.

Naylor, Sean. *Not a Good Day to Die: The Untold Story of Operation Anaconda*. New York: Berkley Books, 2005.

O'Connell, Aaron, ed. *Our Longest War: Losing Hearts and Minds in Afghanistan*. Chicago, IL: University of Chicago Press, 2017.

Rashid, Ahmed. *Descent into Chaos: The United States and the Failure of Nation Building in Pakistan, Afghanistan, and Central Asia.* New York: Viking, 2008.

Rashid, Ahmed. *Taliban: Militant Islam, Oil, and Fundamentalism in Central Asia.* 2nd ed. New Haven, CT: Yale University Press, 2010.

Riedel, Bruce. *What We Won: America's Secret War in Afghanistan, 1979–1989.* Washington, DC: Brookings Institute Press, 2014.

Romseha, Clinton. *Red Platoon: A True Story of American Valor.* New York: Dutton, 2016.

Rubin, Barnett R. *Afghanistan from the Cold War through the War on Terror.* New York: Oxford University Press, 2013.

Simpson, Emile. *War from the Ground Up: Twenty-First Century Combat as Politics.* New York: Oxford University Press, 2012.

Stanton, Doug. *Horse Soldiers: The Extraordinary Story of a Band of US Soldiers Who Rode to Victory in Afghanistan.* New York: Scribner, 2009.

Tanner, Stephen. *Afghanistan: A Military History from Alexander the Great to the War against the Taliban.* Philadelphia, PA: Da Capo Press, 2009.

Tomsen, Peter. *The Wars of Afghanistan: Messianic Terrorism, Tribal Conflicts, and the Failures of Great Powers.* New York: PublicAffairs, 2012.

Wadle, Ryan. *HAMMER DOWN: The Battle for the Watapur Valley, 2011.* Fort Leavenworth, KS: Combat Studies Institute Press, 2014.

Williams, Bryan Glyn. *Afghanistan Declassified: A Guide to America's Longest War.* Philadelphia: University of Pennsylvania Press, 2011.

Woodward, Bob. *Bush at War.* New York: Simon and Schuster, 2002.

Woodward, Bob. *Obama's Wars.* New York: Simon and Schuster, 2010.

Wright, Donald P., ed. *Vanguard of Valor: Small Unit Actions in Afghanistan.* Fort Leavenworth, KS: Combat Studies Institute Press, 2012.

Wright, Donald P., ed. *Vanguard of Valor: Small Unit Actions in Afghanistan, Vol. II.* Fort Leavenworth, KS: Combat Studies Institute Press, 2012.

Wright, Donald P., James R. Bird, Steven E. Clay, Peter W. Connors, Scott C. Farquhar, Lynne Chandler Garcia, and Dennis F. Van Vey. *A Different Kind of War: The United States Army in Operation ENDURING FREEDOM (OEF), October 2001–September 2005.* Fort Leavenworth, KS: Combat Studies Institute Press, 2010.

INDEX

ABOUT THE AUTHOR

Ryan Wadle, PhD, is an associate professor of comparative military studies at the Air Command and Staff College's eSchool of Graduate Professional Military Education at Maxwell Air Force Base, Alabama. He was previously a member of the Afghanistan Study Team at the U.S. Army's Combat Studies Institute at Fort Leavenworth, Kansas. He is the author of *HAMMER DOWN: The Battle for the Watapur Valley, 2011*, published by Combat Studies Institute Press (2014) and the forthcoming book *Selling Sea Power: Public Relations and the U.S. Navy, 1917–1941*, from the University of Oklahoma Press.